Ernst Pauer

A Dictionary of Pianists and Composers for the Pianoforte

With an Appendix of Manufacturers of the Instrument

Ernst Pauer

A Dictionary of Pianists and Composers for the Pianoforte
With an Appendix of Manufacturers of the Instrument

ISBN/EAN: 9783744783484

Printed in Europe, USA, Canada, Australia, Japan

Cover: Foto ©Thomas Meinert / pixelio.de

More available books at **www.hansebooks.com**

NOVELLO, EWER AND CO.'S
MUSIC PRIMERS AND EDUCATIONAL SERIES.
Edited by Sir JOHN STAINER and Dr. C. HUBERT H. PARRY.

A DICTIONARY

of

PIANISTS AND COMPOSERS

for the

PIANOFORTE

WITH AN APPENDIX OF MANUFACTURERS
OF THE INSTRUMENT

by

E. PAUER.

PRICE TWO SHILLINGS.
In Paper Boards, Two Shillings and Sixpence.

LONDON & NEW YORK
NOVELLO, EWER AND CO.

ALL RIGHTS RESERVED.

THE STEINWAY PIANO . . . . .

The entire world has recognized and accepted the **Steinway** Piano as the standard of tone in the art realm of music.

There are other good pianos—excellent ones; but the **Steinway** occupies the unique position of being above the range of classification. It is a creation apart from all others, existent in an atmosphere peculiarly and proudly its own, alone and unclassified.

We are the sole authorized agents for Canada for these superb instruments, and have a large variety on exhibition in both Uprights and Grands in various styles and favorite woods.

A. & S. NORDHEIMER,
15 KING STREET EAST. - - - TORONTO.

LONDON:
NOVELLO, EWER AND CO.,
PRINTERS.

THE NORDHEIMER PIANO . . . .

Recognizing fully the cardinal points which have raised the leading American pianos to the eminent position they now hold, our constant aim has been to reproduce their intrinsic qualities in the Nordheimer Piano.

For some years our instruments have been before the public, and have obtained a most enviable reputation.

Our aim, however, is progress, and during the last few months we have produced our **new scale** piano, which we proudly claim has reached a perfection hitherto unattained in any Canadian manufacture.

So ready have the public been to recognize the qualities of these instruments, that in spite of working overtime in our factory we have been unable to meet the actual demand, and have found it necessary to further increase our staff.

A. & S. NORDHEIMER,
15 KING STREET EAST, - - TORONTO.

THE LIBRARY
BRIGHAM YOUNG UNIVERSITY
PROVO, UTAH

PREFACE.

Of all musical instruments, the Pianoforte is decidedly the most popular, and, with but few exceptions, every composer of instrumental music has written longer or shorter works for it. The interest we take in a composer and performer is certainly enhanced by knowing the country and time of his birth or death, the names, respectively, of his teachers and pupils, what his appointments were, and the distinctions which were conferred on him. To give some short and concise information on these points is the aim of this book, which follows the scheme of the popular and useful "Fach-Lexica," issued at Leipzig by the Bibliographical Institute. It is a *special* book, which deals only with the Piano, and thus the productions of composers in other branches of the musical art are not within its scope.

A great difficulty in compiling a biographical book is to draw the line between names which should be mentioned and those which should be omitted. Although it was my earnest desire to act in the most impartial manner, I am fully prepared to be accused of injustice done to professors who, in a small sphere of activity, have helped to promote the progress of the art and to awaken interest in it. But to become acquainted with the names of musicians and teachers who have not published any of their works is exceedingly difficult.

All articles marked * contain *personal* information. Complete lists of the works of classical composers are given according to the published thematic catalogues.

The pieces marked † have been pointed out either by the composers themselves or selected by myself, according to my experience as teacher, as worthy of notice.

I have to express my sincerest thanks to the following persons who have assisted me in procuring important information. They are:—

Baron A. Pachner-Eggenstorff, Messrs. E. Mandyczewski, E. Streicher, Epstein, Door, and Prosniz (Vienna); Dr. A. Dörffel, Messrs. Senff, Kistner, Rather, and Forberg (Leipzig); E. Bechstein, Bote & Bock (Berlin); J. Strauss (Munich); Dr. Carlo Weber and Signor Ricordi (Milan); Don Mariano Varquez (Madrid); Messrs. Neuparth & Co. (Lisbon); G. Hartmann, Léon Grus, Leduc, Weckerlin, Léon Langlois, Veuve Girod (Paris); Schott frères (Brussels); Mdlle. M. Stachè (Liège); Messrs. W. Hansen, Henrik Hennings (Copenhagen); Lundquist (Stockholm); Warmuth (Christiania); Jürgenson (Moscow); Belaieff (St. Petersburg). I am equally grateful for the kind help offered by Miss E. C. Stainer, Sir George Grove, and Mr. A. J. Hipkins.

May my be found useful and interesting, and may it meet with the favour hitherto accorded to my publications.

E. PAUER.

London, 1895.

The following authorities have been consulted :—

Neues historisch-biographisches Lexicon der Tonkünstler, von E. L. Gerber (Leipzig, 1813).

Encyclopædie der gesammten musikalischen Wissenschaften. Universal-Lexicon der Tonkunst, von Dr. Gustav Schilling (Stuttgart, 1835).

Universal-Lexicon der Tonkunst, von Dr. F. S. Gassner (Stuttgart, 1849).

Neues Universal-Lexicon der Tonkunst, von Dr. Eduard Bernśdorf (Dresden, 1856).

Hand-Lexicon der Tonkunst, von Dr. Oscar Paul (Leipzig, 1870).

Musikalisches - Conversations-Lexicon, von Gathy (Reissmann) (Berlin, 1871).

Schuberth's Musikalisches Conversations-Lexicon, herausgegeben von E. Breslaur (Leipzig, 1891).

Musik-Lexicon, von Dr. Hugo Riemann (Leipzig, 1893).

A Dictionary of Music and Musicians, by G. Grove (London and New York, 1889).

Biographie Universelle des Musiciens, par F. J. Fétis (Paris, 1860), and Supplement de Pougin (Paris, 1878).

Annuario Musicale, Storico-cronologico-universale, di Giovanni Paloschi (Milan, 1876).

Nordisk Musik-Lexicon, H. V. Schytte (Copenhagen, 1888).

Bouillet, Dictionnaire d'histoire et de géographie (Paris).

Conversations-Lexicon, Brockhaus (Leipzig, 1851).

Conversations-Lexicon, Meyer (Leipzig and Wien, 1890).

CATALOGUES.

W. A. Mozart, Thematisches Verzeichniss, von Köchel.

Louis van Beethoven, Thematisches Verzeichniss, von G. Nottebohm.

Franz Schubert, Thematisches Verzeichniss, von G. Nottebohm.

Carl Maria von Weber in seinen Werken, von Friedrich W. Jähns (Leipzig, 1871).

Thematische Cataloge von Mendelssohn, Chopin, and Liszt (Breitkopf and Härtel, Leipzig).

Eitner, Robert, Verzeichniss neuer Ausgaben alter Musikwerke (Berlin, 1871).

Prosniz, Adolph, Handbuch der Clavier-Literatur (Wien, 1884).

Weitzmann, C. F., Geschichte des Klavierspiels und der Klavier-Literatur (1863).

Whistling, C. F., Handbuch der musikalischen Literatur (Leipzig, 1842).

BIOGRAPHIES.

Bach, Sebastian, by Forkel (1802), Hilgenfeldt (1850), Spitta (1873-80).

Beethoven, Louis van, by Schindler (1840), Thayer (1866-79), Nohl (1864-79), Mensch (1870), Dr. Marx (1875).

Händel, G. F., by Dr. Chrysander (1858-67).

Haydn, Joseph, by C. F. Pohl (1875).

Mendelssohn, Felix, by Reissmann (1867 and 1872), Lampadius (1848-86).
Mozart, W. A., by Dr. Otto Jahn (1856-59 and 1862).
Mozart and Haydn in London, by C. F. Pohl (1867).
Schubert, Franz, by Kreissle von Hellborn (1865).
Schumann, Robert, by Reissmann (1867 and 1872), Wasieliewski (1858 and 1880).
Weber, C. M. von, by Max M. von Weber (1866-68).

History of the American Pianoforte, by Daniel Spillane (New York, 1890).
Weltadressbuch der gesammten Musikinstrumenten-Industrie, Paul de Wit (Leipzig, 1890).

PUBLISHERS' CATALOGUES.

André, C. A. (Frankfort o/M.).
Augener and Co. (London).
Bote and Bock (Berlin).
Belaieff, M. P. (St. Petersburg).
Breitkopf and Härtel (Leipzig).
Chappell and Co. (London).
Forberg, R. (Leipzig).
Grus, Léon (Paris).
Hainauer, Julius (Breslau).
Hansen, Wilhelm (Copenhagen).
Haslinger, Carl (Lienau), (Vienna).
Hennings, Hendrik (Copenhagen).
Hofmeister, F. (Leipzig).
Jürgenson, P. (Moscow).
Kahnt, C. (Leipzig).
Kistner, Friedrich (Leipzig).
Leuckart, F. E. C. (Leipzig).
Novello, Ewer and Co. (London).
Peters, C. F. (Leipzig).
Rahter, D. (Leipzig).
Rieter-Biedermann (Leipzig).
Schlesinger (R. Lienau) (Berlin).
Schott, B. and Sons (Mayence o/R., London, and Paris).
Schreiber (Cranz) (Vienna).
Senff, Bartholf (Leipzig).
Siegel, C. F. W. (Leipzig).

ABBREVIATIONS.

Pf.	...	Pianoforte.
Vln.	...	Violin.
V'cello	...	Violoncello.
Vla.	...	Viola.
Cl.	...	Clarinet.
Fl.	...	Flute.
Ob.	...	Oboe.
Bssn.	...	Bassoon.
C.-Bass.	...	Contra-Basso.
Hn.	...	Horn.
Clav.	...	Clavichord.

b.	...	born.
d.	...	died.
maj.	...	major.
min.	...	minor.
Conserv.	...	Conservatoire.
Prof.	...	Professor.

THE PIANO:

COMPOSERS, PERFORMERS, AND MAKERS.

A.

Abeille, Johann Christian Ludwig, b. Feb. 20, 1761, Bayreuth; d. 1832, Stuttgart. Pupil of Boroni and Saemann. Composer of Concertos, Trios, Duets, &c.; among them a Concerto (Op. 6) for 4 hands, which became very popular. His compositions were respected for their gracefulness and melody, and greatly esteemed by C. M. v. Weber.

Abel, Carl Friedrich, b. 1725, Cöthen; d. Jan. 22, 1787, London. Pupil of Seb. Bach (Leipzig). 1759, in London, patronised by the Duke of York, who procured for him the appointment of chamber musician to the Queen. 1782, in Germany, but on account of his dissipated habits had to return (*via* Paris) to London. His works were published, 1760-84, in London, Paris, and Berlin. His principal instrument was the Viol da Gamba. Among his Clavecin works were:—
>Concertos, 6 Quartets, Trios, Op. 2 and 5; Sonata with Vln.; Solo Sonatas.

Abt, Franz, b. Dec. 22, 1819, Eilenburg (district Merseburg); d. March 31, 1885, Wiesbaden. 1841, pupil at the Thomas School (Leipzig); studied theology, but soon devoted himself entirely to music. Conductor at Stuttgart and Zürich; 1852, Hof-Capellmeister at Brunswick. Decorated by several Sovereigns, and Hon. Member of most of the German male choral societies. Composed Variations, Rondos, Bagatelles, and brilliant Dances.

Adam (Johann), Louis (founder of the French school of Pf. playing), b. Dec. 3, 1758, Miettersholz (Lower Rhine); d. April 8 (14?), 1848, Paris. Pupil of the Organist Hepp (Strassburg). 1775, in Paris, patronised by Gluck. With Edelmann (*see* that name) he published the standard work "Méthode pour le Piano," after which publication he was appointed Prof. at the Conserv., which appointment he held for 35 years. Among his pupils were Henri Lemoine, Benoist, Kalkbrenner, Hérold (father and son), and many excellent lady pianists. 1829, Knight of the Legion of Honour; Inspecteur en général des Classes de Piano, and Membre du Comité d'examination. He was universally beloved and respected.
>Sonatas (9); Sonate dans le style dramatique, Op. 10; Sonata for 4 hands; Sonatas (3), with Vln.; Variations, and many Studies.

Adler, Vincent, b. April 3, 1826, Raab (Hungary); d. Jan. 4, 1871, Geneva. Pupil of his father, later of his uncle, Erkel (Pesth); he pursued his studies in Vienna and went later to Paris, where his performances and works were received with great favour. 1865, Prof. at the Conserv. at Geneva. His most popular compositions are:—
>Feuilles d'Album, Op. 13; Valse rococo, Op. 11; 12 Etudes de style, Op. 16; Barcarolle, Op. 26; Grande Marche, Op. 24; Allegro de Concert, Op. 15.

Agrell, Johann, b. Feb. 1, 1701, Löth (Sweden); d. Jan. 19, 1765, Nürnberg. 1723, appointed Kammer-Musiker at Cassel; 1746, after having visited Italy, he settled at Nürnberg.
>Concertos (7), with Quartet accompaniment; Trios (7); Duos for Pf. and Vln., Cl., or Fl.; Solo Sonatas (6).

Agricola, Johann Friedrich, b. Jan. 4, 1720, Dobitschen (Altenburg); d. Nov. 12, 1774, Berlin. 1738-41, pupil of Seb. Bach (Leipzig), as a Clavecinist contemporary with C. P. E. Bach and Nichelmann. 1750, appointed Königl. Hof-Compositeur, and, 1759 (after Graun's death), Königl. Hof-Capellmeister at Berlin. His compositions are out of print.

Agthe, Carl Christian, b. 1762, Hettstädt; d. Nov. 27, 1797, Ballenstädt (Harz Mountains). Highly talented and promising; his compositions were, in their time, admired for their agreeable melodies and solid structure.

***Aguilar,** Emanuel, b. Aug. 23, 1824, Clapham (London). Pupil of Charles Neate and John Goss. Went to Frankfort o/M., where he had lessons from Schnyder von Wartensee (1786-1868) in Composition and Jacques Rosenhain in Pf. He resides in London.
<small>Sonatas (6), Overture, Overture-Scherzo-Fantasia (A min.), Caprice, Etudes, Romanzas, Melodies, Trios (4), Septuor for Pf., Vla., V'cello, C.-Bass, Fl., Ob., and Hn.; Sextet for Pf., Fl., Ob., Cl., Hn., and Bssn.; Duo for 2 Pf.; Fantasia for Organ, 2 Pf., and Vln.</small>

Albanesi, Luigi, b. March 3, 1821, Rome. Pupil of Ernesto Coop. Composed about 50 pieces in various styles. His son—

***Albanesi,** Carlo, b. Oct. 22, 1856, Naples. Pupil of his father and Sabino Falconi (Composition). On the death of Thos. Wingham (1893) appointed Prof. at the R.A.M. (London). Excellent pianist, and composer of—
<small>Sei fogli d'Album, Op. 13; Trio, 2 Solo Sonatas, 12 Preludes, and about 40 smaller pieces.</small>

Albeniz, Don Pedro (founder of the modern Spanish Pf. school), b. April 14, 1795, Logroño (Old Castile); d. April 12, 1855, Madrid. Pupil of Henri Herz (Paris). 1830, Prof. at the (newly established) Madrid Conserv.; 1834, attached to the Royal Court. Received all possible honours. Composer of a great number of Pf. works. Author of a Pf. School adopted by the Spanish music schools.

***Albeniz,** Don Isaac (grand-nephew of the above), b. May 29, 1861, Camprodon (Prov. of Gerona). Pupil of his sister, C. A., of Narciso Oliveras (Barcelona), Marmontel (Paris), Marchyabal (Madrid), Jadassohn and Reinecke (Leipzig), L. Brassin (Brussels), and Liszt (Rome). Teachers of composition: Dupont and Gevaert (Brussels). Excellent performer. Composer of about 220 published pieces (Concerto fantastico). Pianist to the Queen of Spain. Commander of the Orders Carlos III., Isabella la Catolica (Spain), and Christ of Portugal.

Albert, Emile, b. 1823, Montpellier; d. Aug., 1865, at Bagnères-de-Bigorre.
<small>Trios, Sonatas with Vln., about 50 smaller pieces.</small>

Albert, Eugen d', b. April 10, 1864, Glasgow. Pupil of the London National Training School, Newcastle and Queen's Scholar, where his teachers were Pauer, Sullivan, and Stainer. 1880, in Vienna—met Liszt, who superintended his studies until 1883. Eminent performer, who created a great sensation in Germany, Holland, Belgium, Italy, Spain, &c.; went twice to America (inclusive of Mexico); resides now at Berlin. Pianist to the Grand Duke of Saxe-Weimar. Knight of the Saxe-Coburg, Weimar (falcon), Spanish (Carlos V.), Dessau (arts and science) orders, &c.
<small>Composer of Concertos (2), Suite, Sonata (F sharp min.), and different smaller pieces.</small>

Alberti, Domenico (amateur, who resided in Venice), d. 1740, Formia (Caserta). Composer of 8 popular Sonatas and inventor (?) of the easy (broken chords) accompaniment, often adopted, and called "Alberti Bass."

Albrechtsberger, Johann Georg, b. Feb. 3, 1736, Klosterneuburg (on the Danube); d. March 7, 1809, Vienna. 1772, Kaiserl. Hof-Organist; 1792, Organist of St. Stephen's (Cathedral). Eminent theorist; teacher of Eybler, Beethoven, Gänsbacher, Hummel, Umlauf, Weigl, Seyfried, &c. Composer of—
<small>About 80 Fugues; Concerto; Pf. Quartet (1792); Preludes and Fugues for 4 hands; Method for Beginners For Fugues, see Clementi's Practical Harmony.</small>

Alkan, Charles Henri Valentin, b. Nov. 30, 1813, Paris; d. there March 29, 1888. Pupil of Zimmermann (Paris Conserv.). First prize, when only ten years old; 1831, hon. mention for the Grand Prix de Rome. Composer of ingenious, original, and exceedingly difficult pieces, his Etudes Sonates presenting the highest possible degree of technical execution.
<small>Etudes-Caprices, Op. 12, 13, 16; L'amitié, grande Etude; Le Chemin de fer, Etude; 3 grandes Etudes, Op. 15: (a) Aime moi, (b) †Le Vent, (c) Morte; Le Preux, Op. 17; Marche funèbre, Marche triomphale, Op. 26, 27; †Bourrée d'Auvergne, Op. 29; Trio, Pf., Vln., and V'cello, Op. 30; 25 Préludes dans tous les tons, Op. 31; Recueil d'Impromptus, Op. 32; Grande Sonate, Op. 33; Etudes (12), Op. 35; Etudes (12 grandes), Op. 39.</small>

Ambros, Dr. August Wilhelm, b. Nov. 17, 1816, Mauth, near Prague; d. June 28, 1876, Vienna. Studied law and passed his exam. 1840; appointed, 1850, Attorney-General (Staatsanwalt) at Prague; 1872, Prof. of Mus. History at the University of Vienna. Wrote History of Music (4 vols.); finished by Dr. Langhans (Berlin). Composer of interesting Pf. pieces, somewhat

influenced by Schumann. Excellent critic and recipient of many honours and distinctions. Author of—
  Die Grenzen der Musik und Poesie, 1856; Culturhistorische Bilder aus dem Musikleben der Gegenwart, 1860.

Amerbach (Ammerbach), Elias Nicolaus, b. in Saxony (details are wanting). 1570, Organist of St. Thomas's Church (Leipzig). Published, 1571, his "Tabulatur," containing rules for fingering, including the use of the thumb, &c. An essay on this work was written by Wilh. Tappert, "Die älteste Clavierschule," 1887.

Amon, Johann Andreas, b. 1763, Bamberg; d. March 29, 1825, Heilbronn. Composer of—
  Concerto, Op. 34; Trios, Op. 48, 58, and 76; Sonatas for 4 hands; Solo Sonatas (6); Sonate dans le style dramatique, Op. 12.

Anderson, Lucy (*née* Philpot), daughter of Philpot, the Prof. and Musicseller, b. 1790, Bath; d. Dec. 24, 1878, London. Pupil of Windsor (Bath). For many years instructress of Queen Victoria and her children.

André, Johann Anton, b. Oct., 1775, at Offenbach o/M.; d. there April 16, 1842. Pupil of Vollweiler (1770-1847). Composer of many Sonatinas and other educational pieces. Publisher of great importance; owner of most of Mozart's autographs, bought for a trifling sum from his widow. Author of a large work on composition, edited by his pupil, M. Henkel, of Frankfort o/M. The sons of A. were—

André, Carl (August), b. June 15, 1806, Offenbach o/M.; d. Feb. 15, 1887, Frankfort o/M. Musicseller (Mozart-Haus), Pf. manufacturer (Mozart-Flügel), and author of a work on the construction of pianos.

André, Julius, b. June 4. 1808, Offenbach o/M.; d. April 17, 1880, Frankfort o/M. Pupil of his father and Aloys Schmitt. Composer of educational pieces, editor of a valuable collection of classical works, arranged by him for 4 hands. He possessed a thorough knowledge of Mozart's works.

André, Johann Baptist, b. March 7, 1823, Offenbach o/M.; d. Dec. 12, 1882, Frankfort o/M. Pupil of Aloys Schmitt (Pf.), Kessler (Harmony), Frankfort o/M.; later of Taubert (Pf.), Dehn (Composition), Berlin. Brilliant performer and elegant composer. His arrangements of Beethoven's **Symphonies for 4 hands are very much** respected.

Andreoli, Guglielmo, b. April 22, 1832, Modena; d. 1860, Nice. Pupil at the Conserv. of Milan. Eminent pianist, and composer of elegant drawing-room pieces. His brother—

Andreoli, Carlo, b. Jan. 8, 1840, Mirandola (near Modena). Pupil at the Milan Conserv., subsequently appointed Prof. Composer of Nocturnes, Op. 4, 10, 12, 19; Romanzas (4), Op. 16; ditto (4), Op. 17.

Angelet, Charles François, b. Nov. 18, 1797, Ghent; d. there, Dec. 20, 1832. Pupil of Zimmermann (1814) at the Paris Conserv. 1822, first prize. 1829, named pianist to King William of Holland. Excellent pianist, and composer of effective and brilliant pieces.

Anglebert, Jean Henri d', dates of birth and death unknown. Clavecinist to Louis XIV. He published, 1689, a collection of—
  Pièces de Clavecin avec la manière de les jouer, diverses chacones, ouvertures, et autres airs de M. de Lully, mis sur cet instrument. Livre I., chez l'auteur. For an Allemande from this collection, *see* Weitzmann's History of Pf. Playing.

*Arensky, Anton Stepanowitsch, b. July 30, 1862, Novgorod. 1879-82, pupil at the St. Petersburg Conserv. — his teachers were Johannsen and Nicolaus Rimsky-Korsakow. 1882, appointed Prof. of Harmony and Composition at the Imperial Conserv. of Moscow. Compositions (beginning to be very popular) are—
  6 pieces in the form of Canons, Op. 1; Concerto with Orchestra, Op. 2; 6 pieces, Op. 5 (No. 5, †Basso ostinato); Scherzo, Op. 8; Suite for 2 Pf., Op. 15; 3 pieces, Op. 19; †Bigarrures, Op. 20; Silhouettes (Suite for 2 Pf.). Op. 23; 3 Sketches, Op. 24.

Arne, Thomas Augustine, Mus. Doc., b. 1710, London; d. there, March 5, 1778. Composer of Sonatas or Lessons. For Sonata in G, *see* Pauer's "Alte Clavier Musik," Leipzig.

Arnold, Carl, b. May 6, 1794, Neukirchen (Würtemberg); d. Nov. 11, 1873, Christiania. Pupil of Aloys Schmitt (Pf.) and of Vollweiler and Joh. André (Composition), Frankfort o/M. Composer of a Sextet, Sonatas, Variations, &c.

Asantschewsky, Michael von, b. 1838, Moscow. 1861-62, pupil of Rietz and Hauptmann (Leipzig). 1866-70, he resided at Paris. 1870-76, successor of Anton Rubinstein as Director of the Imperial Conserv. of St. Petersburg. Composer of chamber music and solo pieces, mostly published at Leipzig.

*Ascher, Joseph, b. June 4, 1829, Groningen (Holland); d. June 4, 1869, London. Pupil of Mendelssohn and Moscheles (Leipzig). Pianist to the Empress

Eugénie, and composer of many fashionable pieces, some of which became very popular (Fanfare Militaire, Mazurka des traineaux, Sans-souci, &c.).

*Ashton, Algernon, b. Dec. 9, 1859, Durham. Pupil at the Leipzig Conserv., where Heinig, Coccius, and Rob. Papperitz were his teachers for Pf., Iwan Knorr, Jadassohn, and Reinecke for Composition. Teacher of Pf. at the Royal College of Music (London). Among his Pf. works (reaching, 1893, the number Op. 63) are to be mentioned—
  Duets; Spanish, English, Scottish, and Irish Dances; Suite for 2 Pf.; Concerto (4 movements); Sonata; Chamber - music—several works.

Asioli, Bonifacio, b. Aug. 30, 1769, Correggio; d. there, May 26 (18 ?), 1832. 1782 (13 years old), Conductor in his native town. 1787-99, residing partly in Turin and partly in Venice. 1809, Prof. and Inspector of the Milan Conserv. 1813, returned to Correggio, where he founded a music school. Composer of—
  Sextet, Pf., Cl., Bssn., Hn., Vla., and V'cello, Sonata, Pf. and V'cello; Solo Sonata, Capriccios for 4 hands, Capriccios, Fantasias. Author of a "Breve Metodo per Pf."

Assmayer, Ignaz, b. Feb. 11, 1790, Salzburg; d. Aug. 31, 1862, Vienna. Pupil of Michael Haydn. 1808, Organist of St. Peter's (Salzburg); 1815, pupil of Eybler (Vienna); 1824, Regens-chori of the Schottenkirche, Vienna; 1825, Kaiserl. Hof-Organist, and, 1838, Kaiserl. Hof-Capellmeister. Composer of Trios, Sonatas, Rondos, &c.

Attwood, Thomas, b. 1765, London; d. March 28, 1838, Cheyne Walk, Chelsea. 1785-87, pupil of Mozart in Vienna. Composer of Sonatas and Lessons.

B.

Bach, Johann Christoph (son of Heinrich B., 1615-92), b. 1642. Arnstadt (Schwarzburg - Sondershausen); d. March 31, 1703, Eisenach. His compositions consist of—
  12 Variations on a Sarabanda in G; 15 Variations on an Aria by Dan. Eberlin (1630-91).

Bach, Johann Christoph (eldest brother of Sebastian B.), b. 1671, Eisenach; d. Feb. 22, 1721, Ohrdruff. Teacher of Sebastian B. in Clav. playing.

Bach, Johann Ernst (son of Joh. Bernhard B.), b. 1722, Eisenach; d. 1777, Weimar. Capellmeister of the Court. Educated for the law, he devoted himself later to music. Composer of—
  Sonatas (3) with Vln.; Solo Sonatas (2); Fantasia and Fugue in A min.; Sonata in A; and Suite in E min.

Bach, Johann Sebastian (son of the Stadt-Musikus, Ambrosius B.), b. March 21, 1685, Eisenach; d. July 28, 1750, Leipzig. Being 9 years old when he lost his mother, and 10 when his father died, he was educated by his eldest brother, Joh. Christoph B. Studied at the College of Lüneberg (Hanover). 1703, as violinist, member of the Weimar Court Orchestra; 1704, Organist at Arnstadt; 1708-17, Hof-Capellmeister at Cöthen (Anhalt), and, from 1723 until his death in 1750, Cantor of the Thomas School (Leipzig). B. was twice married, and had 11 sons and 9 daughters. Of the sons 5 survived him and the same number of daughters. It is unnecessary to speak about his transcendent and unsurpassed merits as a composer, but it may be of interest to mention the remarks of contemporaries with respect to his playing: "Bach was undoubtedly the greatest performer of his time. The chief feature of his playing was its extreme distinctness in the tones produced from the keys. He held his fingers bent in such a manner over the keyboard that they stood with their points in a downward vertical line, each finger at every moment ready for action. In taking a finger off the keyboard, he drew it gently inwards with a sort of movement very like taking up coin from a table. Only the end joint was moved, all the rest of the hand remained still. Each finger was equally well trained. The tranquil grandeur and dignity of Bach's playing were eminently remarkable. Bach took quick times and yet rendered his performance so intelligible and interesting that it sounded like speech. Passionate passages he never expressed by violent or spasmodic movements, but solely relied on the power the composition itself possessed. His favourite instrument was the clavichord, on which he could give all the expression he desired. He often said that he found no soul in the clavecin, and that the pianoforte, then newly invented, was too clumsy and harsh to please him" (*see* Hilgenfeldt). His works for the Clavecin (Clavichord) are the following:

Das wohltemperirte Clavier—48 Preludes and Fugues in all maj. and min. keys; French Suites (6); English Suites (6); Suites in A min., E flat, and E min.; Suite (Overture in the French style); Partitas (6); Sonatas (3); and Sonata in D; Chromatic Fantasia and Fugue (D min.); Concerto in the Italian style; Fantasias and Fugues in A min., B flat, D (2), B min. (con imitazione), Fantasias in C min.(2), A min., and G min.; Toccatas and Fugues in E, F sharp, C, D, and G min.; Toccata in G; Preludes and Fugues, E flat (Lute or Clav.), F, G, A min., B flat (on the name of Bach), A min., D min., E min., A min.; Fugues, B min. (subject by Albinoni), C min., C (2), D min., D, A, E min., A min., E min. (not finished), and in A (2); Petits Préludes pour les commençants (12); Kleine Praeludien (6); Inventions in 2 parts (15); Ditto in 3 parts (15), sometimes called Symphonies; Duets (4); Menuets (3); Concerti (16), transcribed from Ant. Vivaldi's Vln. Concertos; Aria con (30) Variazioni in G; Aria variata, A min.; †Capriccio sopra la lontananza del suo fratello dilettissimo; Capriccio in E; Overture in F; Das musikalische Opfer; Kunst der Fuge; Sonatas for Clav. and Vln. (6); Suite for Clav. and Vln.; Sonatas for Clav. and Fl. (6); Sonatas for Clav. and Viol da Gamba (3); Concertos for Clavecin (with accomp. of Strings) (6); Concerto for Clav., Fl., and Vln.; Concertanti (with accomp. of Strings); Concerto for Clav. and 2 Fl. (with accomp. of Strings); Concerto for Clav., Fl., and Vla. (with accomp. of Strings); Concerti for 2 Clav. (3); Concerti for 3 Clav. (2); Concerto for 4 Clav. (Transcription of a Concerto for 4 Vln., by Ant. Vivaldi).

Bach, Friedemann (Wilhelm), the eldest and most gifted son of Seb. B.; b. Nov. 22, 1710, Weimar; d. July 1, 1784, Berlin. Pupil of his father. First Organist in Dresden, later in Halle, soon became very dissipated, and led a wandering life, until he died in a state of great misery at Berlin. According to Bitter's biography he composed—

Concertos (10); Fugues (10); Sonatas (10); a Fugue; Grand Fantasias (7); Short Fantasias (4); Polonaises (30?); Variations (12); Sonata for 2 Clavecins in F.

Bach (Carl), Philipp Emanuel (second son of Seb. B.), b. March 14, 1714, Weimar; d. Dec. 14, 1788, Hamburg. Sometimes called the "Berlin" or "Hamburg" Bach. Pupil of his father and at the Thomas School (Leipzig). Studied the law in Leipzig and Frankfort o/Oder. 1740, Cembalist and Kammermusikus to Frederic II. of Prussia (Berlin); 1767, appointed Musik-Director at Hamburg, where he remained until his death. Emanuel B. has often been called the founder of the modern instrumental music, and is decidedly the predecessor of Haydn and Mozart, by whom he was much admired. ("He is the father, we are the boys."—*Haydn*.) His best works were written in Hamburg, and his chief energy was devoted to the Clavecin (Clavichord). The Sonatas, Rondos, and Fantasias for connoisseurs and amateurs, and the so-called Würtemberg Sonatas, are decidedly the best. He was a very prolific composer.

Sonatas (6), Op. 1, 1742-43; Sonatas (6), Op. 2, 1743-44; Sonatas (6) and a Fantasia, 1753; Sonatas (6), with varied repetitions, 1760; Sonatas (12), 1761-63; Easy Sonatas (6), 1766; Sonatas (6), for ladies, 1770; Sonatas (6), for the Harpsichord, 1776; Clavier Sonatas, Rondos, and free Fantasias for connoisseurs and amateurs, 1779-87; 6 Collections, containing 18 Sonatas, 13 Rondos, and 6 Fantasias; Sonatina nuove (6), 1780; Sonata in C min., 1785; Sonatas (2), 1786; Minuet with crossed hands, 1731, etched by the composer; 12 short pieces for 2 and 3 parts, 1770; Clavecin pieces of various kind, 1765 (19 pieces).
Collections, edited and selected by Emanuel B.: 1. Œuvres mêlées (1755-65); 2. Raccolta delle più nuove composizioni di Clavicembalo, 1756-57; 3. Musikalisches Allerley, 9 books, 1760-63; 4. Musikalisches Vielerley, 1762-65; 5. Collection recreative, 1760-61. *Works for Clavecin and other instruments*: Concerto in D (1745); in B flat (1753); in E (1763); 6 Concerti per il Cembalo concertato accomp. da 2 Violini, Violetta e Basso con 2 Corni e 2 Flauti per rinforza, 1772 (dedicated to the Duke of Courland), in F, D, E flat, C min., G, and C; 3 Sonatines for Clavecin, 2 French Hn., 2 Fl., 2 Vln., Vla., and Basso (C, F, E flat), 1764; 2 Trios (Trii), dedicated to Count Schaumburg—the first describes the dialogue between "a Sanguinicus and a Melancholicus"; 6 Sonatas with accompaniment of a Vln. or V'cello, in 2 collections, 1776-77; 6 Sonatas, with Vln. or V'cello, 1778. *Theoretical works*: Versuch über die wahre Art das Clavier zu spielen (Essay on the true manner of playing the Clavecin): First part (1753), second part (1761). Bitter, in his biography of Friedemann and Emanuel B., mentions 146 Sonatas (99 published); shorter pieces, 174 (123 published); Concerti with accompaniment, 52 (9 published); 28 Trios (12 Sonatinas) and smaller pieces 44 (19 published). On the whole, 420 works for the Clavecin, of which 250 were published.

Bach, Johann Christoph Friedrich (the "Bückeburg" Bach), b. June 29, 1732, Leipzig; d. Jan. 26, 1795, Bückeburg. Pupil of his father, Sebastian B., Capellmeister to Count Schaumburg. Composer of—

Sonatas with Fl. or Vln. (6), 1777; Easy Solo Sonatas (6), 1785; Concerti (2), Sonatas, and other pieces (16) in Emanuel B.'s "Musikalisches Vielerley."

Bach, Johann Christian (the "Milan" or "London" Bach), youngest son of Sebastian B.; b. 1735, Leipzig; d.

Jan., 1782, London. Pupil of his father, and, after his death, of his brother Emanuel B. (Berlin). 1759, he settled in London and became teacher of the Queen. Although he had received an excellent musical education, he preferred to write in a popular style and mostly for amateurs.

20 Concerti; Concerto in Tartini's manner; Sextet; Quintets (2); Quartet; Trios (about 25); Sonatas with Fl. (6); Solo Sonatas (6); Sonatas (6), Op. 17; Fugue on the name *Bach*; Sonata for 4 hands; Sonata for 2 Pf., and several other Sonatas.

Bache (Francis), Edward, b. Sept. 14, 1833, Birmingham; d. there, Sept. 14, 1858. Pupil of Sterndale Bennett, London; Plaidy (Pf.), Hauptmann (Composition), Leipzig.

Andante and Rondo with Orchestra; Romanza for Pf. and Vln.; Concerto (MS.), and a number of graceful, elegant, and effective Solo pieces.

Bache, Walter (younger brother of the above), b. June 19, 1842, Birmingham; d. March 26, 1888, London. Pupil of Plaidy and Moscheles (Pf.), Leipzig, and F. Liszt, Weimar and Rome. Prof. at the R.A.M. (London), and an enthusiastic and devoted admirer of Liszt, for the popularisation of whose orchestral and vocal works he worked with noble and indefatigable energy and perseverance.

Bachmann, (Pater), Sixtus, b. July 18, 1754. Kettershausen (Bavaria); d. 1818, Vienna. Brilliant pianist, also composer of Sonatas and Fugues. He possessed a really phenomenal gift of memory.

Badarczewska, Thekla, b. 1838, Warsaw; d. there, 1862. Her reputation rests on a single piece, "La prière d'une Vierge," which made the round of the world, whilst her other pieces remained almost unknown.

*__Bärmann__, Carl, b. July 9, 1839, Munich. Son of the eminent Clarinetist, Carl B., and grandson of the friend and travelling companion of C. M. von Weber, Heinrich B. Pupil of Wanner and Wohlmuth (Pf.), and Franz Lachner (Composition), of Munich. For some time pupil of Liszt (Weimar). Teacher at the Munich Conserv. (now Royal Academy). 1881, he went to Boston (U.S.), where he became a most successful teacher, public performer, and influential authority. His technique is extraordinarily great. Syme of his effective and brilliant pieces were published by André, Offenbach o/M

Bagge, Selmar, b. June 30, 1823, Coburg At first a pupil at the Prague Conserv., later of Sechter (Vienna). 1851, teacher at the Vienna Conserv.; 1863-67, editor of the *Allgemeine Musikzeitung* (Leipzig). 1868, appointed Director of the Music School at Basel (Basle) He published—

Exercises and Studies, Solo pieces, and an excellent Essay on the Minor Keys and Scales.

Baillot, Pierre, b. Oct., 1771, Passy, near Paris; d. Sept. 15, 1842, Paris. Celebrated violinist, who deserves to be mentioned as the composer of a very good Sonata for Pf. and Vln., Op. 32.

*__Baker-Gróndahl__, Agathe, b. Dec. 1, 1847, Holmestrand, Norway. 1856, pupil of Fröken (Miss) With, of Christiania for 2 years; afterwards of Otto Winter Hyelm; 1860, of Halfdan Kjerulf (Pf.) and L. M. Lindemann (Theory); 1863, pupil of Kullak (Berlin). Appeared, 1864, with great success in Christiania; returned to Berlin in order to take lessons in composition from Richard Wüerst. Before 1875 she spent three months in Florence under the guidance of Dr. von Bülow. Afterwards she benefited by Liszt's advice (Weimar). 1875, she married the Prof. of Singing, O. A. Gróndahl. Resides in Christiania, and is one of the most influential musical authorities. Her performances in Leipzig, Copenhagen, Stockholm, London, &c., were received with great warmth and unanimous approval. She is Hon. Member of the "Svendsen" Quartet Society, of the Choral Institution for Sacred Music, Member of the Royal Swedish Academy, and recipient of the Royal Swedish gold medal, "Pro Literis et Artibus." The best known of her compositions are—

6 Etudes de Concert, Op. 11; 3 Morceaux, Op. 15; 4 Sketches, Op. 19; Suite (5 movements), Op. 20. A selection of her works is contained in the "Agathe Gróndahl" Album.

Balakireff, Mily Alexejewitsch, b. 1836, Nishny-Novgorod. Studied at the University of Kasan (on the Volga), but is an entirely self-taught musician. Performed, 1855, for the first time at St. Petersburg. Founded, 1862, with Lamakin, the "Gratis" Music School. 1866, appointed Capellmeister of the Opera (Prague); returned to St. Petersburg, where he conducted, 1867-70, the Concerts of the Imperial Musical Society, and introduced works of Liszt and Berlioz and of the younger Russian composers. Of his Pf. compositions, the Oriental Fantasia,

"Islamei," created a certain sensation, while several of his shorter pieces (l'Alouette de Glinka) are often played in public.

Balbastre, Claude, b. Dec. 8, 1729, Dijon; d. April 9, 1799, Paris. Pupil of Rameau. His pieces enjoyed great popularity.
 Pièces de Clavecin; 4 Suites de Noëls avec Variations; Septuor, &c.

*Banister, Henry Charles, b. June 13, 1831, London (son of the Violoncellist, H. J. B.). 1846, elected King's Scholar of the R.A.M.; re-elected 1848. Pupil of Cipriani Potter. Since 1852, Prof. of Harmony and Composition at the R.A.M. Since 1880, Prof. at the Guildhall School. Examiner in Music and Member of the Board of Studies (Cambridge University). Composer of—
 Fantasia; Allegretto alla Marcia; Sonata for 2 performers; and author of well-known, excellent, and highly-valued theoretical books.

*Barbadette, (Hippolyte), Henri la Rochelle (Sénateur de la Republique Française), b. 1827, Poitiers. Pupil of L. d'Aubigny. Resides at Paris. His name is well known through his biographies of Haydn, Gluck, Weber, Beethoven, Mendelssohn, Chopin, Schubert, Heller, &c., and by his excellent Essays on musical matters. Composer of—
 Sextuor for Pf. and Strings; Sonatas with Vln.; ditto, with V'cello; Scènes d'enfants (12), Op. 113; 25 Etudes mélodiques, Op. 122; !25 Etudes expressives, Op. 125; 25 Etudes de genre, Op. 136; Préludes et pièces fuguées, Op. 118; Esquisses musicales, Op. 95; Sonates et Sonatines.

Barbara, Pierre Henri, b. April 28, 1823, Orléans (Loiret); d. May 9, 1863, Libourne (Gironde). Pupil of Aloys Schmitt (Frankfort o/M.). 1843, he published solo pieces, which were favourably received and obtained considerable popularity.

Barbot, François Cécile Paul, b. 1828, Toulouse, where he resides. With his children he gives Concerts on 6 pianos, performing with great success his effective arrangements of the best works of Beethoven, Weber, &c. Since 1846 he has published upwards of 100 pieces with characteristic titles.

Bargiel, Woldemar, b. Oct. 3, 1828, Berlin. He is a half-brother of Madame Clara Schumann. Pupil of Moscheles (Pf.), Hauptmann, Gade, and Rietz (Composition), at Leipzig. For several years Prof. at the Cologne Conserv., afterwards at the Music School of Rotterdam. Since 1874, Prof. at the Berlin Hochschule. 1875, Member of the Senate of the Royal Academy of Arts and Science. Knight of the Prussian Order of the Red Eagle. Composer of—
 Trios (3); a Sonata, Op. 34; †Bagatelles, Op. 4; Suites (2), Op. 8 and 31; Characteristic Pieces (3); †8 pieces, Op. 32; ditto, Op. 41; Impromptu, Op. 44; Etude and Toccata, Op. 45. His works are distinguished by clearness, melodiousness, and absolute correctness.

*Barnett, Domenico, b. Aug. 25, 1846, London, son of John Barnett (1802-90). Pupil at the Leipzig Conserv of Plaidy and Moscheles (Pf.), Richter and Hauptmann (Harmony), Rietz and Reinecke (Composition). Principal Pf. teacher at the Ladies' College of Cheltenham. His pieces remain unpublished.

*Barnett, John Francis, b. Oct. 16, 1837, London. Pupil of the late Dr. Henry Wylde; 1875, at the Leipzig Conserv., under Moscheles (Pf.), Hauptmann and Rietz (Composition). Since 1861, has resided permanently in London. Teacher at the National Training School, Royal College of Music, Guildhall School, and London Academy of Music (where he is Hon. Vice-President). Excellent performer, and successful composer of—
 Concerto (D min.); Trio (C min.); Sonata (E min.); Impromptus (3); Home Scenes (9 pieces); Tarantella; Berceuse, &c.

*Baroni-Cavalcabo, Julie (first married to the Imperial Councillor von Webenau, secondly to the Brazilian Ambassador, Chevalier de Britto), b. Oct. 16, 1813, Lemberg; d. July 3, 1887, Graz (Styria). Pupil of W. A. Mozart, jun. Brilliant pianist and composer of effective Caprices, Sonatas, Drawing-room pieces, &c. Schumann had a high opinion of her musical attainments, and dedicated to her his "Humoreske," Op. 20.

*Barth, Carl Heinrich, b. July 12, 1847, Pillau (district of Konigsberg). Son of a teacher, who was his first instructor. 1856, pupil of L. Steinmann (Potsdam), later of Bülow, Bronsart, and Tausig (Pf.); Dr. Marx, Weitzmann, and Kiel (Composition). 1871, appointed Prof. at the Hochschule, Berlin. Pianist to the late Emperor Frederick; and Royal Prof. His excellent qualities as a musician and thoughtful pianist, commanding a vast repertory, are well known and warmly appreciated.

Batta, Jean Laurent, b. Dec. 30, 1817, Maestricht (Holland); d. Dec., 1879, Nancy. Brilliant pianist and highly successful teacher.

*Baumfelder, Friedrich, b. May 28, 1836, Dresden. Patronised by the King of Saxony. He was first a pupil of Julius Otto; obtained later a Scholarship at the Leipzig Conserv., where Moscheles, Wenzel, and Hauptmann were his teachers. After leaving Leipzig he settled in Dresden. 1875, Director of the "Robert Schumann" Academy. Very successful teacher and popular composer.

Confidence, Op. 48; Rondo mignon, Op. 49; Rococo, Op. 367; "Tirocinium musicæ" is greatly esteemed.

Baumgart (Expedit), Friedrich (Dr. Phil.), b. Jan. 13, 1817, Glogau; d. Sept. 15, 1871, Warmbrunn (Silesia). Principal teacher at the Matthias Gymnasium and Musical Director of the Breslau University. Excellent theorist; carefully edited Phil. Emanuel Bach's Clavecin works with a highly valuable preface.

Beckmann, Johann Friedrich Gottlob, b. 1737, Celle; d. there, April 25, 1792. He was one of the best performers of his time, and his improvisations were much admired. Composer of—

Sonatas (12); Concertos (6), and many Solo pieces.

Beethoven, Ludwig van, b. Dec. 16, 1770, Bonn; d. March 26, 1827, Vienna. Pupil of Van den Eeden and Neefe (Bonn), and of Haydn, Salieri, and Albrechtsberger (Vienna). See Nottebohm's valuable works: "Beethoven's Skizzenbuch," "B. Studien," "Beethoveniana," and "Neue Beethoveniana." For an exhaustive biography of Beethoven, see Grove's Dictionary, Vol. I., p. 162. The following list mentions his compositions for Pf. :—

Sonatas: Sonatas (3), composed in his 11th year (1783); ditto (3), Op. 2 (1796); Grand Sonata, Op. 7 (1797); Sonatas (3), Op. 10 (1798); Sonate pathétique, Op. 13 (1799); Sonatas (2), Op. 14 (1799); Sonata, Op. 22 (1800); Sonata, Op. 26 (1801); Sonatas Quasi Fantasias (2), Op. 27 (1801); Sonata (commonly called "Pastorale"), 1801; Sonatas (3), Op. 31 (1802); Easy Sonatas (2), Op. 49 (1805); Sonata ("Waldstein "), Op. 53, 1803 (appeared 1805); Sonata, Op. 54 (1803); Grand Sonata ("Appassionata "), Op. 57 (1804); Sonata, Op. 78 (1809); Sonatina, Op. 79 (1810); Characteristic Sonata (l'Adieu, l'Absence, et le Retour), Op. 81a, (1809); Sonata, Op. 90 (1814); Sonata, Op. 101 (1815); Grand Sonata, Op. 106 (1818); Sonata, Op. 109 (1821); Sonata, Op. 110 (1821); Sonata, Op. 111 (1822). Variations (with Opus number): On an original air (6), Op. 34 (1802); 15 and Fugue, Op. 35 (1802); 6, Op. 76 (1810); 33, on the "Diabelli" Valse, Op. 120 (1823); Ditto, without Opus number: 9 Variations on a March by Dressler (1782); 9 on "Quant è più bello," by Paisiello (1796); 6 on "Nel cor più non mi sento," by Paisiello (1795); 12 on Haibel's Minuet à la Vigano (1795); 12 on "Waldmädchen," by Wranitzky (1796); 8 on "Une fièvre brûlante," by Gretry (1798); 10 on "La Stessa," by Salieri (1799); 7 on "Kind willst du ruhig schlafen," Winter (1799); 8 on "Tändeln und scherzen," by Süssmayer (1799); 13 on "Es war einmal," by Dittersdorf (1794); 6 easy on an original air (1801); 6 easy on a Swiss air (1799); 24 on "Vieni amore," by Righini (1790); 7 on "God save the King" (1804); 5 on "Rule, Britannia" (1804); 32 on an original air (1807); 8 on "Ich hab' ein kleines Hüttchen nur." Rondos: 2 in C (1798) and G (1802); Rondo à capriccio, Op. 129 (posth. work); Rondo in A (1784). Bagatelles: 7, Op. 33 (1782); 11, Op. 119 (1820-22); 6, Op. 126 (1821?). Fantasia, Op. 77 (1809). Prelude in F min. (1805); Ditto (2), in all 12 maj. keys (1789). Dances: 6 rustic (1802); 7 ditto (1803); 12 German (1795); 6 Contre-Danses (1802); Minuet in E flat (1805); 6 Minuets; 12 ditto (1795). Military March (1816). Polonaise, Op. 89 (1814). Andante favori (1803). For 4 hands: Sonata, Op. 6 (1797); Marches (3), Op. 45 (1801 or 1802); Variations, 6 (1800); ditto, 8 (1783). For Pf. and Vln.: Sonatas (3), Op. 12 (1798-99); Sonata, Op. 23 (1801); ditto, Op. 24 (1801); Sonatas (3), Op. 30 (1802); Sonata ("Kreutzer"), Op. 47 (1803); Sonata, Op. 96 (1810); Variations (12), 1793. For Pf. and V'cello: Sonatas (2), Op. 5 (1796); Sonata, Op. 69 (1809); Sonatas (2), Op. 102 (1815); Variations: 12 (1793); 7 (1801); Rondo (1807). These may also be played with Vln. For Pf. and Hn.: Sonata, Op. 17 (1800). Trios for Pf., Vln., and V'cello: 3, Op. 1 (1791-92); 2, Op. 70 (1808); Grand Trio, Op. 97 (1811); Short Trio (1812); Trio (1791); Adagio, Variations, and Rondo, Op. 121a (1824); 14 Variations, Op. 44 (1802). Trio for Pf., Cl., and V'cello, Op. 11 (1798). Quartet for Pf., Vln., Alto, and V'cello, arranged from the Quintet for Pf., Ob., Cl., Hn., and Bssn., Op. 16 (1798). Quartets: 3, posth. works (1785), for Pf., Vln., Alto, and V'cello. Concertos: No. 1, Op. 15 (1795); No. 2, Op. 19 (1798); No. 3, Op. 37 (1800); No. 4, Op. 58 (1804); No. 5, Op. 73 (1809) Concerto for Pf., Vln., and V'cello, Op. 56 (1804-5). Concerto (arr. from the Vln. Concerto), Op. 61 (1806). Fantasia with Solos, Chorus, and Orchestra, Op. 80 (1808).

Beethoven's Sonatas, indeed almost all his Pf. works, offer the noblest objects of study for anyone who practises for the sake of the art and not for mere amusement. His Sonatas comprise every feature of characteristic expression; they pourtray every shade of human feeling, and their plastic perfection cannot fail to imbue the performer with ideas of the highest and best style. The sphere of technique is here shown in its purest and loftiest range, for the noblest technical skill is devoted to the service of the noblest thoughts. In every one of his Pf. works we discern the deep interest the illustrious and unrivalled composer took in the instrument itself; and the immediate grand, inspiring and elevating effect they produce on the earnest and loyal interpreter has never been rivalled;

indeed, in Beethoven's Sonatas and the Concertos, Op. 37, 58, and 73, we perceive the climax of all that is grand, noble, masculine, pure, tender, and intrinsically beautiful in the literature of the Pf. The following extract from an article by Carl Ludwig Junker, published Nov. 23, 1791, in Bossler's Musical Correspondence, gives a very quaint description of Beethoven's playing:—". . . I also heard one of the greatest players on the Clavier, that dear, good Bethofen [*sic !*] of whom some things were published as early as 1783, which he composed when only 11 years old. It is true that he did not perform in a public concert, perhaps because the instrument did not satisfy him; it was a Grand by Spath, and he is accustomed, when in Bonn, to play only on one of Stein's. But still, and what I liked all the better, I heard him extemporise, and I was indeed asked myself to give him a theme for variations. The inexhaustible wealth of his ideas, the originality of expression in his playing, and the technical excellence of his performance render, in my opinion, an accurate estimate of the artistic greatness of this dear and modest man. . . . I have frequently and for hours heard Vogler perform on the Fortepiano and always admired his extraordinary technique, but Bethofen's performance, technically quite as high, is much more important and expressive, and touches your heart infinitely more: he is, in consequence, as good at an Adagio as at an Allegro. Even all the members of the band, excellent players themselves, are his admirers, and all ear whenever he plays. And with all this he is modesty itself, and free from all pretension. He confessed, however, that his expectations were but rarely fulfilled when, during the journeys which the Prince allowed him to undertake, he met and heard some of the most reputed and best pianoforte players of the day. His performance, indeed, is so entirely different from the ordinary manner of playing the Pianoforte, that it seems as if he had been determined from the outset to choose a way quite his own, in order to reach the goal of perfection at which he has now actually arrived. Had I followed the pressing invitation of my friend Bethofen to stay another day in Mergentheim, in which he was supported by Herr Winneberger, I believe Herr Bethofen would have played to me for hours, and in the society of these two great artists I would thus have had an opportunity of enjoying another of the sweetest days of my life."

Bègue, Nicolas Antoine le, b. about 1630, Laon; d. July 6, 1702, Paris. Among his works, "Pièces pour le Clavecin" were published 1677, at Paris.

Behr, Franz, b. July 22, 1837, Lübtheen (Mecklenburg). He is one of the most prolific composers of easy, fashionable, and light pieces, which are written in a thoroughly practical manner, and therefore exceedingly popular. He publishes his compositions also under the names of Francesco d'Orso, William Cooper, and Charles Morley.

Belleville-Oury, Emilie, b. 1808, at Munich; d. there, July 23, 1880. Pupil of Charles Czerny. For many years resident in London. Brilliant and elegant pianist, popular composer (really arranger), and highly successful teacher.

Benda, Georg (member of a very musical family), b. 1721, Jung-Bunzlau (Bohemia); d. Nov. 6, 1795, Köstritz (Reuss). His works are distinguished by agreeable melodies and general euphony.

<small>Solo Sonatas (12), Op. 1; 6 Ditto, Berlin (1772); 6 collections of various pieces, Gotha (1780-82); Sextet, Op. 3; Concertos (2); 1 Concertino (1779 and 1783).</small>

Bendel, Franz, b. March 23, 1833, at the Market-place, Schönlinde, near Rumburg (Bohemia); d. July 3, 1874, Berlin. Pupil of Proksch (Prague) and Liszt (Weimar). Exceedingly brilliant pianist, possessing a wonderful technique, and composer of highly effective, melodious, and, in a certain degree, fascinating pieces.

<small>Studies (6); Study in sixths (B flat min.), On the Lake of Geneva (6), Op. 139; Nocturnes, Romanzas, Transcriptions of Songs by Chopin, Rubinstein, Brahms, &c.</small>

Benedict (knighted 1871), Sir Julius, b. Dec. 24, 1804, Stuttgart; d. June 5, 1885, London. Pupil of Hummel and C. M. von Weber. Popular conductor and accompanist. Composer of Concertos, Sonatas, Rondos, Fantasias, Variations, &c. Founder of the annual Monster Concerts. In his later years he received orders of Knighthood from Austria, Sweden, Portugal, Würtemburg, Russia, &c.

Bennett (knighted 1871), Sir William Sterndale (Mus. Doc., M.A., D.C.L.) b. April 13, 1816, Sheffield; d. Feb. 1, 1875, London. Pupil at the R.A.M., his teachers being Charles Lucas, Dr. Crotch, W. H. Holmes, and Cipriani Potter. 1836, he was in Leipzig, received with great kindness by Mendelssohn and Schumann. 1856-66, Conductor of the Philharmonic Society's Concerts; 1856, elected Prof. of Music at Cambridge University; 1866, Principal of the R.A.M. Soon after his election as Prof., the University of Cambridge conferred on him the hon. degree of Mus. Doc., and, 1870, he received from the University of Oxford the degree of D.C.L. As a pianist he belonged to the classical school. As a teacher he enjoyed great popularity in certain circles. His compositions (strongly influenced by Mendelssohn and Dussek) consist of—

Concertos (4); Capriccio, Op. 2; Sextet for Pf. and Strings; Sonata (dedicated to Mendelssohn); ditto (Maid of Orleans); Sonatina, Fantasia (dedicated to Schumann); Musical Sketches (3); Studies, Suite de Pièces, Toccata, Chamber Trio, Sonata for Pf. and V'cello, &c.

Bentayoux (Ben-Tayoux), **Frédéric**, b. June 14, 1840, Bordeaux. Pupil at the Paris Conserv., of Marmontel (Pf.), Emile Durand (Theory), Carafa (Composition). Composer of a considerable number of effective and fashionable pieces.

Berens, Hermann, b. April 17, 1826, Hamburg; d. May 12, 1880, Stockholm. At first pupil of his father, the flautist, Carl B., afterwards of C. J. Reissiger (Dresden), C. Czerny, and Sechter (Vienna). 1845, he travelled with the celebrated singer Marietta Alboni, and went, 1847, to Stockholm; remained till 1849 Musik-Director at Örebro, and was appointed, 1860, Capellmeister at the smaller theatre of Stockholm, and Prof. of Composition at the Royal Music School; Member of the Royal Academy of Sweden. Excellent pianist, and successful composer of excellent Studies and many other Pf. pieces, as well as of Trios and Quartets.

Berg, Conrad Matthias, b. April 27, 1785, Colmar (Alsace); d. Dec. 13, 1852, Strassburg. 1806-7, pupil at the Paris Conserv. He settled later in Strassburg, where he was for many years an influential, successful, and much respected teacher. One of his essays, "On the influence of modern Piano-playing on musical education in general" (Cäcilia, Vol. 17, 1835), created a great sensation. Composer of—

Concertos (3), Sonatas, Variations, Trios (10), and many effective pieces for 4 hands.

***Berger, Francesco**, b. June 10, 1834, London. Resided with his parents at Trieste, where he was a pupil of Luigi Ricci (Harmony), and later, when in Vienna, of Carl Lickl (Pf.). Afterwards private pupil of Hauptmann (Harmony) and Plaidy (Pf.) at Leipzig. Composer of a considerable number of elegant and effective pieces. Prof. of the Pf. at the R.A.M. and Guildhall School of Music. For several years hon. secretary of the Philharmonic Society.

Berger, Ludwig, b. April 18, 1777, Templin, near Frankfort o/Oder; d. Feb. 16, 1839, Berlin. At first a pupil of Gürrlich; 1804, went to Berlin, where Clementi heard him and persuaded him to go with him (1805) to St. Petersburg. John Field, a pupil of Clementi, had, however, greater influence on the development of Berger's playing than the Italian Maëstro. He left Russia in 1812, travelled for two years in Sweden and England, and settled (1814) in Berlin. The loss of his wife and child produced a state of mental despondency from which he could never free himself entirely; added to this, a kind of apoplectic stroke deprived his right arm of its independent movement. Owing to these circumstances he devoted himself entirely to teaching. Among his pupils were Felix Mendelssohn and his sister Fanny (Madame Hensel), Wilhelm Bach (no relation of the "Bach" family). Wilhelm Taubert, Greulich, the Ladies Zeidler, Laidlaw, and others. Berger's works are greatly respected, they are solidly constructed, full of expression, and of considerable originality. A collection of them has been published by Hofmeister (Leipzig). At present only his Studies, a Toccata, and Rondo are played. An exhaustive essay on his life and artistic activity was written by L. Rellstab, and printed in the *Berlinische Zeitung* of Feb. 21, 1839.

***Bergson, Michael**, b. 1820, Warsaw. Pupil of Schneider (Dessau); later of Rungenhagen and Taubert (Berlin). 1840, he visited Paris, and went (1846) to Italy. 1850-53, he resided in Vienna; later, again in Paris. 1863, appointed "Professeur de l'enseignement supérieur du Piano" at the Conserv. of Geneva. 1868, he returned to Paris, but had to leave on account of the war (1870), and settled in London. Among his most important works are—

12 Grandes Etudes, Op. 62; École du mécanisme, Op. 65; Concerto Symphonique; Trio, Op. 5; Polonaise héroique, Op. 72; and a Sonata with Fl.

*Beringer, Oscar, b. July 14, 1844, Fürtwangen (Grand Duchy of Baden). He came (1849) to London. Studied from 1864 to 1866 at Leipzig under Plaidy, Moscheles, and Reinecke, and later with Tausig, Ehlert, and Weitzmann in Berlin. 1869, Tauzig appointed him Prof. at the "Schule des höhern Clavierspiels." A similar establishment, under the name of "School for the higher development of Pianoforte Playing," was started by Beringer (1871) in London. As a composer, he turned his attention more towards the technical department of playing, and his compilation of technical exercises is a very useful book of considerable popularity, founded more or less on Tausig's principles. As a pianist, Beringer is noted for his absolutely correct and clear execution.

Bernard, Moritz, b. 1794, Courland; d. May 9, 1871, St. Petersburg. 1811, he was Field's pupil in Moscow; also had instruction in composition from Haesler. After having finished his studies, he travelled and gave concerts. 1816, he was appointed by Count Potocky, Conductor of his orchestral band (South Russia). 1822, went to St. Petersburg, where he was one of the most popular teachers. 1829, he opened a music warehouse. He composed a quantity of smaller pieces.

Bernard, Paul, b. Oct. 4, 1827, Poitiers; d. Feb. 24, 1879, Paris. He was a most successful teacher, wrote a great number of Pf. pieces, and was the able critic of the Parisian musical journals *Le Ménestrel* and *La Revue et Gazette musicale*.

Bernsdorf, Dr. Eduard, b. March 25, 1825, Dessau. Pupil of Schneider (Dessau) and Prof. A. B. Marx (Berlin). Among his Pf. works are an "Allegro appassionato," Sonatas, Caprices, Fantasias. He is chiefly active, however, as a critic of new works and of the Leipzig concerts; he writes in the *Signale für die musikalische Welt*. He completed Schladebach's "Musikalisches Konversations-Lexicon," in 3 volumes.

Berthold, Carl Friedrich Theodor, b. Dec. 18, 1815, Dresden; d. there, April 28, 1882. Patronised by the King of Saxony; he received lessons in Composition from Julius Otto, and in Pf. playing from Johann Schneider. Went, 1840, with a rich family to Russia; was appointed, 1843, principal teacher of the "Ladies' School" at Charkow; 1849, similar appointment at the "Noble Ladies' College" at St. Petersburg, from whence he returned, 1864, to Dresden. He published a Concerto, many smaller pieces, and wrote (with Fürstenau) a book: "Die Fabrikation musikalischer Instrumente im Voigtland" (Saxony).

Bertini, Henri, b. 1798, London; d. Oct. 1, 1876, at his estate, Meylan, near Grenoble. Pupil of his brother, Benoit Bertini. As a composer he is particularly esteemed for his useful, practical, and thoughtful educational works, such as Studies, Rondos, Fantasias, which are well constructed and devoid of any triviality. His Studies are more or less introductions and supplements to similar works by J. B. Cramer and Czerny:—

    Etudes primaires, Op. 166; 25 Etudes élémentaires, Op. 137; 25 Etudes faciles, Op. 100; 25 Etudes préparatoires, Op. 175; †25 Etudes doigtées, Op. 29; Etudes intermediaires, Op. 276; †25 Etudes doigtées, Op. 32; 25 Etudes spéciales, Op. 177; 25 Etudes doigtées, Op. 134; ditto, Op. 134*bis*; 25 Etudes classiques et normales, Op. 178; 25 Etudes caractéristiques, Op. 66; 25 Caprice-Etudes, Op. 94; 25 Grandes Etudes artistiques, Op. 122; Seb. Bach's 48 Preludes and Fugues arranged for 4 hands.

Besozzi, Louis Désiré, b. April 3, 1814, Versailles; d. Nov. 11, 1879, Paris. Pupil at the Paris Conserv., where he obtained several prizes, and, 1837, the Grand Prix de Rome. Composer of a good many well-written and effective pieces.

Beyer, Ferdinand, b. 1803, Querfurt (Prussia); d. May 14, 1863, Mayence. Prolific writer of popular Pot-pourris, Fantasias, and Arrangements of various Arias and Dances.

Biagi (Biaggi?), Alessandro, b. Jan. 20, 1819, Florence. Pupil of his elder brother, Ludovico B.; later of Geremia Sbolci and Palafuti. 1857, appointed Prof. at the Florence Academy. Composer of several eminent Pf. works.

Bigot de Morognes, Marie (*née* Kiene), b. March 3, 1786, Colmar (Alsace); d. Sept. 16, 1820, Paris. 1804, she married Monsieur Bigot, librarian to Count Rasumoffsky. In Vienna she made the acquaintance of Haydn, Salieri, and Beethoven, all of whom passed highly flattering laudations on her playing. In 1809 she introduced, with Baillot, Mozart and Beethoven's Violin Sonatas to a Parisian public. 1816, during Mendelssohn's stay in Paris, he received some lessons from her. It is not known whose pupil she was.

* **Bird, Arthur**, b. July 23, 1856, Cambridge, near Boston (U.S.). His grandfather, a descendant of William Byrde, left England and settled in Boston. Bird went, 1881, to Berlin, and was a pupil of Haupt, Löschhorn, Urban; 1884-85, of Liszt, in Weimar. 1886, he was engaged to conduct the Milwaukee Festival; since his return he has resided in Berlin, a highly successful teacher. Of his compositions the following deserve attention:—
    Variations and Fugue; 3 Valses, Op. 12; Puppentänze (Dolls' dances), 4 pieces, Op. 10; Sketches; 3 Suites, Ballet Music, Introduction and Fugue, Zwei Poesien, for 4 hands; 3 Characteristic Marches, Op. 11.

Birnbach, Heinrich (Joseph Benjamin), b. 1793, Breslau; d. 18—(?), Berlin. Son of Carl Joseph B. (1751-1805), who was his teacher. 1809, he had become a successful Prof. at Breslau; 1813, in Pesth, as conductor and pianist; playing with great success at concerts; 1815, he returned to Breslau, where he remained until 1821, when he settled in Berlin. He composed Concertos, Sonatas, Fantasias, &c., which were very popular.

Bischoff, Dr. Hans, b. Feb. 17, 1852, Berlin; d. June 12, 1889, Niederschönhausen, near Berlin. Pupil of Dr. Theodor Kullak; studied Philosophy, Mathematics, and modern languages at the University of Göttingen, where he gained the degree of Dr. Ph. Created a well merited sensation as an excellent pianist; 1873-88, teacher at the Academy of Music, and, for a short time, at Stern's Conserv. Edited Bach's, Schumann's, Schubert's, and Mozart's Pf. works; published a new edition of Adolph Kullak's "Æsthetik des Clavierspiels," and was greatly esteemed for his talent and rare accomplishments.

Bizet, Georges (really **Alexandre César Léopold**), b. Oct. 25, 1838, Paris; d. June 3, 1875, Bougival. Pupil of his father-in-law, Halévy. Possessed great talent as a composer; his Pf. playing was admired for its brilliancy and musicianlike expression. Composer of several exceedingly pretty Pf. pieces—"Jeux d'enfants" (12 pieces); "Les chants du Rhin" (6 pieces); "Le Pianiste-chanteur"; 150 pieces of all schools.

* **Blahetka (Plahetka), Marie Léopoldine** (Composer and Pianist), b. Nov. 15, 1811, Guntramsdorf, near Vienna; d. Jan. 17, 1887, Boulogne-sur-Mer. Pupil of Joseph Czerny (no relation to Carl Czerny), Kalkbrenner, and Moscheles for the Pf., and of Simon Sechter for Composition. Brilliant performer and moderately successful composer of effective pieces. From 1840 she resided in Boulogne, where she was very popular and successful as a teacher, and highly esteemed for her excellent and amiable character.

Blassmann, Adolph Joseph Maria, b. Oct. 27, 1823, Dresden; d. June 30, 1891, Bautzen. Pupil of Charles Mayer and Franz Liszt. Teacher at the Dresden Conserv.; 1862-64, Director of the Leipzig Euterpe Concerts; 1867, Hof-Capellmeister at Sondershausen, but soon after returned to his former appointment in Dresden. Ill health obliged him to retire into private life.

* **Bloomfield-Zeisler, Fannie**, b. July, 1866, Bielitz (Austrian Silesia). Received her first lessons at Chicago, and studied afterwards for 5 years with Th. Leschetizki (Vienna). Performed in her tenth year (1876) at Chicago, but made her first important appearance in the same town in Jan., 1884. Her performances in the United States, Germany, and Austria have been received with unusual applause, and there is a unanimous opinion that she is one of the foremost lady pianists of the present time.

Blow, John (Mus. Doc.), b. 1648, North Collingham, Nottinghamshire; d. Oct. 1, 1708, Westminster (London). Composer of Harpsichord lessons. 1669-80 and 1695, Organist of Westminster Abbey. For his works, *see* the publication "Old English Composers," and a volume (British Museum), published 1700, "A Choice Collection of Ayres for the Harpsichord or Spinett," &c. In this collection the first "Sett" is by Blow (Almand, Corant, Minuett, Jigg).

* **Blumenthal, Jacques**, b. Oct. 4, 1829, Hamburg. Pupil of Grund (Hamburg); 1843, of C. W. von Bocklet (Pf.) and Sechter (Composition) in Vienna; afterwards of Halévy (Paris). 1848, in London, where he settled. Brilliant pianist and successful composer of fashionable, melodious, and effective drawing-room pieces:—
    La Source; Fleurs emblematiques (3); Lavisella; Chant du Cygne; Adagio sostenuto e Presto agitato; Ralouka, Marche turque, Op. 80; Chant national des Croates; Marches (2), Op. 17; La Caressante; Les deux Anges; Mazurkas (3), Op. 5 (3), Op. 9; Nocturnes (2), Op. 10; Une nuit à Venise.

*Blumenfeld, Felix, b. April 7, 1863, Cherson (Village Kowalewska). Pupil of Neuhaus (Elizabethgrad), 1881-85, of Th. Stein (Conserv. of St. Petersburg.) 1885, he received the diploma and gold medal for Pf. playing, and was appointed Prof. at the St. Petersburg Conserv.

Allegro de Concert (with Orchestra), Op. 7; Variations caractéristiques, Op. 8; 24 Preludes, Op. 17, &c.

*Blumer, Fritz, b. 1860, Glarus (Switzerland). At first (1871) a pupil at the Geneva Conserv.; gained (1874) the first prize; 1875-77, pupil at the Leipzig Conserv., where Wenzel and Reinecke were his teachers for Pf. and E. F. Richter for Composition; 1877, he received the "Helbig" prize; 1878-79, with Liszt in Weimar and Rome; 1884 and following years, gave successful performances at Pasdeloup's Concerts (Paris) and at the Crystal Palace Concerts; 1885, performed at the "Gewandhaus" Concerts (Leipzig); 1886, appointed Prof. at the Strassburg Conserv. as successor to Paderewski; 1888, performances at Lamoureux's Concerts (Paris).

Boccherini, Luigi, b. Feb. 19, 1743, Lucca; d. May 28, 1805, Madrid. 1785, Composer to the Royal Court of Spain. Author of—

3 Pf. Quintets (Op. 40); 6 ditto (Op. 46); 6 ditto (posthumous works); 12 Trios; a good number of Vln. Sonatas and Solo Sonatas (Op. 4).

Bocklet, Carl Maria von, b. 1801, Prague; d. July 15, 1881, Vienna. Pupil of Zawora (Prague), Hummel (Weimar) for Pf., and Dyonys Weber (Prague) for Composition. Excellent pianist, much admired for his eminent talent of improvisation, and most successful teacher; amongst his best known pupils are Louis Köhler and Jacques Blumenthal.

*Bocklet, Heinrich von (son of the above), b. Nov. 7, 1850, Vienna. Pupil of his father and of Franz Krenn. From 1878 till 1887, Prof. at the Imperial Institute for teachers; since 1887, only private teacher.

Popular method of Pf. playing and editor of Japanese melodies, harmonised, &c.

Böhm, Carl, b. Sept. 11, 1844, Berlin. Pupil of Löschhorn (Pf.), Flodoard Geyer and Aug. Reissmann (Composition). Composed and published a great number of drawing-room pieces, but also important works, such as Sonatas and Trios. Received from the Duke of Anhalt-Dessau the gold medal for art and science.

Böhm, Georg, b. 1661, near Gotha; date of death unknown. He was considered an excellent composer. 1700, Organist at Lüneburg. Of his Clavecin works may be mentioned—

3 Suites, an Overture, and a Fugue.

Böhner, Johann Ludwig, b. Jan. 8, 1787, Töttelstädt (Gotha); d. there, March 28, 1860. A decidedly gifted but erratic musician, whom the well-known author G. T. A. Hoffmann took as model for his "Capellmeister Kreisler." 1810-20, he travelled as a virtuoso, composed a great deal, accused C. M. von Weber of stealing his ideas. Sank—owing to dissipated habits—deeper and deeper, and died eventually in great distress. Before 1830 he had written 5 Concertos—

After 1830 appeared a Sonata, Op. 15, a Fantasia-Sonata, Op. 130 (!) and a Grand Sonata, Op. 188. Of the intervening *Opera* scarcely anything is known. Besides these he published Fantasias, Bagatelles, Caprices, Variations (one set, Op. 3, has been re-published by Breitkopf and Härtel), Aquarellen, &c. He also wrote Studies in all keys, after A. E. Müller's principles. A Fantaisie Romanesque for 4 hands was lately published in a new edition.

Bohrer, Sophie (daughter of the Violinist, Anton B.), b. 1828, Stuttgart; d. St. Petersburg. Excellent pianist. When only six years old she created an extraordinary sensation by her wonderful execution, prodigious memory, and eminent talent for improvisation; at that time she was called "the female Liszt." Her first teacher was her mother (née Dulcken, of Munich). After travelling for several years, she married, 1846, M. Börninghausen, proprietor of an estate in Westphalia. On account of nervous debility, she was treated in Paris by a magnetiser; for reasons unknown she separated from her husband and married, later, an assistant of the magnetiser. Any information about her further life or career is entirely wantnig; neither her Munich nor Stuttgart relations are able to give it. Her memory was in every respect astonishing—nay, phenomenal. It is on record that at a concert given by her in Vienna she presented in the programme a list of not less than 80 pieces, offering to play any of these from memory at the choice of her audience. Among those present were Czerny, Thalberg, and other celebrated musicians, who accordingly selected several of the most complicated and difficult, all of which she rendered without hesitation and to the complete satisfaction of her critical listeners.

Bolck, Oscar, b. March 4, 1839, Hohenstein (East Prussia); d. May 2, 1888, Bremen. 1857, pupil of Moscheles (Pf.) and Jul. Rietz (Composition), in Leipzig; 1861, Prof. at a Music School in Wiborg (Finland); he returned, 1862, to Leipzig; 1866-67, teacher in Liverpool; afterwards again in Leipzig. 1875, appointed Prof. at the Music School in Riga. Composed and published a good many characteristic pieces for Pf., some of which became well known.

Bonewitz (Bonawitz), Johann Heinrich, b. Dec. 4, 1839, Dürckheim (Bavarian Palatinate). Pupil at the Liège Conserv.; then went to America, where he had to rely on his own studies. 1861-66, in Wiesbaden; 1871, in New York, where he established and conducted the Popular Concerts. Returned to Europe and settled in London, where he gave Historical Pf. Recitals. Composed, among other pieces—
  A Grand Fantasia, "Sur la mer," Op. 28; a Concerto with Orchestra, Op. 36; a Sonata for Pf. and Vln. in A min., Op. 40.

Bontempo, João Domingos, b. 1781, Lisbon; d. there 1847. Details as to the instruction he received are wanting. 1806, he settled as a teacher in Paris; went, after a few years, to London, where he remained until 1818. Returned to Paris. At that time about 22 of his works had been published there. Among them were 2 Concertos with Orchestral Accompaniments, Sonatas (Op. 1 and 5), and several Fantasias and Variations (*Fandango*). Returned, 1821, to Lisbon, where he founded a Conserv. and the Philharmonic Society. 1816, he published a method of Pf. playing (London).

Boom, Jan van, b. Oct. 15, 1807, Utrecht; d. April, 1872, Stockholm. Pupil of his father. From 1859-65, Prof. at the Royal Academy of Stockholm. Composed—
  Pf. Duets, Trios, and Studies, which deserve attention.

*****Borwick,** Leonard, b. Feb. 26, 1868, Walthamstow (Essex). Pupil of Henry R. Bird. 1884, entered the Conserv. of Frankfort o/M. and remained till 1890; pupil of Madame Schumann (1885-90), and of Dr. Bernhard Scholz and Iwan Knorr (Composition and Counterpoint). Appeared in London 1890 and has performed since then with increasing success at the Popular and Crystal Palace Concerts, &c.

Boulanger, Ernest Henri Alexandre, b. Sept. 16, 1816, Paris. Pupil of Alkan (Pf.), Halévy, and Lesueur (Composition). His compositions, mostly drawing-room pieces, are highly effective and enjoy a certain popularity.

Boyce, William (Mus. Doc.), b. 1710, London; d. there Feb. 7, 1779. Among his compositions for Clavecin, a Concerto is to be mentioned.

Brahms, Dr. Johannes, b. May 7, 1833, Hamburg. Pupil of Eduard Marxsen. For some time Conductor in Detmold; settled (1862) in Vienna; resided at times in Hamburg, Zurich, Baden, Heidelberg; but from 1869 permanently in the Austrian capital, where he conducted, 1872-74, the Concerts of the Gesellschaft der Musikfreunde. The University of Breslau conferred on him the diploma of Hon. Doc. Phil.; the University of Cambridge offered to confer on him the diploma of Mus. Doc., *hon. causâ*; and Hamburg gave him the freedom of the city. He is a Member of the "Ordre pour le mérite" (Prussia), Knight of the Imperial Austrian Order of Leopold (a distinction never before bestowed on a musician), Member of the Bavarian Maximilian Order for Art and Science, and Knight of several other orders. His compositions are:—
  Sonatas, Op. 1, Op. 2, and Op. 5; Sonatas for Pf. and Vln., Op. 78, Op. 100, and Op. 108; Sonatas for Pf. and V'cello, Op. 38, Op. 99; Trios for Pf., Vln., and V'cello, Op. 8, Op. 40 (also for Vln. and Hn.), Op. 87, Op. 101; Quartets for Pf., Vln., Vla., and V'cello, Op. 25, Op. 26; Quintet for Pf. and Strings, Op. 34; Concertos, Op. 15, Op. 83; Variations on a theme of Schumann, Op. 9, Variations: 1. On an original theme; 2. On a Hungarian Melody, Op. 21; Variations for 4 hands on a theme of Schumann, Op. 23; Variations on a theme of Handel, Op. 24; Variations (28) on a theme of Paganini, Op. 35; Variations for 2 Pf. on a theme of Haydn; Ballades (4), Op. 10; Scherzo, Op. 4; Capriccios and Intermezzi, Op. 76; Rhapsodies (2), Op. 79; Fantasias, Intermezzi, and Capriccios, 2 books, Op. 116; Intermezzi (3), Op. 117; Intermezzi, Romanze, Op. 118; Intermezzi, Rhapsodie, Op. 119; Waltzes (16), for 4 hands, Op. 39; Hungarian Dances for 4 hands (2 books); Gavotte by Gluck, transcribed; Study after Chopin ,Op. 25, No. 2); Study after Weber's Moto perpetuo, Op. 24; Bach's Chaconne, arranged for the left hand; 51 Studies (1893).

*****Brambach,** Carl Joseph, b. July 14, 1833, Bonn-on-the-Rhine. 1851-54, pupil at the Cologne Conserv., as a "Mozart" Scholar, pupil of Hiller. 1858-61, Prof. at the Cologne Conserv.; 1861-69, Musik-Director at Bonn, where he now resides as private teacher. Composer of—
  2 Pf. Quartets, a Sextuor, a Concerto, Sonatas, and a considerable number of Pf. Solo pieces.

Brandes, Emma (wife of Prof. Engelmann), b. Jan. 20, 1854, near Schwerin. Pupil of Aloys Schmitt, jun. (Pf.), and of Goltermann, of Frankfort (Composition) Excellent performer. She was cordially received in London, 1871 and 1872, as well as on the Continent. Resides in Utrecht.

Brassin, Leopold (younger brother of Louis B.), b. May 28, 1843, Strassburg (Alsace). 1857, named Hof-Pianist to the Duke of Coburg. Teacher at the Music School of Berne; went to St. Petersburg, from there to Constantinople, where he died, 1890. Composed Concertos for 1 and for 2 Pf. and many Solo pieces.

Brassin, Louis, b. June 24, 1836, Aix-la-Chapelle; d. May 17, 1884, St. Petersburg. 1847, pupil at the Leipzig Conserv. of Moscheles; 1866, Prof. at the Stern Conserv. (Berlin); 1869, Prof. at the Brussels Conserv.; 1879, in the same capacity at the St. Petersburg Conserv. Excellent pianist and composer of — with regard to technical difficulties—interesting Solo pieces.

*Breitner, Louis, b. March 22, 1854, Trieste. Pupil (took first prize) at the Milan Conserv.; later, pupil of A. Rubinstein and Liszt. Has resided since 1876 at Paris. Composer of a Quartet and shorter pieces. Officier de l'instruction publique en France, and Knight of the Order of Charles III. of Spain. President of the musical society "la Gallia."

Breslaur, Emil (Prof.), b. May 29, 1836, Kottbus (district of Frankfort o/Oder). He studied modern languages, the Hebrew grammar, Talmud religious code, &c., literature, and music, and was elected teacher of religion and preacher of the Synagogue of his native town. Settled, 1863, in Berlin; was for four years pupil at the Stern Conserv , under Jean Vogt and Ehrlich (Pf.), Kolbe, Weitzmann, and F. Geyer (Composition). 1868-79, Prof. at Kullak's Academy and musical critic to several Berlin papers; Knight of the Order of the Prussian Crown, the Italian Order of St. Mauritius and Lazarus, the Brunswick Order of the Lion, &c., and editor of the journal *Der Clavierlehrer*. Of his works the best known are: "Technische Grundlagen des Clavierspiels" (technical basis of Pf. playing, 4 editions), "Technische Uebungen" (technical exercises), "Methodik des Clavier-Unterrichts," "Clavierschule," 8 editions, and many Solo pieces.

Breunung, Ferdinand, b. March 2, 1830, Brockerode (Thuringia); d. Sept. 22, 1883, Aix-la-Chapelle. 1844, pupil of Mendelssohn and Hauptmann, in Leipzig. 1855, Prof. at the Cologne Conserv.; 1865, Musical Director at Aix-la-Chapelle, where he did much for the improvement of the different musical societies and for public taste in general.

*Bright, Dora, b. Aug. 16, 1863, Sheffield. Pupil at the R.A.M. from 1881-88. From 1884, Sub-Prof. in the classes of Walter Macfarren (Pf.) and Ebenezer Prout (Harmony and Composition). Among her compositions are 2 Pf. Concertos, a Quartet, 3 Duets for 2 Pf.; all of them were performed at public concerts with eminent success.

*Brissler, Friedrich Ferdinand, b. July 13, 1818, Insterburg; d. July 30, 1893, Berlin. He went, 1836, to Berlin, in order to complete his studies; became teacher at the Stern Conserv., and made his name known by his excellent arrangements of classical works.

Brisson, Frédéric, b. Dec. 25, 1821, Angoulême (Charente). Since 1846, resident in Paris. Composer of a great number of fashionable pieces. In his piece, "La Rose et le Papillon," he was the first to introduce the device of engraving the melody in large and the accompaniment in smaller notes; thus in the above piece all that concerns the *Rose* is in large notes, whilst the part of the *Papillon* (butterfly) is in smaller type. This piece was published in 1848. The same device has been adopted by Thalberg in his "l'Art du Chant."

Bronsart von Schellendorf, Hans, b. Feb. 11, 1830, Berlin. 1849, pupil of Dehn for Harmony, and of Theodor Kullak for Pf. 1854-57, with Liszt, in Weimar; 1860, Conductor of the Euterpe Concerts in Leipzig; 1867, Director of the Royal Theatre of Hanover. He went, 1870, as a volunteer to the French war and obtained the Iron Cross.
Trio, Op. 1; various Solo pieces (Aus der Jugendzeit, Op. 2); a Concerto in F sharp min.; a Fantasia, &c.

Bronsart, Ingeborg (*née* Starck), wife of the above; b. Aug. 24, 1840, St. Petersburg. At first pupil of Martinoff and Decker, later of Henselt; and, 1858, of Liszt, in Weimar.
Concertos, Sonatas, Studies, Fugues, and Drawing-room pieces.

Bruch, Max, b. Jan. 6, 1838, Cologne. At first a pupil of his mother; later, obtained the "Mozart" Scholarship of Frankfort o/M., and so was for three years pupil of Hiller. 1862, in Mannheim; 1865, in Coblentz; 1867, Hof-Capellmeister to the Prince of Sondershausen; 1870, in Berlin; 1872, in Bonn; 1878, Director of the Stern Choral Society of Berlin; 1880-82, Conductor of the Liverpool Philharmonic Society; 1882, of the Orchestral Society of Breslau; 1889, he settled in Berlin and is now Royal Prof. of the "Akademische Meisterschule für Composition," and, as such, Member of the Senate of the Royal Academy; Member of the Royal Bavarian Maximilian Order for Art and Science, Knight of the Order of the Prussian Crown, Hon. Mus. Doc. of the Cambridge University (June 13, 1893). Among his Pf. compositions may be mentioned—

A Fantasia for 2 Pf., Op. 11; 6 smaller pieces, Op. 12; a Romanza and Phantasiestück, Op. 14, &c.

*****Brüll, Ignaz**, b. Nov. 7, 1846, Prossnitz (Moravia). Pupil of Julius Epstein (Pf.), Rufinatscha (Composition), and Dessoff (Instrumentation). Received the Würtemberg gold medal for Art and Science on the Riband of the "Friedrich" Order of Merit. Hon. Member of the "Société Philharmonique" of Athens; one of the Directors and principal Prof. of the Pf. at the "Horak" School (Vienna). Composer of—

Concertos, Op. 10 and Op. 24; a Rhapsody, Op. 65, with Orchestral accompaniments; a Suite, Op. 60; Studies (9), Op. 61; Theme and Variations, Op. 39; ditto, Op. 45; Scherzi (2), Op. 20; a great many Mazurkas (Op. 35, in G, a great favourite); Impromptus, Romanzas, Album Leaves, Caprices, &c. For 2 Pf., he composed; Tarantella, Op. 6; Sonata, Op. 19; and Duo, Op. 64.

Brunner, Christian Traugott, b. Dec. 12, 1792, Brünlos, near Stollberg (Saxony); d. April 14, 1874, Chemnitz. He wrote a great number of educational works which still enjoy, in some parts of Germany, a deserved popularity owing to the correctness of their style and practicability of execution.

Bruyck, Carl Debrois van, b. March 14, 1828, Brünn (Moravia). 1842, pupil of August Mittag (Pf.); 1850, of Rufinatscha (Composition). His essays on Schumann created considerable interest, and his technical and æsthetical analyses of Bach's 48 Preludes and Fugues were received with great favour. His pamphlet, "The development of Piano-music from Seb. Bach to Schumann," is written in a masterly style and deserves translation into English. Pf. compositions: Variations in A, Op. 21, and Variations in D flat, Op. 22.

Bülow, Dr. Hans Guido von, b. Jan. 8, 1830, Dresden; d. Feb. 12, 1894, Cairo. At first a pupil of Mdlle. Schmiedel, afterwards of Wieck and Litolff (Pf.), Max Eberwein and Hauptmann (Theory and Composition); 1846-48, pupil at the Stuttgart College; 1848, student at the Leipzig University; 1850, at the Berlin University, in order to study law; 1851, in Weimar, with Liszt; 1854, principal teacher at the Stern Conserv.; 1854, in Russia; 1865, in Munich as Court Pianist to the King of Bavaria; 1866, went to Basle, but on receiving, Dec. 30 of the same year, the appointment as Royal Capellmeister and Director of the Royal Music School at Munich, he returned to the Bavarian capital and remained there until 1869, when he resigned on account of family dissensions. 1869-72, he resided in Florence. After 1872 he again gave public concerts in almost all European countries; 1875, he went to America; 1876, he was in England; 1877-80, he was Royal Capellmeister at Hanover; 1880-84, Intendant (Director) of the Meiningen Theatre and Orchestra. Latterly he conducted the Philharmonic Concerts of Berlin and Hamburg. His edition of Beethoven's Sonatas (beginning with Op. 53) is most valuable; less so his edition of Emanuel Bach and Domenico Scarlatti's Sonatas, which suffers from anachronisms. The King of Prussia conferred on him the title of Pianist to the Court, which appointment he resigned; the University of Jena made him Dr. Ph., *hon. causâ*, and many sovereigns bestowed on him Orders of Knighthood. As a pianist he was universally admired for the acuteness of his understanding, phenomenal memory, extraordinary technique, and lucidity of phrasing. Of his Pf. compositions, only a few became generally known.

Bürgel, Constantin, b. June 24, 1837, Liebau (Silesia). Pupil of Brosig (Breslau) and Kiel (Berlin). 1869-70, Prof. at the Kullak Academy in Berlin, where he now resides. Among his compositions, a Sonata in A, Op. 5; Suite, Op. 6; and Phantasiestücke, Op. 13, became well known.

Bungert, August, b. March 14, 1846, Mühlheim o/Ruhr. At first a pupil of H. Kufferath (Pf.); later, studied at the Cologne Conserv. He was afterwards for two years at the Paris Conserv., under Matthias. After leaving Paris he was for four years Musical Director at Kreuznach, but settled ultimately in Pegli, near Genoa. His compositions for Pf. enjoy a considerable popularity, particularly his "Pictures of Italian travel" (2 books).

*Buonamici, Giuseppe, b. Feb. 12, 1846, Florence. Pupil of his uncle, Ceccherini, in Florence, and of Dr. von Bülow in Munich. For three years a teacher at the Royal Music School of Munich. His compilations of technical figures found in Beethoven's Pf. and Chamber music (Passaggi estratti dalle opere per Pianoforte solo o con altri istrumenti, aggruppati, dileggiati e metti in forma di Studii giornalieri), his edition of Bertini's Studies in graduating difficulty, and of Bach's smaller Preludes and Fugues, are very much esteemed. He is also the editor of Ricordi's *Biblioteca del Pianista*. Only 3 of his original compositions are published.

*Burchard, Carl, b. Sept. 21, 1818. Hamburg. Pupil of Julius Otto and J. J. F. Dotzauer. Since 1842, has resided at Dresden. His name is well known by his successful, practical, and effective arrangements of classical pieces, more particularly for 4 performers on 2 pianos.

Burckhardt, Salomon, b. Nov. 3, 1803, Tripitis (near Weimar); d. Feb. 19, 1849, Dresden. Greatly esteemed as an excellent teacher and as a composer of well-written and useful educational pieces.

Burgmein, J. *See* Ricordi, Giulio.

Burgmüller, Friedrich, b. 1806, Regensburg (Ratisbon); d. Feb. 13, 1874, Beaulieu (France). His Studies— particularly Op. 100 and 105—and smaller pieces are very popular for their practical and useful contents.

Burgmüller, Norbert (brother of the above), b. Feb. 8, 1810, Düsseldorf; d. May 7, 1836, Aix-la-Chapelle. Pupil of Spohr and Hauptmann (Cassel). Composer of noteworthy works; a Concerto, Sonatas, and Quartets. The Sonata, Op. 8, and Rhapsody, Op. 13, are particularly esteemed.

Burney, Dr. Charles, b. April 7 (? 12), 1726, Shrewsbury; d. April 12, 1814, Chelsea College. Among his Clavecin works are 6 Sonatas, a Sonata Trio with accompaniment of Vln. and V'cello, and 2 books of Duets (4 hands), 1778.

Burrowes, John Freckleton, b. April 23, 1787, London; d. there, March 31, 1852. Pupil of William Horsley. Author of a Pf. Primer and many Pf. pieces.

*Busoni, Ferruccio Benvenuto, b. April 1, 1866, Empoli (Florence). Pupil of his mother; was already giving Concerts when only 8 years old. 1880-81, pupil of Dr. Meyer-Rémy, of Graz (Styria). He travelled for two years in Italy and received from his native town a gold medal, struck in his honour. 1888, principal Prof. at the Helsingfors College of Music. 1890, he received the "Rubinstein" Prize for composition; has since become Prof. at the Moscow Conserv. Composed many works for the Pf.

Bussmeyer, Hans, b. March 29, 1853, Brunswick. Pupil (now Prof.) at the Munich Conserv. and of Liszt (Weimar). Pianist of distinction, composer of a good number of pieces, editor of Studies (Kessler, &c).

Bussmeyer, Hugo (elder brother of the above), b. Feb. 26, 1842, Brunswick. Pupil of Carl Richter and H. Litolff (Pf.) and Methfessel (Composition). 1860, in South America; after journeys to Monte Video, Buenos Ayres, Chili and Peru, he went, 1867, to New York and Paris; in 1868, to South Mexico, and then settled permanently in New York, where he performs at concerts and teaches. His compositions for Pf. are not very numerous.

*Buths, Julius, b. May 7, 1851, Wiesbaden. Pupil of his father and Fr. Gernsheim (Pf.), at Freudenberg, and Hiller (Composition) at Cologne, and later of Fr. Kiel (Berlin). 1871-72, Conductor of the St. Cecilia Society (Wiesbaden); gained, 1873, the "Meyerbeer" Scholarship; 1873-74, he sojourned in Milan and Paris; 1875-79, Conductor in Breslau; 1879-90, in Elberfeld; since 1890, Conductor of the musical societies of Düsseldorf. Brilliant pianist and composer of a Suite, Sarabande, and Gavotte, Novelletten, Concerto, Quintet, &c.

Buttstedt, Johann Heinrich, b. April 25, 1666, Erfurt; d. there, Dec. 1727. Pupil of Pachelbel. He was noted for his excellent performances. Of his compositions, the "Musikalische Clavierkunst und Vorrathskammer" was published, 1716, in Leipzig. The work consists of 4 Preludes and Fugues, Aria with 18 Variations, and 2 Parthien (Suites) of Clavecin pieces.

Byrd (Byrde, Bird), William (performer on the Virginal), b. about 1538, London; d. there, July 4, 1623. Pupil of Tallis. The "Virginal Book of Queen Elizabeth" and "Lady Nevill's Virginal Book" contain his short pieces. Refer to "Parthenia" and Pauer's "Old English Composers."

C.

*****Calkin,** John Baptiste, b. March 16, 1827, London. Pupil of his father, James C. Prof. at the Guildhall School of Music.
> Sonatas, Studies (Concert Study in double notes), Minuets, Caprices Mélodiques, 6 Caprices, "Youth and Age," Op. 100; Pieces for 4 hands, &c.

Callcott, William Hutchins, b. 1807, Kensington; d. there, Aug. 4, 1882. Son of Dr. John Wall C. His compositions are written in a popular style and mostly for educational purposes. His "Half-hours with the best Composers" have had a large circulation.

Carpentier, le. *See* Lecarpentier.

Carreño, Teresa (Madame d'Albert), b. Dec. 22, 1853, Venezuela. Pupil of her father, later of Gottschalk in New York and George Matthias in Paris. After having resided for some time in London, she travelled, 1889-90, in Germany, and obtained after 1891 a great reputation by her brilliant and effective performances. 1893, appointed Court Pianist of Saxony.

Castello, Dario. Dates of birth and death not known. His published compositions are—
> Sonate Concertante in stilo moderno per sonar nel Organo, ovverro Spinetta con diversi stromenti. Libro Primo. In Venetia, 1629. Libro secondo sec., 1644.

Castello, Giovanni. Dates of birth and death not known. He published—
> Neue Clavier-Übung, bestehend in einer Sonate. Caprice, Allemande, Corrente, Sarabande, &c. Wien, 1721.

Catel, Charles Simon, b. June, 1773, l'Aigle (Orne); d. Nov. 29, 1830, Paris. Pupil of Gobert and Gossec. 1795, Prof. at the newly-founded Paris Conserv.; 1810, Inspector; retired, 1814; 1817, elected a Member of the Academy.
> 3 Sonatas, Op. 1; ditto with Vln., Op. 4; Sonatinas.

*****Cavallo,** Peter (son of the Royal Bavarian Court-musician, I. N. C.), b. Dec. 23, 1819, Munich; d. April 19, 1891, Paris. Showed, when only in his tenth year, uncommon talent. At first a pupil of Madame Golliet (Pf.) and Caspar Ett (Composition). 1836, at Vienna, pupil of Sechter (Composition); and a highly successful teacher; 1842, he settled in Paris. His Pf. works number about 84.

Chambonnières, André (Jacques ?) Champion de, b. about 1600; d. 1670 (?). Came from a musical family. Clavecinist to Louis XIV.; teacher of Hardelle, Le Bègue, d'Anglebert, and François Couperin.
> Pièces de Clavecin, 2 books (Paris: Ballard, 1670). Reprinted by Farrenc, in the "Trésor du Pianiste."

*****Chaminade,** Cécile, b. Aug. 8, 1861, Paris. Pupil of Le Couppey and Savard. She is at the present time undoubtedly recognised as the foremost French lady composer.
> Concertos, Trios, and highly effective solo pieces; Concert Studies; "Automne," Op. 35; "Fileuse," Op. 35; "Marine," Op. 38; "Toccata," Op. 39; "Arabesque," "Les Sylvains," "La Moreña," Op. 67; "Tarantelle," Op. 35; and a Gigue, Op. 43.

Chaulieu, Charles (composer of educational pieces), b. June 21, 1788, Paris, d. 1849, London. Pupil of Adam (Pf.) and Catel (Composition). 1840, he settled in London. Among his many educational works, a collection of Studies, "l'Indispensable," enjoyed a certain reputation.

Cherubini, Luigi Maria Carlo Zenobio Salvatore, b. Sept. 14, 1760, Florence; d. March 15, 1842, Paris. Pupil of Sarti (Bologna). 6 Sonatas and a Fugue.

Chopin, Frédéric François, b. March 1, 1809, Zelazowa Wola (near Warsaw); d. Oct. 17, 1849, Paris. Pupil of Zywny (Pf.) and Joseph Elsner (Composition). 1830, he travelled to Breslau, Dresden, Prague, Vienna, Munich, and to Paris, where he remained until his death, with exception of 1838 when, on account of ill-health, he went to Majorca. A monument was erected to him, 1869, in Warsaw, and a second one has been erected (1894) in his native place. A collection of his letters appeared, 1877 (Franz Ries, Dresden). His extraordinary merits, striking originality, and the impetus he gave to technical execution, romantic and poetic feeling, have often been recognised with sincere enthusiasm. He founded an entirely new school. The popularity of his Nocturnes, Ballades, Impromptus, Scherzos, Valses, and Polonaises becomes greater with every year; and the actual indispensability of his wonderful Studies as a means to become an accomplished pianist is now universally acknowledged. He is decidedly the most original of all composers for the Pf., his technical figures are entirely new, his ornaments graceful, at times almost ethereal, the basses noble and independent, the harmonies rich, the modulations free and natural, the rhythmical part fresh and fascinating, the melodies distinguished; indeed, many points of extreme beauty meet here, and it is therefore not astonishing that his works are among the most popular in existence :—

Concertos: No. 1 in E min., Op. 11; No. 2 in F min., Op. 21. *Trio* in G min., Op. 8. *Sonatas:* No. 1 in C min., Op. 4; No. 2 in B flat min., Op 35; No. 3 in G min., with V'cello, Op. 65; No. 3 in B min., Op. 58. Allegro de Concert in A, Op. 46. *Ballades:* No. 1 in G min., Op. 23; No. 2 in F, Op. 38; No. 3 in A flat, Op. 47; No. 4 in F min., Op. 52. *Impromptus:* No. 1 in A flat, Op. 29; No. 2 in F sharp, Op. 36; No. 3 in G flat, Op. 51. *Scherzi:* No. 1 in B min., Op. 20; No. 2 in B flat min., Op. 31; No. 3 in C sharp min., Op. 39; No. 4 in E, Op. 54. *Polonaises:* No. 1 in C (arranged by Czerny), Op. 3; No. 2 in E flat (with orch. accomp.), Op. 22; Nos. 3 and 4 in C sharp min. and E flat min., Op. 26; Nos. 5 and 6 in A and C min., Op. 40; No. 7 in F sharp min., Op. 44; No. 8 in A flat, Op. 53; No. 9 (Fantaisie) in A flat, Op. 61. *Preludes:* (24), Op. 28; Prelude in C sharp min., Op. 45. *Mazurkas:* (4), Op. 6, Nos. 1, 2, 3, 4; (5), Op. 7, Nos. 5, 6, 7, 8, 9; (4), Op. 17, Nos. 10, 11, 12, 13; (4), Op. 24, Nos. 14, 15, 16, 17; (4), Op. 30, Nos. 18, 19, 20, 21; (4), Op. 33, Nos. 22, 23, 24, 25; (4), Op. 41, Nos. 26, 27, 28, 29; (3), Op. 50, Nos. 30, 31, 32; (3), Op. 56, Nos. 33, 34, 35; (3), Op. 59, Nos. 36, 37, 38, (3), Op. 63, Nos. 39, 40, 41. *Valses:* No. 1 in E flat, Op. 18; Nos. 2, 3, 4 in A flat, A min., F, Op. 34; No. 5 in A flat, Op. 42; Nos. 6, 7, 8 in D flat, C sharp min., A flat, Op. 64. *Variations:* in B flat (Là ci darem la mano), Op. 2; Variations in B flat (Je vends des Scapulaires), Op. 12; Variations in E (Hexameron). *Berceuse* in D flat, Op. 57. *Barcarolle* in F sharp, Op. 60. *Bolero* in C, Op. 19. *Nocturnes:* Nos. 1, 2, 3 in B flat min., E flat, B, Op. 9; Nos. 4, 5, 6 in F, F sharp, G min., Op. 15; Nos. 7, 8 in C sharp min. and D flat, Op. 27; Nos. 9, 10 in B and A flat, Op. 32; Nos. 11, 12 in G min. and G, Op. 37; Nos. 13, 14 in C min. and F sharp min., Op. 48; Nos. 15, 16 in F min., E flat, Op. 55; Nos. 17, 18 in B and E, Op. 62. *Rondos:* No. 1 in C min., Op. 1; No. 2 in F, Op. 5; No. 3 in F, Op. 14 (Krakowiak); No. 4 in E flat, Op. 16. *Tarantelle* in A flat, Op. 43. *Fantasias:* No. 1 in A (Polish melodies), Op. 13; No. 2 in F min., Op. 49; No. 3, Fantaisie Polonaise, Op. 61 (*see* Polonaises, No. 9). *Etudes:* (12), Op. 10; Etudes (12), Op. 25. *Without Opus number:* Duo Concertante, Pf. and V'cello; Mazurkas, Nos. 42, 43. *Posth. Works:* Fantaisie-Impromptu in C sharp min., Op. 66; Mazurkas (4), Op. 67; ditto, Op. 68; Mazurkas (5); Polonaises (3), Op. 71; Polonaises (2), G sharp min. and B flat min.; Valses (2), Op. 69; Valses (3), Op. 70; Valses (2), E maj. and min.; Nocturne (No. 19) in E min., Op. 72; Marche funèbre in C min.; Ecossaises (3); Rondo for 2 Pf., Op. 73; Variations (Thème allemand).

Chotek, Franz Xaver, b. 1800, Liebisch (Moravia); d. May 5, 1852, Vienna. Educational composer of great popularity in Austria.

Christiani, Adolph Friedrich, b. March 8, 1836, Cassel; d. Feb. 10, 1885, Elisabeth (United States). Director of a Music School. His work, "The principles of musical expression in Pianoforte-playing," was translated into German by Dr. H. Riemann.

Chwatal, Franz Xaver, b. June 19, 1808, Rumburg (Bohemia); d. June 24, 1879, Elmen (district of Magdeburg). Composer of many valuable educational works.

Clasing, Johann Heinrich, b. 1779, Hamburg, d. there, Feb. 8, 1829. Pupil of Schwencke. Trios, Sonatas, Fantasias, Rondos, which enjoyed in their time a considerable reputation.

Clauss (Szárvády), Wilhelmine, b. Dec. 13, 1834, Prague. Pupil of Proksch (Prague). Her brilliant, excellent, and musicianly performances were greatly admired. 1855, she married the Hungarian author Szárvády, who died 1882. For some years she has resided at Paris and occupies herself with teaching.

Clementi, Muzio, b. 1752, Rome; d. March 10, 1832, at his country house in Evesham (Worcestershire). Pupil of Buroni (Clavecin), Cordicelli and Carpini (Composition). 1766-70, resided with Mr. Beckford on his estate in Dorsetshire. Played after this with enormous success in London, &c.; 1780, went to Paris; 1781, to Vienna; returned to London and remained there until 1802. John Baptist Cramer was (1783) for one year his pupil. In 1802 he left for the Continent Among his pupils was John Field, who went with him to St. Petersburg. As Field decided to remain in Russia, Clementi took Zeuner as a pupil, and travelled with him to Dresden and Berlin. Aug. Alex. Klengel (Dresden) and Ludwig Berger (Berlin) became his pupils, and accompanied him on his return to St. Petersburg. After a sojourn of some time, Clementi came (1810) again to London. 1817, he published his well-known "Gradus ad Parnassum." 1820-21, he left once more for the Continent, remained a long time in Leipzig, where two of his Symphonies were performed. From 1821 until his death he resided in England. His compositions are very numerous. Breitkopf and Härtel, of Leipzig, have published 64 Sonatas and Sonatinas; these are:—

Nos. 1,† 2, 3, Op 2; Nos. 4, 5, 6,* Op. 7; Nos. 7, 8, 9, Op. 9; Nos. 10, 11, 12, Op. 10; Nos. 13, 14, 15, 16,* Op. 12; Nos. 17, 18, 19,* Op. 14; No. 20, Op. 17 (La Chasse); No. 21, Op. 19: No. 22, Op. 20; No. 23, Op. 21; Nos. 24, 25, 26, Op. 24; Nos. 27, 28, 29, Op. 25; Nos. 30,* 31,* 32, (p, 26; No. 33, Op. 27; Nos. 34, 35, 36, Op. 30; Nos. 37, 38, 39, Op. 33; Nos. 40, 41, Op. 34; Nos. 42, 43, Op. 35; Nos. 44, 45, 46, Op. 36 (Sonatinas); Nos. 47, 48, 49, Op. 37 (Sonatinas); Nos. 50, 51, 52, Op. 38; Nos. 53, 54, 55, Op. 39; Nos. 56,* 57, 58, Op. 40; No. 59, Op. 46 (dedicated to Fr. Kalkbrenner); Nos. 60, 61, Op. 47 (No. 61 was played before the Emperor Joseph II. in the presence of Mozart); Nos. 62, 63,* 64* (Didone abbandonata), Op. 50 (dedicated to Cherubini). The Sonatas marked (*) are the most celebrated and best known 7 Sonatas for 4 hands; 2 Sonatas for 2 Pf., Op. 12 and 46; about 40 Sonatas with Vln. or Fl ; between 30 and 40 Trios for Pf., Vln. (Fl.), and V'cello; Studies: Gradus ad Parnassum, ou l'art de jouer le Pianoforte, demontré par des Exercices dans le style sévère et dans le style élégant. 3 vols., 100 numbers. The 1st part appeared 1817. Méthode de Pianoforte, en 2 Parties (Paris); Introduction à l'art de toucher le Pianoforte, avec 50 leçons (London, 1797); Préludes et Exercices dans tous les tons majeurs et mineurs (1790); 8 Cadences; Grand Exercice doigté (Czerny); Caprices, Préludes et Point d'orgue, composés dans le goût de Haydn, Mozart, Kozeluch, Merkel, Wanhal et Clementi, Op. 19; 5 Caprices, Op. 18, 35 (or 36), and Op. 47; Toccata in B flat; 6 Fugues; 12 Books of Variations, Op. 48, Op. 19, Op. 43; Rondeaux, Divertissements, and about 60 Dances (Minuets, Waltzes, Monferines).

*Coenen, Willem, b. Nov. 17, 1837, Rotterdam. First taught by his father and sister, later by Ernst Lübeck and Sigismund Thalberg. Since 1862, resident in London. Travelled in the West Indies, North and South America. Among his compositions is a Caprice for 16 performers on 8 pianos.

Colizzi, Giovanni Andrea, b. about 1740 (where?); d. (when?). He lived for many years in England and Holland. 2 Concertos, Op. 2 (Hague and London);

Sonatas with Vln., 3 with Vla., and a Solo, "La bataille d'Ivry" (Heckel, Mannheim).

Concone, Giuseppe, b. 1810, Turin; d. there in June, 1861. Although Prof of Singing, he composed a good many educational Pf. works, among which his Studies obtained popularity:—

25 Etudes mélodiques, Op. 2; 20 Etudes chantantes, Op. 30; 15 Etudes expressives, Op. 44; 15 Etudes de genre, Op. 25; and 15 Etudes de style, Op. 31. The whole collection is entitled, Ecole mélodique.

Coop, Ernesto Antonio Luigi, b. June 17, 1802, Messina; d. Nov. 1, 1879, Naples. His power as a composer was devoted to popular pieces, of which about 130 are published by Ricordi and Lucca, of Milan.

Cooper, William. See Behr, Franz.

Corette (Corrette), Michel, called himself in his earlier works, Zipoli; b. 1685. He lived in Paris, and amongst his published works are—

Sonata d'intavolatura per Organo o cembalo; Toccate, versi, canzone, &c. (Roma, 1716); and Livre de Pièces pour le Clavecin, Œuvre 12 (Paris).

Couperin, Armand Louis (nephew of François C. le grand), b. Feb. 25, 1725, Paris; d. there, 1789. His wife (née Blanchet) was an excellent Clavecinist, who enjoyed a great reputation as a performer.

2 Sonates, Op. 1; † Trios (2) for Clavecin and Vln. (Violins ?), Op. 3. According to Fétis, these compositions are very solid, but dry and uninteresting.

Couperin, François (generally called Le Grand), son of Charles C. (1632-69); b. 1668, Paris; d. there, 1733. Pupil of Chambonnières; and the most distinguished of the French Clavecinists. Composer of the following works: Pièces de Clavecin, 4 Books: Livre I. (1713); Livre II. (1716, also 1722); Livre III. (1722!); Livre IV. (1730). Paris, gravé par F. du Plessy. Their contents are—Liv. I., 1-5 : Ordre (Suites) and Explication of the Agrémens (Grâces) et Signes. Liv. II., 6-12: Ordre (amongst them a piece for 2 Clavecins). Liv. III., 13-19: Ordre and 4 Concerts Royaux, with orchestral accompaniments. Liv. IV., 20-27: Ordre. The 27 Ordres (Suites) contain 208 short pieces and 4 Concertos. Other works of C. are: "L'art de toucher le Clavecin" (Paris, 1716), almost the only copies of this valuable work are possessed by the National Library of Paris and the Royal Library of Berlin; "L'Apothéose de l'incomparable Lully" (Paris, 1724), "Les goûts réunis ou nouveaux Concerts, augmentés de l'Apothéose de Corelli,

en Trio" (2 Vln. and Bass), Paris, 1717, also 1730. All the short pieces have characteristic titles, and in his preface he declares them to be musical portraits of distinguished, elegant, and amiable persons. *See* the preface to his Liv. I. The names of the pieces are as follows:
1, l'Auguste; 2, I. Courante; 3, II. Courante; 4, La Majestueuse; 5, Gavotte; 6, La Mylordine; 7, Menuet; 8, Les Sylvians; 9, Les Abeilles; 10, La Nanette; 11, Les Sentiments; 12, Les Blondes; 13, Les Brunes; 14, La Bourbonnaise; 15, La Manon; 16, L'Enchanteresse; 17, La Fleurie ou la tendre Nanette; 18, 19, Les plaisirs de Saint Germain en Laye; 20, La Laborieuse; 21, I. Courante; 22, II. Courante; 23, La Prude; 24, L'Antonine; 25, Gavotte; 26, Menuet; 27, Les Canaries; 28, Passepied; 29, Rigaudon; 30, La Charoloise; 31, La Diane; 32, Fanfare pour la Suite de la Diane; 33. La Terpsichore; 34, La Florentine; 35, La Garnier; 36, La Babet; 37, Les Idées heureuses; 38, La Mimi; 39, La Diligente; 40, La Flatteuse; 41, La Voluptueuse; 42, Les Papillons; 43, La Ténébreuse; 44, I. Courante; 45. II. Courante, 46, La Lugubre; 47, Gavotte; 48, Menuet; 49, Les Pélerines; 50, Les Laurentines; 51, L'Espagnolette; 52, Les Regrets; 53, Les Matelotes Provençales; 54, La Favorite; 55, La Lutine; 56, La Marché des Gris-vêtus; 57, Les Bacchanales; 58, La Pateline; 59, Le Réveille-Matin; 60, La Logivière; 61, I. Courante; 62, II. Courante; 63, La Dangereuse; 64, La Tendre Fanchon; 65, La Badine; 66, La Bandoline; 67, La Flore; 68, L'Angélique; 69, La Villers; 70, Les Vandangeuses; 71, Les Agréments; 72, Les Ondes. Other pieces by Couperin are called: Les grâces naturelles; L'Artiste; Les barricades mystérieuses; La Nointèle, and Les Bergeries. Of new editions, that revised and edited by Johannes Brahms is the only complete one.

*Cramer, Heinrich (Henri), b. Feb. 16, 1809, Stuttgart; d. May 31, 1877, Frankfort o/M. Pupil of P. Lindpaintner and Molique (Stuttgart), and later of Seyfried (Vienna). Chiefly known by his very popular Potpourris and Fantasias, &c., on airs of well-known operas.

Cramer, John Baptist, b. Feb. 24, 1771, Mannheim; d. April 16, 1858, Kensington (London). Was the eldest son of the well-known violinist and composer, Wilhelm C. (1745-99). Pupil of Benser, later (1782-83) of Schröter and of Clementi (one year only); C. F. Abel (1725-87), a pupil of Seb. Bach, was his teacher for Composition. 1788, he travelled a great deal and became celebrated as an eminent performer. 1832, he opened with Addison and Beale a business as musicseller; the firm still exists in London (Cramer and Co.). After having lived from 1832 till 1845 in Paris, he resided permanently in London. His chief fame rests on the great merit of his useful, beautiful, harmonious, and generally original Studies—of which Nos. 1-42 are the best known; Nos. 43-84, although most excellent, are less popular; and the Nos. 85-100, very beautiful works, would never obtain the celebrity of the first instalment. Schumann wrote in 1831 a most interesting account of these 16 supplementary Studies. As a composer C. was very prolific: he wrote 105 Sonatas for Pf. solo, with accompaniment for another instrument (generally Vln.). Of the solo Sonatas about 60 have been published. Of these the best known are:—

Grand Sonata, Op. 20, dedicated to Clementi; a Sonata, Op. 23, dedicated to J. Haydn; 3 Sonatas, Op. 25, 27, 29; "La Gigue," Op. 39 and Op. 40, which has been published by several firms. A Sonata which created considerable sensation is "La Parodie," Op. 43; also "L'Ultima," Op. 53; "Les Suivantes" (3 Sonatas, 57, 58, 59); "Le Retour de Londres," Op. 62, and a Grand Sonata, Op. 63, dedicated to Hummel. For 4 hands he wrote 2 Sonatas, a Duo Brillant, 12 Etudes en forme de Nocturne, and a few other pieces. With Orchestral accompaniment he produced (before 1828) 8 Concertos and a Concerto da Camera; "Le Retour à Vienne," Grand Variations, Introduction and Andante Varié. Of chamber music, 2 Pf. Quintets and 1 Quartet; about 40 Trios for Pf., Vln., and V'cello; 2 Serenades for Pf., Harp, Fl., and 2 Hns. Besides these greater works, there are a large number of Variations, Rondos, Divertissements, Adagios, Impromptus, Toccatas, Valses, &c.

None of these works, however, obtained anything like the great and well-deserved popularity his excellent and beautiful Studies enjoy even at present; whilst in Clementi's Gradus the technical part stands foremost, Cramer's Studies present the harmonious and melodious principle, and thus interest the student's mind and ear; indeed, it might be said that C. introduced the philanthropic and pleasing side of the study as a form. C. was a Knight of the Legion of Honour and Hon. Member of the Royal Academy of Stockholm.

Crotch, William (Mus. Doc.), b. July 5, 1775, Norwich; d. Dec. 29, 1847, Taunton. He was one of the most wonderful prodigies that ever existed, on whom Dr. Burney wrote in the Philosophical Transactions a "Paper on Crotch, the infant musician." He received his first regular instruction from Prof. Knyvett, of Cambridge, and later at St. Mary's College, Oxford, where he received his Doctor's degree and became Prof. at the University. In London he gave lectures and lessons, and filled the post of Prof.

Among his compositions for Pf. are Sonatas, which, however, are not so greatly esteemed as are his excellent arrangements of some of the instrumental works of Haydn, Mozart, and Beethoven. Other original works are -

> A Concerto for the Harpsichord or Pf., with an accompaniment for 2 Vln. and Bass, dedicated to Dr. Burney; Original Airs in various and familiar styles, Divertimento (2 books); Introduction and Fugue on a subject of 4 notes; Fugue for Pf. on a subject of Muffat's; Prelude and Air; 12 Fugues (published 1835-37); 30 Rondos, intended as an introduction to playing from score and reading the various clefs.

*Cui, Cesar Antonowitsch, b. 1835, Wilna. Pupil of Moniouszko. Before he devoted himself entirely to music, was an engineer, and Prof. of the engineering sciences (Imperial appointment) at St. Petersburg. Among his Pf. compositions, several obtained considerable popularity—

> Etude-Arabesque; Tarantelle (transcribed by Liszt); Petite Suite for Pf. and Vln.; 3 Valses, Op. 31; 3 Impromptus, Op. 35.

Cumann, Harriet Johann Louise, b. Dec. 26, 1851, Copenhagen. Was, 1872-75, one of Neupert's best pupils (Conserv.) and created in her country a decided sensation by her artistic and refined performances. She is considered to be one of the foremost pianists of the present time.

*Cusins, (since 1892, Sir) William George, b. Oct. 14, 1833, London; d. Aug. 31, 1893, Remonchamps (Ardennes). Entered the Chapel Royal as Chorister in 1842. Pupil at the Brussels Conserv. (1844), where Michelot was his Pf. teacher. Gained, 1847, the King's Scholarship at the R.A.M., London; re-elected, 1849; pupil of Bennett (Pf.), Cipriani Potter (Composition), and Sainton (Vln.). After completing, in 1851, his studies at the R.A.M., he was for many years Prof. at that Institution. 1849, Organist at Covent Garden Opera and of Her Majesty's Private Chapel; 1867, appointed Conductor of the Philharmonic Society's concerts, which post he held until 1884; 1870, appointed Master of Music to the Queen, which appointment he resigned, May, 1893; 1875, Prof. of Instrumental Music, Queen's College; 1885, Examiner at the Royal College of Music; 1885, Prof. of Pf. at the Guildhall School of Music. As a pianist he appeared in London, Leipzig, and Rome. In 1892 he received the honour of Knighthood.

> Concerto (A min.); Septet for Pf. and Wind instruments; Trio (E min.); Sonata, Pf. and Vln., and many smaller pieces.

Czerny, Carl, b. Feb. 20, 1791, Vienna; d. there, July 15, 1857. Son of Wenzel Czerny (1752-1832). Pupil of his father, afterwards enjoyed the advice of Beethoven. He began to teach when in his 14th year, and became, by degrees, the most popular and successful Pf. teacher in Vienna. Among his most celebrated pupils were Franz Liszt (1818-21), Theod. Döhler, Theod. Kullak, Madame Belleville-Oury, Leop. von Meyer, Alfred Jaell, &c. His chief merit consists in having produced most excellent, useful, and practically written Exercises and Studies, which are actually indispensable and have—with regard to their practicability—not yet been rivalled. Among the best known and universally used are—

> The School of Velocity, Op. 299 (40 Studies); The School of Legato and Staccato, Op. 335 (50 Studies); The School of Ornaments, Op. 355 (70 Studies); The School of the Left Hand, Op. 399 (10 Studies); The School of Fugue Playing, Op. 400 (24 Studies); The School of the Virtuoso, Op. 365 (4 books); Die Kunst der Fingerfertigkeit, Op. 740 (50 Studies); The Higher Degree of Virtuosity, Op. 834; Forty Daily Exercises, Op. 337.

Besides these, there is a great variety of special Studies for the shake, runs, arpeggio, thirds, octaves; indeed, for every imaginable feature of technique. In all, he wrote about 800 Studies. He composed a great number of Rondos, Fantasias, Divertissements, Sonatinas, Sonatas, and many pieces for 4 hands on 1 or 2 pianos. His collective works inclusive, the number of his *opera* reaches 1,000. To give an idea of his industry it may be mentioned that in his collective works, "Décaméron" contains 30 pieces; the "Souvenir Théatrale," Collection de Fantasies, fills 90 books; the "Musical Gallery of Flowers" gives 1,000 "tone-flowers" of celebrated composers; and "Les plaisirs du jeune Pianiste" consists of 160 récréations, &c.

Czerny, Joseph (no relation of the above), b. June 17, 1785, Horritz, Bohemia; d. Sept. 22, 1831, Vienna, where he resided. Was a teacher, musicseller, and composer. Among his best known pupils was Léopoldine Blahetka (*see* this name).

Czerwinski, Wilhelm, b. 1838, Vienna; d. Feb. 13, 1893, Lemberg. Pupil of Fischhof, Mikuli (Pf.), and Nottebohm (Theory). Was both excellent as a pianist and esteemed as a composer. He resided as a teacher in Lemberg.

D.

*Dachs, Joseph, b. Sept. 30, 1827, Regensburg (Ratisbon). At first, pupil of Kreutner (Pf.) and Mettenleiter (Harmony), of Regensburg. Went, 1884, to Vienna, became a pupil of Halm and Czerny (Pf.) and Simon Sechter (Composition). Performed with great success in Vienna and other towns, and was appointed, 1861, Prof. at the Vienna Conserv. Among his pupils may be named— Hans Schmitt, the late Joseph Rubinstein (no relation of Anton R.), Vladimir de Pachmann, Madame Laura Rappoldi (née Kahrer), Princess Bibesco, &c. Editor of several valuable educational works.

Dalberg, Johann Friedrich Hugo von (Dean of the Cathedrals of Trier, Worms, and Speyer), b. May 17, 1752, Coblenz; d. July 26, 1812, Aschaffenburg. Pupil of Ignaz Holtzbauer (1711-83), of Mannheim. Eminent pianist and composer.
<small>Quartet for Pf., Ob., Hn., and Bssn., Op. 25; Trios; Sonatas with Vln. Solo; Sonatas, Op. 9 and 20; a Sonata for *five* hands, Op. 19; and Sonatas for 4 hands.</small>

Damm, Friedrich, b. March 7, 1831, Dresden. Pupil of E. Krägen (Pf.) and Julius Otto; later also of A. Reichel (Counterpoint and Composition). His compositions, mostly intended for educational purposes, enjoy considerable popularity, whilst his activity as a teacher is highly appreciated and successful.

Dandrieu, Jean François, b. 1684, Paris; d. there, Jan. 16, 1740.
<small>Premier livre de pièces de Clavecin, contenant plusieurs Divertissements dont les principaux sont les caractères de la guerre, ceux de la chasse et la fête du village. Dédié au Roi (Paris, 1724). Also second and third books.</small>

*Dannreuther, Edward, b. Nov. 4, 1844, Strassburg, in Alsace. Was taught by F. L. Ritter, at Cincinnati, U.S.A. In 1856 he entered the Conserv. at Leipzig, and remained there till 1863, under Moscheles, Plaidy, Richter, and Hauptmann. Settled in London in 1863, where he was the first to play the Concertos of Liszt, Brahms, Grieg, Scharwenka, Tschaikowsky, Parry, &c. Founded the Wagner Society in 1872, and conducted its two series of concerts in 1873-74. Started concerts of chamber music in 1875, the twenty-third series of which was given in 1893. Wrote the articles on the principal pianists, from Couperin to Chopin, also the article on Wagner, in Grove's Dictionary of Music. He has repeatedly lectured at the Royal Institution on matters connected with the Pf. and its precursors, and has published essays on Beethoven, Chopin, Bach, and a historical treatise on Musical Ornamentation, of which the first part covers the period extending from Diruta to J. S. Bach, and the second, from C. Ph. E. Bach to the present time.

Daquin (Aquin d'), Louis Claude (Clavecinist and Organist), b. July 4, 1694, Paris; d. there, June 15, 1772. Patronised by Louis XIV., he performed at Court, and received good appointments. Premier livre de Pièces de Clavecin (Paris), 1735 (?).

*Davenport, Francis William, b. 1847, Wilderslowe, near Derby. Pupil of G. Macfarren. 1879, appointed Prof. at the R.A.M., and, 1882, at the Guildhall School of Music.
<small>6 pieces for Pf. and V'cello, 4 others ditto, and Trio in B flat.</small>

David, Félicien, b. April 13, 1810, Cadenet (Departement Vaucluse); d. Aug. 29, 1876, Paris. Pupil at the Paris Conserv. Membre de l'Académie, Chevalier de la Légion d'Honneur. Librarian of the Conserv.
<small>Short pieces; "Les Brises d'Orient," Recueil de mélodies pour Piano; "Les Minarets," 3 Mélodies pour Piano.</small>

Davies, Fanny, b. June 27, 18--, Guernsey. In Birmingham, pupil of Miss Welchmann and Charles Flavell (Pf.), Dr. Gaul (Composition). 1882-83, pupil at the Leipzig Conserv., of Reinecke and Paul (Pf.) and Jadassohn (Fugue and Counterpoint); 1883-85, pupil of Madame Schumann at the Hoch Conserv., of Frankfort o/M., where she also took lessons in fugue and composition from Dr. B. Scholz. She appeared in London for the first time on Oct. 17, 1885, and since this time her success as a pianist in England, Germany, and Italy has been continual.

Decker, Constantin, b. Dec. 29, 1810, Fürstenau (Brandenburg); d. Jan. 28, 1878, Holp (Pomerania). Pupil of Dehn. Resided, 1835-38, in Berlin, later at St. Petersburg (where Madame Ingeborg Stark-Bronsart was his pupil), and after 1859 at Holp.
Souvenir de la Pologne, Op. 24; Lui et Elle, Op. 25, I., and Nocturnes, Op. 25, II.

*__Delaborde,__ Eraim Moriam, b. Feb. 8, 1839, Paris. Pupil of Henselt and Moscheles, but mostly self-taught. 1873, appointed Prof. at the Paris Conserv. as successor to Madame Farrenc. Received the Legion of Honour in 1885. He is particularly well known for his excellent performances on the pedal piano.
12 Petits Préludes, Cadences pour les Concerts de Beethoven, Etude de Concert, Valse, Menuet d'Arlésienne, Fantaisie sur Carmen, Morceau romantique pour Piano et instruments à cordes, Overture "Attila" for 4 hands.

*__Delioux,__ Charles de Savignac, b. April, 1830, Lorient (Morbihan). Pupil of Barbereau (Harmony), Halévy (Composition), and Le Couppey (Pf.). Gained, 1846, the "Grand Prix pour Contrepoint." Composer of many effective and popular pieces, published in France, England, and Germany. His "Cours complet de Mécanisme pour le Piano" is used in the Paris Conserv.
Marche Hongroise, Fête à Seville, Le Ruisseau, †Mandoline, †Carnaval espagnol, Les Bohémiens, Les Matelots, 6 Pensées Musicales, and Allegro agitato.

*__Del Valle de Paz,__ Edgar (Samuel), b. Oct. 18, 1861, Alexandria. Pupil at the Conserv. of Naples, where B. Cesi (Pf.) and P. Serrao (Composition) were his teachers. He is at present Prof. of the Elementary Class of the "Istituto Musicale regio di Firenze" (Florence); and is the author of a "Scuola practica del Pianoforte" adopted by the Italian Music Schools.
Prize Sonata, Pieces with Orchestra, Suite dans le Style ancien, and a great number of elegant and popular Solo pieces, which were published in London.

Deppe, Ludwig, b. Nov. 7, 1828, Alverdissen (Lippe-Detmold); d. Sept. 5, 1890, Pyrmont. Pupil of Gensendorf for Pf., and of Marxsen (Hamburg) and Lobe (Leipzig) for Composition. From 1849, he resided in Hamburg as a teacher; from 1874 until his death he lived in Berlin, where his system of teaching found many sympathetic students.

Deprosse, Anton, b. May 18, 1838, Munich; d. June 23, 1878, Berlin. 1853-55, pupil at the Munich Conserv. of Werner (Wanner?) and Leonhard (Pf.), Dr. J. G. Herzog (Organ), Wohlmuth, Julius Mayer, and, later, of Stunz (Composition). 1861-64, teacher at the Conserv.; settled, 1875, at Berlin. Composer of several Pf. works of distinction.

Dessauer, Joseph, b. May 28, 1798, Prague; d. July 9, 1876, Mödling (near Vienna). Pupil of W. Tomaschek (Pf.) and Dionys Weber (Composition). His parents wished him to become a merchant, but yielded to his desire to study music only, and to devote his decided talent to it. Most of his works are vocal, but amongst his pieces for the Pf. are—
Rimembranze di Napoli; Composizioni sopra Motivi originali Napolitani, Op. 2; Caprices, Op. 30, I., II.

Dessoff, Otto, b. Jan. 14, 1835, Leipzig; d. Oct. 28, 1892, Frankfort o/M. Pupil of Moscheles (Pf.), Hauptmann and Rietz (Composition). He was an excellent Conductor, and filled the post of Capellmeister at the Imperial Opera of Vienna; the Court Theatre of Carlsruhe (Baden), and, lastly, at the Opera of Frankfort o/M., with eminent success. Quartet, Quintet, Sonatas.

Diabelli, Anton (Composer), b. Sept. 6, 1781, Mattsee (near Salzburg); d. April 7, 1858, Vienna. Pupil of Michael Haydn. His parents desired him to become a priest, but although he passed excellent examinations in several theological seminaries, his love for music was so great that, on the recommendation of Michael Haydn, he was allowed to devote himself to composition and music. 1803, he went to Vienna, was kindly received by Joseph Haydn and succeeded, by giving lessons in Pf. and guitar-playing, in saving a little capital, with which he opened, with Cappi, a publishing business. 1824, he became sole proprietor of the firm, which was intimately associated with the names of Beethoven, Schubert, Czerny, Hummel, Moscheles, and other celebrities. 1854, the firm, Diabelli and Co., changed into that of C. Spina and Co. Diabelli's name, as a composer of solid, practical, and melodious Sonatinas for 2 and 4 hands, is a very popular one; his educational works are still appreciated by teachers and their melodiousness and charming simplicity readily recognised by pupils.

*Diémer, Louis, b. Feb. 14, 1843, Paris. Pupil at the Conserv. of Marmontel (Pf.); obtained, 1856, the first Pf. prize; he had Ambroise Thomas and Bazin as teachers for Composition; gained (1859) the first Harmony prize, the second Organ prize, and (1860) first prize for Fugue and Counterpoint. After having finished his studies, he appeared with great success as a performer at the Alard, Pasdeloup, and Conserv. Concerts. 1887, he succeeded Marmontel as Prof. at the Conserv.; performed at the great Colonne and Lamoureux Concerts pieces written for him by Widor, Lalo, Bernard, Saint-Saëns, &c. As a pianist, his refined and distinguished playing, the simplicity of his style, and the irreproachable purity of his technique have won for him a well-deserved reputation. 1889, he was promoted to the rank of Chevalier of the Legion of Honour.

Concerto, Septuor for Pf. and Wind instruments, Characteristic pieces, Promenade pastorale (Op. 30), Quatrième and Cinquième Orientale (Op. 38 and Op. 40), Deuxième Caprice (Op. 24), Grand Valse de Concert (Op. 37).

*Dietrich, Albert Hermann, b. Aug. 28, 1829, Golk, near Meissen (Saxony). 1842-47, he was taught by Julius Otto (Dresden); 1847, pupil of Rietz and Hauptmann (Leipzig); 1851, he went to Düsseldorf, where he enjoyed the friendship and advice of Robert Schumann. 1855, Conductor of the Orchestral Concerts in Bonn; 1861, Conductor of the Court Theatre of Oldenburg, where he resides. Since 1888, is a member of the Royal Academy of Arts (Berlin); received the Cross of Merit, 1st Class, and Gold Medal of Art and Science (Oldenburg).

4 Pi ces, Op. 2; 6 ditto, Op. 6; Sonata for Pf. and Vln., Op. 15; Trios, Op. 9 and 14, and Sonata for 4 hands.

Dietz, Kathinka von, b. 1816, Munich; d. (no information to be obtained). Even in her sixth year she created a great sensation by her performances, which induced King Maximilian of Bavaria to send her to Paris in order to take lessons from Fr. Kalkbrenner. 1838, she gave most successful Concerts in Paris, returned some time after to Munich, where she was highly esteemed for her amiable and sterling character and her finished and truly artistic performances.

Dobrszinsky, Felix (son of the eminent violinist, D.), b. 1807, Romanow (Volhynia); d. Oct. 10, 1867, Warsaw. 1827, pupil of Elsner (Warsaw). He enjoyed a great reputation as a brilliant pianist.

Rondos, Fantasias, Variations, Mazurkas, Nocturnes, Studies, mostly published by Hofmeister (Leipzig).

Döhler, Théodore, b. April 20, 1814, Naples; d. Feb. 21, 1856, Florence. Pupil of J. Benedict (Naples); 1827, of Czerny (Pf.) and Sechter (Composition), in Vienna. 1830, he received the title of "Court Pianist" to the Duke of Lucca, and was also decorated by him. 1837, in London and Paris; after journeys in Holland, Denmark, Hungary, and Poland, he went, 1845, to St. Petersburg. On his return to Italy, Rossini instructed him in instrumentation; 1846, he remained in Paris, but signs of a severe illness (consumption) showed themselves, and, 1848, he took up his permanent residence in Florence. His compositions are written in an elegant and popular style; his so-called Fantasias are copies of Thalberg; indeed, it seems that he took him for his model. His playing was noted for extreme clearness, correctness, fluency, and brilliancy, but lacked warmth.

Nocturnes, Op. 24, 25, 31; Tarantella, Op. 39, 46; 12 Etudes de Concert, Op. 30; 50 Etudes de Salon, Op. 42; Œuvres posthumes (4 books); Fantasias, Variations, Valses, Op. 26; 6 Mélodies sans paroles, Op. 44.

*Dörffel, Dr. Alfred, b. Jan. 24, 1821, Waldenburg (Saxony). Pupil of J. A. Trube (Pf.) and L. Mallder (Theory and Violin). 1835, he went to Leipzig, where he was for a short time a pupil of C. Kloss, and, later, of C. Günther. 1843, he established himself, warmly encouraged and recommended by Mendelssohn, as music teacher in Leipzig. 1865, appointed Custos of the town library. 1885, the Leipzig University conferred on him the diploma of Dr. Phil., *honoris causâ*. His reputation as a scholar, teacher, author, and musician is well deserved.

*Döring, Carl Heinrich, b. July 4, 1834, Dresden. Became Prof. at the Royal Conserv. there. 1852-55, pupil at the Leipzig Conserv., where he had Plaidy and Moscheles as teachers of Pf., Rietz, Hauptmann, E. F. Richter, and Lobe, of Composition. 1864, Pope Pius IX. created him "Knight of the Golden Spur," the Duke of Saxe-Coburg-Gotha conferred on him the Gold Medal of Art and Science, and the King of Saxony named him, 1875, Königl. Prof.

25 Easy and Progressive Studies, Op. 8; O tave and other Studies, Op. 24 and 25; Rhythmical Studies, Op. 30; 20 Shake Studies, Op. 33.

C

*Door, Anton, b. June 20, 1833, Vienna. Pupil of Czerny (Pf.) and Sechter (Composition). Went, 1857, to Stockholm, where he received the title of Pianist to the Royal Court, and was named Member of the Royal Swedish Academy. 1859, succeeded Nicolas Rubinstein as teacher at the Imperial Institute, and, 1864, became Prof. at the Imperial Conserv. of Moscow. Since 1869 has been Prof. of the highest Pf. class at the Vienna Conserv., where Robert Fischhof, Mottl, Steinbach, Schwickerath, Sichel, Adele Margalies, Benno Schönberger, and Marie von Timoni were among his pupils. He is temporary President of the Society of Musicians (Vienna). His editions of classical and educational works are greatly esteemed.

Dorn, Alexander Julius Paul (son of the Composer and Hof-Capellmeister Heinrich D., of Berlin), b. June 8, 1833, Riga. Pupil of his father. Resided, 1855-65, at Cairo and Alexandria as a teacher and performer. 1865-68, Director at Crefeld; settled, 1868, at Berlin as Prof. at the Kön. Hochschule (High School); received the diploma of Königl. Prof. The Viceroy of Egypt gave him the Order of Medidjie. He is the composer of many brilliant and effective pieces.

Dorn, Edouard. *See* Röckel.

*Dorrel, William, b. Sept. 5, 1810. Pupil at the R.A.M., London, where his teachers were Haydon and Cipriani Potter for Pf., Charles Lucas, Dr. Crotch, and Potter for Harmony and Composition. 1842, he gave under high patronage an orchestral concert, conducted by Sterndale Bennett, and played on several other occasions in public. 1844, he went to Paris to study under Kalkbrenner and Stephen Heller. After his return to London he was appointed Prof. of Pf. at the R.A.M., which post he filled for almost forty-five years. Out of modesty he never published any of his compositions. Respected and beloved by his pupils, he is not less a great favourite of his colleagues and of all who have the privilege of knowing him and his eminent qualities as a man and artist.

D'Orso, Francesco. *See* Behr, Franz.

Dotzauer, Justus Bernhard Friedrich (son of the well-known Violoncellist, Justus J. F. D.), b. May 12, 1808, Leipzig; d. Nov. 30, 1874, Hamburg, where he was esteemed as a most excellent teacher and successful composer.

*Draeseke, Felix, b. Oct. 7, 1835, Coburg. 1852-55, pupil at the Leipzig Conserv., where he studied Composition with Rietz. 1862-67, in Dresden; 1869-76, in French Switzerland; between 1867-69 he studied with Bülow in Munich; since 1876, he has resided in Dresden as Prof. at the Royal Conserv. and Principal of the Theoretical Classes. Knight of the Royal Saxon Order of Albert and of the Saxe-Coburg Order, and Hon. Member of several societies.

Sonata, Op. 6; Concerto, Op. 36; and shorter pieces, which bear the numbers of Op. 13, 14, 15, 22, 43, and 44.

Dresel, Otto, b. 1826, Andernach on the Rhine; d. July 26, 1890, Beverly, U.S. Pupil of Hiller and Mendelssohn; he went, 1848, to New York, where he established himself as a teacher; remained there until 1851, when he left for Boston. Here he opened with great success a music school, and did much for the furtherance of the best music and the improvement of public taste.

Arrangements of Schumann's String Quartets and Beethoven's Symphonies for 4 hands; Trios and Quartets for Pf. and Strings.

Dreszer, Anastasius Vitalis, b. April 28, 1845, Kalisch (Poland). 1859-62, pupil at the Dresden Conserv., where he studied with H. Döring, E. Leonhardt, and C. Krebs. After having resided for some time in Leipzig, Paris, and again in Leipzig, he settled, 1868, in Halle, o/S., where he founded a music school.

2 Sonatas, and a good number of effective smaller pieces.

Dreyschock, Alexander, b. Oct. 15, 1818, Zack (Bohemia); d. April 1, 1869, Venice. He appeared, when only in his eighth year, at Concerts, and created a great sensation. 1831, he went to Prague, and became a pupil of Wenzel Tomaschek. 1838, he made his first journey to North Germany. From 1840-42 he was in Russia, visited (1846) Belgium, Paris, England, Holland, and Austria, and was everywhere successful. The great brilliancy and certainty of his technique, the wonderful facility and rapidity of his octave playing, and the till then unknown feat of playing with the left hand alone, created in every place the greatest sensation. J. B. Cramer used to say: "Dreyschock has no left hand, but two right ones." 1862, he went to St. Petersburg, where he received the title of Pianist to the Russian Court, was appointed Prof. at the newly-established Conserv., and Director of the Music School of the

Opera; but in 1868 he had to leave the Russian capital, and was ordered to pass the winter in Venice, where he died. Dreyschock was Knight of many European orders, Pianist to the Courts of Austria, Russia, Hesse-Darmstadt, and Mecklenburg, and Hon. Member of many societies and academies. His compositions, mostly written to exhibit his wonderful technique, do not possess any intrinsical artistic value.

Nocturne, Op. 28; l'Inquiétude, Op. 29; Grande Sonate, Op. 30; Salut à Vienne, Op. 32; Saltarello, Op. 43; Andantino et Allegro appassionata, Op. 47; Allegro spirituoso, Op. 57.

Dreyschock, Felix (nephew of the above), b. Dec. 27, 1860, Leipzig. Was a pupil of Grabau, Ehrlich, Taubert, and Kiel, of Berlin. His performances are much admired for their refinement, taste, elegance, and brilliancy, and his melodious, effective, and well-written pieces (particularly Op. 17) enjoy considerable popularity. At present he is Prof. at the Stern Conserv. (Berlin).

Dubois, Théodore, b. Aug. 24, 1837, Rosnay (Marne). Pupil at the Paris Conserv. of Marmontel (Pf.), Bazin (Harmony), Benoist (Organ), and Ambroise Thomas (Fugue and Counterpoint). 1861, he gained the Grand Prix de Rome. At present he is Conductor at the "Madeleine," and succeeded Saint-Saëns as Organist of the same church. 1871, appointed Prof. of Harmony, succeeding Elwart; and, 1891, Prof. of Composition on the death of Délibes. He is also "Inspecteur de l'enseignement musicale," Chevalier de la Légion d'Honneur, Officier de l'Instruction publique, and Officer of the Royal Order, Saviour of Greece.

Chœur et Danse des Lutins; Scherzo in F sharp min.; Scherzo et Choral; Recueil de 12 pièces; Chaconne; Réveil; Clair de lune; Recueil de 20 pièces; Poëmes Sylvestres, and Concerto capriccioso.

Dulcken (*née* David), Louise, b. March 29, 1811, Hamburg; d. April 12, 1850, London. Sister of the violinist, Ferdinand David. Pupil of Schwencke and Grund (Hamburg). She gave her first Concert in Hamburg at the age of ten; appeared, 1825, with her brother in Leipzig; married, 1828, and went to London, where she was very successful as a performer and teacher.

Dumonchau, Charles François, b. April 11, 1775, Strassburg; d. Dec. 21, 1820, Lyon. Pupil of Baumeyer (Pf.) and Berg (Composition). Later, pupil at the Paris Conserv., taking also private lessons from Woelfl. 1809, he settled in Lyon, where he remained until his death; most successful as a teacher.

Grande Sonate et la Coquette, Op. 19; 3 Sonates and 3 Fugues dans le style de Mozart, Haydn, and Clementi, Op. 30; 6 Bagatelles, Op. 36; and 3 Sonates de différents styles, Op. 32.

Dupont, Auguste, b. Feb. 9, 1828, Ensival; d. June 26, 1867, Haarlem. Pupil of Jalheau at the Conserv. of Liége. Returned, 1844, to Ensival, and studied with great industry and perseverance until he went, 1850, to Brussels, where he appeared in public; he visited also London and different towns of Germany, until he was appointed Prof. at the Brussels Conserv., which post he held until his death. He was one of the most brilliant and effective performers, an excellent teacher, and successful as a composer of popular pieces of drawing-room music. The King of Belgium created him an Officer of the "Leopold" Order.

Pluie de Mai, Op. 2; Barcarolle, Op. 17; †Une Chanson de jeune fille, Op. 18; Chanson Hongroise, Op. 27; Danses caractéristiques dans le style ancien, Op. 45; Roman en dix pages, Op. 48; 4 Esquisses, Op. 57; Fantaisie and Fugue (for the right hand), Op. 41.

Durante, Francesco, b. March 15, 1684, Frattamaggiore (Naples); d. Aug. 13, 1755, Naples. 6 Sonate per Cembalo, divise in studi e divertimenti (Naples, 1732).

Dušek or **Duschek**, Franz, b. Dec. 8, 1736, Chotěborky (Bohemia); d. Feb. 12, 1799, Prague. Pupil of Wagenseil (Vienna); returned (1763) to Prague, where he settled, and was the most celebrated pianist and most successful teacher of Bohemia. Among his pupils were Leop. Kozeluch, Vincenz Maschek, J. N. Wittasek, Fr. von Nostic, &c. He was esteemed and beloved by every artist who went to Prague, and Mozart testifies in his letters (1787) how much he respected Duschek. Composed Trios, Quartets, Concertos, and Sonatas; but only a Sonata (1773), several others (1774), a characteristic Sonata (1799), and a Concerto (Op. 1) were published.

Dussek, Johann Ladislaus, b. Feb. 9, 1761, Czaslau (Bohemia); d. March 20, 1812, St. Germain-en-Laye. Studied at first Theology, then went as Organist to Malines, later to Bergen-op-Zoom; 1782, went to Amsterdam as tutor to the sons of the Governor (Hague). In Hamburg he made Emanuel Bach's acquaintance, who persuaded him to devote himself entirely to music. In Berlin, St. Petersburg, and Paris he was eminently successful as a pianist and performer on the harmonium. He lived for some time in Italy, returned to Paris, but left—on account of the Revolution — for London, where he began with Corri, his father-in-law, a music business. After failing as a publisher he went (1800) to Hamburg; visited, after an absence of 29 years, his native town Czaslau; and met in Magdeburg the genial Prince Ferdinand of Prussia, whose teacher he became. After the Prince's death, in 1806, he was appointed Pianist by the Prince of Ysenburg, and later by Prince Talleyrand of Paris.

Sonatas for Piano Solo: Nos. 1, 2, and 3, Op. 9; Nos. 4, 5, 6, Op. 10; Nos. 7, 8, 9, 10, 11, 12, Op 20; No. 13, Op. 23; Nos. 14, 15, 16, Op. 35; Nos. 17, 18, 19, Op. 39; No. 20, Op. 43; No. 21, Op. 44, dedicated to M. Clementi; Nos. 22, 23, 24, Op. 45; Nos. 25, 26, Op. 47; No. 27, Op. 61 (Elégie harmonique sur la mort du Prince Louis Ferdinand de Prusse, en forme de Sonate); No. 28, Op. 69; No. 29, Op. 70 (Le Retour à Paris); No. 30, Op. 75; No. 31, Op. 77 (L'Invocation); No. 32 (La Chasse). *Sonatas for 4 hands:* No. 1, Grande Sonate, Op. 32; No. 2, Grande Sonate, Op. 48; No. 3, Grande Sonate, Op. 72; No. 4, Grande Sonate, Op. 73; No. 5, Grande Sonate, Op. 74. *Sonatas for Pf. and Vln.:* 3 Sonatas, Op. 4; 3 Sonatas, Op. 5; 3 Sonatas, Op. 8; 3 Sonatas, Op. 12; 3 Sonatas, Op. 13; 3 Sonatas, Op. 14; 3 Sonatas, Op. 17; 3 Sonatas, Op. 18; 3 Sonatas, Op. 28 (easy); Grande Sonate, Op. 36; 6 Sonatas, Op. 46 (easy); 3 Sonatas, Op. 51 (also for Fl.); 3 Sonatas, Op. 69. *Sonatas for Pf. and Fl.:* 3 Sonatas, Op. 7; 6 Sonatas, Op. 19; 6 Sonatas, Op. 20 (also for Vln.); 3 Sonatas, Op. 25 (also for Vln.). *Sonatas (Trios) for Pf., Vln. (or Fl.), and V"cello:* 3 Sonatas, Op. 2; Sonata, Op. 21 (Pf., Fl., and V'cello); 3 Sonatas, Op. 24; 3 Sonatas, Op. 31; 3 Sonatas, Op. 34. Sonate favorite, Op. 37; Grande Sonate for Pf., Fl., and V'cello, Op. 65; Quartet for Pf., Vln., Alto, and V'cello, Op. 56; Grand Quintuor for Pf., Vln., Alto, V'cello (obbligato), and C.-Bass (ad lib.), Op. 41. *Concertos:* No. 1, Op. 3; No. 2, Op. 14; No. 5, Op. 22; No. 6, Op. 26; No. 7, Op. 29; No. 8, Op. 40 (Concerto militaire); No. 9, Op. 50; No. 10, Op. 63 (for 2 Pf.); No. 11, Op. 66; No. 12, Op. 70. 12 Leçons progressives, Op. 16; the celebrated "Consolation," Op. 62; Recueil d'Airs connus variés (6), Op. 71; Fantaisie in F, Op. 76; Les Adieux; Air russe; Alla tedesca; l'Amusoire; Anna; Air varié; Chanson de la Comtesse de Sutherland; Partant pour la Syrie, Variations; 3 Fugues à la Camera (for 4 hands.)

Duvernoy, Henri Louis Charles, b. Nov. 16, 1820, Paris. In his eighth year he entered the Conserv. as a pupil of Zimmermann (Pf.) and Halévy (Composition). Composer of about 100 popular, mostly easy, pieces. He is no relation of the well-known educational composer, Jean Bapt. D., Officier de l'Instruction publique.

Duvernoy, Jean Baptiste. About this decidedly meritorious educational composer it is—in spite of inquiries addressed to the original publishers of his works in Paris, and other publishers in Mayence, Berlin, and Leipzig—impossible to obtain any reliable information as to the details of his birth and death. There are no relations of D.

A, B, C du pianiste, Op. 137; 6 petites Etudes élémentaires, Op. 137; 25 Etudes primaires, Op. 176; 20 Études préparatoires de la vélocité, Op. 276; 25 Etudes progressives (pour les petites mains), Op. 298; 15 Etudes du mécanisme, Op. 120; 25 Etudes de moyenne force, Op. 299; 25 Études caractéristiques, Op. 300; Gammes harmonisées, Op. 210A; Exercices journaliers, Op. 240B; 20 Etudes speciales, Op. 240C; 12 Etudes d'égalité et de goût, Op. 263.

Duvernoy, Victor Alphonse, b. Aug. 30, 1842, Paris; Pupil at the Conserv. Excellent and brilliant performer. He founded, 1869, a Society for the performance of chamber music.

Concerto and many characteristic pieces.

Dvořák, Anton, b. Sept. 8, 1841, Mülhausen (Moravia). Went, 1857, to Prague and studied in the School of Organists. He received from the Emperor of Austria a stipend, which enabled him to devote himself entirely to composition. The University of Prague conferred on him the hon. degree of Doc. Phil; the University of Cambridge the degree of Mus. Doc.; the Academy of Berlin elected him Hon. Member, and the Emperor of Austria made him a "Knight of the Iron Crown." At present he resides in the United States.

Slavonic Dances, Op. 46 and 72; Waltzes, Op. 54, Op. 59; Legends (arr.), Op. 65; Trio (F min.), Op. 68; Aus dem Böhmerwalde, characteristic pieces, Op. 81; Quintet for Pf. and Strings; Op. 87, Quartet for ditto.

E.

Eberl, Anton, b. June 13, 1766, Vienna; d. there, March 11, 1807. At first only an amateur, his decided talent for Pf. playing induced his father, a high Imperial functionary, to allow his son to devote himself entirely to music. He enjoyed Mozart and Gluck's friendship. 1796, he went to St. Petersburg, but returned (1800) to Vienna. His performances are described as effective and brilliant. The Sonatas, Op. 12, 16, 27, 39, and 43 were much admired. The two sets of Variations on the air "Zu Steffen sprach im Traume" and "The manly heart," which appeared with Mozart's name, are by Eberl.

Eberlin, Johann Ernst, b. 1716, Jettenbach (Swabia); died, 1776, Salzburg. Of his life and career little is known. It is, however, certain that he was (1747) Organist to the Prince Archbishop Sigismond, at Salzburg.

    Toccatas and Fugues, 1747 (*see* Clementi's Practical Harmony). Besides these, 2 Sonatas appeared in Haffner's Œuvres mêlés, 1760; and, lastly, a Prelude and Fugue.

Ebers. Carl Friedrich, b. March 25, 1770, Cassel; d. Sept. 9, 1836, Berlin. Entirely self-taught, he had to fight against many vicissitudes, and for this reason he had in later years to devote his decided talent to arrangements, potpourris, and other small pieces. Among his more important works may be mentioned—

    3 Sonates Brillantes, Op. 43, and a Grande Polonaise, Op. 62.

Ebner, Wolfgang, Composer and Hof-Organist to the Emperor Ferdinand III. of Austria. Published, 1648, at Prague.

    36 Variations on an air by this Emperor. These variations were republished (1810) at Vienna, by Tobias Haslinger. All other information s wanting.

*****Echeverria**, José Maria, b. Feb. 2, 1855, Lafarte, near San Sebastian (Spain). Pupil at the Conserv. of Madrid of Miguel Galiana (Harmony) and Manuel Mendizabal (Pf.). 1873, *primer premio* (first prize) for Pf. playing. Resides at present as teacher in San Sebastian.

    La Serenata Espan͂ole, La Seconde Mazurka, La Gavota, Dos Habaneras, Enskal (Basque Air), Etudio Capricho.

Eckard, Johann Gottfried, Clavecinist, &c., b. 1734, Augsburg; d. Aug., 1809, Paris. Too poor to have lessons from a master, he taught himself and achieved, through his marvellous industry and perseverance, decided success. The organ-builder, Stein, of Augsburg, took him (1758) to Paris, where he soon became one of the most popular teachers.

    6 Sonatas, Œuvre 1, Paris, 1763 (also printed in Leipzig, 1773); 2 Sonatas for the Harpsichord, Op. 2, London; and Menuet with Variations, "Le maréchal de Saxe."

Edelmann (Edlmann), Johann Friedrich, b. May 6, 1749, Strassburg; d. (under the guillotine) July 17, 1794, Paris. At first a Doctor of the Law, he finally devoted himself entirely to music, and performed with great success in Paris, where he settled, 1782.

    Concertos, a Quartet, Trios, Sonatas with Vln., and Sonatas for Pf. solo.

*****Eggeling**, Eduard, b. July 30, 1813, Brunswick; d. April 8, 1885, Harzburg. Pupil of Griepenkerl. His educational works, published by Breitkopf and Härtel (Leipzig), are of decided value; in particular his

    Studies for the higher development of Pf. playing, his Mechanical Studies, the Study of the Scale for children, ditto for advanced players. Of original compositions he published "Erhebung," a Fantasia, and another Fantasia called "Der Frühling."

*****Egghard**, Julius (*nom de plume* for Count Hardegg, of the branch Hardegg-Glatz), b. April 24, 1834, Vienna; d. there, March 23, 1867. Pupil of Czerny (Pf.) and Preyer (Composition). Composer of a great number of popular drawing-room pieces.

Ehlert, Louis, b. Jan. 13, 1825, Königsberg (Prussia); d. Jan. 4, 1884, Wiesbaden. He studied in Leipzig, Berlin, and Vienna. After spending several years in travelling, he settled, 1869, in Berlin, where he was, until 1871, teacher at Tausig's Music-school; was afterwards tutor to the sons of the Duke of Meiningen, who gave him the title of Prof. His literary works are: "Letters to a Friend about Music" (translated into several languages) and "Letters from the Tone-world" (Briefe aus der Tonwelt), essays, which were published in 2 volumes.

    Sonata in A min.; Capriccio, Op 3; Sonate romantique, Op. 5; Lyrische Skizzen, Op. 12 (6 pieces); and Rhapsodies, Op. 15.

Ehrlich, Heinrich, b. Oct. 5, 1822, Vienna. Pupil of Henselt, Bocklet, Thalberg (Pf.), and Sechter (Composition). For some time Pianist to King George of Hanover. 1864-72, teacher at the Stern Conserv., Berlin, from which appointment he retired, but resumed it again in 1886.

Among his pupils were Felix Dreyschock, Mannstaedt, &c. He is musical critic to the *Berliner Tageblatt* and *Die Gegenwart*. Of his literary works, the books " Wie übt man Klavier ? " (How does one practise the Piano ?) and " Musik-Æsthetik " are of considerable importance.

> 12 Studies, a Concertstück in ungarischer Weise, Lebensbilder, Variationen über ein eigenes Thema. Editor of Tausig's technical Studies, with the addition of a preface and annotations

Eichner, Ernst (Composer). According to Fétis, b. Feb. 9, 1740, Mannheim; d. 1777, Potsdam.

> 2 Concertos, Op. 5 (Amsterdam); ditto, Op. 9 (Mannheim); Sonatas with Vln. and V'cello ; Sonatas with Vln., and Solo Sonatas.

* **Eibenschütz, Albert**, b. April 15, 1857, Berlin. Pupil at the Leipzig Conserv. of Reinecke (Pf.) and Dr. Oscar Paul (Composition). The Leipzig Conserv. conferred on him the Diploma of Honour. 1867-80, Prof. at the Music School of Charkoff (South Russia); 1880-84, Prof. at the Leipzig Conserv.; 1884, appointed Prof. at the Cologne Conserv. He resides at Cologne. Brilliant performer.

> Sonatas, Pieces for 4 hands (Op. 6-13), Staccato Study, Paraphrases, &c. Besides these he is the editor of several works of Emanuel Bach (Breitkopf and Härtel).

* **Eibenschütz, Ilona** (cousin of the above), b. May 8, 1872, at Buda-Pesth. Even in her fifth year she showed uncommon talent, and played in a public concert with Liszt, who advised her to pursue her studies at the Vienna Conserv. From her 6th to 13th year she was a pupil of Hans Schmitt. After travelling in Russia, Denmark, Sweden, Norway, France, and Germany, she went to Frankfort o/M., and, 1885-89, was pupil of Madame Schumann. During these years she retired from public life. 1890, she resumed her journeys with great success and has chosen Vienna for her residence. Her performances in London have met with unqualified approval.

Eitner, Robert (musical Archæologist), b. Oct. 22, 1832, Breslau. Pupil of Brosig. Settled, 1853, in Berlin. 1867, he obtained the prize for a Biographical-Bibliographical Lexicon of Dutch composers, and received from the Government of Holland the order to write the history of Dutch musicians. From 1869, editor of the *Monatshefte für Musikgeschichte*. 1873, he initiated the publication of works belonging to the 15th and 16th centuries..

Elewyck, Xavier Victor, Chevalier van (musical Historian), b. April 24, 1825, Ixelles les Bruxelles; d. April 18, 1880, Louvain. He published the work " Matthias van den Gheyn, le plus grand organiste et carilloneur belge du 18 siècle." Besides this he published, at Brussels, 2 volumes containing Gheyn's and other Flemish composers' works, books of great interest and decided historical importance. The Kings of Holland and Belgium bestowed upon him high orders.

Elkamp, Heinrich, b. 1812, Itzehoe (Holstein); d. 1868, Hamburg. Pupil of Clasing (Hamburg) and Zelter (Berlin). Settled in Hamburg and remained there until his death, with exception of the years 1842-52, which he spent in St. Petersburg. His compositions are written for educational purposes, and consist of Sonatinas (Op. 7-12), Fantasias, &c. As a teacher he was most successful, and enjoyed a great reputation.

Enckhausen, Heinrich Friedrich, b. Aug. 28, 1799, Celle; d. Jan. 15, 1885, Hanover. His compositions, mostly easy pieces, are very popular and much used; they are melodious, practical, well-harmonised, and, in their way, effective.

> Progressive Studies, Op. 63; Sonatinas, Op. 75 and 76; and Rondos.

Engel, Carl (musical Historian), b. July 6, 1818, Thiedenwiese (Hanover); d. Nov. 17, 1882, London. Pupil of Hummel (Pf.) and Lobe (Composition) of Weimar. 1846, he settled in London, active as a teacher and author. Among his works is a Pf. School for beginners, which appeared in 12 editions; author of " The Music of the most Ancient Nations," " Musical Myths and Facts," &c.

* **Epstein, Julius**, b. Aug. 14, 1832, Agram (Croatia). Pupil of Lichtenegger of Agram; Halm (Pf.) and Rufinatscha (Composition) of Vienna. Eminent pianist and most successful teacher. Among his pupils are Ignaz Brüll, Marcella Sembrich (at first pianist), &c. Since 1867, Prof. at the Vienna Conserv.

Erdmannsdörfer, Max, b. June 14, 1848, Nürnberg. Pupil at the Leipzig Conserv., and later of Rietz (Dresden). 1871, Conductor of the Sondershausen Orchestra as successor to Max Bruch; 1882, Conductor of the Concerts of the

Imperial Musical Society of Moscow; at present (since 1889) Conductor of the Philharmonic Concerts of Bremen. Brilliant pianist and composer of highly effective solo pieces.

Erdmannsdörfer (*née* Fichtner), Pauline (wife of the above), b. June 28, 1851, Vienna. Pupil of Eduard Pirkhert (Pf.), later of Liszt (Weimar). Distinguished pianist, on whom the Grand Dukes of Saxe-Weimar and Hesse-Darmstadt conferred the title of "Court Pianist." She resides at Bremen.

Eschmann, Johann Carl, b. April 12, 1826, Winterthur; d. October 27, 1882, Zürich. Pupil of Moscheles (Pf.) and Mendelssohn (Composition), both of Leipzig. Among his most popular educational works are—

> The first, second, and third year of Pf. playing; 100 Aphorisms; Guide through the literature of the Pf., of which the newest edition is revised by Ruthardt (Leipzig); Technical Studies and excellent arrangements of classical pieces (Haydn, Mozart, and Beethoven).

*Eschmann, Carl Dumur (cousin of the above), b. July 6, 1835, Wädersweil, Zürich. Pupil of his cousin. Prof. of the higher classes of Pf. playing at the Musical Institute of Lausanne. His most important work is—

> "Guide du jeune Pianiste, classification méthodique et graduée d'œuvres diversées pour Piano" (second edition). He published also: "Rhythme et Agilité," Exercices techniques.

Essipoff (Essipowa), Annette von, b. Feb. 1, 1851, St. Petersburg. Pupil at the Conserv., where Leschetizki, whom she married 1880, was her teacher. Brilliant pianist, who obtained everywhere great success. 1885, she received the title of "Pianist to the Prussian Court."

Evers, Carl, b. April 8, 1819, Hamburg; d. Dec. 31, 1875, Vienna. Pupil of Jacques Schmitt (Pf.) at Hamburg, Zieger (Theory) at Hanover, Carl Krebs (Composition) at Hamburg, and of Mendelssohn (1839) at Leipzig. He never had a fixed appointment, until he established himself (1858) as a musicseller at Graz (Styria). As a pianist he possessed considerable technical execution, and was everywhere favourably received. "Chansons d'amour," describing the characteristic expression of the European national melodies.

Eybler, Joseph von (Composer), b. Feb. 8, 1765, Schwechat, near Vienna; d. July 24, 1846, Vienna, when Imperial Capellmeister. Pupil of Albrechtsberger, and a friend of Haydn and Mozart. He chiefly devoted himself to church music.

> Sonatas, Concertos, Trios, Dances, 4 Italian scenes, &c.

F.

Faisst, Dr. Emmanuel (Gottlob Friedrich), Composer and Author; b. Oct. 13, 1823, Esslingen (Würtemberg); d. June 5, 1894, Stuttgart. Pupil of Silcher (Tübingen) and Dehn (Berlin). 1857, he assisted in the constitution of the Stuttgart Conserv., where he was active as Prof. and Director. From the University of Tübingen he received the diploma of Hon. Doc. Phil. for an essay on the history of the Sonata. With Lebert he edited the "Cotta" edition of classical Pf. works. The King of Würtemberg bestowed upon him several distinctions.

Farrenc, Jeanne Louise (*née* Dumont), b. May 31, 1804, Paris; d. there, Sept. 15, 1875. Pupil of Hummel, Moscheles (Pf.), and Reicha (Composition). Married (1821) Jacques Hyppolite Aristide Farrenc, publisher of the "Trésor du Pianiste." She obtained great success both as a performer and teacher, and was elected (1842) Prof. at the Conserv. Madame F. is regarded as one of the best female composers of France.

> Sonatas, Quintets, Trios, Fugues, 30 Etudes, Op. 26; 12 Etudes brillantes, Op. 41; and 20 Etudes de moyenne difficulté, Op. 42.

Fasch, Carl Friedrich Christian (Composer, and founder of the Berlin Sing-Akademie), b. Nov. 18, 1736, Zerbst; d. Aug. 3, 1800, Berlin. Pupil of Hertel (Strelitz). 1756, Cembalist to Frederic II. of Prussia, alternating with Eman. Bach. Among his works for Clavecin several Sonatas have been published in the collections—

> "Musikalisches Mancherley" (1762) and "Musikalisches Vielerley" (1770). 4 Posth. Sonatas were published by Rellstab. An Arietta with 14 variations, and other sets of Variations appeared at Berlin. A Concerto remained unpublished.

Favarger, Réné, b. 1815, Paris; d. Aug., 1868, Etretat (Havre). His fashionable compositions (mostly so-called Fantasias) enjoyed great popularity in

England, France, and Germany; and in London, where he resided for many years, he obtained considerable success as a teacher.

Fesca, Alexander (Ernst), second son of the well-known violinist, Friedr. Ernst F. (1789-1826); b. May 22, 1820, Carlsruhe (Baden); d. Feb. 22, 1849, Brunswick. Pupil of Taubert (Pf.), Berlin, and of Schneider and Rungenhagen (Theory). As a pianist he created (1839-40) a great sensation in Germany, Austria, and Hungary. As a composer he obtained considerable reputation; his pieces are written with fluency and elegance, but lack finish and depth.

Trios, Sonatas, Fantasias, Drawing-room pieces.

Fétis, François Joseph, b. March 25, 1784, Mons; d. March 26, 1871, Brussels. Pupil of Rey, Boieldieu, and Pradher (Paris). 1813, teacher at the Music School of Douai; he went (1818) to Paris and was appointed (1820) Prof. at the Conserv. 1826, he founded the journal *La Revue Musicale*. 1833, he became Director of the Brussels Conserv., which post he filled for 39 years. He was Custos of the Royal Belgian Library, Member of the Academy, and Commander of high orders. For Pf. he wrote—

Several Fantasias; 3 Suites de Préludes progressifs; Fantaisie chromatique; 3 Sonates faciles à quatre mains; grand Duo for Pf. and Vln.; Marche variée; Sextuor pour Pf. à quatre mains, deux Violons, Alto, et Basse, Op. 5. He is the author of the "Méthode des Méthodes de Piano," of which Moscheles edited the practical part.

Fibich, Zdeněk, b. Dec. 21, 1850, Seborschitz, near Czaslau (Bohemia). At first instructed in Prague; 1865, at the Leipzig Conserv.; later a pupil of Vincenz Lachner (Mannheim). 1876, second Capellmeister of the National Theatre (Prague); 1878, Director of the Choir of the Russian Church.

Op. 7, 4 Ballads, Op. 8, Quartet; Op. 10, Romance for Pf. and Vln.; Op. 11, Quartet; Op. 19, Mignons for 4 hands: 1. Valse, 2. Scène Orientale, 3. *,*, 4. Rococo Gavotte; the same for 2 hands, Op. 20; Vigiliæ, 2 characteristic pieces for 4 hands.

***Fiedler,** August Max, b. Dec. 31, 1859, Zittau. Pupil of his father, the Pf. teacher, Carl Aug. F, and of G. Albrecht (Theory and Organ-playing). 1877-80, pupil at the Leipzig Conserv., where he gained the "Holstein" scholarship. 1882, appointed teacher at the Hamburg Music School.

5 Pieces, Op. 2 (Phantasiestück, Romanze, Gavotte, Phantasiestück, Scherzo); 4 pieces, Op. 6 (Phantasiestück, F min.; Waltzer, A flat; Phantasiestück, A flat; Waldstück, F sharp).

Field, John, b. 1782, Dublin; d. Jan. 11, 1837, Moscow. At first pupil of his grandfather, an Organist in Dublin; later of Clementi, whom he accompanied to St. Petersburg. When Clementi had left, good times began for Field. He was the favourite teacher of the aristocracy, and had plenty of engagements for Concerts; but, owing to rather disorderly habits, he had to leave the Russian capital and settled in Moscow, where he met with an enthusiastic reception. 1831, he revisited Dublin, where he found his aged mother. Soon after he went to Paris, where his success was not so great as elsewhere. Disappointed in Paris, he went to Vienna, Milan, and other Italian towns, where he was much *fêted*. In Naples a Russian family, sympathising with Field—now ill and feeble—took him (1834) to Moscow, where—suffering from a fearful cough and inflammation of the intestines—he died, 1837. He was a most excellent pianist — famous for his beautiful singing tone and sweet touch, admired for the independence of his fingers, the correctness and clearness of his execution, and the fascinating and captivating manner of his entire style of performance. Of the now highly popular form, "The Nocturne," Field may be called the inventor.

Concertos, No. 1, in E flat; No. 2, in A flat; No. 3, in E flat; No. 4, in E flat (very popular); No. 5, in C; No. 6, in C; No. 7, in C min.; Sonatas in A, E, and C min.; Sonata in B; 2 Airs en Rondeaux, Air russe, Air russe varié (4 hands), Chanson russe varié (D min.), Polonaise in E flat, "Reviens, Reviens," Romanza and Cavatine in E, Romance in E flat, 3 Romances, Rondeau in A, 2 Rondeaux Favori in E and A, Rondeau with 2 Vln., Alto, and Bass; "Since then I'm doomed," Variation in C; "Speed the Plough," Rondo in B flat; Divertissements, with 2 Vln., Alto, and Bass, in E and A; 2 Fantasias, in A and G; Exercise; Exercice modulé dans tous les tons majeurs et mineurs; 18 Nocturnes, of which Nos. 1-10 appeared before 1828.

Fischer, Johann Caspar Ferdinand (Composer and Conductor to the Margrave of Baden), lived about 1720. Gerber mentions that Fischer was one of the strongest executants on his instrument (clavecin), and to him belongs the merit of having made known in Germany the meaning and execution of the graces.

Musikalisches Blumenbüschlein (Musical flowerbushlet) bestehend in (consisting of) 8 Partien, u.s.w., Op. 2. The Musical Parnassus, or an entirely new work, consisting of 9 Partitas (Suites) with the name of the 9 Muses (Augsburg, 1738).

Fischer, Michael Gotthardt (Composer), b. June 3, 1773, Village Alach (Erfurt); d. Jan. 12, 1829, Erfurt. Pupil of Kittel (pupil of Bach). After having spent some years at Jena, Baron Dalberg (*see* page 23) called him to Erfurt as Conductor of the Winterkonzerte. His works enjoyed in their time a great reputation and were praised for their solidity and excellent workmanship.

<small>A Clavier-Quartet, Op. 6; Sonatas, Op 3; a Capriccio, Studies, and a Sonata for 4 hands Op. 12.</small>

Fischhof, Joseph, b. April 4, 1804, Butschowitz; d. June 28, 1857, Baden, near Vienna. His parents desired him to become a physician, but on his giving proofs of decided talent for music they allowed him to have Anton Halm as teacher of Pf. and von Seyfried as instructor in Composition. 1833, elected Prof. at the Vienna Conserv. He was one of the musical authorities of Vienna, well acquainted with Robert Schumann, Liszt, Thalberg, Donizetti —in short, with every artist of distinction who visited the Austrian capital. As a pianist he was esteemed for the musicianly qualities of his performances, and as a teacher respected for the thoroughness of his knowledge. He wrote an essay on the history of the Pf.

<small>Rondos, Op. 10, 12, 19; a Fantaisie caractéristique, Op. 18. Editor of "Classische Studien," pieces by Händel, Bach, Mozart, and Scarlatti.</small>

Fischhof, Robert (nephew of Joseph F.), b. 1857, Vienna. Pupil of Door, R. Fuchs, Krenn, and Bruckner (Vienna Conserv.); later of Liszt. 1874, he appeared for the first time in public and continued to give highly successful concerts in Austria and Germany. 1884, appointed Prof. at the Conserv. (Vienna). A Concerto of his own composition was performed by him in Berlin and Paris. Other pieces appeared in Vienna, Berlin, and Paris.

***Fissot, Alexis Henri**, b. Oct. 24, 1843, Airaines (Somme). At Paris pupil of Marmontel (Pf.), Bazin (Harmony), Benoit (Organ), and Ambroise Thomas (Composition); he gained the first prize in every class. Since April, 1887, Prof. at the Conserv. (Paris).

<small>3 Feuillets d'Album, 12 Pièces de Genre, 12 Préludes, 3 Morceaux (Op. 4), Adagio et presto, Fantaisie impromptu, Ballades (2), Arabesques (6), Caprice héroïque (Op. 18), Allegro symphonique (Op. 20), Scherzi, 1, 2, and 3.</small>

***Flügel, Ernst**, b. Aug. 31, 1844, Halle a/d/Saale. Pupil of his father, Gustav F., Löschhorn, Bülow, Geyer, and Kiel. 1879, he settled in Breslau, where he is Cantor of the Bernhardin Church and critic to the Silesian journal, *Schlesische Zeitung*. The King of Prussia conferred on him the title of Königl. Musik-Director. The *opera* 16, 31, 32 are considered by the author to be his best works.

***Flügel, Gustav** (father of the above), b. July 2, 1812, Nienburg a/d/Saale. Pupil of Thiele (Altenburg); from 1827-30, of Fr. Schneider (Dessau). 1840, appointed Musik-Director at Stettin, which town he left (1850) for Neuwied, where he remained until 1859, when he returned to Stettin as Organist and Cantor of the Schlosskirche. 1856, he received the title of Königl. Musik-Director. His principal works for Pf. are—

<small>5 Sonatas, Op. 4, 7, 13, 20, 36; his most popular pieces are decidedly "Nachtfalter" (Moths), Op. 14.</small>

Fodor, Anton (youngest brother of the violinist, Joseph F.), b. 1759, Venloo (Holland); d. Feb. 23, 1849, Amsterdam. He resided until 1790 in his native place, but settled later in Amsterdam. Appointed Conductor of the Concerts "Felix meritis."

<small>Concertos (published in Paris), Quartets for Pf. and Strings, Trios, Sonatas with Vln., a Sonata for 4 hands, one ditto for 6 hands, Solo Sonatas, Fantasias, Variations, &c.</small>

Förster, Alban, b. Oct. 23, 1849, Reichenbach (Saxony). 1863-65, pupil of R. Blume; 1866-69, pupil, and, 1881-82, Prof. at the Dresden Conserv.; 1882, Hof-Capellmeister of Mecklenburg-Strelitz (at Neu-Strelitz). His compositions are mostly of an educational character.

<small>Op. 12, Miniatures (20); Op. 13, Gedenkblätter (3); Op. 14, Musikalische Plaudereien (Musical chattings), 10 pieces; Op. 32, 8 easy characteristic pieces for 4 hands; Op. 40, Album of Dances; Op. 41, Wander-Skizzen; Op. 53, Aus der Jugendzeit (8 pieces); Op. 60, Trio in an easy style.</small>

Förster, Emanuel Aloys, b. 1757, Neurath (Austrian Silesia); d. Nov. 19, 1823, Vienna. Received his musical education in Prague, from whence he went, 1779, to Vienna; he received the title of Capellmeister, and was active as a teacher of Pf. and Composition. It is said that Beethoven respected him very much. His work, "Anleitung zum Generalbass" (Leipzig, 1805), is considered a book of great merit.

<small>Sestet, Op. 9 (1796), 4 Quartets, Sonata for 4 hands, Fantasia and grand Sonata, Op. 15; several other Sonatas, 50 Preludes in 3 books, &c. The 10 Variations in A maj. on Sarti's air "I finti eredi," generally believed to be by Mozart, are by Förster, who published them (1802) in Vienna.</small>

Fontaine (Henri Louis Stanislas), Mortier de, b. May 13, 1816, Wiesriowiec (Volhynia, Russia); d. May 10, 1883, Balham, near London. 1832, he performed for the first time at a concert in Dantsic; went, 1833, to Paris, where he was warmly welcomed by Chopin; and played in public with great success. 1837, he travelled in Italy; returned, 1842, to Paris, and went, 1850, to Russia; settled, 1853, in St. Petersburg, and remained there till 1860 as a teacher; from 1860 till 1868 in a similar capacity at Munich. In 1873 he resumed his artistic journeys, and remained during the last years of his life in London. His accomplishments as a pianist were very considerable.

Fontana, Jules de, b. 1810, Warsaw; committed suicide in Paris on December 31, 1869. He was a fellow-pupil of Chopin in Warsaw. After a sojourn in Paris, he travelled with the violinist Sivori in America, afterwards returning to Paris, where he published Chopin's posthumous works. There is a difference of opinion about Fontana's loyalty in doing this.

2 Caprices, Marche Funèbre and L'Inquiétude, Op. 1; Rêverie, Op. 2; Elégie, Op. 7; 12 Etudes de Style, Op. 8; ditto, Op. 9; and a Ballade, Op. 17.

Forkel, Dr. Johann Nicolaus (the son of a shoemaker), b. Feb. 22, 1749, Meeder, near Coburg; d. March 17, 1818, Göttingen. 1762, appointed chorister at the principal church of Lüneburg; 1766, Director of the Schwerin Choir. 1769, he entered the University of Göttingen, where he studied law; but as he found that the historical studies of music afforded greater attractions, he devoted himself entirely to music; became (1778) Musical Director of the University; founded (1780) the so-called Winter Concerts, received the diploma of Hon. Doc. Phil., and remained active as a Conductor until 1815, when he retired and devoted his time to teaching and writing. As a composer he was less successful than as an author. He published:

6 Sonatas, 2 books (Göttingen, 1778-79); 3 Sonatas, with accompaniment (London); 24 Variations on "God save the King"; Trios, Op. 2 (1780); a Concerto (1782). According to his MS. catalogue he composed 22 Concertos and a Duo for 2 clavecins. His book, "Joh. Seb. Bach's Life, Art and Works," was published at Leipzig, 1802. Only 2 volumes of his General History of Music appeared.

Franck, César Auguste, b. Dec. 10, 1822, Liège; d. Nov. 8, 1890, Paris. Pupil at the Liège Conserv. until 1837, when he entered that of Paris and became a pupil of Zimmermann (Pf.) and Leborne (Counterpoint). 1838, first prize for Pf.; 1839, second prize for Composition. Remained permanently at Paris as a Pf. teacher; was Prof of Organ at the Conserv. and Organist of St. Clotilde.

3 Trios, Op 1; Trio, Op. 2; Eclogue, Op. 3; Duo for 4 hands, Op. 4; Sonata, Op. 6, &c.

*****Franck**, Dr. Eduard, b. Oct. 5, 1817, Breslau; d. Dec. 1, 1893, Berlin. Received his general and musical education in his native town. Went, 1843-46, to Italy, afterwards to Berlin, where he performed with great success at public concerts. Appointed Prof. at the Cologne Conserv., but accepted (1859) the post of Musik-Director at Berne, where the University conferred upon him the diploma of Hon. Doc. Phil.; 1867-78, Prof. at the Stern Conserv.; since 1878, Prof. at the Breslau Conserv. of Berlin. He received the titles of Königl. Prof. and Musik Director.

Concerto, Op. 13; 2 Trios; Quintet, Op. 45; Sextet, Op. 41; Sonata, with V'cello, Op. 42; Duo for 2 Pf., Op. 46; 6 Solo Sonatas, Op. 40, &c.

*****Frescobaldi**, Girolamo (Composer), b. 1580, Ferrara; d. March 22, 1644, Rome. Pupil of Luzzasco Luzzaschi, he went for further studies to the Netherlands. Became, 1607, Organist of S. Rombaut (Malines); returned to Italy, and was appointed, 1608, successor of Pasquini, Organist of S. Pietro (Rome)—according to Fétis he obtained this post only in 1614. 1628, he went to Florence for several years as Organist to Ferdinand II. of Toscana, but returned (1635) to his former post at Rome; remained there till 1643; was for one year Organist of S. Laurentius in Montibus. Among his pupils, Froberger was decidedly the best.

Il primo libro di Fantasie a due, tre e quattro (in Milano, 1608). Ricercari e canzoni francesi, fatti sopra diversi obblighi, in partitura (Rome, 1637). Previous publications of this collection appeared in 1615 and 1627. Il secondo libro di Toccati, Canzoni, Versi d'Hinni, Magnificat, Gagliarde, Correnti et altre partite d'intavolatura di Cembalo ed Organo (Rome, 1637). First edition, 1616. Fiori musicali di diverse Compositioni, Toccati, Kirie, Canzoni, Capricci e Ricercari in Partitura a Quattro, utile per Sonatori, Op. 12 (Venezia, 1635). (See Pauer's "Alte Meister," Leipzig.)

Freund, Robert, b. 1852, Buda-Pesth. Pupil of Huber. 1865, he entered the Leipzig Conserv., where Moscheles and Coccius (Pf.), Richter and Papperitz (Harmony) were his teachers. For one year he studied with Tausig (Berlin), and was (1870-72) a pupil of Liszt in Buda Pesth. 1876, appointed Prof. at the Music School of Zürich, where he resides. His performances are very much admired for their refinement and warmth of expression.

Freystädtler (Freystädler), Franz Jacob, b. Sept. 13, 1760, Salzburg; d. about 1836, Vienna. Pupil of Lipp (Organ and Clavecin), he was appointed Organist of St. Peter's, Salzburg; went, 1784, to Munich, where he remained as teacher until 1786. From this year until his death he settled (owing to the invitation and encouragement of his townsman, Mozart) in Vienna, where he soon was actively engaged as a teacher.

Easy Concerto; Sonatas with Vln.; "The Siege of Belgrad" and "The Siege of Valenciennes," with Vln.; 18 original Valses for 4 hands; several Caprices and sets of Variations; 50 Preludes, and the Fantasias " Mittag und Abend" (Noon and Evening) and "Der Frühlingsmorgen" (Spring morning).

*Frickenhaus (née Evans), Fanny (Pianist), b. June 7, 1849, Cheltenham. Pupil of George Mount, later of Aug. Dupont (Brussels). Appeared for the first time in 1879 in London, where she has played with continued success at the best public concerts (Philharmonic, Crystal Palace, Popular). She introduced many interesting works of living composers in her chamber music concerts, and is considered one of the foremost English pianists.

*Friedheim, Arthur, b. Oct. 26, 1859, St. Petersburg. Pupil of Rubinstein for one year. 1877, he went to Dresden, in order to finish an opera, already begun in St. Petersburg ; afterwards, for 8 years, a pupil of Liszt. Excellent performer, possessing a phenomenal execution, and a talented Conductor. He resides in New York.

Froberger, Johann Jacob (Organist, Clavecinist, and Composer), b. 1605 (?), Halle (?) ; d. May 7, 1667, Héricourt (Haute Sâone). Pupil of Frescobaldi. The details of his life are very scanty and uncertain. According to Mattheson ("Grundlage einer Ehrenpforte"), a Swedish Ambassador was so pleased with his singing, when 15 years old, that he took him to Vienna, where Ferdinand III. commanded him to be sent to Rome to study under Frescobaldi. On his return he was, 1641-45, and again, 1653-57, Court Organist at Vienna, when he was dismissed (for unknown reasons) from the Imperial service, and went to Mayence; later, he found a generous patroness in the Duchess Sybilla of Würtemberg, who appointed him her " Musikmeister und Musiklehrer." At what time he came to Héricourt, the residence of the Duchess, is unknown. It is also unknown whether he went (1657) from Vienna direct to England. See Grove 1., 565, Fétis and Mendl, about a romantic incident which is said to have happened in Westminster Abbey. It is, however, certain that he lived during his later years in comfortable circumstances at the Court of the Duchess, who called him " her dear, honest, faithful, and industrious master." Of his works the following appeared :—

Diverse curiose e rarissime Partite di toccate, ricercate capricci e fantasie dall' Eccelentissimo e Famosissimo Organista Giovanni Giacomo Froberger, per gli amatori di Cembali, Organi e Istrumenti (Mainz Ludw. Bourgeat, 1693, 1695, 1699). Diverse ingegniosissime, rarissime e non mai più viste curiose partite di toccate, canzone, ricercate, alemande, correnti, sarabande e gigue di cembali, organi e istrumenti (Mainz, 1714). Phantasia supra, ut, re, mi, fa, sol, la, Clavicymbalis accommodata, in Athan. Kircher's Musurgia, Rome, 1650. The Imperial Court Library of Vienna possesses the following works in MS. 1st vol., 8 toccate, 5 capricci e canzone per l'Organo; 2nd vol., Libro secondo di Toccate, Fantasie, Canzone, &c. (Contenente Pezzi per il Cembalo, et a 4 voci, 1649) ; 3rd vol., Libro terzo di Capricci e Ricercati ; 4th vol., Libro quarto di Toccate, Capricci, &c. (Pezzo per il Cembalo et a 4 voci), Vienna, 1656 ; 5th vol., Lamento sopra la dolorosa perdita della R.M. di Ferdinando IV., Rè de Romani, Per il Cembalo, 1649 MS. of Fugues, Caprices, Toccatas, and Suites: MS., 1 vol., with 26 Clavecin pieces, Suites by Froberger (but also by Biber and Schmelzer), 1681.

*Frugatta, Giuseppe, b. May 26, 1860, Bergamo. Pupil at the Milan Conserv. of Antonio Bazzini (Composition) and Carlo Andreoli (Pf.). Prof. at the " Collegio Reale delle Fanciulle " and at the Conserv. (Milan).

Sonata, Trio (both received prizes), Fantasia, Schizzi di Valzer, Polonaise de Concert, Moments poétiques, three Morceaux de Concerts, &c.

*Fuchs, Robert, b. Feb. 15, 1847, Frauenthal. Pupil at the Vienna Conserv., where, 1875, he was appointed Prof. of Theory, and, 1893, Director.

Sonatas, Sonata with V'cello, Trios, 2 Sonatas with Vln., Variations, very melodious pieces for 4 hands, a Concerto, &c.

Fumagalli, Adolfo, b. Oct. 19, 1828, Inzago; d. May 3, 1856, Florence. Pupil of Angeleri. Most excellent and highly distinguished pianist, who composed in a fluent style a good many elegant, graceful, effective, and well-written pieces, mostly published by Ricordi, of Milan, and Schott Sons, of Mayence.

Fumagalli, Disma (elder brother of the above), b. Sept. 8, 1826, Inzago; d. March 2, 1893, Milan. Pupil at the Milan Conserv., where he was afterwards Prof. Prolific composer, who published above 250 pieces.

Fumagalli, Luca (younger brother of Adolfo F.), b. May 29, 1837, Inzago. Also a pupil at the Milan Conserv. Played, 1860, with great success in Paris, and published many elegant and pleasing drawing-room pieces.

Fux, Johann Joseph (the celebrated author of the "Gradus ad Parnassum sive manuductio ad compositionem musicae regularem"), b. 1660, Hirtenfeld, near St. Marein in Styria; d. Feb. 14, 1741, Vienna, where he was Kaiserlicher Obercapellmeister. He served under Leopold I. (1640-1705), Joseph I. (1678-1711), and Carl VI. (1685-1740), and was greatly honoured and even beloved by each of these sovereigns. *See* Köchel's Biography of Fux (Vienna, 1871). His Gradus was published 1725. For Clavecin he wrote—

Sei Sonate, Capriccio, Fughe.

G.

Gabler, Christoph August (son of a clergyman), b. March 15, 1767, Mühldorf (Voigtland, Saxony); d. April 15, 1839, St. Petersburg. He studied theology at Leipzig, but followed up with zeal his musical studies. 1800, music-teacher in Reval, where his performances were very successful. 1836, he settled in St. Petersburg.

3 Sonatas, Op. 19; Sonata, Op. 26; Sonatine, Op. 46; Adagio and Rondo, Op. 50; and several sets of Variations, &c.

Gade, Niels Wilhelm, b. Feb. 22, 1817 (*not* Oct.), Copenhagen; d. there, Dec. 21, 1890. Pupil of Weyse. 1841, he gained the first prize for the Overture "Nachklänge an Ossian," which was soon performed under Mendelssohn in Leipzig. King Christian VIII. of Denmark gave him a stipend, which enabled him to travel in Germany. 1843, he spent in Leipzig. 1845-46, he participated with Mendelssohn in the direction of the Gewandhaus Concerts. 1848, he returned to Copenhagen, was appointed Conductor of the Musical Society, Hof-Organist, Hof-Capellmeister, and Prof. The amiable, harmonious, correct, pure, and thoroughly sympathetic character of his compositions was everywhere acknowledged and welcomed—in short, he was one of the few composers who had only friends and no enemies. The Danish Court recognised his merits by bestowing upon him the Commandership of the Danebrog, and from several Academies and Societies he received the diplomas of Hon. Membership. He was Hon. Dr. Phil., Member of the Prussian order *pour le mérite;* and, during his later years, Director of the Copenhagen Conserv. His works are only slightly tinged with Scandinavian expression.

Frühlings-Phantasie for Pf., Orchestra, and 4 solo voices; Trio, Op. 42, in F; Sonata, Op. 2ª, in E min.; Sonata, with Vln., in A, Op. 6; ditto in D min., Op 21; Aquarellen, Op. 19 (10 pieces); Frühlingsblumen, Op. 2 (3 pieces); Album leaves (3 pieces); Christmas pieces, Op. 36 (5 pieces); Arabeske, Op. 27; Volkstänze, Op. 31.

Gänsbacher, Johann Baptist, b. May 8, 1778, Sterzing (Tyrol); d. July 13, 1844, Vienna. 1796, he fought as a volunteer against the French and became first lieutenant; but his desire to devote himself to music was greater than the wish to follow up his military career. 1802, he went to Vienna, where Abbé Vogler gave him some advice. His patron, Count Firmian, and his pupil, Count Erdödy, paid for his instruction by Albrechtsberger. 1810, he went to Darmstadt, where he was, with C. M. von Weber and Meyerbeer, a pupil of Vogler. 1823, appointed Principal Organist of St. Stephen's, Vienna, which post he filled until his death. For his merits as a soldier he received, 1796, the medal for bravery, and, 1817, the great gold medal of merit.

Trios, Sonatas with Vln.; Variations for 4 hands, Op. 9; Divertissements, Op. 20 and 29, and Sonate facile, Op 30.

Gallenberg, Wenzel Robert, Count, b. Dec. 28, 1783, Vienna; d. May 13, 1839, Rome. Pupil of Albrechtsberger. With Barbaja he was co-administrator of the Vienna Opera, for which he had to furnish the ballet-music. He married Countess Giulietta Guicciardi, to whom Beethoven dedicated, 1802, the well-known Sonata, Op. 27, No. 2, commonly called the "Moonlight" Sonata. Several of Gallenberg's themes were used for variations—for instance, the "Gallenberg" Valse, by Charles Mayer, Moscheles, Czerny, and others.

Fantasie, Op 4; Rhapsody, Op 5; Fantasie der Trauer, Op. 35; Grande Sonate, Op. 15; Characteristic Marches for 4 hands, Op. 11; and a grand Triumphal March.

Galuppi, Baldassare (called Buranello), composer; b. Oct. 18, 1706, Burano; d. Jan. 3, 1785, Venice. Pupil of Lotti. Lived, from 1741 till 1743, in London; was appointed, 1765, Capellmeister at St. Petersburg; and went, 1768, to be Conductor of San Marco, at Venice. His Sonatas (of which several are reprinted in Pauer's "Alte Clavier Musik" and "Alte Meister") are distinguished by great freshness and fluency.

*****Ganz**, Wilhelm, b. Nov. 6, 1833, Mayence on the Rhine. Pupil of C. Eckert (Berlin) and Anschütz (Coblenz). Prof. at the London Guildhall School. Composer of fashionable pieces, and a popular Conductor. Received decorations from the King of Prussia and the Duke of Saxe-Coburg-Gotha.

Gaschin-Rosenberg, Countess Fanny (excellent pianist), b. 1818, Thorn. Pupil of Liszt, Thalberg, and Henselt. Although an amateur, she created a great sensation by her excellent and brilliant performances.

Rêverie (very popular); 2 pieces: Charme brisé, Poëme Harmonique; Mazourka, and Bourrasque (fit of passion) musicale.

*****Gayrhos**, Eugen, b. 1843, Kempten (Bavaria). Pupil of D. Pruckner (Pf.) and Dr. Faisst (Composition), of Stuttgart; held appointments at Munich, 1862-67, later at Basle, as successor to Bülow, and is at present Prof. at Lausanne.

Gebel, Georg, sen., b. 1685, Breslau; d. there, 1749. Greatly respected for his organ performances. He made himself a name as the inventor of a clavichord with quarter-tones, and a clavicembalo with manual, pedal, and compass of 6 octaves. He published not less than 24 Concertos. His eldest son—

Gebel, Georg, jun., b. Oct. 15, 1709, Brieg (Breslau); d. Sept. 24, 1753, Rudolstadt. Pupil of his father. Very clever executant on Hebenstreit's Pantaleon (an improvement of the so-called Dulcimer). Although a very prolific composer for the orchestra (he wrote in six years not less than 100 Symphonies) he composed for the clavecin only a few Concertos and a Partita, published in Rudolstadt.

Gelinek, Abbé Joseph (composer), b. Dec. 3, 1757, Selcz, Bohemia; d. April 13, 1825, Vienna. His first instruction he received from his father, a schoolmaster, later from Segert. 1786, he was ordained. Mozart chanced to hear him, and was so struck by his gift of improvising that he recommended him to Count Kinsky, who, when travelling in Italy, appointed him house-chaplain and music-teacher of his family. On his return to Vienna he took lessons from Albrechtsberger. From 1795 until his death he was house-chaplain of Prince Esterhazy. Soon he became the most popular Pf. teacher and began to write his—in their time fashionable—Variations.

Sonatas, Trios, Fantasias, Dances, Marches, and 120 Sets of Variations.

Gerke, Anton, b. 1814, in Poland; d. Aug. 27, 1870, St. Petersburg. He was one of the most influential and successful teachers of the Russian capital.

10 Characteristic Pieces, Op. 14; Amusement, Op. 19, I., II.; Divertimento, Op. 22; Souvenir, Op. 23; and 12 Scherzi à la Mazurek.

Gerke, Otto (really a violinist), b. Jan. 13, 1807, Lüneburg; d. June 28, 1878, Paderborn. Pupil of Spohr and Hauptmann.

Sonata, Op. 32; Fantaisie et Rondeau, Op. 21; Invitation à la Danse, Rondeau Brilliant, Op. 3; Salut à la Newa, and several shorter pieces.

*****German**, Edward, b. 1862, Whitchurch, Shropshire. Pupil at the R.A.M. (London). Although chiefly a composer for orchestra, his Pf. works deserve mention:

Suite (1-6), Valse in D flat, Polish Dance, Intermezzo in A min., Valsette, Album Leaf, Graceful Dance, Minuet in G, Suite for 4 hands. His other works for Pf. are arrangements from his highly successful music to "Richard III.," "Henry VIII.," and the "Tempest."

Germer, Heinrich, b. Dec. 30, 1837, Sommersdorf (Province of Saxony). Pupil of the section for Composition of the Berlin Academy. After finishing his studies he settled in Dresden as a music-teacher, and is at present chairman of the "Musikpädagogischen Verein." He published "Rhythmical Problems," "The Technique of Pianoforte-playing," "The Musical Ornamentation," Studies, and a Method of Pf. playing. He edited some of Czerny's and Cramer's Studies and Beethoven's Sonatas;

there is a great difference of opinion as to the necessity, propriety, and practicability of interfering with the originals, as it may be rightly maintained that Beethoven, Czerny, and Cramer knew well what they meant themselves.

Gernsheim, Friedrich, b. July 17, 1839, Worms. From 1847-49, pupil of Pauer (Mayence); 1849-52, Rosenhain (Pf.) and Hauff (Composition), Frankfort o'M; 1852, at the Leipzig Conserv.; 1861, appointed Musik-Director at Saarbrücken; 1864, Prof. at the Cologne Conserv., and, 1874, Director and Prof. of the Conserv. of Rotterdam; 1890, Director of the Stern Choral Society, and artistic Director of the Stern Conserv. (Berlin). 1872, the Duke of Saxe-Coburg-Gotha conferred on him the title of Prof., and the Grand Duke of Hesse the Order of Philipp. His compositions are distinguished by excellent workmanship, practical writing, effective treatment, and a thorough absence of shallowness or triviality.

Concerto, Trios (2); Quintet, Op. 35; Quartet, Op. 6; Sonatas with Vln.; ditto with V'cello; Dances (4 hands), Op. 30; 6 Preludes, Op. 2; Variations, Op 18 and Op. 22; Fantasia, Op. 27; Suite, Op. 8; Romanza, Op. 15, &c.

Gheyn, Matthias van den (organist, carilloneur, and composer), b. April 7, 1721, Tirlemont; d. June 22, 1785, Louvain. His Sonatas and Divertissements (2 vols.) were published by the Chevalier d'Elewyck (Brussels: Schott frères). The preface to the first volume contains a detailed description of his life.

Giannini, Salvatore, b. Dec. 24, 1830, Naples. Pupil of Giuseppe Lillo. Ricordi and Lucca, of Milan, published about 270 of his pieces.

Gibbons, Orlando, b. 1583, Cambridge; d. June 5, 1625, Canterbury. His pieces are published in "Parthenia" and "Old English Composers."

*Giehrl, Joseph, b. Sept. 18, 1857, Munich; d. there, April 24, 1893. At first a pupil at the Munich Conserv., later a pupil of Liszt (for one year in Rome). Prof. at the Royal Academy of Music (formerly Conserv.) of Munich. He was considered one of the foremost performers of his time and was a leading artist of the Bavarian capital.

Giordani (called Giordanello), Giuseppe, b. 1753, Naples; d. 1794, Lisbon. Pupil at the Conserv. of Loreto of Naples. Resided for some years in London.

Concertos, Quartets, and Quintets; Sonatas with Vln.; 3 Sonatas for 4 hands; Leçons pour les commençants et Préludes.

*Glazounow, Alexander, b. July 29 (Aug. 10), 1865, St. Petersburg. Pupil of Narciss Jelenkowski (Pf.) and Nicolai Rimsky-Korsakoff (Composition). He holds no appointment. A medal for his compositions was awarded to him by the Jury of the Chicago Exhibition, 1893.

Op. 2, Suite; Op. 22, 2 Morceaux; Op. 23, Walzer; Op. 25, Prélude et 2 Mazurkas; Op. 31, 3 Etudes; Op. 37, Nocturne; Op. 41, Grande Valse de Concert; Op. 42, Miniatures.

Glinka, Michael Ivanowitsch de, b. May 20, 1804, at the village Novo Spaskoië (Government Smolensk); d. Feb. 3, 1857, Berlin. 1833, pupil of Dehn (Berlin). He returned to Russia, was appointed Imperial Capellmeister and Director of the Opera and of the Church Choir of St. Petersburg. 1840-50, he spent in travels, visited also Spain, but resided mostly in Paris. 1856, he went to Berlin, and studied with Dehn the East Roman Church Music. He died suddenly. 1870, a monument to Glinka was erected at St. Petersburg.

Due Ballabile nel Ballette "Chao Kang," with Variations, a Rondino brillante, and several sets of Variations.

Gobbaerts, Jean Louis (his compositions appear under the name "Streabbog") b. Sept. 28, 1836, Antwerp; d. April 28, 1886, Saint Gilles. Pupil at the Brussels Conserv. Published a Method of Pf. playing, and a great number of easy, popular pieces (mostly published by Schott, of Mayence).

Gobbi, Heinrich, b. June 7, 1842, Buda-Pesth. Pupil of Dunkl (Pf.), Robert Volkmann (Composition), and later of Liszt, whose private secretary he was for two years. 1860, appointed Prof. of Pf. at the Pesth (Royal) Conserv. Was influential in making the compositions of Schumann and Brahms known.

8 Waltzer, Sonata in the Hungarian style, Phantasiestücke, Album leaves, and other pieces.

Godard, Benjamin Louis Paul, b. Aug. 18, 1849, Paris; d. Jan. 9, 1895, Cannes. Pupil of Reber and Vieuxtemps.

Trio, Concerto, various characteristic Studies, Mazurkas; Contes de la veillée (6) for 4 hands, Op. 67; Nocturnes, Op. 68; Premier Mai, Scènes italiennes (3), Op. 126.

*Goddard, Arabella, b. Jan. 12, 1836, St. Servan (Brittany). She studied under a local master, Mr. Louel, afterwards in Paris with Kalkbrenner, and when she came to London she received lessons from Thalberg, Mrs. Anderson, and J. W. Davison, the musical critic of the *Times*, to whom she was married in 1859. Her first appearance in public was at St. Malo, where she played at a charitable concert when four and a half years of age. She made her first appearance in London at fourteen, at the National Concerts conducted by Jullien. She was the first pianist to introduce the Grand Sonata in B flat (Op. 106) of Beethoven to the London public, at a concert of her own at Willis's Rooms, at seventeen years of age, entirely from memory. Some months later she made a tour through Germany and Italy. In 1872 she took part at the inauguration of the Royal Albert Hall, playing on that occasion Beethoven's Concerto in E flat ("Emperor"), Sir Michael Costa conducted the orchestra. In June of the same year she was invited to play at the Boston Centennial Jubilee of the United States, and in February of the year following she bade farewell to the English public, and made a tour of three years round the world, visiting Australia, New Zealand, India, China, California, and America. She took part in the English concerts conducted by Sir Arthur Sullivan at the Paris Exhibition of 1878, being the recipient on that occasion of a medal from the Musical Committee of the Exhibition. The Philharmonic Society presented her with a gold medal, bearing the bust of Beethoven on one side and an appropriate inscription from the Society on the other. Arabella Goddard has played before the Queen on several occasions; the first time she did so was when she was quite a little girl, before she had appeared at the National Concerts, the Princess Royal being present. She has also played before the late German Emperor and the Empress William. When the Royal College of Music was founded she was asked to join the professorial staff. She resides now at Tunbridge Wells.

Godefroid (Dieudonné Joseph Guillaume), Félix (harpist), b. July 24, 1818, Namur; resides at Paris. Composer of a great number of elegant and popular drawing-room pieces, of which the best known are:

Danse des Sylphes, Op. 31; Le Chamelier, Chanson arabe, Op. 32; Nuits d'Espagne, Op. 40; several Tyroliennes, and an educational work (3 books) called École chantante.

Goethe (Wolfgang), Walther von (grandson of Joh. Wolfgang von Goethe), composer; b April 9, 1817, Weimar; d. April 15, 1885, Leipzig. Pupil of Mendelssohn and Weinlig (Leipzig), and later of Löwe (Stettin). He spent a long time (until 1850) in Vienna, where he came into contact with the best artists. He resided later, as Chamberlain to the Duke of Saxe-Weimar, in his native town, but abstained from following the direction which music took in Weimar when guided by Liszt. Several of his compositions for Pf. have been published at Leipzig, such as an Allegro (Op. 2) and several shorter pieces. His essays on music, and correspondence about musical matters in towns he had visited, appeared, 1849, in the *Berliner Musikzeitung*, and are of great interest.

Götz, Hermann, b. Dec. 7, 1840, Königsberg (Prussia); d. Dec. 3, 1876, Hottingen (Switzerland). Pupil of L. Köhler; later, of Bülow (Pf.), Ulrich (Composition), and Stern (reading from full score). 1863, Organist at Winterthur; 1870, relinquished this appointment on account of severe illness, from which he never recovered. For Pf. he published:

Trio, Op. 1; 3 easy pieces, with Vln., Op 2; Quartet for Pf., Vln., Vla., and V'cello, Op. 6; Lose Blätter, 2 books of Pf. pieces, Op. 7; 2 Sonatinas, Op. 8; 6 pieces, Op. 13. After his death appeared a Sonata for 4 hands and a Quintet for Pf., Vln., Vla., V'cello, and C.-Bass. Among his most popular pieces are decidedly his charming Sonatinas.

Götze, Heinrich, b. April 7, 1836, Wartha (Silesia). 1859-61, pupil at the Leipzig Conserv. of Plaidy and Moscheles (Pf.), Hauptmann and Richter (Composition). After having had appointments in Russia, Breslau, and Liebenthal, he became, 1885, music-teacher at the Seminary of Ziegenhals (Silesia). 1889, he received the title of Königl. Musik-Director.

Trio and other pieces, and author of an essay on Pf. playing, and another book on "Musical Dictation."

Goldbeck, Robert, b. 1835, Potsdam. Pupil of Litolff (Brunswick), and later, following Meyerbeer's advice, of various Paris teachers. From Paris he went, armed with weighty recommendations from Alex. von Humboldt, to London, gave a concert at Devonshire House, and published several of his compositions. 1857-66, he was active as a teacher in New York; 1867, in Boston, where he founded a Conserv., which he left to one of his assistants, and settled in Chicago, where he opened another Conserv.

Concertos, Aquarellen (12), Sentiments poétiques (8 books), Nocturne (la Violette), 3 Mélodies, &c.

Goldberg, Johann Gottlieb (?). According to Reichardt, he lived between 1730 and 1769. Nothing certain about the place or year of his birth is known, nor is any information to be got about his death. All that we know is, that about the middle of the 18th century he was Kammer-Musikus to Count Brühl, of Dresden. As he was Bach's best, most industrious, and talented pupil, he must have resided in Leipzig. Bach's well known Variations (30) in G were written for Goldberg, and are therefore known as the "Goldberg" Variations. Gerber relates that he suffered from melancholia and extraordinary obstinacy, from which his family had often to suffer. Of his works, 24 Polonaises, a Sonata, Variations, two Concertos, Preludes and Fugues are mentioned, but did not appear in print.

Goldmark, Carl, b. May 18, 1830, Keszthely (Hungary). 1847-48, pupil at the Vienna Conserv. Till 1857 he studied mostly by himself, and left, 1858, for Pesth; but not finding in the Hungarian capital sufficient sympathy, he returned to Vienna, where he succeeded in making the Viennese public acquainted with his chamber music.

Trio, Op. 4; Sonata for Pf. and Vln., Suites for ditto, Dances for 4 hands, and 9 characteristic pieces: "Sturm und Drang," Op. 5.

*Goldschmidt, Otto, b. Aug. 21, 1829, Hamburg. Pupil of Jacob Schmitt and F. W. Grund, of Hamburg, where he played (1840) for the first time in public (11 years old). 1842, he was examined by Mendelssohn (Leipzig), who advised him to enter (1843) the newly-established Conserv.; he remained in Leipzig until 1846 and studied under Mendelssohn, Robert and Clara Schumann, Hauptmann, Plaidy, and Hiller. 1847-48, he established in Hamburg a series of Pf. Chamber Music concerts. 1848, he went to Paris, in order to study with Chopin, but as, on account of the French Revolution, Chopin left Paris for England, this plan was frustrated. 1848, he went to England, to Manchester and London, played on July 31 at the concert gi·en by Jenny Lind in Her Majesty's Theatre on behalf of the Brompton Hospital for Consumption. 1848-49-50, he continued the Hamburg Chamber Music concerts, played also at the Gewandhaus concerts of Leipzig, and in Ella's Musical Union *Matinées* (London). In May, 1851, he went to New York and replaced Jules Benedict as pianist and accompanist of Mdlle. Jenny Lind's concert-party in her tour through the North of the United States and Canada. Married Mdlle. Jenny Lind on Feb. 5, 1852, at Boston (Mass.), and returned with her to Europe. The years from 1852 until 1863 were occupied by journeys in Austria, Germany, Holland, Ireland, and the English provinces, where the celebrated singer was successfully supported by her devoted husband. 1863, Prof., and, from 1866-68, Vice-Principal of the R.A.M. (London); 1863 and 1866, he conducted the Lower Rhenish Festivals; 1866, the Hamburg Musical Festival; 1876-85, Conductor of the Bach Choir; 1883-85, Examiner of the R.A.M., original Member of Council, Royal College, Member of the Philharmonic Society. 1864, Member of the Swedish Royal Academy of Music (Stockholm), Hon. Member of R.A.M., and Royal College of Organists, &c.; 1870, Knight of the Swedish Vasa Order, Great Medal for Art and Literature with Commander Ribbon of Polar Star, Sweden, &c.

12 great Studies, Op. 13; Concerto, Op. 10; Trio with Vln. and V'cello, Op. 12; Duets for 2 Pf., Op. 21 and 22, &c.

Goldschmidt, Sigismund, b. Sept. 28, 1815, Prague; d. Sept. 26, 1877, Vienna. Pupil of W. Tomaschek. 1845-49, he resided in Paris, where his performances and compositions were received with great favour. After his return to Prague, he had, on the death of his father, a rich banker, to take charge of the firm, and consequently to give up his artistic career. He was a Member of the Stockholm Academy.

12 Etudes de Concert, 6 ditto, Nocturne, Scène de Bal, Sonatas, Concertos, &c.

Golinelli, Stefano, b. Oct. 26, 1818, Bologna; d. there, July 3, 1891. For many years active as Prof. at the Bologna Lyceum, and at the same time a prolific composer. His name is held in high respect by the Italians, while he received every kind of distinction on the part of his Sovereign. The number of his works reaches 200, mostly of a light, elegant, graceful, and highly effective character.

Grande Sonate, Op. 53; ditto, Op 54; and Sonata in B min., Op. 70; Fantaisie romantique, Op. 58; "Vittoria," Morceau de Concert, Op. 59; Valse brillante, Op. 61; 24 Préludes, Op 69; Fantasia elegiaca in C min., Op. 75; second Fantaisie romantique, Op. 76; 12 Studies, Op. 15; and Prima Fantasietta.

Goria, Alexandre (Edouard), b. Jan. 21, 1823, Paris; d. there, July 6, 1860. Pupil at the Conserv., which he entered in his 8th year; Laurent and Zimmermann were his teachers of Pf., and

Dourlen and Reicha of Composition. 1834, he received the second, and, 1835, the first prize for Pf. playing; left the Conserv., 1839.
> Caprice Nocturne, Op. 6; Etude de Concert, Op. 7; and 'Olga" Mazurka (made the round of the world). Etudes (some of them, Op. 15, 23, 39, 43, of great merit), Fantasias on operatic airs, Rêveries, Nocturnes, and Transcriptions of Songs (Schubert's "Plaintes de la jeune fille," Beethoven's "Adelaide," "Les Adieux de Maria Stuart," by Niedermeyer, &c.).

Gottschalk, Louis Moreau (Maurice ?), b. May 2, 1829, New Orleans; d. Dec. 18, 1869, Rio de Janeiro. From 1841-46, pupil of Hallé and Chopin (?) at Paris; performed, 1847, for the first time in Paris; travelled afterwards in France, Spain, Switzerland, Italy; and returned, 1853, to America. He settled in New York as a teacher; went, 1866, to California and Brazil; returned to New York, and died on a second visit to Brazil. He was an excellent executant—elegant, graceful, and brilliant.
> Le Bananier, la Bamboula, la Savane, le Mancenillier, la Moissonneuse (very popular).

Gounod, Félix Charles (composer), b. June 17, 1818, Paris; d. there, Oct. 18, 1893. Pupil of Reicha and Halévy.
> La Pervenche, le Ruisseau, le Calme, Chanson de printemps, l'Angélus, Menuet, les Pifferari, Musette, le Bal d'enfants, Sérénade, Menuet Royal, l'Invocation, Marche Pontificale (Op. 43), Valse des fiancés, le Rendezvous (Op. 46), Souvenance, &c. Some of these are Transcriptions of his songs.

Gouvy, Théodore, b. July 21, 1822 (according to Fétis, 1819), Goffontaine, near Saarbrücken. He first studied law, but devoted himself later entirely to music; went to Paris, where Billard was his teacher, and Elwart instructed him in Composition. He went several times to Germany, where some of his works were performed at Leipzig, Cologne, &c. His compositions enjoy great esteem in Germany.
> 2 Studies, appeared 1845, at Berlin; Sérénades, Op. 3, 4, 5, 6, 7, 10, 27 (containing 3); Sonatas, Op. 17, 29, and 36 (for 4 hands); Trios, Op. 8, 18, 19, 22, 32; and Quintet for Pf., 2 Vln., Vla., and V'cello, Op. 24.

Graedener, Carl G. P., b. Jan. 14, 1812, Rostock; d. June 10, 1883, Hamburg. He held the appointment of Musical Director of the Kiel University; went, 1851, to Hamburg, where he founded a music school; left, 1862, for Vienna, appointed Prof. at the Conserv.; returned, 1865, to Hamburg. He is also the author of different essays on musical matters.
> Concerto, Quintet, Op. 7; 3 Sonatas with Vln., Op. 11; Variations, &c.; several Trios.

Graedener, Hermann, jun., b. May 8, 1844, Kiel. Pupil of his father and at the Vienna Conserv.; is at present Prof. at that Conserv., and enjoys considerable respect as a composer.
> Trios, Quintet, Sonata for 4 hands, and several shorter pieces.

Grammann, Carl, b. June 3, 1844, Lübeck. 1867, pupil at the Leipzig Conserv., where he remained until 1871. He settled in Vienna.
> Trios, Sonatas, and a good many shorter pieces.

Graun, Carl Heinrich, b. May 7, 1701, Wahrenbrück (Saxony); d. Aug. 8, 1759, Berlin. Pupil of I. K. Schmidt (Dresden). 1725, appointment at Brunswick; 1740, Capellmeister to King Frederic II. of Prussia.
> 12 Concertos with accompaniment, in 4 books; also a Gigue in B flat min.

Graupner, Christoph, b. Jan., 1683, Kirchberg (Saxony); d. May, 1760. Pupil at the Thomas School, Leipzig, where he was instructed by Kuhnau. 1706, went as cembalist to Hamburg; 1710, appointed by the Landgrave of Hesse, Capellmeister in Darmstadt. He became blind in 1750. He was a very prolific composer, as is testified by the Catalogue of the Darmstadt Court Library, which records not less than 50 Concertos for different instruments, 80 Overtures, 114 Symphonies, &c.
> 8 Suites for Clavecin (1718), ditto (1726); Monatliche Clavier-Früchte (Monthly Clavecin fruits), 1722; Die vier Jahreszeiten (The Four Seasons), 4 Suites (1733).

Grazioli, Giovanni Battista, b. about 1755, Venice; d. there, 1820. There are no details about his education or musical career, except that he was appointed Organist of San Marco.
> 6 Sonatas, Op. 1, and ditto, Op. 2, for Solo Clavecin; and 6 Sonatas with Vln., which appeared 1799.

*Greef, Arthur de, b. Oct. 10, 1862, Louvain. Pupil of Louis Brassin. Since 1888, Prof. at the Brussels Conserv. Eminent pianist and a successful composer, to whom Liszt and Moszkowski dedicated some of their pieces.

*Greis, Herbert, b. April 29, 1839, Maischoss a/d/Ahr. Pupil of Ferd. Hiller and Breunung (Cologne). Resides in Breslau, where he is active as a teacher and influential in furthering the interests of art. Of his compositions a good many shorter ones have appeared during the last few years.

Greulich, Adolph, b. 1819, Posen; d. 1868, Moscow. Pupil of W. Fischer (Brieg). In Breslau he continued his studies with the greatest perseverance and industry until he succeeded in obtaining the appointment of tutor in an aristocratic family of Warsaw. After having made the acquaintance of Liszt in Weimar, who gave him excellent advice, he was appointed teacher at a college at Schitomir, in South Russia, and finally Prof. at the Catharina Institute (for Ladies) in Moscow. His compositions enjoyed considerable popularity.

Greulich, Carl Wilhelm, b. Feb. 13, 1796, Kunzendorf (Silesia); d. 1837, Berlin. Pupil of his father, a Cantor and Organist, and of Kahl (Hirschberg); 1816, of B. Romberg, Bernh. Anselm Weber (Composition), and L. Berger (Pf.) He was one of the foremost pianists of Berlin, highly successful as a teacher, and of some importance as a composer.

Sonata, Op. 21; 5 Rondos, 12 Studies for the left, and both hands; Variations, Divertissements, &c.

Grieg, Edvard Hagerup, b June 15, 1843, Bergen (Norway). 1859-62, pupil at the Leipzig Conserv., where Wenzel, Reinecke, and Moscheles were his teachers; 1863, pupil of Gade (Copenhagen). 1867, he founded a Musical Society in Christiania for the promotion of a "Northern School"; 1879, he performed his Concerto, Op. 16, at the Gewandhaus concerts, Leipzig; 1893, the University of Cambridge desired to name him Hon. Mus. Doc., which distinction he could only accept in 1894. His compositions have obtained unusual popularity, and their special national character created great attention and curiosity, although it cannot be denied that moving in such a small circle as Norwegian music allows must sometimes lead to repetition. He is decidedly a most intensely national composer.

Lyric Pieces, Op. 12, 38, 43, 47; Humoresken, Op. 6; Nordische Tänze und Volksweisen, Op. 17; Aus dem Volksleben, Op. 19; Album leaves, Op. 28; Holberg Suite, Op. 40; Sonata, Op. 7; Romanze (4), Op. 10; Concerto in A min., Op. 16; Elegiac Melodies, Op. 34; Norwegian Dances, Op. 35; Sonata with Vln., Op. 8; Sonata with V'cello, Op. 36; Ballade, Op. 24.

Griepenkerl, Friedrich Conrad, b. 1782, Peine (Brunswick); d. April 6, 1849, Brunswick, where he was appointed Prof. at the "Carolinum." Author of "Æsthetics," and, with Roitzsch, editor of Bach's works.

*Grimm, Dr. Julius Otto, b. March 6, 1827, Pernau (Livland), the son of German parents. 1844-48, he studied Philology in Dorpat, and was, till 1851, private tutor to a family in St. Petersburg. After 1851, a pupil at the Leipzig Conserv., where Plaidy, Moscheles, David, E. F. Richter, Hauptmann, and Rietz were his teachers. 1855, he settled in Göttingen as a private teacher and Conductor of a Choral Society. Since 1860, Conductor of the Oratorio and Symphony Concerts, Königl. Musik-Director of the Academy, and Prof. at Münster (Westphalia). Doc. Phil., hon. causâ.

4 pieces, Op. 2; 4 Scherzi for 4 hands, Op. 4 and 5; 3 Elegies. Op. 6; 4 pieces in the form of free Canons, Op. 9; Sonata for Pf. and Vln., Op. 14; also the arrangement of 2 Orchestral Suites (in form of Canons), Op. 10 and 16; and of 2 grand Marches, Op. 17.

Grünfeld, Alfred, b. July 4, 1852, Prague; pupil of Höger (Prague) and Kullak (Berlin) One of the most excellent pianists of the present time. Travelled in Germany, France, United States, &c. He is pianist to the Imperial Courts of Austria and Prussia; Knight of the Orders of Russ. St. Stanislaus and of Saxe-Coburg; also Officer of the Roumanian Crown.

Octave-Study, Op. 15; Minuet, Op. 31; Humoreske, Op. 35; Spanisches Ständchen, Op. 37; Barcarolle, Op. 38; Impromptu, Op. 39.

Grund, Friedrich Wilhelm, b. Oct. 7, 1791, Hamburg; d. there, Nov. 24, 1874. Pupil of Schwencke. His left hand having been disabled, he devoted himself to teaching. Founded, 1819, the Sing-Akademie; became, 1828-62, Director of the Philharmonic concerts. Among his pupils were Berens, O. Goldschmidt, and Blumenthal.

Sonatines (3), Op. 14; 12 grandes Etudes, Op. 21 (a good book); Grande Sonate, Op. 27; Rondo espressivo, Octet for Pf. and Wind instruments, Sonatas with Vln., ditto with V'cello, Divertissement for 4 hands, &c.

*Guelbenza, Don Juan Y Fernandez, b. Dec. 27, 1819, Pamplona; d. Jan. 8, 1886, Madrid. Pupil of his father. When his talent developed in an astonishing manner, he was sent to Paris, where he studied with Emile Prudent; entered, later, the Conserv. as pupil of Zimmermann and C. V. Alkan. Having the opportunity of hearing Chopin, Thalberg, and Liszt, he made extraordinary progress; became, 1841, pianist to Doña Maria Cristina de Borbon, at that time a resident in Paris. She encouraged him to settle in Madrid, where he became, 1844, teacher of the King, and, on the death of Don Pedro Albéniz (1855), first Organist of the Royal Chapel. Soon after, he endeavoured to acquaint the public with the beauties of Haydn, Mozart, Beethoven and Mendelssohn's chamber music. At the time of creating (through Guelbenza's instrumentality) a musical section of the "Academia de Bellas Artes de San Fernando," King Alfonso XII. bestowed upon him the Grand Cross of the Order of Isabel la Catolica, the King of Portugal the Order of la Concepcion, and the Academy created him a Member (Academico de Número). His compositions, mostly elegant and graceful pieces, were published at the expense of the Infanta Doña Isabel de Borbon.

Guglielmi, Pietro, b. May, 1727, Massa-Carrara; d. Nov. 19, 1804, Rome.
Concerto (pour les commençant), 6 Clavecin Quartets, 6 Sonatas with Vln., and 6 Solo Sonatas (London).

Guiraud, Ernest, b. June 23, 1837, New Orleans; d. May 8, 1892, Paris. Pupil of Marmontel; since 1876, Prof. at the Conserv., Paris. Composed very effective solo pieces.

*Gurlitt, Cornelius, b. Feb. 10, 1820, Altona. Pupil of Reinecke, sen. (Altona), Courländer and Weyse (Copenhagen). Received, 1857, the diploma of Prof. from the Papal Music Academy of Rome; 1864, Organist of the principal church (Altona). 1874, the King of Prussia conferred on him the title of Königl. Musik-Director. Knight of the Prussian Crown. Composer of a great number of instructive works, studies, characteristic pieces, valses, sonatinas for 2 and 4 hands, &c.

Gutmann, Adolph, b. 1818, Heidelberg; d. Oct. 27, 1882, Spezia. Son of a hotel-keeper of Heidelberg, where Chopin, when ill, was nursed with great care; whereupon, recognising young Gutmann's decided talent, he took him to Paris and instructed him gratis; indeed, treated him as a sincere friend.
10 Etudes caractéristiques, Op. 12; about 10 Nocturnes; a Ballade, Op. 19; Marche Hongroise, Op. 22; several Mazourkas, Op. 9 and 14, &c.

Gyrowetz, Adalbert, b. Feb. 19, 1763, Budweis (Bohemia); d. March 19, 1850, Vienna. With Ignaz Pleyel he was, in his time, a most popular composer among amateurs. From 1804-27 he was Conductor of the Imperial Opera, Vienna.
Concertos, almost 80 Trios, Sonatas, Divertimentos, Notturnos (La Chasse), Sonatas with Vln., a Sonata for 2 Pf., Solo Sonatas, and many Variations.

H.

*Haan, Willem de, b. 1849, Rotterdam. Pupil of S. de Lange, Woldemar Bargiel, and C. Reinecke. 1873, appointed Musical Director at Bingen-on-the-Rhine; 1876, Conductor of the "Mozart" Society. Since 1878, Capellmeister of the Court Theatre, Darmstadt.
Pieces for 4 hands, Op. 1, and 4 Idyls, ditto; a Sonata with Vln., Op. 3; Fantasiestücke, Pf. and Vln., Op. 15; and Sketches for Andersen's Picture Book without Pictures, Op. 5.

*Haas, Alma (née Holländer), b. Jan. 31, 1847, Ratibor (Silesia). From 1857-62, pupil at the "Wandelt Institute" (Breslau), in which Logier's system was introduced. From 1862-68, pupil at Th. Kullak's Academy (Berlin); 1872, married to Dr. Ernst Haas, librarian of the British Museum. Performed with great success in many German towns, at the Popular Concerts and Henschel's Concerts, London, in Scotland and the provinces. Prof. of Bedford and King's College.

Haberbier, Ernst, b. Oct. 5, 1813, Königsberg, Prussia; died during a performance on March 12, 1869, Bergen (Norway). Pupil of his father. His method of dividing the most intricate and difficult figures between two hands and thus realizing an enormous, almost incredible speed, created a decided sensation. He was most successful in all his public performances, and his beautiful and original "Etudes Poésies," Op. 53, and a second series of them, will for a long time to come be much admired. From 1832 to 1850 he resided at St. Petersburg, where he was the favourite teacher of the Russian aristocracy.

Händel, Georg Friedrich, b. Feb. 23, 1685, Halle; d. April 13, 1759, London. Pupil of Zachau. His biography is so well known that any further notice is unnecessary. The original editions of his works are:
Suites de pièces pour le Clavecin, comp. par G. F. Händel, Vol. I. (London, printed for the Author, 1720). Suites de Pièces pour le Clavecin, Vol. II. (London, J. Walsh, 1733). Pièces de Clavecin (Amsterdam, Witvogel, 1723). 6 Fugues or Voluntaries for the Organ or Harpsichord, 3me Ouvrage (London, Walsh, 1735). Six Concertos for

the Harpsichord or Organ (London, Walsh, 1738), G min., B flat, G min., F, F, B flat, Op. 4. Second Collection, appeared 1740, contains arrangements. Third Collection (B flat, A, B flat, D min., G, B flat), Op. 7, appeared 1760. Fourth Collection, published by Arnold, 1797, contains 3 Concertos, most likely arrangements. The Clavecin or Harpsichord pieces as published by the German Händel Society, in 1 volume, contains:—First Collection: 8 Suites: A, F, D min., E min., E, F sharp min., G min., F min. Second Collection: No. 1, Prelude, Aria con Variazoni, B flat; No. 2, Chaconne, G; No. 3 (Suite), Allemande, Allegro, Air, Gigue, Menuetto, D min.; No. 4 (Suite), Allemande, Courante, Sarabande, Gigue, D min.; No. 5 (Suite), Allemande, Sarabande, Gigue, E min.; No. 6 (Suite) Allemande, Courante, Gigue, G min.; No. 7 (Suite), Allemande, Courante, Sarabande, Gigue, B flat; No. 8 (Suite), Allemande, Allegro, Courante, Aria, Menuetto, Gavotte, Gigue, G; No. 9, Chaconne, with 62 Variations in G. Third Collection: No. 1, Suite in D min.; No. 2, Suite in G; No. 3, Capriccio in G min.; No. 4, Fantasia in C; No. 5, Chaconne in F; No. 6, Lesson in A min.; No. 7, Courante e due Menuetti; No. 8, Capriccio in F; No. 9, Preludio e Allegro; No. 10, Sonatina; No. 11, Sonata; and No. 12, Sonata. Fourth Collection: 6 Fugues in G min., G, B flat, E min., A min., and C min.

Hässler (Haesler), Johann Wilhelm, b. March 29, 1747, Erfurt; d. March 25, (29?), 1822, Moscow. Pupil of his uncle, Kittel, and Seb. Bach's last pupil. Excellent performer and good composer. He travelled a great deal, returned for several years to his native town, where he established (1780) Philharmonic concerts; 1782, he left Erfurt for St. Petersburg; was appointed pianist to the Grand Duke Paul and teacher of the Grand Duke's children; 1791, he was in London, played at Court and in public; particularly successful in performing Concertos by Mozart, whom he had met (1787) at Dresden. After leaving St. Petersburg he settled in Moscow, where he was a most successful and universally respected teacher.

Sonatas (36), the set, Op. 13 and 14, are still known; Grande Gigue in D min.

Hallé, Sir Charles (Carl Halle), knighted 1888; b. April 11, 1819, Hagen (Westphalia). At first a pupil of his father, Capellmeister H.; 1835, of Rinck and Gottfried Weber (Darmstadt). 1836, he went to Paris, where he became the friend of Chopin, of Salvator Cherubini (son of the celebrated composer), and also of Cherubini himself, of Berlioz, Stephen Heller, &c.; 1842, he gave his first public concert in Paris, met Mendelssohn in Frankfort o/M. in the same year, and paid his first visit to England in 1843; 1847, he introduced (with Alard and Franchomme), Chamber Music concerts in Paris; 1848, he settled in England, appeared in London and Manchester, and was appointed Conductor of the Gentlemen's Concerts (Manchester) in 1850; he established his own orchestral concerts in 1857; his chamber concerts in London and provinces were commenced in 1859, and continued with unabated success for many years. His numerous performances of classical music at his own, the Popular, and other concerts have convinced the public of his great merit not only as an excellent and thoroughly finished executant, but also as a thoughtful, appreciative, accomplished musician, endowed with liberal views—indeed, he was instrumental in acquainting English audiences with the most recent and interesting works of modern composers. He received the honour of knighthood in 1888, the University of Edinburgh elected him LL.D., and many societies named him Hon. Member. He founded the Manchester Royal College of Music in 1893; edited Bach's 48 Preludes and Fugues, Mozart and Beethoven's Sonatas, and published the well-known Practical Pf. School. Of his mostly short compositions, only a few were published at Leipzig and Manchester.

Halm, Anton, b. June 4, 1789, Altenmarkt (Styria); d. 1872, Vienna. Until his 22nd year he served in the army, and could devote himself only later to musical studies, which he did with so much perseverance and energy that he became one of the most respected musicians in Vienna. Among his pupils were Stephen Heller and Eduard Pirkhert. He was an intelligent, thoughtful, and liberal-minded artist, who knew how to appreciate all that was good and deserving of praise.

Trios (6), Op. 12 and Op. 58; Sonatas, with Vln.; Solo Sonatas, Op. 15, 43, 51; a good many other pieces. Grandes Etudes de Concert, Op. 59; Etudes mélodiques, Op. 60; Etudes pathétiques, Op. 61; and Etudes héroiques, Op. 62.

***Handrock**, Julius, b. June 22, 1830, Naumburg a/d/Saale; d. Jan. 5, 1894, Halle o/S. He studied at the Leipzig Conserv. Since 1857 he has resided as a successful teacher at Halle.

"Mechanical Exercises" and the Studies, Op. 99 and Op. 100. He published also Sonatas and shorter pieces. Of these the "Waldlieder," Op. 2, and the "Reiselieder," Op. 6, have obtained great popularity.

Hansen, Agnes Charlotte Dagmar, b. Feb. 9, 1865, Copenhagen. Her first instruction she received from her father, Carl Emilius H., a distinguished violoncellist. For half-a-year a pupil of Neupert; afterwards, for three years, instructed in the Conserv. (Copenhagen), and finally by Aug. Winding. Since her first appearance in "Musikforeningen," in 1882, she has been esteemed as one of the best Danish lady-pianists, equally successful in solo and *ensemble* performances.

*Harmston, John William, b. 1823, London; d. Aug. 26, 1881, Lübeck. Pupil of Sterndale Bennett. Settled, 1848, at Lübeck. After a very checkered career, first as a teacher of English, later as a photographer, he succeeded, by great industry and perseverance, in teaching himself composition. His Op. 14 to 24 were favourably received. His Op. 22 (the "Song of the Bird") became very popular, and his works were eagerly sought by the publishers of North Germany. About 230 of his (mostly drawing-room) pieces were published.

Hartknoch, Carl Eduard, b. 1775 (?), Riga; d. 1834, Moscow. Pupil of J. N. Hummel. Excellent pianist and successful teacher.
<small>Solo Sonata; Sonata with Vln.; Studies; 3 Nocturnes (caractéristiques), Op. 8; and 9 Grandes Valses, Op. 9.</small>

Hartmann, Johann, Peter Emilius, b. May 14, 1805, Copenhagen. Pupil of his father. He is one of the Directors of the Conserv. and Prof. of Organ and Theory. Amongst the Danish composers he is certainly one of the most eminent. Gade married one of Hartmann's daughters. The King of Denmark conferred on him the "Danebrog" Order, and from the University of Copenhagen he received (1874) the diploma of Hon. Doc. Phil.
<small>Grande Sonate Concertante, with Vln., Op. 8; Little Characteristic Pieces, with Introductory Poetry by Hans Christian Andersen, Op. 50; 6 Fantasiestücke, Op. 54. and a Suite for Pf. and Vln., Op. 66.</small>

Hartmann, Emil (son of the above), b. Feb. 21, 1836, Copenhagen. Pupil of his father and his brother-in-law, Niels W. Gade. Since 1871, Organist of the Royal Castle. Like his father, he is a "Knight of the Danebrog."
<small>Pf. Concerto; a Trio, Op. 10; several Suites and other solo pieces; "Nordische Tonbilder," Op. 11 (very popular); 3 Mazurkas, Op. 28.</small>

Hartog, Eduard de, b. Aug. 15, 1828 (1826?), Amsterdam. Pupil of Döhler, Litolff, and Heinze. 1852, he settled in Paris, but took up his abode later at Wiesbaden. Among his numerous works, those written for children are very popular.

"Aus dem Kinderleben," Op. 53; 7 pieces, and a second set (Op. 54), 5 pieces. He published likewise Suite de Chorals célèbres de J. S. Bach, Graun, Mendelssohn, &c., 4 hands; Impromptu Mazurka, with V'cello, Op. 55; la Danse des Willis, Op. 23; and Vilanelle, Op. 25.

*Hartvigson, Frits, b. May 31, 1851, Grenaae, Iylland (Denmark). At first a pupil of his mother, later of Anton Rée (pupil of Chopin), of Gade (for the performance of Bach and Beethoven's works), and of Gebauer (Theory). In 1858 he undertook a tour through Norway. Assisted by the Danish Government, he studied (1859-61) at Berlin under Dr. von Bülow. 1861, he played at one of the Gewandhaus concerts (Leipzig) and, 1863, under Gade's direction in Copenhagen. 1864, he appeared, under Bennett's direction, at a Philharmonic concert, and was re-engaged 1872. 1873-75, he resided at St. Petersburg, played there, in Moscow and in Helsingfors; went afterwards to Munich, and settled (1875) in London. 1873, appointed pianist to the Princess of Wales; 1875, Prof. at the Royal Normal College for the Blind (Upper Norwood), and, 1888, at the R.A.M. He has often appeared at the Crystal Palace and Richter concerts, and his performances have always been received with well-merited sympathy.

*Hartvigson, Anton (brother of the above), b. Oct. 16, 1845, Aarhus (Denmark). First a pupil of his mother, later of Edmund Neupert and Carl Tausig. He visited England in 1873, and settled in London, 1882. In his annual Recitals he introduced many compositions of Liszt.

Hasert, Rudolph, b. Feb. 4, 1826, Greifswald; d. Jan. 4, 1877, Gristow, near Greifswald. Intended for a lawyer, he studied music only as an amateur, but devoted himself later entirely to it. Studied, 1848-50, under Kullak and Dehn (Berlin). For several years he was unable to play on account of muscular pain. 1861, he settled in Berlin, where he was active as a teacher at Kullak's Academy, but decided to study theology; passed (1870) his examination, received a living first at Straussberg, and later at Gristow.
<small>Sonatas, Studies, Drawing-room pieces, Transcriptions, &c</small>

Haslinger, Tobias, b. March 1, 1787, Zell (Upper Austria); d. June 18, 1842, Vienna. He succeeded S. A. Steiner as proprietor of the well-known publishing house, Tobias Haslinger, a firm intimately connected with Beethoven, Czerny, Hummel, Seyfried, Liszt, Joh. Strauss, &c. Among his compositions, mostly written for educational purposes, his Sonatinas and Rondos obtained great popularity.

Haslinger, Carl (only son of the above), b. June 11, 1816, Vienna; d. there, Dec. 26, 1868. Pupil of Czerny and Seyfried. Excellent pianist and a talented composer. Succeeded his father, 1842, as sole proprietor of the publishing business, under the name Carl Haslinger, quondam Tobias. Among the works he published were some by Schubert, Schumann, Liszt, Thalberg, Döhler, Czerny, Bargiel, Strauss, Lanner, Labitzky, Kullak, Moscheles, and many others. During the winter he gave weekly Soirées, at which the most celebrated musicians of Vienna, and other European celebrities passing through the Austrian capital, assembled and listened to most exquisite performances. Haslinger was one of the most efficient musicians of Vienna, a friend and patron of young artists, and universally beloved for his innate kindness and delightful geniality.

Hasse, Johann Adolph, b. May 25, 1699, Bergedorf (Hamburg); d. Dec. 16, 1783, Venice. Of his compositions for clavecin were published.

6 Sonatas (Paris) and Concertos (Favourite Concertos, London).

Hauk (Hauck), Wenzeslaus, b. Feb. 27, 1801, Habelschwerdt (Glatz); d. Nov. 30, 1834, Berlin. Pupil of the Organist Deutsch, later of Birnbach (Breslau), and, 1825, of Hummel (Weimar). Settled, 1828, in Berlin; much respected and esteemed for his excellent qualities and eminent performances.

Sonatas, Rondos, Divertissements, Variations.

Hauptmann, Moritz, b. Oct. 13, 1792, Dresden; d. Jan. 3, 1868, Leipzig. 1811, pupil of Spohr (Cassel); 1812, appointed violinist at the Dresden Opera; 1815, tutor to the children of Prince Repnin (Russia); 1822, violinist at the Cassel Opera; 1842, Cantor of the Thomas School (Leipzig); and, later, Prof. at the newly founded Conserv. 1857, the University of Göttingen conferred upon him the diploma of Hon. Doc. Phil. and Arts (freie Künste). He received numerous other distinctions.

Sonatas with Vln., Op. 5, 6, and 23; Concerto facile, Op. 20; and 12 Pièces detachées, Op. 12.

Haydn, Joseph, b. March 31, 1732, Rohrau (Lower Austria); d. May 31, 1809, Vienna. Pupil of Porpora, but mostly self-taught. 1759, Capellmeister to Count Morzin; 1761-90, in the same capacity to Prince Esterhazy (Eisenstadt, in Hungary); settled, 1790, in Vienna; 1790-92, in England; 1794, he paid his second and last visit to London. 1791 (July 8), he received the diploma of Hon. Mus. Doc. from the University of Oxford; the Magistrate of Vienna conferred on him the great gold medal of St. Salvator and the freedom of the town. His Sonatas are always fresh, cheerful, and healthy, sometimes full of a sweet and charming expression, and at other times indicating a quaint humour and a playful spirit which is quite delightful. They are highly original, containing many traits and passages almost startling in their novelty. Although not so brilliant as those of Beethoven or Clementi, they are invaluable for teaching purposes and for inducing a healthy, vigorous, and natural train of musical thought in the mind of the student. His works for Pf. are very numerous:—

Sonatas (34): †No. 1 in E flat, 4/4 (1790); No. 2 in E min., 6/8 (1777); †No. 3 in E flat, 3/4 (1790); No. 4 in G min., 4/4 (1786); No. 5 in C, 4/4 (1780); †No. 6 in C sharp min., 4/4 (1786); †No. 7 in D, 4/4 (1780); No. 8 in E flat, 4/4 (1786); No. 9 in E flat, 4/4 (1780); No. 10 in A flat, 4/4 (1786); No. 11 in D, 4/4 (1767); No. 12 in B flat, 2/4 (1767); No. 13 in G, 6/8 (1784); No. 14 in B flat, 4/4 (1784); No. 15 in D, 3/4 (1784); No. 16 in C, 3/4 (1786?); No. 17 in F, 3/4 (1789); No. 18 in G, 2/4 (1776); †No. 19 in C min., 4/4 (1771); No. 20 in D, 2/4 (1767); No. 21 in G, 4/4 (1766); No. 22 in D, 2/4 (1777); No. 23 in G, 2/4 (1780); No. 24 in E flat, 3/4 (1776); No. 25 in F, 4/4 (1776); No. 26 in A, 2/4 (1767); No. 27 in E, 4/4 (1776); †No. 28 in B min., 4/4 (1776); No. 29 in C, 2/4 (1773); No. 30 in E, 4/4 (1774); No. 31 in F, 2/4 (1774); No. 32 in D, 4/4 (1777); No. 33 in A, 2/4 (1776); No. 34 in E, 4/4 (1767). *Smaller pieces:* Andante varié in F min., 2/4; Arietta con Variazioni in E flat, 3/4; Arietta con Variazioni in A, 3/4; Tema con Variazioni in C, 2/4; Air varié in C min. (La Roxelane), 2/4; Adagio in F, 3/4; Fantasia in C, 3/8; Capriccio in G, 3/4; Il maëstro e lo scolare, Andante and Variations for 4 hands. *Sonatas with Vln.:* No. 1 in G, 6/8; No. 2 in D, 3/4; No. 3 in E flat, 4/4; No. 4 in A, 4/4; No. 5 in G, 4/4; No. 6 in C, 6/8; No. 7 in F, 4/4; No. 8 in G, 4/4 (for Fl. or Vln.). *Trios with Vln. and V'cello:* No. 1 in G, 2/4; No. 2 in F sharp min., 4/4; No. 3 in C, 4/4; No. 4 in E, 4/4; No. 5 in E flat, 2/4; No. 6 in D, 4/4; No. 7 in A, 4/4; No. 8 in C min., 2/4; No. 9 in A, 3/4; No. 10 in E min., 4/4; No. 11 in E flat, 4/4; No. 12 in E min., 4/4; No. 13 in B flat, 4/4; No. 14 in G min., 2/4; No. 15 in E flat min., 2/4; No. 16 in G min., 4/4; No. 17 in E flat, 4/4; No. 18 in C, 6/8; No. 19 in D min., 2/4; No. 20 in E flat, 2/4; No. 21 in D, 2/4; No. 22 in B flat, 4/4; No. 23 in F, 4/4; No. 24 in A flat, 2/4; No. 25 in F, 2/4; No. 26 in C, 4/4; No. 27 in F, 4/4; No. 28 in G, 3/4; No. 29 in F, 4/4 (for Fl.

(Vln.) and V'cello); No. 30 in D, 4/4 (for Fl. (Vln.) and V'cello); No. 31 in G, 4/4 (for Fl. (Vln.) and V'cello) *Concertos*: No. 1 in F (1771, Le Duc, Paris); No. 2 in G, published in Amsterdam and Paris; No. 3 in D, published at Schott's (Mayence) and Artaria, 1784 (Vienna).

*Heap, Swinnerton Charles (Mus. Bac., Mus. Doc.), b. 1847, Birmingham. Pupil of Dr. Monk (York), and, as Mendelssohn Scholar (1865), of Moscheles, Richter, and Reinecke (Leipzig). Among his compositions are—
> Trio, Sonata for Pf. and Cl., Quintet for Pf. and Wind instruments, Sonata for Pf and Vln., Solo Sonata, 3 Valses, 2 Nocturnes, Romanza, &c.

Hecht, Eduard, b. Nov. 28, 1832, Dürckheim (Rhine - Palatinate); d. March 7, 1887, Manchester. Pupil of his father, a clever musician residing at Frankfort o/M., and Jacques Rosenhain (*see* this name) for Pf., Messer and Hauff for Composition. Excellent pianist and a highly talented and clever composer. Settled (1854) in Manchester, where he was a successful teacher and public performer.
> Pieces for Chamber Music, Caprices, Marches, and several very effective Drawing-room pieces.

*Hegner, Otto, b. Nov. 18, 1876, Basle (Switzerland). Pupil of Dr. Hans Huber (*see* this name) for Pf. and Alfred Glaus for Harmony. As a child he created great and deserved attention by his extraordinary dexterity and thoroughly musicianly performances, which were heartily applauded in Germany, England, and America. At his own desire his compositions are not mentioned.

Heinlein, Paul, b. April 11, 1626, Nürnberg; d. there, Aug. 6, 1686. A son of the celebrated physician, Heinlein, he received an excellent education; was sent (1646) to Linz and Munich and (1647) to Italy, where he studied for three years. He was considered one of the best performers on the clavecin.
> Toccatas, Fantasias, Fugues, and Ricercaris (published at Nürnberg).

Heller, Stephen, b. May 15, 1815, Pesth; d. Jan. 15, 1888, Paris. 1824, pupil of Anton Halm, in Vienna, where he remained for two years, giving concerts; resided for several years in Augsburg, and settled, 1838, in Paris. He was a most excellent pianist, who appeared, however—owing to extreme nervousness—but seldom in public, and preferred to teach and compose. Among Pf. composers he occupies a foremost rank. All his compositions are distinguished by nobility of expression, correctness and clearness of style, and considerable originality.
> Studies, Op. 16, 45, 46, 47, &c.; Character Pieces, Dans les Bois, Promenades d'un solitaire, Nuits blanches, Tarantellas; Blumen-Frucht und Dornenstücke; Valses, Sonatas, Preludes, Overtures, Barcarelles, Fantasias, Pensées fugitives (written in conjunction with H. W. Ernst), 21 Technical Studies, Op. 154, preparatory to Chopin's works; Paraphrases of Schubert's Songs (la Truite, la Poste, &c.), Saltarello on an Air of Mendelssohn, Op 77; Concert Transcriptions of some of Mendelssohn's Songs.

Henkel, Dr. Heinrich, b Feb. 14, 1822, Fulda. Pupil of Aloys Schmitt (Pf.) and André (Theory) at Frankfort o/M.; later (1846), of Julius Knorr (Pf.), Leipzig. Founded, 1849, a Music School in Frankfort o/M. A successful teacher and respected author. Obtained, 1883, the title of Königl. Musik-Director. The University of Marburg gave him the diploma of Hon. Doc. Phil.; the Grand Duke of Hesse and the Duke of Coburg conferred on him the gold medals for Art and Science, &c. Among his compositions, Op. 15, 16, 17, 19, 27, 38, and 51 have obtained considerable popularity Author of a "Klavierschule" and highly useful technical Studies.

Hennes, Aloys, b. Sept. 8, 1827, Aachen (Aix-la-Chapelle); d. May 8, 1889, Berlin. 1844-52, appointed a "Post-official," and therefore only able to devote himself later to the study of music. Studied under Hiller and Reinecke at the Cologne Conserv., and afterwards gained his living by giving lessons in Creuznach, Alzey, Mayence, and Wiesbaden. Settled, 1872, in Berlin; appointed, 1881, a teacher at Xaver Scharwenka's Conserv. Hennes obtained a good reputation by the publication of his "Clavier Unterrichtsbriefe" (was translated into English), and by his decidedly practical and useful Studies.

*Henschel, Georg, b. Feb. 18, 1850, Breslau. Pupil at the "Wandelt" Institute (Breslau), of Moscheles, Richter, and Götze (Leipzig); later (1870) of Kiel (Berlin). At first he intended to become a pianist, but devoted himself later to singing, without, however, losing command over the keyboard, a result of which is apparent in his masterly accompaniments, aided by a phenomenal memory. The "Maatschappy tot Bevordering der Toonkunst" of Holland elected him an Hon. Member.
> Pieces (3), Op. 2; ditto (2), Op. 5; an Etude Impromptu, Op. 6; Pieces in the form of Canons, Op 9 and 18; 6 Pieces (nach Genrebildern), Op. 13; 2 Nocturnes, Op. 35; and a Mazurka, Op. 48.

Hensel, Fanny Cecile (sister of Felix Mendelssohn-Bartholdy), b. Nov. 14, 1805, Hamburg; d. May 17, 1847, Berlin. Pupil of L. Berger. Several of her compositions (mostly songs) appeared under the name of her illustrious brother, but were published later with her own name. 4 Songs without words, Op. 8; Trio, Op. 11.

Henselt, Adolph von, b. May 12, 1814, Schwabach (Middle Franconia, Bavaria); d. Oct. 10, 1889, Warmbrunn (Silesia). Was first a pupil of Madame de Fladt, an excellent amateur pianist of Munich, then received pecuniary aid from the Bavarian Court, and went to Weimar in order to study with Hummel, afterwards to Vienna to take lessons from Simon Sechter in Composition. Settled (1838) in St. Petersburg; appointed pianist to the Empress and teacher of the Imperial children. The Emperor conferred on him the Order of St. Vladimir with the patent of nobility, named him Imperial Councillor with the title Excellency, and appointed him Chief Inspector of the Imperial Ladies' Colleges. His works for Pf. are very much admired, not only for their thoroughly musicianly qualities, roundness of form, beautiful harmonisation, ingratiating melodies, and considerable originality, but also for their entirely new (almost orchestral) effects. In his great Studies, Op. 2 and Op. 5 (composed before he went to Russia), he was the first to introduce poetical mottos giving a clue to their character; whilst in his two sets of Variations, Op. 1 and 11 ("Elisir d'amore" and "Robert le Diable"), he produces a decidedly new technical treatment. By nature exceedingly modest and simple, he disliked appearing in public, and could only be prevailed on to play before a small, select circle. By Schumann he was called the "German Chopin." His style of playing was extraordinarily fine, noble, and effective; he combined unusual physical force with the greatest suavity and delicacy, and a wonderful *legato*. In his transcriptions from Weber and other composers he succeeded in realizing a fulness hitherto unknown.
Concerto in F min., Op. 16; Duo for Pf. and V'cello; Poëme d'amour; Impromptu, Op. 7; Pensée fugitive, Op. 8; Scherzo, Op. 9; Toccata, Nocturnes, Spring Song, Valses, 12 Etudes, Op. 2; 12 Etudes, Op. 5.

Hering, Carl Gottlieb, b. Oct. 25, 1766, Schandau; d. Jan. 3, 1853, Zittau. Pupil of Schicht. Since 1798, principal music teacher at the Stadt-Schule (Zittau). He became well known by his excellent educational works.
Instructive Variations (1802), Progressive Variations (1809), a Method for Children (Leipzig, 1804-7), and a Practical School for inventing Preludes (1812-14). Studies for 4 hands, 6 Books (Peters, Leipzig).

Hérold, Louis Joseph Ferdinand (only son of Franç. Jos. H., a pianist of Emanual Bach's School), b. Jan., 1791, Paris; d. there, Jan. 19, 1833. 1806, pupil at the Conserv., where Louis Adam (Pf.), Catel and Méhul (Composition) were his teachers; gained the first prize for Pf. playing and obtained, 1812, the "Grand Prix de Rome." 1814, pianist to Queen Caroline (Naples). After a short stay in Vienna he returned to Paris. During 1827 and the following years he composed a quantity of pieces for Pf. (about 59), of which may be named—
3 Concertos, Sonatas, one in A flat; another, "L'Amante disperato"; Variations, Rondos ("Le dernier soupir"), Andantes, &c.

Herz, Henri (younger brother of the following), b. Jan. 6, 1806, Vienna; d. Jan. 5, 1888, Paris. At first a pupil of his father and the organist Hünten, at Coblenz. 1816, pupil of Pradher at the Paris Conserv., where he obtained the first prize. 1818, his first compositions were very favourably received. In company with the violinist Lafont, he travelled in Germany, and later in England. Very popular as a public performer and an excellent teacher. 1837, Chevalier de la Légion d'Honneur (later Officer) and Knight of the Belgian Leopold Order. Appointed, 1842, Prof. at the Paris Conserv., which appointment he held until 1874. He joined the Pf. maker (1825) Klepfa, in a Pf. manufactory, which speculation, however, turned out very disastrously and compelled him to undertake a journey through the United States, Mexico, California, and the West Indies, lasting from 1845 until 1851. His experiences and adventures are described in the amusing book, "Mes voyages," &c. (Paris, 1866). In his later established Pf. manufactory he was eminently successful (*see* Piano Makers). As a pianist he was admired for his elegant, fluent, correct, and brilliant performances; he never occupied himself much with playing classical pieces, but relied more on the interpretation of his own works, of which he wrote a very large number:—
Studies: Etudes du Conservatoire (24), Op. 151; ditto, Op. 152 (15); Op. 119, I.; ditto, Op. 119, II.; Grandes Etudes de Concert

(18), Op. 153; Etudes de l'agilité, Op. 179; Collection des Gammes, 1,000 Exercices pour l'emploi du Dactylion, Fantasias, Variations Souvenirs, Rondos, &c.

Herz, Jacques Simon, b. Dec. 31, 1794, Frankfort o/M.; d. Jan. 27, 1880, Nice (Nizza). 1807, pupil at the Paris Conserv. under Pradher. He resided for many years, a highly successful and popular teacher, in Paris; settled later in London.

Valses (La Coquette, Op. 51; Valse brillante, Op. 57; La Fiancée, Op. 69); Mazurkas, Redowa brilante, Op. 60, Fantaisies, and Variations on operatic airs.

Herzogenberg, Heinrich von, b. June 10, 1843, Graz (Styria). 1862-65, pupil at the Vienna Conserv., where Otto Dessoff was his teacher; remained from 1865 till 1872 in Graz, settled afterwards in Leipzig, where he became, 1875, Conductor of the Bach Society. 1885, appointed as a teacher at the Berlin Hochschule; 1890, elected a Member of the Royal Academy of Arts.

Fantasiestücke, Op 4; Fantasia for Pf. and Vln., Op 15; Duos for Pf. and V'cello, Op. 12; Quintet, Op. 17; Trio, Op. 24, and several shorter pieces.

Hess, Charles Léon, b. Jan. 28, 1844, Lorient (Departement Morbihan). Pupil at the Paris Conserv. He is one of the most popular French writers of light and fashionable pieces.

Hesse, Adolph Friedrich (son of an organ - builder). b. Aug. 30, 1809, Breslau; d. there, Aug. 5, 1863. Pupil of Berner and Ernst Köhler (Breslau), and later of Hummel (Weimar). Although his reputation as an excellent organist was very great, he distinguished himself also as a brilliant pianist, and among his works for Pf. are—

Sonata for 4 hands, Concerto, and several shorter pieces.

Heuschkel, Johann Peter, b. Jan. 4, 1773, Harres (Eisfeld); d. 1853, Biebrich on the Rhine. 1797, appointed musician of the princely orchestra of Hildburghausen, where (1796-1797) C. M. von Weber was his pupil. Weber writes of him: "I have to thank him for the true and firm foundation, the even development of both hands, and the future correct and characteristic style which he, the energetic, strict, and severe teacher, taught me."

***Heymann-Rheineck, Carl August,** b. Nov. 24, 1852, Castle Rheineck on the Rhine. Pupil of Rudorff, Isidor Seiss, and Ferd. Hiller (Cologne). 1869-71, pupil at the Berlin Hochschule, of Rudorff (Pf.) and Kiel (Composition). Since 1875 Prof. at the Hochschule.

Novelletten, Op. 5; Fantasiestücke, Op. 3; and other highly effective pieces.

Heymann, Carl (no relation to the above), b. Oct. 6, 1853, Amsterdam. Pupil at the Cologne Conserv. of Gernsheim (Pf.) and Hiller (Pf. and Composition). 1879, Prof. at the Hoch Conserv. (Frankfort o/M.), which appointment he had to relinquish on account of a mental malady. Most excellent pianist, and graceful, elegant composer.

Concerto; the popular "Elfenspiel"; other short and highly effective pieces.

Hiller, Ferdinand (von), b. Oct. 24, 1811, Frankfort o/M.; d. May 10, 1885, Cologne. At first a pupil of Aloys Schmitt (Frankfort o/M.); 1825, of Hummel (Weimar). 1828-35, he lived in Paris, enjoying the friendship of Liszt, Chopin, Rossini, Meyerbeer, Bellini, Cherubini, Döhler; in short, of all the Parisian celebrities. 1836, he returned to Frankfort o/M. in order to conduct the "St. Cecilia" Society. 1840, he spent in Leipzig and conducted (1842) the "Gewandhaus" Concerts; 1847, Capellmeister at Düsseldorf; 1850, elected Director of the newly-established Conserv. and Conductor of the "Gürzenich" concerts of Cologne. He paid repeated visits to London, where his performances and compositions found many admirers. His improvisations and the manner in which he played Bach and Mozart were most excellent. He was very prolific as an author, and his "Feuilletons" for the *Cologne Gazette* were much admired for their elegant style and amusing wit. The King of Würtemberg ennobled him, the Prussian, Saxon, and other Sovereigns conferred orders of Knighthood upon him, and he also received the "Maximilian" Order for Art and Science (Bavaria); was a Member of the Berlin Academy, as well as of other non-German academies and societies. The University of Bonn named him (1868) Hon. Doc. Phil., and the town of Cologne amply provided for his family. He composed largely for the Pf., and his works testify to the interest he took in the instrument. Among the best known of his Pf. works are—

Concerto in F sharp min., Sonatas, Suites, Sonatinas, Op. 95; Variations, Op. 98; an Operetta without words (for 4 hands), excellent Studies, Impromptus, Suite for Pf. and Vln.; 5 Trios, 5 Quartets, and many shorter pieces (Op. 57, 59, 66, 191).

Hiller (Hüller), Johann Adam, b. Dec. 25, 1728, Wendisch-Ossig (Görlitz); d. June 16, 1804, Leipzig. Pupil of Homilius (Dresden). As a composer he chiefly devoted himself to operas and operettas; was also Conductor of the "Gewandhaus" concerts of Leipzig. For clavecin he published—
  Sonatas and short pieces (Leipzig, 1760 and 1762), and a collection of small pieces called "Musikalischer Zeitvertreib."

Himmel, Friedrich Heinrich (founder of the German "Singspiel"), b. Nov. 20, 1765, Treuenbrietzen (Brandenburg); d. June 8, 1814, Berlin. Intended to study theology, but his talent for playing and composing was noted by Frederic William II. of Prussia, who persuaded him to devote himself entirely to music, and allowed the necessary sums for furthering his studies. Pupil of Naumann (Dresden). 1792, he went to Italy; 1795, appointed Royal Capellmeister at Berlin. After short journeys to Stockholm and St. Petersburg, he remained, from 1801, permanently in Berlin.
  Concertos, Sextet, Quartet (Leipzig); 3 Trios, Op. 16, and 6 others without opus number; Grand Sonata with Fl., Op. 14; Sonata for 2 Pf.; another for 4 hands; Fantasias, Variations, &c. (Peters, and Breitkopf & Härtel, of Leipzig).

Hitz, Franz, b. July 17, 1828, Aarau. Pupil at the Paris Conserv. of Zimmermann and Laurent (Pf.), Reber (Harmony). Composer of about 200 short drawing-room pieces, of which the most popular are the Romances "Souviens toi" and "Bon soir," Op. 150.

Hoffmeister, Franz Anton, b. 1754, Rothenburg on the Neckar; d. Feb. 10, 1812, Vienna. 1768, in Vienna, in order to study the law; but his inclination to become a musician was so great that he devoted himself entirely to music. He opened a music business in Vienna, which he gave up in 1798 in order to travel. 1799, in Leipzig, where he founded (1800), with Kühnel, the well-known Bureau de Musique, which was taken later by Peters. He returned after some time to Vienna, where he occupied himself entirely with composing. The Viennese gave him the nickname of the "Flute-Pleyel."
  12 Concertos, Quartets, 44 Trios, Sonatas with Vln. or Fl., Solo Sonatas, Rondos, Pieces for 4 hands, &c; 156 Quartets for Strings and Fl., 96 Duets for Fl.

Hofmann, Heinrich, b. Jan. 13, 1842, Berlin. Pupil of Theodor Kullak (Pf.), Dehn and Wüerst (Composition). Highly successful as a composer. He is a Member of the Berlin Royal Academy of Arts, has received several decorations, and obtained the title of "Professor." Among his best known works are—
  Sonata for Pf. and Vln., Op. 67; Trio, Op. 18; the solos: Der Trompeter von Säkkingen, 6 pieces, Op. 52; Aus meinem Tagebuch, 12 pieces, Op. 46; Stimmungsbilder, Op. 88. For 4 hands: English Songs; Silhouetten aus Ungarn; Chants and Danses russes, Suite Hongroise, Op. 16; 3 characteristic pieces, Op. 35; 6 ditto, Op. 70; 2 Serenades, Op. 54; Ekkehard-Sketches, Op. 57; Italienische Liebesnovelle, Op. 19; Ländler und Walzer, Op. 23; Norwegian Songs and Dances; new Hungarian Dances; Souvenirs d'autrefois, Op. 66; Am Rhein, 4 Sketches, Op. 43, &c.

*__Hofmann, Joseph__, b. Jan. 20, 1877, Cracow (Austrian Poland). Pupil of his father. Played as early as 1882 at a charity concert in Warsaw, where he himself gave (1883) several concerts. 1885, he performed Beethoven's Concerto (Op. 37) and Liszt's arrangement of Weber's Polacca, with orchestra; and, with Michalowski, Schumann's Variations for 2 Pf. The sensation he produced was unprecedented, and was repeated in Vienna, Paris, England, Germany, Norway, Sweden, Denmark, and America. His extraordinary gifts and modest, amiable, and natural manners were everywhere admired. For three years he enjoyed Rubinstein's tuition, and after seven years' retirement resumed, on his advice, his career as a virtuoso. He also shows considerable talent as a composer, and several of his published works (Hainauer, Breslau) exhibit natural and correct feeling and a thorough absence of triviality.

*__Hol, Richard__, b. July 23, 1825, Amsterdam. Pupil at the Amsterdam and, later, at the Leipzig Conserv. Since 1862, Director of the Utrecht Music School; Conductor of the Cecilia Society and "Diligentia" concerts of Utrecht; Conductor of the classical concerts given in the Amsterdam "Crystal Palace." Knight of the Orders "Crown of Oak" and "Lion," Officer of the French Academy.
  Sonatas, Sonatinas, Trios, Duets for 4 hands, Novelletten, and a Method of Pf. playing

Holmes, William Henry, b. Jan. 8, 1812, Sudbury (Derbyshire); d. April 23, 1885, London. Pupil at the R.A.M. under Cipriani Potter as early as 1822, when he gained two gold medals; became, 1826, Sub-Prof. and subsequently Prof. He was a highly successful teacher; among his pupils were Sterndale Bennett, George and

Walter Macfarren, J. W. Davison, and others. As a pianist he was likewise successful, and many of his compositions show decided ability. 1880, he was appointed Prof. at the newly-established Guildhall School of Music. Like Potter, he had very liberal ideas about new composers and took great interest in the advance of modern Pf. playing.

*Holten, Carl von, b. July 26, 1836, Hamburg. Pupil of Jacques Schmitt, Avé Lallemant, and Grädener. Went, 1853, to Leipzig, where he studied, until 1855, under Moscheles and Plaidy (Pf.), and Julius Rietz (Composition). Since 1874, Prof. at the Conserv. of Hamburg. 1857, he began to give an annual series of Chamber Music concerts at Hamburg and Altona.
Sonata with Vln., Concerto, 6 Concert Studies, Children's Symphony, and several short solo pieces.

Horn, August, b. Sept. 1, 1825, Freiberg, Saxony; d. March 23, 1893, Leipzig. Pupil at the Leipzig Conserv., and one of the best instructed musicians of the present time. He made his name well known by his excellent arrangements of classical pieces for Pf. (2 and 4 hands), which are particularly distinguished by their practicability and absolute faithfulness. His own compositions (Fantasias, &c.) became but little known, although they show in every instance the cultivated musician. His death was deplored by a large circle of sincerely attached friends, who understood how to value his sterling qualities.

Horsley, Charles Edward, b. Dec., 1822, Kensington; d. Feb. 28, 1876, New York. Pupil of Moscheles in London; 1839, of Hauptmann in Cassel, and, later, of Mendelssohn in Leipzig.
Trio, Sonata for Pf. and V'cello in G, Op. 3; Sonata for Pf. and Vln. in F, Op. 14; 6 Lieder ohne Worte, Op. 11, &c.

*Horzalka, Johann Evangelist, b. Dec. 6, 1798 (not 1778), Triesch (Moravia); d. Sept. 9, 1860, Penzing, near Vienna. Son of a schoolmaster and organist, his father sent him to Vienna, where he made the acquaintance of Moscheles, who gave him lessons gratis and introduced him to the musical circles of Vienna. From Emanuel Alois Förster he received instruction in composition. 1819, he gave his first public concert, in which he introduced with decided success several of his own works. The critics praised his performances and spoke highly of his "free Fantasias." For many years he was one of the most successful teachers.
Sonata, Op. 9; Fantasia Pastorale, Fantasia on themes of Beethoven's Sonata Pathétique, Op. 60; excellent Studies, many Rondos, a Fugue in E min., and a Fantasia for 4 hands, Op. 22.

*Huber, Dr. Hans, b. June 28, 1852, Schoenewend (Solothurn). 1870-74, pupil at the Leipzig Conserv., under Ernst Wenzel, C. Reinecke, and Dr. Oscar Paul. 1874-76, private teacher at Wesserling (Alsace). Settled, 1876, in Basle (Switzerland). At present Prof. at the Basle Music School. 1892, the University of Basle conferred on him the diploma of Hon. Doc. Phil. Among his best known pupils are Otto Hegner and Schelling.
2 Concertos, 3 Trios, 4 Sonatas with Vln., 2 with V'cello, Sonata for 2 Pf., Quartet with strings, and several pieces for 2 and 4 hands.

Hüllmandel, Nicolaus Joseph, b. 1751, Strassburg; d. Dec. 19, 1823, London. After having learned the elements of Pf. playing and composition, he went to Hamburg, where he became a pupil of Emanuel Bach. 1775, he was in Italy; 1776, in Paris, where his performances were much admired. 1787, for some time in London; but returned to Paris, where he married a rich lady and retired from public life. His devotion to the Royal family brought him into discredit with the Republicans, and he had to fly (1790) to London, where—although his confiscated estate was restored to him by the first Consul —he remained till his death, giving lessons and composing.
6 Sonatas for Pf., Vln., and V'cello, Sonatas with Vln. (ad lib.), Solo Sonatas, Petits Airs Faciles and Progressives.

Hünten, Franz, b. Dec. 26, 1793, Coblenz; d. there, Feb. 22, 1878. Son of the organist, Daniel H., teacher of Henri Herz, who, on his side, persuaded Daniel to send his son (1819) to Paris, where he could assist him in his career. He became there a pupil at the Conserv. under Pradher and Reicha, made astonishing progress as an executant, and succeeded in getting from the Parisian publishers many orders for little, easy, and fashionable pieces, earning by them very respectable sums. Soon he disposed of his works not only in France, but also in Germany, Italy, and England, and after eighteen years' hard work he had earned sufficient to live quietly and comfortably with his relations in Coblenz. His compositions are by no means interesting, but are correctly and practically written, and afforded pleasure to pupils and amateurs. None of them are so brilliant or effective as those of his friend Herz, but they are in their way useful and possess decided merit.

> 18 Studies, Op. 80; 12 melodious Studies, Op. 81; and 25 Etudes progressives, Op. 114. About 200 other pieces consist of Variations, little Fantasias, Rondos, Sonatinas (3), Op. 6, and easy transcriptions of favourite French (Puget), German (Schubert, Proch), and Italian songs.

Hummel, Johann Nepomuk, b. Nov. 14, 1778, Pressburg (Hungary); d. Oct. 17, 1837, Weimar. For two years pupil of Mozart, he went (1788) with his father to different countries, giving successful concerts. 1795, he returned to Vienna, and studied with Albrechtsberger, Salieri, and Joseph Haydn. 1803-11, Capellmeister to Prince Esterhazy (succeeding Joseph Haydn); 1816, Hof-Capellmeister at Stuttgart; and from 1820 until his death (1837) Hof-Capellmeister at Weimar. He travelled much, and gathered honours and distinctions in Russia, Holland, England, France, Austria, and Germany. Member of the Academies of Stockholm and Paris, decorated with the Legion of Honour and many other orders, and generally respected for his uprightness, constancy in friendship, and goodwill to his younger colleagues. According to Czerny, he was one of the most brilliant executants of his time; admired for the beauty of his touch, his excellent *legato* style, great taste and elegance of ornaments — and, indeed, for the general harmonious quality of his style of playing. Many of his contemporaries testify that he was the only one who came near to Beethoven in his art of improvising. In his compositions the influence of Mozart is particularly recognisable in the beauty of his harmonies and the roundness of his forms; the excellent qualities of his part-writing show the tuition of Albrechtsberger, whilst Salieri encouraged him in writing with elegance, and Haydn was his model for freshness. In his works there is, however, a strange absence of feeling, more conventionality — so to say, diplomatic politeness. Among his pupils are to be named Ferd. Hiller, Adolph Henselt, Julius Benedict, and Rudolph Willmers.

> *Works with Orchestra*: Concerto (C), Op. 34; Concertino (G), Op. 73; †Concerto (A min.), Op. 85; †Concerto (B min.), Op. 89; Concerto (Les Adieux in E), Op. 110; †Concerto (A flat), Op. 113; Concerto (posthumous); Concerto for Pf. and Vln. (G), Op. 17; †Rondo (A), Op. 56; Rondo (B flat), Op. 98; Rondo (D), called "Society Rondo," Op. 117; Rondo (F), "Le retour de Londres," Op. 127; Variations on "Castor and Pollux," Op. 6; Variations on an Air russe, Op. 97; Variations on the "Fest der Handwerker," Op. 115; †Grande Fantasia, "Oberon's Zauberhorn," Op. 116. *Chamber music*: †Grand Septuor for Pf., Fl., Ob., Hn., Vla., V'cello, and C.-Bass, Op. 74 (also arranged by the composer as Quintet with Strings); Septet militaire for Pf., Fl., Vln., Cl., Trumpet, V'cello, and C.-Bass (in C), Op. 114; †Quintet for Pf. and Strings in E flat min., Op. 87; Quartet in G (posthumous); 2 Grandes Sérénades for Pf., Vln., Guitar, Cl., and Bssn., Op. 63 and 66 (these are also arranged as Trios with Fl. and V'cello); La Sentinelle for Pf., Voice, Vln., and Guitar, or V'cello, Op. 71. *Trios*: †No. 1 (E flat), Op. 12; 2 (F), Op. 22; 3 (G), Op. 35; 4 (G), Op. 65; †5 (E), Op. 83; †6 (E flat), Op. 93; 7 (E flat), Op 96, Adagio, Variations, and Rondo on the Russian air "Schöne Minka," for Pf., Fl., and V'cello, Op. 78. *For Pf. and Vln. or V'cello*: 3 Sonatas, Op. 5; Sonata, Op. 25; 4 Sonatas with Vln. or Vla. or Fl.; Sonata with Vln. or Mandoline; grand Sonata with V'cello (A), Op. 104. *Solo Sonatas and Fantasias*: †No. 1, Sonata in E flat, dedicated to Haydn, Op. 13; 2, Sonata in F min., dedicated to Magdalene von Kurzbeck; 3, Sonata in C, Op. 30 (38); †4, Sonata in F sharp min., Op. 81; †5, Sonata in D, Op. 106; 3 Sonatas (G, A flat, and C) without number; Sonata (C), Op. 2, No. 3; †Fantasia (E flat), Op. 18. *For 4 hands*: †Grande Sonate (A flat), Op. 92; Sonate ou Divertissement (E flat), Op. 51; †Notturno in F (with 2 Hn. *ad lib.*), Op. 99; Introduction and Rondo for 2 Pf. (posthumous). *Variations*: 3 Airs variés, Op. 1; 2 Airs variés, Op. 2; 3 Airs variés, Op. 3 (appeared 1794, when he was 16 years old). Variations on a Dutch Song, Op. 21; 3 Thèmes variés, Op 34; Les charmes de Londres, 3 thèmes variés, Op. 119; Variations on an Air from Gluck's "Armide," Op. 57; Variations on an Austrian air in G, Op. 8; †Variations on an air from Rossini's "La Cenerentola" (C); Variations on the March from Cherubini's "Les deux journées," Op. 9. *Rondos*: †Rondo (E flat), Op. 11; Rondo quasi Fantasia (E), Op. 19; Rondo (C), Op. 52; †Rondo brillant (B min.), Op. 109; Rondo La Galante (E flat), Op. 120; Rondo Villageois, Op. 122. Several smaller Rondos. *Studies*: 24 Etudes, Op. 125; Préludes dans tous les tons, maj. et min., Op. 67; 60 Exercises from the great School. *Fantasias, &c.*: Fantasia on an air from Mozart's "Figaro," Op. 124; Fantasia (Recollection de Paganini); †Polonaise, La bella capricciosa (B flat), Op. 55; Caprice (F), Op 49; Capriccio (E flat min.), Œuvre posthume; Bagatelles, Op. 107; 7 Cadenzas for Mozart's Concertos; Pièces faciles, Op. 42 and 111; Amusements, Op. 105 and 108; 3 Grandes Valses en forme de Rondeaux, Op. 103; 6 Polonaises, Op. 70; several books of German Dances Grand Pf. School, with 2,200 examples in music (German, Italian, and French).

***Hummel, Ferdinand,** b. Sept. 6, 1855, Berlin. Pupil of Kullak, Rudorff, Bargiel, and Kiel.

> Sonatas (4) with V'cello; Quintet, Op. 47; Concerto, Op. 35; Scherzo, Op. 34; Serenade

("In the Spring"), Op. 37 (both for 4 hands); 5 pieces for the left hand, Op. 43; and 3 pieces, Op. 44 (No. 2).

Hurlebusch, Conrad Friedrich (son of Heinrich Lorenz H.), b. 1696, Brunswick; d. 1768 (date uncertain), Amsterdam. At first a pupil of his father, a sound musician; he went, 1718, to Italy; returned, 1721, to Germany (went to Munich, where he was received with great distinction), and went, 1722, to Stockholm, which town he left, 1727, for Hamburg, where he settled for ten years as a teacher; 1738, he received and accepted an offer of a post in Amsterdam. He was one of the most brilliant performers of his time, and an industrious composer. His contemporaries, however, thought more of his playing than of his compositions, which they declared eccentric and not natural.

6 Sonatas (1746), 12 Solo (?) Concertos, another collection of 12 Sonatas and 8 Overtures, 6 Concertos with orchestral accompaniment, 18 Suites, &c.

I.

Indy, Paul Marie Théodore Vincent d', b. March 27, 1851, Paris. Pupil of Diémer and Marmontel (Pf.), of Lavignac (Composition). An excellent executant and highly talented composer. Among his works for Pf. may be mentioned a—

Quartet in A for Pf. and Strings, a Symphony on an Alpine air for Pf. and Orchestra, and several smaller solo pieces.

J.

Jadassohn, Salomon, b. Aug. 13, 1831, Breslau. Pupil (1848) at the Leipzig Conserv., he went (1849) to Liszt (Weimar), but returned later to Leipzig to study under Hauptmann. 1867-69, Conductor of the Euterpe concerts; 1871, Prof. at the Conserv.; and Hon. Doc. Phil. of the University of Leipzig. Among his Pf. compositions, those written in the form of Canons have been very favourably received. They are—

Sérénade, Op. 8, and Sérénade, Op. 35 (8 Canons); Ballet Music, Op. 58 (6 Canons). Besides these he published a Quartet, Op. 70; Trios, Op. 20 and 59; Improvisations, Op. 48 and 75; Bal masqué, 7 Airs de Ballet, Op. 26; Variations sérieuses, Op. 40; Capriccietto e Scherzo, Op. 21; Album leaves (6), Op. 71; and a Sérénade for 4 hands, Op. 64.

Jadin, Louis Emanuel, b. Sept. 21, 1768, Versailles; d. July, 1853, Paris. Pupil of his younger brother, Hyacinthe, and his successor as Prof. at the Conserv. He is the inventor of the so-called "Mélanges" or "Potpourris," but besides these he wrote also—

Concertos, Quintets, Quartets, Trios, &c. His Sonates faciles, Rondos, and Fantasias were very popular; one of the latter was called "La grande bataille d'Austerlitz, un fait historique."

Jadin, Hyacinthe, b. 1769, Versailles; d. Oct., 1800, Paris. Pupil of Hüllmandel. He was the first Pf. Prof. at the Paris Conserv. (1795). As an executant, teacher, and composer he was very popular. Several of his works, Concertos, Sonatas with Vln., Solo Sonatas, Studies, and 2 Sonatas for 4 hands, were published at Paris.

Jaell, Alfred, b. March 5, 1832, Trieste; d. Feb. 27, 1882, Paris. Pupil of his father, he played when only in his eleventh year in public, and travelled almost all his life. 1852-54, he was in America, and resided, after his return to Europe, either in Paris, Brussels, or Leipzig. He was a most excellent pianist, had a beautiful touch, played with great refinement, taste, and elegance, and was, on the whole, a sound musician. Because of his restlessness he was called jokingly "Le Pianiste Voyageur." His original compositions consist of little Romanzas, Notturnos, Valses, &c. Besides these he published a great many (highly effective) transcriptions of Wagner, Mendelssohn, and Schumann's airs and songs.

***Jaell-Trautmann,** Marie (wife of the above since 1866), b. 1846, Steinseltz, near Weissenburg (Alsace). 1861, pupil of Henri Herz at the Paris Conserv., where she gained the first prize. Most excellent pianist. Of her compositions the best known are—

A Concerto; Waltzes for 4 hands; the pieces: Voix du Printemps, Sphinx, Prismes, Promenade nationale, Valses mélancoliques, Valses mignonnes, &c. She is also the author of a new method, "Le toucher," which created considerable attention in Paris.

Janko, Paul von, b. June 2, 1856, Totis (Hungary). Pupil at the Vienna Conserv., where he was taught by Hans Schmitt. 1881-82, he attended the University Lectures on Mathematics at Berlin, and became a pupil of H. Ehrlich. He is the inventor of the new keyboard called the "Janko Claviatur," which offers to the executant a good many advantages; his device consists of six keyboards, which are placed in rows one above the other. This arrangement allows: 1, a smaller compass of the intervals (an octave on Janko's keyboard is but ⅔ of that on another piano); 2, the same fingering for all the scales; 3, greater facility for skips and great stretches; 4, most surprising tonal effects, which are not to be realised on an ordinary instrument, such as glissando chromatic scales. The manufacturers, Bösendorfer of Vienna, Franke and Blüthner of Leipzig, have in many instances improved on Janko's original idea. He has explained in a book the whole system, has arranged several well-known works with his fingering, and has instructed several performers in order to exhibit in a practical manner his undoubtedly highly ingenious invention.

*__Janotha, Natalie__, b. Warsaw. Studied at the Berlin Hochschule (Joachim, Rudoff), under Clara Schumann, Dr. Brahms (for short time), and Princess Czartoryska. In Harmony she was instructed by Prof. F. Weber (Cologne) and W. Bargiel (Berlin). Pianist to the Court of the German Emperor; highest diploma of the St. Cecilia Academy (Rome), Hon. Member of the Academies of Cracow, London, Rome, &c. Victoria Badge from H.M. the Queen.

> Gavottes, Mazurkas, Mountain Scenes (dedicated to Madame Schumann), Ave Maria (dedicated to Leo XIII.), &c.

Jedliczka, Dr. Ernst, b. June 5, 1855, Poltava (S. Russia). Pupil of his father. From 1872-77 he studied Physics and Mathematics (University of St. Petersburg). 1877, he went to Moscow (pupil of Klindworth and Tschaikowsky). Appointed Prof. at the Conserv. by Nicolaus Rubinstein; left, 1887, for Berlin as teacher of the upper class in the Scharwenka-Klindworth Academy.

Jensen, Adolph, b. Jan. 12, 1837, Königsberg (Prussia); d. Jan. 23, 1879, Baden-Baden. For two years only, pupil of Ehlert and Marpurg (Berlin); he mostly taught himself, and worked with such restless energy that his health suffered. His compositions for Pf. are throughout noble, full of expression, and of considerable originality. Among the pieces which have obtained great popularity are—

> Op. 2, Innere Stimmen; †Op. 8, Romantic Studies; Op. 12, Berceuse; Op. 15, Jagdscene; Op. 16, Der Scheidenden (To the parting), 2 Romanzas; †Op. 17, Wanderbilder (2 books); Op. 19, Prelude and Romanza; Op. 25, Sonata; Op. 31, 3 Valses Caprices; †Op. 32, 25 Studies; †Op. 33, Songs and Dances (2 books); Op. 36, 6 German Suites; Op. 38, Nocturne; †Op. 43, Idyllen (particularly the charming "Dryade"); Op. 44, Eroticon; †Op. 45, Hochzeitsmusik (Wedding Music) à 4 mains; Op. 48, Erinnerungen (Recollections).

Joseffi, Raphael, b. 1852, Pressburg (Hungary). Pupil at the Leipzig Conserv., where Reinecke was his teacher. After finishing his studies in Leipzig he became a pupil of Tausig (Berlin), and created considerable sensation in Germany and Austria by his eminent technical execution. For several years he has been established in New York, where he is an active teacher, and greatly admired as a performer. He composed and published several drawing-room pieces.

*__Jungmann, Albert__, b. Nov. 14, 1824, Langensalza (Prussia); d. Nov. 7, 1892, Vienna. Pupil of G. W. Körner (the well-known publisher of organ works) at Erfurt, and later, for several years, of Dr. I. A. Leibrock (Brunswick). He was for a long period active as a Prof. at the St. Cecilia Academy of Rome; settled, 1853, in Vienna; became manager of the music warehouse of C. A. Spina (formerly Diabelli and Co.), and established himself with Lerch, as the firm Jungmann and Lerch, C. A. Spina's successors. He published over 400 educational works, which became very popular, as they are, without exception, written in a practical manner, are melodious, and devoid of any triviality. Among these, "Heimweh" (Home sickness) made the round of the world.

*__Jungmann, Ludwig__, b. Jan. 2, 1832, Weimar; d. there Sept. 20, 1892. Pupil at the Teachers' Seminary (Weimar); later, of Dr. Töpfer (Composition) and Liszt (Pf.). Since 1869, Prof. at the Grand Ducal "Sophia" Institute for Ladies. Among his Pf. works the best known are—

> Scherzo (F min.), Variations on an original air, and Phantasiestücke. He also composed several Trios.

K.

Kafka, Johann Nepomuk, b. May 17, 1819, Neustadt (Bohemia); d. Oct. 28, 1886, Vienna. At first intended to study law, but then resolved to devote himself entirely* to music. His practically-written drawing-room pieces—particularly those on Austrian airs—are very popular, but devoid of merit in an artistic sense.

*Kafka, **Heinrich**, b. Feb. 25, 1844, Stražowitz (Bohemia). Pupil of Joseph Krejči and Prof. Mildner (Prague). He resides in Vienna. Composer of—
Sonatas with Vln., ditto with V'cello, Trios, and a goodly number of shorter solo pieces.

*Kahn, **Robert**, b. July 21, 1865, Mannheim o/Rhine. Pupil of Ernst Frank, Vincenz Lachner (Mannheim), Kiel (Berlin), and Rheinberger (Munich). His compositions testify to uncommon talent, and excellent work may be expected from him. Since 1891 he has resided at Leipzig, and is now appointed teacher at the Hochschule (Berlin). He published—
6 Solo pieces, Op. 11; ditto, 7, Op. 18; 8 pieces for 4 hands, Op. 13; Sonata for Pf. and Vln., Op. 5; Pf. Quartet, Op. 14.

Kalkbrenner, Friedrich Wilhelm Michael, b. 1784, on a journey between Cassel and Berlin, a son of the eminent musician Christian K.; d. June 10, 1849, Enghien-les-Bains. Pupil of his father until he went (1798) to Paris, where he studied the Pf. with A. Adam and Composition with Catel. He gained several prizes at the Conserv. Published (about 1800) his first compositions, and gained his livelihood by teaching. 1803, he went to Vienna, where he met Clementi, who, by his marvellous technical execution, made such a deep impression upon him that, on his return to Paris, he tried with the greatest energy and perseverance to gain an equally high degree of technical efficiency. Not only Clementi's, but also Dussek and Hummel's style of playing impressed him very much, and he was anxious to profit by their example. 1814, he went to London, where he was well received, and was very successful as a teacher; indeed, the pecuniary results of his work in London enabled him to acquire a fine property at Rambouillet (France), where he annually spent a few months. In 1823 he undertook a great and long tour in Germany, and was highly successful in most of the larger towns. 1824, he returned to Paris, became a partner in the Pf. manufactory of Pleyel, which business profited very much by his practical advice. Another tour, in 1833, in Germany and Belgium was not less successful than that undertaken ten years earlier. From 1834 he remained permanently in Paris, busily engaged with teaching and composing. Among his most celebrated pupils was Madame Marie Pleyel. He was attacked by cholera in 1849, and died at Enghien-les-Bains on June 10 of that year. A contemporary mentions that Kalkbrenner's playing was most perfect with regard to technical execution; his fingers were all equally strong, producing a rich, full tone, which he could exhibit in the most different gradations, his conquering of the most intricate and complicated technical figures being no less admirable than the wonderful clearness and unfailing correctness with which they were exhibited. His style was graceful and elegant, at times full of energy and force; but generally lacking real warmth, depth and natural feeling. His compositions are solidly constructed, the part-writing is unexceptionable, and the melodies agreeable, but never original. On the other hand, he was happy in inventing new technical figures, and for this reason his Studies have decided merit and are of undeniable interest to pianists.

Studies: 24 Etudes dans tous les modes, Op. 20; 24 Préludes dans tous les tons, Op. 88; 12 Etudes préparatoires, Op. 126; †25 Etudes de style et de perfectionnement, Op. 143; 12 Etudes progressives, Op. 161; Etudes faciles et progressives, Op. 169; 4 Toccatas, Op. 182; Ajax, grande Etude; Méthode pour apprendre le Piano à l'aide du guide-mains, Op. 108. Sonatas: 3 Sonatas, Op. 1; 3 ditto, Op. 4; Sonata, Op. 13; Sonata Fantasia, Op. 28; Sonata, A maj., Op. 35; Sonata, A min., Op. 48; Sonata, F min., Op. 56; Sonata pour la main gauche principale, A flat, Op. 42; 3 Sonatas, Op. 3, 79, and 80 for 4 hands. Concertos: †D min., Op. 61; E min., Op. 85; A, Op. 107; A flat, Op. 127. For Two Pf. Op. 125, Gage d'amitié, Rondo, Op. 66; Fantasia and Variations, Op. 72, &c. Chamber Music: Septuors, Op. 15 and Op. 132; Sextets, Op. 58 and Op. 135; Quintets, Op. 30 and Op. 81; Quatuors, Op. 2, 136, and 176; Trios (7); Duets with Vln. Of his smaller solo pieces (about 22), "Le Fou" and "La femme du marin" are the best known and have retained their popularity.

Kalliwoda, Johann Wenzel, b. March 21, 1800, Prague; d. Dec. 3, 1866, Carlsruhe (Baden). Pupil at the Prague Conserv. From 1822 till 1853 Capellmeister to Prince Fürstenberg at Donaueschingen. He was a highly talented composer, who wrote with great facility and smoothness; but the inability to hear other composers' works had a detrimental effect upon his productions, which showed by degrees merely a certain routine. Schumann dedicated his Intermezzi, Op. 4, to Kalliwoda.

> Rondos; Op. 10, 11, 23; 3 Marches (very good), Op. 26; Divertissement in F, Op. 28; and Valses, Op. 27 and 169.

Kalliwoda, Wilhelm (son of the above), b. July 19, 1827, Donaueschingen; d. Sept. 8, 1893, Carlsruhe (Baden). Pupil at the Leipzig Conserv., and an especial favourite of Mendelssohn. His published compositions are very pleasing and thoroughly well written. As a pianist he possessed many sterling qualities, such as excellent technical execution, a beautiful, singing touch, and exquisite refinement. His gift of memory was quite extraordinary, for he played Bach's Suites, the 48 Preludes and Fugues, and many other classical works with ease, certainty, and correctness without book. 1853-75, he was Hof-Capellmeister at Carlsruhe, but owing to feeble health he was pensioned, and retired in the year 1875 from public life.

Kanne, Friedrich August, b. March 8, 1778, Delitsch (Saxony); d. Dec. 16, 1833, Vienna. At first he studied medicine, and later theology, but gave up these studies in order to devote himself entirely to music. He went to Vienna in the first decade of this century, and made the acquaintance of Prince Joseph Lobkowitz, who took great and kindly interest in him. An almost invincible inclination to lead a disorderly life prevented his following up his studies, and although many kind friends, who admired his rare gifts as a musician and poet, did their utmost to rescue him from poverty and misery, he died at last in great distress.

> Trio with Fl. and Vla.; several Sonatas with Vln.; 3 Solo Sonatas, Op. 18, 32, and 100; Sonata for 4 hands, Op. 31; Rondos, Variations, and Marches. His best known work is "Wellington in Wien," 6 Triumphal Marches, Op. 99.

Karr, Henri, b. 1784, Zweibrücken; d. Jan. 10, 1842, Paris. Pupil of L'Etendart (Pf.). Having lost his father very early, he lived in very distressed circumstances, until his teacher, Etendart, succeeded (1808) in getting him an appointment in the firm Erard, where he had to try the instruments for intending buyers. He was the father of the celebrated *littérateur,* Alphonse Karr. His light, rather shallow but effective pieces were in their time very popular, and he was never without orders from publishers.

> Sonatas, many Fantasias, Divertissements, so-called Mélanges (on motives from Operas), a good many drawing-room pieces for 4 hands, Duo for 2 Pf., &c.

Kauer, Ferdinand, b. Jan. 18, 1751, Klein-Thaya (Moravia); d. April 13, 1831, Vienna. Almost self-taught, as he had only a few lessons in Counterpoint from Heidenreich (Vienna). Although always most industrious and modest in his life, he was throughout his career pursued by misery, and even the immense success of his Operetta "Das Donauweibchen" did not improve his income or his social position. For the Pf. he wrote—

> Dramatic Sonatas with the titles: La Prise d'Oczakow, the Battle of Würzburg, Nelson's Great Battle, &c; Sonatas with Vln., Fantasias, Variations, Hungarian Air for 4 hands, and a Method for Pf.

Kellner, Johann Peter, b. Sept. 24, 1705, Gräfenroda (Thuringia); d. there, 1788. Pupil of Nagel, Schmidt, and Quehl.

> Suites called "Manipulus musices, oder eine Handvoll Zeitvertreib vors Clavier" (Or a handful of pastime for the Clavecin) were published (1752) at Nürnberg, and 6 Suites, "Certamen Musicum," were published at Arnstadt, 1748-49.

Kellner, Johann Christoph (son and pupil of the above), b. Aug. 16, 1735, Gräfenroda; d. 1803, Cassel. Pupil of Benda (Gotha). Of his compositions, which were in their time highly esteemed, about 10 Concertos were published by André (Offenbach o/M.) and 6 Trios at Cassel. His principal instrument was the organ.

Kelway, Joseph, b. 17—, London; d. there, 1782. Pupil of Geminiani. His extemporaneous performances on the organ and his playing of Scarlatti's lessons on the harpsichord were very much admired, but less so his published Sonatas, which are reproached with dryness, stiffness, and want of charm.

Kerl, Johann Caspar von, b. 1628, Gaimersheim, near Ingolstadt (Bavaria); d. 1693, Munich, where a monument in his honour was erected in the Theatiner-Church. Pupil of Valentini (Vienna), later of Carissimi (Rome). 1658, Hof-Organist in Munich; 1677, Organist of St. Stephen's Cathedral in Vienna, from whence he returned to Munich. His harpsichord compositions are—

"Toccata tutta da salti" in C, published in Pauer's "Alte Claviermusik," and the Fugue, "Egypt was glad when they departed," which Handel appropriated in his "Israel in Egypt," published at Amsterdam, also in Hawkins's History, chap. 124.

Kessler (Kötzler), Johann Christian, b. Aug. 26, 1800, Augsburg; d. Jan. 13, 1872, Vienna. Studied in Moravia, and later at Vienna; was for several years music teacher to Count Potocki's family at Lemberg; went to Breslau, Warschau, and settled (1857) in Vienna. He was an excellent pianist, which is testified by his ingenious (but very dry and musically uninteresting) Studies, Op. 20 and 51. These were strongly recommended by Liszt, and some of them were introduced in Moscheles and Kalkbrenner's Pf. Schools. The original edition of the Studies appeared at Vienna and Paris, but selections from them were lately published at Munich and London.

Nocturnes, Variations, Preludes, Bagatelles.

Ketten, Henry, b. March 25, 1848, Baja (Hungary); d. April 1, 1883, Paris. Pupil of Marmontel and Halévy (Paris).

Romance sans paroles, Tranquillité, Scherzoso, Mélancolie, Chasse au papillon, Op. 10.

*****Ketterer, Eugène**, b. 1831, Rouen; d. Dec. 18, 1870, Paris. Pupil at the Conserv. He published not less than 290 pieces, of which the following became the most popular :

Grand Caprice hongrois, Op. 7; l'Argentine, Op. 21; Grand Galop de Concert, Op. 24; "Oh, dites lui," Romance favorite, Op. 66; La Châtelaine, Op. 90; Chanson espagnole, Op. 100; Gaëtana, Op. 101; and Rondo orientale, Op. 102.

Kiel, Friedrich (son of a schoolmaster), b. Oct. 7, 1821, Puderbach on the Lahn; d. Sept. 14, 1885, Berlin. Almost self-taught; the teacher of the Seminary of Soest persuaded Kiel's father to allow his son to devote himself entirely to music, more particularly to the Vln. After having received theoretical instruction from Kaspar Kummer of Coburg, he was appointed (1840) Concertmeister, and received from King Friedrich Wilhelm IV. of Prussia a stipend for 3 years, which he used for taking lessons in Counterpoint from Dehn at Berlin, where he remained until his death. 1865, elected Member of the Royal Academy of Arts; he received (1868) the title of Königl. Prof.; was, for 3 years, a teacher at the Stern Conserv.; and, 1870, Prof. at the Hochschule and Member of the Senate of the Royal Academy.

Concerto, Op. 30; 4 Sonatas with Vln.; Sonata with V'cello, Op. 52; **Sonata with Vla, Op. 67**; 7 Trios, Op. 3, **22, 24, 33, 34, 65** (2); 3 Quartets, Op. 43, 44, 50; 2 Quintets, Op. 75 and 76; 2 easy Sonatas for 4 hands, Op. 6; 4 easy Fugues in 2 parts, Op. 10; 16 easy pieces for 4 hands, Op. 13; 2 Caprices, Op. 26; 3 Gigues, Op. 36; Souvenirs de Voyage (4 pieces), Op. 38; Humoresques (4) for 4 hands, Op. 42; 3 Valses, Op. 45; Tema con Variazioni, Presto, Romance sans paroles, Op. 71; 6 Morceaux, Op. 72.

Kienzl, Dr. Wilhelm, b. Jan. 17, 1857, Waitzenkirchen (Upper Austria). Pupil of Burva (Graz), Ignaz Uhl, Mortier de Fontaine, and W. A. Rémy. 1875, he went to Prague and studied with Krejči; 1876, he attended the Lectures of Springer, Overbeck, and Paul. 1879, he received for his essay, "Musical Declamation," the diploma of Dr. Phil. from the University of Vienna. 1881-82, he travelled as pianist, and acted as Capellmeister in Amsterdam and Crefeld; appointed (1886) Director of the Music School of Graz, and is now engaged as Conductor of the Hamburg Opera.

Op. 7, Phantasiestücke for Pf. and Vln.; Op. 3, 9 Sketches; Op. 15, From my Diary (3 pieces); Op. 10, Bunte Tänze (various dances); Op. 21, Tanzweisen (Dance Melodies), 30 pieces; and Op. 30, Kinder-Liebe und Leben (Children's love and life), 12 pieces.

*****Kirchner, Fritz**, b. Nov. 3, 1840, Potsdam. Pupil of Theodor Kullak (Pf.) and Richard Wüerst (Composition). From April, 1864, until Oct., 1889, teacher at the New (Kullak) Academy. After the dissolution of this popular College, was a teacher of Pf. and Theory in the school "Mädchenheim" (Berlin). Composer of a great number of educational and popular pieces; among them 24 Preludes, Ball Scenes, &c.

Kirchner, Theodor, b. Dec. 10, 1824, Neukirchen, near Chemnitz (Saxony). Almost the first pupil at the Leipzig Conserv. After having finished his studies, was appointed Organist in Winterthur, where he remained until 1862; 1862-72, Conductor and teacher of the Zürich Music School; 1872-73, in Meiningen, and 1873-75, Director of the Würzburg Conserv. Since 1875 he has resided in Leipzig. With regard to the beauty of his smaller works, he is considered to be a rival of Schumann, by whom and Mendelssohn he was greatly patronised and esteemed. The following are his most popular works :—

Op. 2, 10 pieces; Op. 5, †Gruss an meine Freunde; Op. 7, †9 Album leaves; Op. 8, Scherzo; Op. 9, †Preludes; Op. 11, †Sketches; Op. 12, Adagio quasi Fantasia; Op. 13, Songs without words; Op. 14, Phantasiestücke; Op. 16, Kleine Lust und Trauerspiele; Op. 17, †New "Davidsbündler"

Dances; Op. 18, Legenden; Op. 19, Phantasi-stücke; Op. 21, Aquarellen; Op. 22, Romanzas; Op. 23, Waltzes; Op. 25, Nachtbilder; Op. 26, Album; Op. 27, Caprices; Op. 28, Nocturnes; Op. 29, †From my Sketch-book; Op. 30, Studies and pieces; Op. 36, Fantasian; Op. 37, 4 Elegies; Op. 38, 12 Studies; Op. 39, Village Stories; Op. 41, Verwehte Blätter; Op. 43, 4 Polonaises; Op. 46, 30 Dances for children and artists; Op. 48, Humoresques; Op. 49, †New Album leaves; Op. 52, A new book for Pf.; Op. 53, Florestan and Eusebius; Op. 54, Scherzo; Op. 55, New Scenes for children; Op. 56, In quiet hours; Op. 65, 60 Preludes; Op. 70, 5 Sonatinas; Op. 71, 100 small Studies. Kirchner's transcriptions of Songs by Mendelssohn, Schumann, Brahms, &c., belong to the very best. Among his Duets for 4 hands the collection of 36 pieces, called "Old friends in new dresses," is particularly to be recommended.

Kirmair, Friedrich Joseph, b. 1770, Munich; d. 1814, Gotha. Pupil of his father, Wolfgang K. Travelled in Germany, Italy, Holland, France, and was everywhere favourably received and esteemed as one of the best performers of his time. 1795, teacher of the Prussian Crown Princess (Berlin); later, appointed in Cassel, and, from 1803 until his death (1814), Concertmeister at Gotha. He published many Sonatas, Variations, &c.

Kirnberger, Johann Philipp, b. April 24, 1721, Saalfeld, district of Königsberg (Prussia); d. July 28, 1783, Berlin. Pupil of Kellner (1705-88), Gerber (1702-75), and, 1739, of Sebastian Bach (Leipzig). 1751, he went to Dresden; 1754, to Berlin, appointed Capellmeister, and teacher of Princess Amalia.

"Clavierübungen nach der Bach'schen Applicatur" (Exercises with Bach's fingering), 4 books, Berlin, 1762-64; 8 Fugues (1777); 24 pieces (1779). Several of his pieces have been republished in Pauer's "Alte Meister" and "Alte Claviermusik."

Kittl, Johann Friedrich, b. May 8, 1809, Worlick (Bohemia); d. July 20, 1868, Lissa (Posen). Pupil of Tomaschek (Prague). On the death of Dionys Weber (1843), appointed Director of the Prague Conserv., which office he retained until 1863.

3 Scherzi, Op. 6; Romanza, Op. 10; and a Grand Septuor for Pf., Fl., Ob., Cl., Hn., Bssn., and C.-Bass Op. 25. For his opera, "Bianca e Giuseppe," the libretto was written by Richard Wagner.

Kjerulf, Halfdan, b. Sept. 17, 1818, Christiania; d. there, Aug. 11, 1868. Pupil at the Leipzig Conserv.; lived, highly esteemed and beloved, as music teacher in his native town, where, 1874, a monument in his honour was erected. One of his pupils was Madame Baker-Gröndahl. His reputation rests on his beautiful songs.

Capriccio, Scherzo, Frühlingslied (Spring Song), Hirtengesang (Shepherd's Song), Polka, Idyl, Wuggewise (Cradle Song), Album leaf, Elfentanz (Dance of Elves), 40 Norske Folkeviser (Northern people's Songs), Scherzino, Intermezzo, Berceuse, a Rondino (Op. 22), 6 Sketches, Polonaise (Op. 13), and March (Op. 211 for 4 hands. Their characteristic expression is notably a Norwegian one.

Klauser, Carl, b. 1823, St. Petersburg. Has resided since 1850 in Farmington, Connecticut (U.S.). He made his name known by his excellent arrangements of works by Schumann (Symphonies) and Liszt, and also by his editions of Mozart, Beethoven, Chopin, Schumann, and Weber's Pf. works.

Klauwell, Adolph, b. Dec. 31, 1818, Langensalza (Thuringia); d. Nov. 21, 1879, Leipzig. Well known as an excellent teacher and author of educational pieces, which obtained great and deserved popularity. Among them the "Golden Melody Album" is a favourite book in Germany. His nephew is—

*****Klauwell,** Dr. Otto, b. April 7, 1851, Langensalza (Thuringia). 1865-70, pupil at the Schulpforta College; he participated (1870) in the Franco-German war; 1871, he studied Mathematics and Natural Science at the Leipzig University, but, 1872, devoted himself entirely to music. 1872-74, pupil of C. Reinecke (Pf.) and E. F. Richter (Theory); 1874, his essay, "The Historical Development of the Canon," brought him from the University of Leipzig the diploma of Hon. Doc. Phil. 1875, appointed Prof. of Pf., History and Theory at the Cologne Conserv. Since 1885, Director of the Seminary of Teachers connected with the Conserv.

Variations in D min., Op. 22; ditto in B min., Op. 27; Phantasiestücke, Op. 17; sundry pieces, Op. 31; several works of chamber music. Among his literary works deserve to be known: "Der Vortrag in der Musik" (1883), "Der Fingersatz" (1885), "Musikalische Bekenntnisse" (1891), "Formen der Instrumental Musik" (in the Press).

*****Klee,** Ludwig, b. April 13, 1846, Schwerin. Pupil of Th. Kullak (1864-68) in Berlin, and later, until 1875, teacher in Kullak's Academy. Since 1875, Director of his own School. He has the title of Musik-Director to the Duke of Saxony. Author of "Die Ornamentik der Klassischen Klaviermusik" (The ornaments of classical Pf. music). In this book the ornaments or graces are described and explained from Bach up to Beethoven. Besides this book, his editions of "Klassische Vortragsstücke," in 3 volumes, containing pieces by Heller and Mayer, Sonatas by Dussek, Diabelli, and Kuhlau, enjoy a good name in Germany and America.

Kleeberg, Clotilde, b. June 27, 1866, Paris. 1876, pupil of Madame Emile Retz at the Conserv., where she received the first medal after her first year there. Later, a pupil of Madame Massart, and obtained the first prize although the youngest of thirty-five competitors. At the age of twelve she played at Pasdeloup's Concerts and created a sensational success. Since her fifteenth year she has visited Denmark, Russia, Austria, Holland, and England, being everywhere received with genuine favour. Her teacher in reading chamber music was Mr. Massart, and she studied harmony with Mr. Théod. Dubois. She is decidedly one of the foremost lady pianists of the present time and is equally well at home in the works of Bach or in those of Chopin or Liszt. Jan., 1894, named "Officier de l'Académie."

Kleffel, Arno, b. Sept. 4, 1840, Pösneck (Thuringia). Pupil (for one year only) at the Leipzig Conserv., more especially under Dr. Hauptmann, from whom he received private instruction. 1863, Director of the Musical Society of Riga. He returned (1867) to Germany and held appointments as operatic Conductor in Cologne, Amsterdam, Bremen, Breslau, Stettin, Berlin; resided at Cologne as Conductor of the opera, but is at present in Berlin.

Une fête d'enfants, 8 characteristic pieces for 4 hands, Op. 5; Valses and Ländler, Op. 21; Ritornelles, Op. 26; Petite Suite, Op. 29; Impromptu in C min., Op. 27; Nuits italiennes, 6 pieces for 4 hands, Op. 28; Toccata, Lied, &c., Op. 37; Jungbrunnen, 30 short educational pieces, Op. 41.

Klein, Bernhard Joseph, b. March 6, 1793, Cologne; d. Sept. 9, 1832, Berlin. Studied first at Cologne, but went (1812) to Paris and became a pupil of Cherubini. After returning to Germany he was appointed Conductor of the Cologne Cathedral; 1819, Prof. at the newly founded Institute of Sacred Music at Berlin, and Music Director of the University.

3 Sonatas, Fantasia (Op. 8), **Variations, and Grand Sonata for 4 hands.**

Kleinheinz, Carl Franz, b. July 3, 1772, Mindelheim (Württemberg); d. 1832, Pesth. Pupil of Albrechtsberger (Vienna). Composer of

Concerto, Sonatas with Vln. (1789), Fantasia with Vln. (Op. 19), Grand Sonata for 4 hands (Op. 12), Sonata for 2 Pf., Toccata, and Solo Sonatas.

Kleinmichel, Richard, b. Dec. 31, 1846, Posen. Pupil at the Conserv. of Leipzig. For several years teacher in Hamburg. 1876, Conductor of the Leipzig Opera, later of that of Magdeburg. He resides at present in Berlin. His Pf. works enjoy considerable popularity, and among them more particularly—

8 Easy characteristic pieces, Op. 8; Album pour la jeunesse, Op. 14; Notturno-Serenade, Op. 16; †Valse-Caprice, Op. 18; 10 Arabesques, Op. 19; 9 Character-Bilder, 4 hands, Op. 21; †Kinder-Frühling, 18 pieces for 4 hands, Op. 42; Roses sans épines (6 Morceaux de Danse à 4 mains), Op. 45; Album de chants nationaux Français, Russes, Anglais. He has also arranged from the original scores not less than 34 old Italian, French, and German operas (Leipzig, Senff); he also published an easier Pf. arrangement of Wagner's later operas.

Klengel, August Alexander, b. Jan. 29, 1784 (1783?), Dresden; d. there, Nov. 22, 1852. Son of the celebrated landscape painter, Prof. Joh. Ch. K. The names of his first teachers are not known. Clementi, who came (1803) to Dresden, heard the young artist and persuaded him to accompany him as pupil to St. Petersburg; before, however, going to Russia they travelled on the Rhine, in Bavaria, and Prussia. Clementi, who married (1804) in Berlin, went with his young wife to Italy, and parted with Klengel After losing his wife, Clementi returned to Germany and again went with Klengel to St. Petersburg. The latter remained in the Russian capital (1805-11), giving lessons and studying by himself. 1811, he went to Paris, where he remained till 1813, but left, on account of the warlike times, for Italy; returned (1814) to Dresden, passed one year (1815) in England, and was appointed (1816) Organist of the Roman Catholic Hofkirche at Dresden. As a pianist he was famous for his splendid legato style, the, so to say, individual independence of his fingers, and the beautiful style in which he executed Canons and Fugues. Among his compositions are—

48 Canons and 48 Fugues, published after his death by Dr. Hauptmann (1876-1881). A previous work, published before 1840, called "Les Avant-coureurs," consists of 24 Canons; 2 Concertos, Quintet, Polonaise concertante with Orchestra, grand Trio, Solo Sonatas (Op. 2, 7, and 9), Variations, Rondos, Fantasias, Nocturnes, Romanzas (3) (Op. 34), Le départ et le retour (Op. 30), 15 progressive lessons (Op. 21), and 16 Studies.

Klindworth, Carl, b. Sept. 25, 1830, Hanover. Pupil of Liszt (Weimar). He resided from 1854 till 1868 in London as a teacher, and was also active as a Conductor. 1868, he went to Moscow, where he edited Chopin's works. Resides at present in Berlin, where he is Director of a Music School, now united with the Scharwenka School. At the same time he is Conductor of the "Wagner" concerts. He arranged Wagner's "Nibelungen" Trilogy for Pf., and also edited Beethoven's Sonatas.

Knecht, Justin Heinrich, b. Sept. 30, 1752, Biberach (Würtemberg); d. there, Dec. 1, 1817. Pupil of Kramer and greatly patronised by the celebrated author, Wieland, who persuaded Knecht's father to allow his son to devote himself entirely to music. 1807, appointed Conductor of the Stuttgart Opera, which appointment he soon relinquished, on account of intrigues by which he was greatly harassed, and returned to his native place. His Pf. works are mostly educational—
"Kleine praktische Clavierschule" (4 parts), "Kleine theoretische Clavierschule" (2 parts) (1800-1802), 48 Preludes, Variations, Sonatinas, and easy Studies.

Knorr, Julius, b. Sept. 22, 1807, Leipzig; d. there, June 17, 1861. At first a pupil of Neudeck (Pf.). 1834, he founded, with Schumann and Schunke, the *Neue Zeitschrift für Musik*. His educational works are very important.
"Guide of Piano music," "Methodischer Leitfaden für Clavierlehrer," "Materialien für das mechanische Clavierspiel" (a most useful book), Guide for Pianists in the beginning. The most important artistic terms explained. Editor of Cramer's Studies, &c.

Koczalski, Raoul, b. Jan. 3, 1885, Warsaw. At first a pupil of his mother, later of Gadowski (Warsaw). When only in his fourth year he played at a Charity concert; was very successful in Paris; travelled through the greater part of Europe, and received many decorations and art medals. The Shah of Persia named him Court Pianist, with a permanent pension of 3,000 francs a year. His wonderful performances of classical and modern works have everywhere created an extraordinary sensation, heightened by the modesty and natural manners of the richly gifted child. Among his greater compositions is a one-act opera, "Hagar."
Gavotte, Waltzes, and several shorter pieces.

Köhler, Louis, b. Sept. 5, 1820, Brunswick; d. Feb. 16, 1886, Königsberg (Prussia). Pupil of A. Sonnemann (Pf.), Chr. Zinkeisen, sen., and J. A. Leibrock (Theory) in Brunswick. 1839-43, he studied in Vienna with C. M. von Bocklet (Pf.), Sechter and Seyfried (Theory and Composition). 1847, he settled in Königsberg, where he founded a highly successful school for Pf. playing and Theory. 1880, he received the title of Königl. Prof. As a composer he was most successful in his useful Studies, the greater part of them is used in almost all the different Conservs. His Practical Pf. School, Op. 300; his School for the Left Hand, Op. 302; and his "Kinder-Clavierschule" enjoy a good reputation. As an author he made himself well known by his "Der Clavierlehrer" (the Pf. Teacher, translated into English); "Systematische Lehrmethode für Clavierspiel und Musik," Vol. 1, 2nd edition, 1872; and "Musiklehre, Metrik, Harmonik," &c., Vol. 2, new edition, 1883. This second volume was highly esteemed by M. Hauptmann, who mentions its first appearance in his letters to Franz Hauser. His "Guide to Pf. literature" is, however, somewhat one-sided, and written more in the interest of the publisher than in that of the student. He was for many years the industrious critic, and reviewer of new works which appeared, for the Leipziger *Signale für die Musikalische Welt*. As a critic he was thoroughly impartial, his style being distinguished by clearness, conciseness, and a total absence of bombastic expressions. He suggested (1859) the foundation of the "Allgemeine Deutsche Tonkünstler-Verein," of which Liszt, Wagner, Von Bülow, Dr. Brendel, Dr. Riedel, Gille, Stern, and others became members. The bye-laws of this at present important society were written by Köhler.
Preliminary Studies, Op. 151; "Little School of Velocity," Op. 242; First Studies, Op. 50; Daily Studies, Op. 150; "New School of Velocity," Op. 128; Studies on English, Scotch, Irish, and Welsh Melodies, Op. 289; Special Studies, Virtuosen-Studien, Op. 120; and besides these the Studies Op. 47, 79, 112, 152, 175, 190, 270, and 280 are for furthering technical proficiency.

*Koning, David, b. March 19, 1820, Rotterdam; d. Nov. 6, 1876, Amsterdam. Pupil of Aloys Schmitt (Frankfort). 1840, appointed Conductor of the Choral Society "Felix meritis," of Amsterdam. Hon. Member of the Society St. Cecilia (Rome), of the Dutch Society, "Bevordering der Toonkunst," and President of the (Dutch) Society St. Cecilia.
7 Studies in the style of Schmitt, Clementi, Cramer, &c.; Sonatas, Friedensmarsch, &c.

Kontski, Antoine de, b. Oct. 27, 1817, Cracow. His wonderful execution created everywhere a sensation, but not in so great a degree his accomplishments as a composer and musician. 1854-67, he resided in St. Petersburg, later in Paris, Berlin (appointed Pianist to the Prussian Court), and for some time in London. He was decorated by most of the European Sovereigns. He resides at present in Buffalo, State of New York.

"Reveil du Lion," Op. 115; Valses, "La Victorieuse," Op. 89, and "Souvenir de Biarritz," Op. 278; Grande Polonaise, Op. 271, and "La nuit sur la mer," Op. 259.

Kowalski, Henri, b. 1841, Paris. For a short time a pupil of Marmontel (Pf.) and Reber (Composition).

Polonaise de Concert, Op. 10; Marche hongroise, Op. 13; 12 Caprices en forme d'Etudes, Op. 16 (of these the "Danse des Dryades" is a great favourite); "Sur l'Adriatique"; Barcarolle, Op. 9, "Sur le fleuve jaune"; Barcarolle chinoise, Op. 68; and Sérénade japonaise, Op. 79.

Koželuch (Kotzeluch), Leopold, b. 1753 (1754 ?), Wellwarn (Bohemia); d. May 7, 1811, Vienna. Pupil of his cousin, Joh. Ant. K. (1738-1814). 1778, he went to Vienna, where he became teacher to Princess Elisabeth of Würtemberg, later Empress of Austria. He was the favourite teacher of the aristocratic and court circles. 1792, appointed (as successor of W. A. Mozart) Composer to the Austrian Court. His daughter, Madame Cibbini, a clever pianist, was a highly influential lady at the Imperial Court, but was, like her father, suspected of intriguing against other artists. His many compositions are now well-nigh forgotten; they are shallow, cold, and uninteresting.

Of 40—nearer 50—Concertos, only 12 were published; 3 Concertos for 4 hands, 1 for 2 Pf.; about 80 (!) Trios; 40 Sonatas—of these the 3 Sonatas, Op. 51, 3 ditto, Op 53, were popular; Sonatas (about 15) for 4 hands; a great many Dances and smaller pieces.

*Krause, Anton, b. Nov. 9, 1834, Geithain (Saxony). Pupil of Fritz Spindler and Friedr. Wieck (Dresden). 1850-53, pupil at the Leipzig Conserv., where he studied the Pf. with Moscheles and Theory and Composition with Rietz, Hauptmann, and Richter. 1859, appointed Music Director of Barmen, where he still resides; received (1877) the title of Königl. Musik-Director, and (1892) the Order of the Prussian Crown. As a composer of educational works he enjoys a well-merited reputation.

His Solo Sonatas are Op. 1, 10, 12, 19, 21, 24 (18 in all); his Sonatas for 4 hands, Op. 3, 18, 22, 26, 27, 30 (13 in all); a Sonata for 2 Pf., Op. 17; his Studies (Shake), Op. 2, 4, 5, 9, 15 (especially for strengthening the left hand); 10 melodious Studies for advanced players, Op. 28; 12 Studies for young performers, Op. 31. Besides these original works, he edited Czerny's Studies, Op. 139, 299, 636, and 740; published a collection of Sonatinas by classical composers; and the "Library for 2 Pf." (18 books).

*Krause, Dr. Eduard, b. March 15, 1837, Swinemünde; d. March 28, 1892, Berlin. Pupil of Hauptmann (Leipzig) and F. Kroll (Berlin). He resided for some years at Stettin, was appointed in August, 1875, first Prof. at the Conserv. of Geneva, but was obliged to relinquish his appointment on account of illness.

Op. 80, School of the left hand; Op. 81, Album leaves and Sketches; Op. 62, †Carmen, Paraphrase de Concert; Op. 30, 8 Phantasiestücke; Op. 21, Berceuse; Op. 24, Grand Sonata.

*Krause, Emil, b. July 30, 1840, Hamburg. Pupil at the Leipzig Conserv. Settled, 1860, in his native town as a teacher, composer, and critic. As a composer he chiefly devoted himself to educational works which are—like his Studies (Op. 38 and 57)—of considerable value. His pieces for children are melodious and practical.

Op. 38, Beitrag zum Studium der Technik; Op. 70, Clavierschule; Op. 57, Grundlage zur höhern Ausbildung; Op. 75, Ergänzungen (Supplements) für Op. 38 and 57; Op. 25, 8 Studies; Op. 71, Cadences and Preludes in all keys; Op. 67, 24 Studies in all keys; Op. 31, Variations; Sonatas, Op. 3 and 67; 15 works of shorter dimensions, for 4 hands, Op. 13, 28, 29, and 45.

Krebs, Carl August (really Miedke), b. Jan. 16, 1804, Nürnberg; d. May 16, 1880, Dresden. Adopted by the singer, Krebs, he studied in Vienna with Seyfried; was appointed (1826) Capellmeister of the Imperial Opera (Vienna); 1827, in a similar capacity at Hamburg; and, 1850, Hof-Capellmeister of the Dresden Opera. His compositions for Pf. are mostly written in a popular style, but never obtained the popularity enjoyed by his songs.

Krebs, Mary (Madame Brenning), daughter of the above; b. Dec. 5, 1851, Dresden. Pupil of her father. Excellent pianist, who created a great sensation in Germany, Austria, and America. After returning from her travels, she was appointed Court Pianist to the King of Saxony, and devotes herself at present to teaching.

Krebs, Johann Ludwig (the favourite pupil of Seb. Bach), b. Oct. 10, 1713, Buttelstädt; d. Jan. 4, 1780, Altenburg. Pupil at the Thomas School of Leipzig, where he enjoyed the private tuition of Seb. Bach. Appointed Organist at Zwickau, Zeitz, and Altenburg. His compositions for clavecin are—

Clavierübung in 4 books, containing Chorales, Choral-Fugues, a Suite, 6 Sonatas (1743-49); 6 Preludes (1740), Suite (1741), Overture (1741), Concerto (1743), 6 Suites, Op. 4; Musikalischer Zeitvertreib (2 Sonatas, and 6 Sonatas with Fl.); 6 "Sonate da Camera per il Cembalo obligato con Flauto (o Violino)" (1762).

Kreutzer, Conradin, b. Nov. 22, 1780, Messkirch (Grand Duchy of Baden); d. Dec. 14, 1849, Riga. His talent developed very early, and although his father, a miller (who died 1797), intended him to become a physician, young Kreutzer resolved to devote himself entirely to music. He went (1804) to Vienna, where he was a pupil of Albrechtsberger. After having filled appointments as operatic Capellmeister—1812, at Stuttgart; 1817, at Donaueschingen; 1825, 1829-32, 1837-40, at Vienna (Imperial Opera); 1832, 1837, at the theatre in the suburb Josephstadt; 1840-46, at Cologne; 1846-49, again in Vienna—he went with his daughter, Cecilia, a distinguished singer, to Riga. His chief activity was devoted to Operas, of which he wrote no less than 24.

3 Concertos, Quartet in E min., Trios (of which Op. 43 is for Pf., Clar., and Bssn.), several Duos, Pieces for 4 hands, 3 Solos for Pf., 2 ditto, Divertissements, Fantasias, Polonaises, Variations, and about 18 easy pieces, of which the "Celebrated Minuet" in G became a great favourite.

Krieger, Johann, b. Jan. 1, 1652, Nürnberg; d. July 18, 1736, Zittau. At first a pupil of Schwemmer (Sebald's School), and later, for seven years, of Wecker. After having finished his studies at Nürnberg, he went to his brother, Joh. Philipp K. (Org. at Weissenfels), who taught him Counterpoint, &c. 1678, Capellmeister at Greitz; 1681, Organist and Conductor at Zittau. Mattheson, in his "Vollkommene Capellmeister," calls him one of the best counterpoint scholars of his time. The titles of his works are here given in the original text—

VI. Musikalische Partien, bestehend in Allemanden, Couranten, Sarabanden, u.s.w., allen Liebhabern des Claviers, auf einem Spinet oder Clavichordis zu spielen, nach einer ariösen Manier aufgesetzt. (Nürnberg, 1697). Anmuthige Clavier-Übungen in Ricercaten, Praeludien, Fugen, einer Ciaccone und einer aufs Pedal gerichteten Toccata (Nürnberg, 1699).

Kroll, Franz, b. June 22, 1820, Bromberg; d. May 28, 1877, Berlin. Pupil of Liszt (Weimar and Paris). Settled (1849) in Berlin, where he was greatly esteemed as a pianist. 1863-64, Prof. at the Stern Conserv. Well known as the editor of Seb. Bach's Preludes and Fugues, and of other classical pieces

Krommer, Franz, b. Dec. 5, 1759, Kamenitz (Moravia); d. Jan. 8, 1831, Vienna. With the exception of a few lessons he received in the rudiments of music from his uncle, an organist, he was entirely self-taught. He held several appointments in Simonthurn and Fünfkirchen (Hungary), accompanied Prince Grassalkowitz as Capellmeister to Vienna, and became (1818) successor of L. Koželuch as "Imperial Composer." His compositions, now entirely forgotten, were in their time very popular.

Quartet (Op. 95), 2 Trios (Op. 84 and 87), 6 Sonatas with Vln., Polonaises, Marches, Valses, &c.

Krüger, Wilhelm, b. Aug. 5, 1820, Stuttgart; d. there, June 16, 1883. Pupil of C. Ziegele (Pf.) and Lindpaintner (Theory and Composition). He resided, 1845-70, a popular teacher and admired performer, in Paris, but he had to leave on account of the Franco-German war. 1870, appointed Pianist to the Court of Würtemberg and Prof. at the Conserv. of Stuttgart. His compositions (they reach the number of 168) are mostly—

Transcriptions, Illustrations, Fantasias, &c., of operatic works, Etudes (les six jours de la semaine, Op. 32), Caprices, Nocturnes, &c. Of his original works the "Harpe Æolienne," Guitare, Polonaise-Bolero, Op. 97, have become very popular. A work of decided merit is his edition of Händel's Clavecin works, 2 vols.

Krufft, Baron Nicolaus, b. Feb. 1, 1779, Vienna; d. there, April 16, 1818. It was his father's wish that he should follow the career of an employé of the State, and he actually became before his death Imperial Councillor. Pupil of Albrechtsberger Excellent pianist.

3 Caprices, Op. 33; 12 Exercices en forme des Ecossaises; 24 Préludes et Fugues dans tous les tons, Liv. 1-4 (this work was much esteemed), Adagio and Variations, Sonata, and eleven sets of Variations on national airs and themes of Cherubini, Pleyel, Rossini, &c.

*__Krug__, Dietrich, b. May 21, 1820, Hamburg; d. there, April 7, 1880. Pupil of Melchert (b. 1810 at Altona), but mostly self-taught. 1840, he made the acquaintance of Jacques Schmitt, at that time a highly renowned artist, to whom he played, whereupon Schmitt advised him to call himself a pupil of his, as it might be useful to his career; but he was not really his pupil. With regard to composition, he was entirely self-taught; as a pianist (Hummel-Kalkbrenner period) he was very distinguished and much admired for his delightful touch and brilliant execution. His educational works are very

melodious, their style is correct and clear, and their technical part practical and brilliant, without offering any great difficulties. He published also a Method of Pf. playing, a Collection of Studies (School of Velocity), and a great many arrangements of classical works. His son—

*Krug, Arnold, b. Oct. 16, 1849, Hamburg. Was a pupil of his father and of Cornelius Gurlitt of Altona. 1868, he went to Leipzig and became a pupil of C. Reinecke. After this he remained for several years in Berlin studying with Kiel and Eduard Frank, and was appointed teacher at the Stern Conserv. 1869, he obtained the Scholarship of the Mozart foundation (Frankfort o/M.), and, 1877, the "Meyerbeer" prize. He is now Prof. at the "Hamburg" Music School and Director of the Altona Sing-Akademie. As a composer he enjoys a well-deserved reputation.

Trio, Op. 1; 4 Phantasiestücke, Op. 3; 5 Impromptus, in form of Valses, Op. 4, for 4 hands; Quartet in C min., Op. 16; 3 Clavierstücke, Op. 17; the Duets "Fahrende Musikanten," Op. 20; and Album leaves, Op. 31 (6 pieces). Besides these he arranged his "Roumanian Dances," Op. 22, for 4 hands.

Küffner, Johann Jacob Paul, b. 1713, Nürnberg, d. 1786, Regensburg (Ratisbon), Capellmeister to the Prince of Thurn and Taxis. Excellent organist and clavecinist.

2 Sonatas, Op. 1 (a second edition appeared, 1762, at Nürnberg); 9 Sonatas with Vln.; a collection of short pieces and Sonata for 4 hands. 10 Concertos remained in manuscript.

Kündinger, Rudolph, b. March 2, 1832, Nördlingen (Bavaria). Pupil of his father. Settled (1850) in St. Petersburg, where his performances were greatly admired, and led to the post of instructor to the Czaritsa and the children of the Grand Duke Constantin Nicolajevič.

Trio, Op. 10; Mazurka-Fantaisie, Op. 16; Nocturnes, Concert pieces, &c.

*Kufferath, Hubert Ferdinand, b. June 10, 1818 (not 1808, as given by many dictionaries), at Mülheim a/d/Ruhr (Germany). At first a pupil of his elder brother, Joh. Hermann (1797-1864), afterwards of Hartmann (Cologne) for Vln.; later, of Ferd. David and of Mendelssohn (Vln and Composition) in Leipzig. 1841-44, Conductor of the Male Choral Society (Cologne); he settled (1844) in Brussels, where he became teacher of Princess Charlotte (later, Empress of Mexico), Count and Countess of Flanders, and other members of the Royal Belgian family; 1872, appointed Prof. of Counterpoint and Fugue at the Royal Conserv. of Brussels, and (1885) Knight of the Order of Leopold. His compositions for Pf. are—

Capriccio, Op. 1; Concerto, Op. 24; Trio, Op. 9; Quartet, Op. 12; Etudes de Concert, Op. 2, Op. 8, Op. 35; Characterstücke, Op. 30; Valses (4 hands), Op. 40.

His brother—

*Kufferath, Louis, b. Nov. 10, 1811, Mülheim a/d/Ruhr; d. March 2, 1881, Brussels. Pupil of his elder brother, Joh. Hermann, later of Friedr. Schneider (Dessau). 1836-50, Director of the Conserv. of Leeuwarden (Holland); he settled (1850) in Ghent as a teacher, but removed later to Brussels. He was a brilliant pianist and excellent teacher. Only a few of his compositions were published.

Trios, Morceaux de Salon, Variations.

*Kuhe, Wilhelm, b. Dec. 10, 1823, Prague. Pupil of Proksch, Tomaschek, and Thalberg. With the singer Pischek he went (1845) to London; settled there, dividing his duties as a teacher between Brighton and London. 1870-82, he gave in Brighton very successful annual Festivals. 1886, appointed Prof. at the R.A.M., London. The King of Prussia conferred on him the Order of the Crown. His compositions consist of drawing-room pieces, operatic Fantasias, Romanzas, &c., some of which have obtained great popularity.

Feu follet, Gondola, Etude de Concert, and Rosée du Soir.

Kuhlau, Friedrich, b. March 13 (Sept. 11?), 1786, Ülzen (Hanover), d. March 18 (12?), 1832, Copenhagen. Pupil of Schwenke in Hamburg. He went (1810) to Copenhagen; was appointed Flautist of the Royal Orchestra, and, later, promoted to a Professorship and to officiate as Composer to the Court. For the Pf. he composed—

Sonatas, Op. 4, 5, 8 (12-15); Sonatas (3), Op. 52; Sonatas (3), Op. 60; Grande Sonate brillante, Op. 127; Sonatinas (16), Op. 20, 55, 59; Sonatinas with Vln. ad lib., Op. 88; several Sonatas with Vln. (or Fl.); 3 Quartets; Concerto, Op. 7, Allegro pathétique, Op. 123; Sonatas and Sonatinas for 4 hands, Op. 8, 17, 44, 66; many Rondos and Variations.

Kuhnau, Johann, b. April, 1667 (1666?), Geysing (Saxony); d. June 5, 1722, Leipzig. Pupil at the Kreuzschule (School of the Cross) in Dresden, but he left for his native place on account of the pestilence breaking out. For some time Organist in Zittau, he was (1684) successor of Kühnel as Organist of the Thomas Church of Leipzig, and was elected (1700) Director of Music of the Leipzig University and Cantor of the Thomas School, where Seb. Bach succeeded him. He was not only an excellent musician, but a highly accomplished scholar; he had studied the law, translated from the Greek, Hebrew, &c. With Froberger, Pachelbel, and Buxtehude, Kuhnau was decidedly the most worthy predecessor of Bach.

> The "first" Sonata in B flat, 1695; Neuer Clavierübung erster Theil, bestehend in 7 Partien aus dem Ut, Re, Mi oder Tertia majore eines jedweden Toni, &c., Allen Liebhabern zu sonderbarer Annehmlickeit aufgesetzet und verleget von J. Kuhnauen (Leipzig, 1689). Neuer Clavierübung anderer Theil—das ist, 7 Partien, &c.; benebenst einer Sonata aus dem B (flat). See above. (Leipzig, 1695.) Frische Clavierfrüchte oder 7 Suonaten von guter Invention und Manier, auf dem Claviere zu spielen (Leipzig, 1696). Musikalische Vorstellung einiger biblischer Historien in 6 Sonaten, auf dem Clavier zu spielen: Sonate 1. The fight between David and Goliath; 2. Saul cured by David through music; 3. Jacob's wedding; 4. The deadly ill and again healthy Hiskias; 5. The Saviour of Israel, Gideon; 6. Jacob's death and funeral.

Kullak, Dr. Adolph, b. Feb. 23, 1823, Meseritz; d. Dec. 25, 1862, Berlin. Studied philosophy at the Berlin University; was a pupil of Agthe and Dr. B. Marx. Appointed teacher at his brother's Academy, contributor to several musical journals, and author of the following important works:

> "Das Musikalische Schöne" and "Aesthetik des Clavierspiels," of which the third edition was revised (1889) by Dr. Hans Bischoff. About 15 solo pieces, amongst them a Nocturne (Op. 37), Ballade (Op. 38), Le Chant des Océanides (Op. 23).

Kullak, Dr. Theodor, b. Sept. 12, 1818, Krotoschin; d. March 1, 1882, Berlin. Through the interest of Prince Radziwill (composer of the music to Goethe's "Faust," b. 1775; d. 1833) he played at Court when only eleven years old. Pupil of Agthe (Posen), Dehn (Harmony) at Berlin; 1842, pupil of Czerny (Pf.), Sechter and Otto Nicolai (Theory and Composition) at Vienna. After having finished his studies in Vienna, he travelled; having settled in Berlin, he became teacher to the Royal Family, was appointed (1846) Court Pianist; founded (1850), with Julius Stern and Dr. Bernh. Marx, the Berlin (later, Stern) Conserv., dissolved (1855) the partnership, and started the eminently successful "Neue Akademie der Tonkunst," which existed for 25 years, and at which Xaver and Philipp Scharwenka, M. Moszkowski, Alfred Grünfeld, Sherwood, Martha Remmert, Dr. Hans Bischoff, Dr. O. Neitzel, C. Sternberg Erica Lie, and Helen Geissler were pupils. Kullak's eminent qualities as a teacher were generally admired and his excellent performances enthusiastically applauded. 1861, he received the title of Königl. Prof., was named Hon. Member of the Royal Philharmonic Academy of Florence, Knight of the Orders "Red Eagle" and "Prussian Crown," and of several other orders. As a composer he was very industrious. His son, Franz Kullak, b. April 12, 1842, continued the Academy, but dissolved it, 1889.

> "Materials for Elementary Instruction" and "School of Octaves" (a highly important work) are considered very useful; Concerto, Op. 55; 7 Octave Studies, Op. 48; Pastorales, Op. 75; Kinderleben, I., II. (a charming collection), Op. 62; Ballade, Op. 54; Impromptu-Caprice, Op. 97; 2 Polonaises caractéristiques, Op. 103; 4 solo pieces, Op. 104; Hymn, Op. 85, &c. His Transcriptions of national songs (Airs nationaux russes, Op. 108; Romances du vieux temps, Op. 111) are very effective, and his "Arpèges" and "Gazelle" have often been played at concerts.

Kunz, Conrad Max, b. Dec. 30, 1812, Schwandorf (Bavaria); d. Aug. 3, 1875, Munich. Conductor of the Royal Opera Choir. Although his reputation rests principally on his works for male voices, his 200 short Canons (Op. 14) are too important to be passed over; for with Seb. Bach's Duets and two-part Inventions they are the most practical introduction for a correct performance of Fugues. Actually intended only for beginners, more advanced performers will also derive great benefit from studying them with attention.

*****Kwast, James,** b. Nov. 23, 1852, Nijkerk (Holland). Pupil of his father, later of Reinecke and Richter (Leipzig), Kullak and Wüerst (Berlin), L. Brassin and Gevaerts (Brussels). 1874, appointed Prof. at the Cologne Conserv., which appointment he changed for a similar one at the Hoch Conserv. of Frankfort o/M.

> Trio, Concerto, Romanza in F sharp, &c.

L.

Lachner, Vinzenz, b. July 19, 1811, Rain (Bavaria); d. Jan. 22, 1893, Carlsruhe (Baden) Like his brothers, Franz and Ignaz L., he was at first instructed by his father, a poor schoolmaster, and had afterwards to depend entirely on his own exertions. In his 17th year he accepted the appointment of tutor, in a Polish family living at Posen. Afterwards he came to Vienna, received the post of Organist of the Lutheran Church, and was (1836) called to Mannheim o/Rhine to succeed his brother Franz as Capellmeister of the Opera, which post he retained until 1873, when he retired and went to Carlsruhe (Baden), occupying himself with teaching and composing. He was one of the best and most widely instructed musicians of our age—well acquainted with history, taking lively interest in natural science, well read in poetry and literature; he was, at the same time, an excellent and sharp, yet kind critic, from whom his pupils learned much by his explaining deficiencies in the plainest manner and showing the means for improvement. Of his compositions for Pf. not many have been published. These are:—

†Prelude and Toccata in D min.; ‡Rustic Dances; 42 Variations on the C maj. scale, Op. 42; 7 Pieces in the form of Valses; †Impromptu and Tarantelle, Op. 52; Bunte Blätter; Quartet (prize) with Strings, Op. 10.

*Lack, Théodore, b. Sept. 3, 1846, Quimper (Finisterre). Pupil and Lauréat of the Paris Conserv., where Marmontel (Pf.) and Bazin (Harmony) were his teachers. He has resided, since 1863, as a teacher in Paris. 1881, named Officier de l'Académie; 1887, Officier de l'Instruction publique.

Op. 30, Etudes élégantes; Op. 85, Etudes de Mdlle. Didi, I., II.; Op. 20, Tarantelle; Op. 27, Boléro; Op. 40, Valse espagnole; Op. 61, Scènes enfantines; Op. 106, Souvenir d'Alsace. For 2 Pf.: Polonaise de Concert.

Lacombe, Louis Brouillon, b. Nov. 26, 1818, Bourges (Departement Cher); d. Sept. 30, 1884, St. Vaast-la-Hougue. 1829, he entered the Paris Conserv., became at once a pupil of Zimmermann and gained, after two years, the first prize for playing. After leaving Paris he went to Germany and Vienna, where Czerny, Fischhof, and Sechter gave him lessons, and where he was able to become more thoroughly acquainted with classical music. In his concerts he was everywhere successful, for his playing was considered most satisfactory and highly interesting. When he returned to Paris he obtained a large circle of industrious pupils, to whom he was a sympathising and encouraging teacher. His best-known works are—

Op. 8, 4 Nocturnes; Op. 40, Etudes en Octaves; Op. 45, Choral, Grande Etude de Concert; Op. 50, 2 Nocturnes; Op. 52, 6 Romances sans paroles, and the charming Lullaby " Dors, mon enfant."

Lacombe, Paul, b. 1837, Carcassonne (Departement Oude). Pupil of Teysseyre in his native place, but mostly relying on his own exertions and industry. He made his name favourably known by—

Sonatas for Pf. and Vln., Op. 8 and 17; 4 Duos for Pf. and V'cello, Op. 10; a Trio, Op. 12; a Suite (A min.), Op. 15; Etudes, Op. 18; 5 Arabesques, Op. 16; and the "Aubade aux Mariés," Op. 56.

Ladurner, Ignaz Anton Franz Xaver, b. Aug. 1, 1766, Aldein (Tyrol); d. March 4, 1839, Paris. 1777, he went to the monastery of Benediktbeuren, where he began his first compositions and practised the clavecin with rare energy. 1782, on the death of his father, he had, in order to sustain his mother, to accept the appointment of organist at Algund near Meran, until his younger brother, Joseph Aloys L., succeeded him. He went to Munich, continued his studies, and found in the Countess Haimhausen (a good pianist) a kind patroness, who took him to her Château Longeville (Champagne), where he remained until 1788, when he went to Paris and soon found a large number of pupils. His industry must have been marvellous, for during 40 years he occupied 15 hours out of the 24 with teaching. One of his pupils was Auber.

Sonatas, 3, Op. 1; 3, Op. 2; 3, Op. 4; 3 for Pf. and Vln., Op. 5; 3 ditto, Op. 7; Sonata for 4 hands, Op. 6; 3 Sonatas followed by a Caprice, Op. 11. Besides these he wrote Variations and Divertissements.

*Laidlaw, Anna Robena (Mrs. Thomson), b. April 30, 1819, Bretton, Yorkshire. She was educated at Edinburgh, where Robert Müller was her musical teacher. 1830, her parents took her to Königsberg (Prussia), where she made such rapid progress that it was decided to let her become an artist. 1834, she came to London and had lessons from Henri Herz; 1836, she went to Berlin, where she enjoyed the friendship and advice of Ludwig Berger; 1837, she made in Leipzig the acquaintance of Robert Schumann, who was so fascinated by her performances that he inscribed to her his beautiful Phantasiestücke, Op. 12. She then gave most successful concerts in Vienna, Breslau, Hanover (appointed Pianist to the Queen), and other towns. 1840, she returned to London and remained there for two years as a teacher. 1842, she started for a lengthened concert tour to Paris, Brussels, the Dutch towns, Frankfort o/M., &c., and was everywhere received by the crowned heads with unusual kindness and with the warmest sympathy and every mark of sincere appreciation by the public. *Viâ* Berlin she went to Königsberg, giving in this town a concert in aid of charity, and returned, 1845, to London, when she invited her parents (her father having failed as a merchant) to join her. She supported them until 1852, when she married a Scotch gentleman, Mr. Thomson, and retired into private life. All reports agree about the fine, correct, graceful, elegant, and thoroughly musicianly qualities of her interesting performances, and the letters which Schumann addressed to her are the best proof of how high she stood in his esteem and admiration.

Lalo, Edouard (Victor Antoine), b. Jan. 27, 1830, Lille; d. April 23, 1892, Paris. Excellent violinist (also viola). Pupil of Baumann (Lille).
   2 Trios, Sonata with V'cello, ditto with Vln., and characteristic pieces with Vln.

*Lamont, Frederic, b. Jan. 28, 1868, Glasgow. At first a pupil of his brother, David L.; 1882, pupil at the Raff Conserv., Frankfort o/M., where Max Schwarz (Pf.), Urspruch (Composition), Heermann (Vln.) were his teachers. 1884-85, he received lessons from Dr. von Bülow in Frankfort o/M., Berlin, and Meiningen; 1885-86, pupil of Liszt at Weimar and Rome. He played with distinguished and decided success in England, Germany, and other countries, and is one of the foremost pianists of the day.
   8 Clavierstücke, Op. 1, and a Trio, Op. 2. Several other Chamber music works have not yet been published.

Lampert, Ernst, b. July 3, 1818, Gotha; d. there, June 17, 1879. Pupil of Hummel (Weimar), Hauptmann and Spohr (Cassel). 1844, appointed Concertmeister and (1855) Hof-Capellmeister at Gotha. From his Duke he received the Cross of Merit, and from the King of Prussia the gold medal for Art and Science. His compositions for Pf. and Vln., and other string instruments, are well and solidly constructed.

*Lange, Gustav, b. Aug. 13, 1830, Schwerstedt, near Erfurt; d. July 19, 1889, Wernigerode. Pupil of Wilh. Bach, Grell, and Albert Löschhorn. Composer of more than 400 light, easy, and effective pieces, which were in great demand and published in England, America, France, and Germany. Their style is correct, and nowhere suffers from vulgarity. His most popular pieces are—
   Message of the Swallow, Op. 58; Boatman's Serenade, Op. 61; Zither Echoes, Op. 67; Brahms's Cradle Song, Op. 190a; In jungen Jahren, Op. 316; With flying flags, Op. 318; Mazeppa Galop, Op. 327; Farewell to the Alm, Op. 334; Love of long ago, Op. 335; The Dulcimer, Op. 355; Jean et Jeanette, Gavotte, Op. 362; Musical Box, Op. 384; Love on the Alm, Op. 393; Woodland round, Op. 406. Also, Op. 344, 347, 366, 371, 375, 376, and 399.

*Lange, Samuel de, b. Feb. 22, 1840, Rotterdam. Pupil of his father, J. F. Dupont, Joh. J. H. Verhulst (Rotterdam), Alex. Winterberger (Vienna), B. Damcke (Brussels), and C. Mikuli (Lemberg). 1856-57, he travelled with the famous violoncellist, François Servais, in Austria and Poland; 1857-58, with his brother in Galicia; 1860-63, active as a teacher in Lemberg; 1869-72, went as organist to the principal German towns, Paris, and Vienna; 1873-74, appointed teacher at the Music School of Rotterdam; 1874-75, in a similar capacity at Basle; 1876-85, at the Cologne Conserv., Prof. of Pf., Organ, and Harmony, and Conductor of the celebrated Male Choral Society; 1885-93, Conductor of the Society "Promotion of Music" at The Hague.
   Concerto, 3 Sonatas with Vln., Sonata with V'cello, Sonata for Pf. solo, Trio and Quintet with strings.

*Lara, Adelina de, b. Jan. 23, 1872, Carlisle (her grandparents were Spanish). 1885, she went to Frankfort o/M. in order to study with Clara Schumann, with whom she remained for five years. Before this she had lessons from Fanny Davies. Her teacher in Composition and Counterpoint was Iwan Knorr (Frankfort o/M.). Her appearances in London and the provinces were eminently successful.

Lauska, Franz (Seraphinus), b. Jan. 13, 1764, Brünn; d. April 28, 1825, Berlin. Although his father intended him to become a gentleman farmer, his love for music was so great that he devoted almost all his time to its study and received permission to go (1784) to Vienna, where Albrechtsberger was his teacher. The Duke of Serbelloni engaged him to accompany him to Rome, and after his return the Palatine of Bavaria elected him Kammer-Musikus. 1794, he went, *viâ* Frankfort o/M. and Hamburg, to Copenhagen, where he created a great sensation, and resided there as a teacher for four years. 1798, he arrived in Berlin, where his name was already well known; the Court engaged him as a teacher, and the number of his pupils was so great that he scarcely found time for composing. Among his pupils was Meyerbeer. His style of playing was elegant, fluent, brilliant, full of grace and refinement. His compositions were popular and much played.

<small>24 Sonatas (Op. 1, in C min.; Op. 4, Grande Sonata; Op. 43, Sonata pathétique). Sonata with V'cello, Op. 28. Several pieces for 4 hands: Sonata, Op. 31, in B flat; Polonaise in C; 6 easy and agreeable pieces, &c.; Rondeaux, Polonaise, and Variations for 2 hands. With Beczwarsowsky he published a Method of Pf. playing.</small>

Lazare, Martin, b. Oct. 27, 1829, Brussels. Pupil of Van der Does (Hague) and Zimmermann (Paris).

<small>6 Concert Studies, 6 Etudes de genre, Sicilienne (Op. 16), and some Valses de Salon.</small>

***Le Beau**, Louise Adolpha, b. April 25, 1850, Rastatt (Baden), daughter of an officer. Pupil of Wilh. Kalliwoda (Carlsruhe) and Clara Schumann in Baden. Composition and Counterpoint she studied in Munich with Prof. Sachs and J. Rheinberger; from Dr. Franz Lachner she received advice about Instrumentation. Up to 1885 she conducted a private school for Pf. playing and theory; after 1885 she resided for a few years at Wiesbaden, and has lived, since 1890, permanently in Berlin. Her performances in Munich, Berlin, Leipzig, Baden, and Vienna were greeted with sincere cordiality and warm applause; but more than this, her excellent compositions, solidly constructed, melodious, and interesting, were an agreeable surprise for the critical public of these towns.

<small>Trio, Op. 15; Fantasia with Orchestra, Op. 25; Quartet with strings, Op. 28; Solo Sonata for Pf., Op. 8; Sonata with Vln., Op. 10; ditto with V'cello, Op. 15; Variations on an original theme, Op. 3; Improvisata for the left hand alone, Op. 30; and Gavotte, Op. 32 (very popular).</small>

Lebert (really Levy), Sigismund, b. Dec. 12, 1822, Ludwigsburg (near Stuttgart); d. Dec. 8, 1884, Stuttgart. Pupil of Tomaschek, Dionys Weber, Tedesco, and Proksch (Prague). He was, with great success, for several years active as a teacher in Munich, and founded (*see* Stark), with Dr. Faisst, Brachmann, Stark, and Speidel, the Stuttgart Conserv., in which he had many opportunities of exhibiting his rare accomplishments as a teacher. He published with Stark the great Method of Pf. playing, which has been translated into English (3 editions), and an instructive edition of the Classics, although in several instances of doubtful merit. The University of Tübingen conferred on him the diploma of Hon. Doc. Phil., and the late King of Würtemberg gave him the title of Königl. Professor. For the "Method" he wrote many Studies.

Le Carpentier, Adolphe Clair, b. Feb. 17, 1809, Paris; d. there, July 14, 1869. Pupil of Lesueur and Fétis at the Conserv. (1818); he gained several prizes and established himself (1833) as a teacher. His patience, experience, and general kindness as an instructor brought him numerous pupils, and his educational pieces were soon popular in France, England, Belgium, and Germany.

<small>His "Méthode de Piano pour les enfants" is a standard work, and his 25 Etudes élémentaires, Op. 59, are excellent; likewise his collection, Le progrès, 24 Etudes. His pieces (about 270) on operatic and national airs are very often used; they are written with care, and not difficult.</small>

Le Couppey, Félix, b. April 14, 1814, Paris; d. there, July, 1887. In his tenth year (1824) he entered the Conserv. as a pupil of Dourlen, whom he succeeded in 1843. When only in his seventeenth year Cherubini entrusted him with a preparatory class for Dourlen and Leborne. 1848, when H. Herz went to America, Le Couppey was selected as his substitute. A special class for ladies was arranged for him, and amongst his fair pupils we find the names of Madame Montigny-Rémaury, Vidal, and Mdlle. Coudère. He received the Legion of Honour, and his pupils remember him with sincere affection. His educational works are well known:

<small>"École du mécanisme du Piano," 24 Etudes primaires, Op. 10; L'art du Piano, 50 Etudes with remarks; and a pamphlet, "De l'enseignement du Piano; conseils aux jeunes Professeurs" (1865).</small>

***Ledent**, Félix Etienne, b. Nov. 17, 1816, Liège; d. there, Aug. 23, 1886.

Pupil at the Liège Conserv., 1827; later of Daussoigne-Méhul (Paris). 1843. he received the second prize of Rome. 1844, appointed Prof. at the Liège Conserv., and received later the Order of Leopold and other distinctions. He was an excellent pianist, of whom the Liègois were very proud. As a composer he did not make any great mark.

Leduc, Alphonse, b. March 9, 1804, Nantes; d. June 17, 1868, Paris. Was a pianist, composer, teacher, and musicseller. His father, an excellent bassoon player, taught his son several instruments; thus he could play in a concert on the bassoon, flute, or guitar. For several years a pupil at the Paris Conserv. 1841, he established the publishing and musicselling business, which still exists. He wrote above 1,000 small pieces. Of his educational works the best known are—

Méthode élémentaire de Piano, à l'usage des pensions (about 20 editions); 25 petites Etudes, &c., Op. 156; Etudes élémentaires, Op. 128; Etudes mélodiques, Op. 146; Etudes de mécanisme, Op. 100, &c.

Lefébure-Wély, Louis James Alfred, b. Nov. 13, 1817, Paris; d. there, Jan. 1, 1870. At first a pupil of his father, Antoine L.-W., Organist at St. Rochus Church; later at the Conserv., where Benoist (Organ), Zimmermann (Pf.), Berton and Halévy (Composition) were his teachers. When only in his eighth year he acted as substitute for his father, and when only fourteen years old he became his successor. He received several prizes at the Conserv., became in time Organist of the Madeleine (1847), but resigned (1858) this post in order to devote himself entirely to composition. 1863, he accepted the post of Organist of St. Sulpice, as successor to his private teacher, Séjan. 1850, he received the Legion of Honour and (1859) the Spanish Order of Charles III.

50 Etudes; 3 Etudes de Salon, Op. 44; Etude moyen-âge, Op. 76; Saltarelle, Etude, Op. 57; la Retraite militaire, Op. 68; la Garde montante, Op. 31; Larmes du cœur, Op. 84; Pensées intimes, Op. 91 (3); Après la Victoire, Marche, Op. 87; les Cloches du Monastère, la Chasse à courre, Op. 64; la Sérénade du Gondolier, Op. 88.

Leitert, Johann Georg, b. Sept. 29, 1852, Dresden. Pupil of Krägen and Reichel (Pf.), Rischbieter (Harmony). 1865, he played with eminent success in Dresden; 1867, he went to England; 1869, to Liszt, with whom he remained for 2 years in Rome; 1871, he returned to his native town, Dresden, and accompanied (1872) the violinist Wilhelmj on a tour to the towns of East Prussia and Russian Poland. 1879-81, was a teacher at Horak's Piano School (Vienna). Of his merits as an executive artist, some critics speak in enthusiastic terms and declare his memory to be a phenomenal one.

Esquisses, Op. 12; Chants du crépuscule, Op. 24; Rayons et ombres, Op. 31; Valse Caprice, Op. 43; Feuilles d'Amour, Op. 37; Lose Blätter, Op. 38.

Lemoine, Henri (fourth son of the guitarist and music-publisher, Antoine Marcel L.), b. Oct., 1786, Paris; d. there, May 18, 1854. Pupil at the Conserv., of Berton, Dourlen, and Catel; he received prizes in 1805, 1806, 1807, 1809. 1821, he took lessons of Reicha, to whom he owes more than to his former teachers; 1817, he succeeded his father as a publisher. As a composer he made himself known by

Sonate à 4 mains; Polonaise, Op. 5; Etrennes, Sonatines faciles; several books of Variations; 36 books of "Bagatelles"; 50 Etudes enfantines, Op. 37; several books of "Récréations." His principal work is "Méthode pratique" and Tablettes du Pianiste, Memento du Professeur de Piano (1844).

Lentz, Heinrich Gerhard, b. 1764, Cologne; d. Aug. 21, 1839, Warsaw. He was a pupil of his father, an excellent organist. 1784, he went to Paris, where he had the rare luck to perform one of his own Concertos at the Concerts spirituels. 1791, he went to London, where Clementi, Salomon, and even Joseph Haydn showed him every possible attention. 1795, he returned to Germany, went first to Hamburg, but then was (1796) invited by Prince Louis Ferdinand of Prussia to join him at Berlin. He was on intimate terms with the Prince until 1802, when Dussek appeared and put Lentz into the background. He left Berlin, went to Halle, Lemberg, and lastly to Warsaw, where he was appointed Prof. at the Conserv. (1826-31). He was a popular teacher, much sought after.

3 Concertos (Paris), 9 Trios, Sonatas with Vln., Sonata for 4 hands, Preludes, Variations, &c.

***Leschetizki**, Theodor, b. 1830, Langert (Austrian Poland). At first a pupil of his father, an eminent and favourite teacher at Vienna; afterwards of C. Czerny and Sechter (Composition). He completed his studies at the College (Gymnasium) and attended the University in order to study Philosophy, but owing to the Revolution of 1848 the University was closed. He began when in his fifteenth year to teach; and he appeared with great success in concerts (1842-48 and 1852). In 1852 he left for St. Petersburg, where he was (with but few exceptions) working for 27 years, not only as a teacher—private and at the Conserv.—but also as a public performer and composer, and, during the absence of Rubinstein, as *Maëstro di capella* to the Grand Duchess Helena. After having been married a first time—which union was dissolved—he married (1880) his former pupil, Annette Essipoff (Essipowa). 1878, his impaired health obliged him to leave Russia; he visited London (where he appeared at the Musical Union and New Philharmonic concerts), Holland, Germany, and again Vienna, where he remained as a private teacher, receiving pupils from all parts of the world. His merits have been recognised by the Sovereigns of Austria, Russia, Sweden, and Roumania, who all conferred on him high Orders. Of his published compositions the best known are—

Souvenirs d'Italie (6 pieces), 4 Morceaux pour Piano, Suite à la Campagne, Menuetto capriccioso, Mazurkas (Op. 24), Les deux Alouettes (Op. 22), †Valse chromatique, Second Nocturne (Op. 12), La Petite Coquette (Op. 12, VI.), Souvenir de St. Pétersbourg (Op. 15).

Lessmann, W. J. Otto, b. Jan. 30, 1844, Rüdersdorfer Kalkberge (near Berlin). At first educated at Magdeburg, where his father had a music business; pupil of A. J. Ritter; in Berlin of H. von Bülow (Pf.) and Kiel (Composition). 1866, teacher at the Stern Academy; later (until 1871) at Tausig's Academy of Pf. playing; for a short time proprietor of a similar Academy; since 1872 Director of the Musical Instruction at the Empress Augusta Institute for Ladies at Charlottenburg, and, since 1881, teacher at Scharwenka's Academy. 1882, he began to publish the *Allgemeine Musik-Zeitung*. He is known as an intelligent and impartial critic.

Polonaise, Op. 13; Erinnerungen (Recollections), 6 characteristic pieces, Op. 16; also Transcriptions (6) from Beethoven's Trios for String Instruments, and 6 ditto from Schubert's String Quartets.

Leybach, Ignace, b. July 17, 1817, Gambsheim (Alsace); d. May 23, 1891, Toulouse. He received his first instruction in Strassburg, afterwards in Paris, from Pixis, Kalkbrenner, and Chopin. 1844, appointed Organist of the Cathedral of Toulouse. He was an excellent teacher and favourite composer of easy, unpretentious, and pleasing pieces (255 numbers).

Of these the Nocturnes, Op. 3 and 4; Aux bords du Gange (Mendelssohn), Op. 42; Boléro brillant, Op. 64; Ballade, Op. 19; Valse poétique, Op. 216; and Les batelières de Naples, are well known.

*****Liadow**, Anatole, b. April 29, 1855, St. Petersburg. Pupil of Johansen (Counterpoint and Fugue), Rimsky-Korsakow (Musical Forms and Instrumentation). Appointed teacher of theory at the St. Petersburg Conserv. and to the Imperial Chapel.

Op. 3, 6 Morceaux, Books 1 and 2; Op. 4, Arabesques (4); Op. 7 and 8, Intermezzi; Op. 13, Préludes (4); Op. 20, Novellette; Op. 21, Ballade; Op. 27, Préludes (3); Op. 31, Deux Morceaux. Besides these, Mazurkas, Impromptus, Bagatelles, Valses, Idyls, Sketches, &c.

*****Liapounow**, Sergi, b. Nov. 18, 1859, Jaroslaw. Pupil of Klindworth and Pabst (Pf.) and Hubert (Theory and Composition) at Moscow. At present Sub-Director of the Imperial Choir.

Concerto, 3 pieces, &c.

Lickl, Carl Georg, b. Oct. 28, 1801, Vienna; d. there, Aug 31, 1877. Pupil of his father.

3 Sonatas, 8 Rondeaux, 4 books of Variations, † the Ischler-Bilder (Op. 57), Gasteiner-Blüthen (Op. 59), 6 Elegies (Op. 63), Novellettes (Op. 66). Very popular.

Lie, Erika (Madame Nissen), b. Jan. 17, 1845, Kongsvinger (near Christiania). Until her fifteenth year she received instruction from her mother and sister. 1860, Halfdan Kjerulf gave her lessons in Christiania; 1861, she went with her sister to Berlin, and became a pupil of Theodor Kullak. During her stay in Berlin she lost her mother, and this determined her to remain longer, in order to profit as much as possible. Kullak engaged her as a teacher in his Academy, and persuaded her to give a concert, which was eminently successful, and encouraged her to extend her artistic journeys to other German towns, and to Copenhagen and Stockholm (where she was elected Hon. Member of the Royal Academy). She was everywhere received with genuine applause. At present she resides in Christiania, where she teaches, and delights her countrymen with her artistic and refined performances.

*****Liebling**, Max (Emil), b. Sept. 22, 1846, Hultschin (Upper Silesia). Pupil of Krug (Posen) and Heinr. Ehrlich (Berlin). 1878-79, he made with Wilhelmj (the celebrated violinist) a *tournée* to the West of the United States, and created a *furore* by his brilliant performances and dazzling technique. He resides in New York. His compositions are light and popular.

Silver Wedding, Polonaise, La Coquette, Polka, "On the wing."

*Liebling, Sally, b. April 8, 1859, Posen. Pupil of Franz Bendel and Theodor Kullak (Pf.), Wüerst and Weitzmann (Composition), Berlin. When only in his twelfth year he gave concerts in the principal towns of Germany, and went, 1875, to North America, where he appeared in the orchestral concerts of Thomas; travelled in turn with Ole Bull, Wilhelmj, Reményi, Clara Luise Kellog, and Emma Thursby, and remained until 1883, when he returned to Berlin, anxious to put himself under Bülow, who, however, declined to take him as a pupil, declaring that he had only to learn from himself, or, perhaps, to follow Rubinstein's advice. 1884, he went to Liszt (Weimar), where he enjoyed, in company with M. Rosenthal, E. Sauer, A. Friedheim, and A. Siloti, the good advice of the illustrious master. 1888, he founded the New Conserv. of Music at Berlin.

*Liebling, Georg (youngest brother of the above), b. Jan. 22, 1865, Berlin. Pupil of Theodor and Franz Kullak, H. Ehrlich (Pf.), Heinrich Urban (Composition) in Berlin, and of Liszt (Weimar). From his sixteenth to his twenty-first year he was teacher in Kullak's Academy. With Dengremont, A. Senkrah, Teresine Tua, A. Materna, Sembrich, Barbi, Nikita, and Mierzwinski he made journeys in all European countries. 1890, the Duke of Saxe-Coburg-Gotha named him Pianist to the Court. His best known pieces are—

Air de Ballet and Romance, Gavotte, "Liebling's" Walzer, and Octave Study.

Lindemann, Ole Andres, b. 1768, Surendalen (Norway); d. 1855, Trondhjem. Pupil of Wernicke, and himself teacher of Tellefsen. Farrenc, of Paris, published, in his "Trésor du Pianiste," the works of Lindemann.

Liszt, Franz (von), b. Oct. 22, 1811, Raiding (Hungary); d. July 30-31, 1886, Bayreuth. At the age of six he commenced to study the Pf. under the supervision of his father, progress being so satisfactory that the boy when nine years old made his *début* at a concert in Oedenburg (Hungary). At another concert, at Pressburg, he so impressed several Hungarian noblemen that they granted him a sum of 600 florins (£60) annually, for a period of six years, towards the continuation of his musical studies. It was at once decided (1821) to send the boy to Vienna to study under Czerny, with whom his progress was marvellous. Beethoven was so enchanted with his playing that he publicly embraced him at the boy's Farewell concert (1823), on his leaving Vienna for Paris. Liszt's conscientious father intended him to continue his education at the Paris Conserv., but this was impossible, owing to the Director's (Cherubini) aversion to prodigies. He refused Liszt admission to the school, giving his foreign nationality as an excuse for his decision. Thus publicity became his chief instructor. He was received in the most distinguished society and "le petit Litz" soon became the *enfant gâté* of Parisian salons. After having electrified Paris audiences, father and son visited London twice. In 1827, when on a concert tour through the French provinces, the father died at Boulogne. From that day forth Liszt was responsible for his own and his mother's sustenance, private lessons enabling him to fulfil his filial duties. The presence in the French capital of artists such as Paganini, Chopin, Berlioz, &c., strongly influenced his artistic development and characteristics. In 1836, when Thalberg created a sensation in Paris, great rivalry existed between the two artists, Liszt, however, eventually proving victor in the contest. The following years (particularly 1839-47) witnessed his greatest triumphs as a performer. During this period he visited all important European countries. In 1847 he accepted the post of Hof-Capellmeister at Weimar, and remained there until 1861; Weimar becoming, under his influence, a musical centre of great importance. 1861-70, he lived in Rome. It was here that Pope Pius IX., who had always manifested a keen interest in Liszt's artistic and personal qualities, conferred upon him (1865) the dignity of Abbé. This distinction was much prized by Liszt, who had always evinced a strong inclination towards clerical life. The last years of his life were spent alternately in Rome, Pesth, and Weimar; the latter town, during his presence, being crowded with admirers and pupils from all countries. His last visit to London was paid in the year of his death (1886). He was the father of three children, who were the issue of his *liaison* with the Comtesse d'Agoult—known as an authoress under the name of Daniel Stern. His daughter, Cosima, has become celebrated by her marriage with Richard Wagner. Liszt occupies a unique position in the history of the Pf., his influence absolutely commanding the modern phase of execution. As a performer, as well as a composer, he stands alone. Unrivalled up to the present day as an executant, and as an interpreter of all kinds and classes of music, he may be said to be the founder of modern Pf. playing. His compositions and transcriptions completely transformed the nature of the instrument, enriching its capacities to a degree hitherto unknown; through him the Pf. has become a worthy representative of the orchestra (*vide*, for instances, his transcription of Beethoven's Symphonies). It is impossible to enumerate the various qualities and characteristics of Liszt's playing; suffice it to say that the King of Pianists is looked upon and honoured by all players as the unsurpassable ideal of an artist Together with Rubinstein and Brahms, Liszt has received the highest distinctions possible from sovereigns, cities, universities, academies, and learned societies; indeed, the collection of his orders, presents, diplomas and addresses formed a little museum, which was, during his lifetime, one of the sights of Weimar, to the Court of which he was attached as Chamberlain. A monument to him was erected (1893) at Oedenburg (Hungary).

Etudes (12) d'exécution transcendante, Trois grandes Etudes de Concert, Grandes Etudes de Paganini (6), Ab-Irato, Etude de perfectionnem nt, Harmonies poétiques et religieuses (10), Années de Pélerinage (9), ditto (5'), Sonata, Grosses Concerto Solo, Concerto (with orchestra), No. 1 in E flat, No. 2 in A; "Todten-Tanz," Paraphrase on "Dies irae," Grand Duo for Pf. and Vln. sur "le marin"; Scherzo and March, Ballades (2), Apparitions (3), Consolations (6), Heroischer Marsch (im ungarischen Styl), Fest-Marsch (1842), Polonaises (2), Mazurka brillante, Caprices - Valses (3), Valse-Impromptu, Feuilles d'Album, Grand Galop chromatique, Waldesrauschen, Gnomentanz, Arbre de Noël (12 pieces), Romance oubliée, Hymne du Pape, Venezia e Napoli (Gondoliera-Tarentelle); Impromptu (1), St. François d'Assise (2), St. François de Paul; Liebesträume (3), Canzone napolitana, Hungarian Rhapsodies (15), Capriccio alla Turca, Rhapsodie espagnole. *Fantasias*: Les Huguenots, Robert le diable, La Juive, Don Juan, Somnambula, Norma, I Puritani (2), La Fiancée (Auber), Muette de Portici, Lucrezia Borgia (2), Lucia di Lammermoor, Illustrations du Prophète (3). *Transcriptions*: Tannhäuser, Lohengrin, Flying Dutchman, Rienzi, Meistersinger, Parsifal, Nibelungen (Wagner), King Alfred (Raff), Benvenuto Cellini (Berlioz). *Paraphrases de Concert*: God save the Queen, Wedding March and Elfin Dance (Mendelssohn), Gaudeamus igitur, Marche funèbre, Dom Sebastian (Donizetti), Swiss melodies, Contrabandista, Cavatine de Pacini, La Serenata e l'orgia (Rossini), Pastorella e li Marinari (Rossini), Hussiten Lied. *Transcriptions of*: Beethoven's Symphonies, Beethoven's Septuor, Episode de la Vic d'un Artiste, Harold en Italie (Berlioz). *Overtures*: Oberon, Jubel, Freischütz (Weber), William Tell (Rossini), Les Francs-Juges, Roi Lear (Berlioz), Tannhäuser (Wagner). *Transcriptions of Songs* by Schubert (57), Beethoven, including " Liederkreis " (15), Mendelssohn (7), Robert Franz (12), Schumann, Dessauer, Weber, Meyerbeer, Liszt. *Other Transcriptions*: Soirées musicales (12), Stabat Mater (2) de Rossini, Amusements (6) on Airs by Mercadante, 3 ditto on Airs by Donizetti, Glanes de Woronince (3), Mélodies russes (2), Mélodies hongroises d'après Schubert, Marches by Schubert and G inka, Soirées de Vienne on Valses by Schubert (9), Bunte Reihe by David (24), La Romanesca, 6 Preludes and Fugues, Fantasia e Fuga, by Bach.

Litolff, Henri Charles, b. Feb. 6, 1818, London; d. Aug. 5, 1891, Paris. His father, a violinist from Alsace, settled in London; confided the musical education of his highly-talented son to Moscheles, under whose care he made such rapid progress that he played in public when only twelve years old. He was throughout his life somewhat erratic, and to this disposition must be attributed his marriage when only in his seventeenth year. This event forced him to leave London to find a living in Paris. However, he did not succeed, and had to content himself with a modest appointment in Melun, a small French town. It was in 1840 that he drew the attention of the Parisians to his splendid performances and interesting compositions. The idyl of his early life—his marriage—was destroyed; he left his wife and travelled in Belgium. 1841-44. he was Conductor in Warsaw, after which he travelled in Germany and Holland, passed the stormy days of 1848 in Vienna, escaped the rigour of the military prosecutions, and arrived, somewhat broken-hearted and dispirited, in Germany. 1850, he settled in Brunswick, married the widow of the music publisher Meyer, and changed the name of the firm to H. Litolff, publishing cheap editions which found their way to all countries of Europe. 1860, he transferred the business to his adopted stepson Theodor, and went again to Paris, where in the excitement and turmoil of the French capital he felt happy Having made the acquaintance of the Countess Larochefoucauld, he dissolved his union with his second wife, and married the Countess. His compositions are interesting, in some degree even original, and for a while fascinating, but they have no lasting value; he never got rid of a certain impetuosity, which prevented him from examining his works with discrimination, and from using the pruning knife in order to eliminate many prolixities.

Concerto-Symphonie, Op. 22; ditto, Concert National Hollandais; Trios, Op. 47 in D min. and Op. 56 in E flat; 3 Duets with Vln. (with Léonard), Op. 53; 6 Etudes de Concert, Op. 18; Opuscules, Op. 25, 1-6; Invitation à la Tarentelle, Op. 36; Nocturne, Op. 62; 6 Characteristic Pieces, Op. 65; †Spinnlied.

Lobe, Johann Christian, b. May 30, 1797, Weimar; d. July 27, 1881, Leipzig. Pupil (as flautist) of Riemann, later of A. E. Müller (Weimar). Appointed a viola player in the orchestra; he left this post in 1842, when he established a music school, which he conducted until 1846; then left Weimar for Leipzig, where he remained until his death. He was a highly intelligent author and a thoroughly well-educated musician.

Quartets (2); Caprice, Op. 15; Variations, Op. 16; †Le Buffon, characteristic piece, Op. 23; Blumen-Frucht und Dornstücke, Op. 24; †Rondoletto ungheriano, Op. 28; and 6 pieces for 4 hands.

***Loder, Kate** (Lady Thompson), b. Aug. 22, 1826, Bath. Daughter of the excellent musician, George Loder (who died at the age of thirty-three) and niece of John Loder, for many years leader of the Philharmonic Society. When only three years old she could tell any notes that were struck on the Pf., and it was decided to train her for the musical profession. After having studied in Bath with Henry Field, she played there in 1838 for the first time in public; came (1839) to London, where she studied the Pf. with Mrs. Anderson and Harmony with Charles Lucas; gained twice the King's Scholarship, and played each year at the Academy concerts. 1847, she appeared at the Philharmonic concerts and continued doing so until 1854, when she made her last public appearance, having married (1851) the eminent Surgeon, Mr. (now Sir) Henry Thompson.

Trio, 2 Sonatas, 2 books of Studies, several smaller pieces, and Duets.

Löhlein, George Simon, b. 1727, Neustadt (Coburg); d. 1782, Leipzig. There is no information concerning his musical education, but it is related that in travelling (1743) to Copenhagen, when passing through Potsdam, he was—owing to his extraordinary height—seized and forced into the Prussian grenadiers. He had to take part in the battle of Collin, was left among the fallen on the battlefield, but was attended to by the Austrians, who, after his recovery, allowed him to proceed to Jena in order to continue his studies. 1761, appointment in Weimar; 1763, left for Leipzig, where he soon made himself a reputation as a performer and talented composer. He published the following works (some of which he engraved himself on copper plates):

Clavecin School (the 6th edition revised by A. E. Müller); 6 Partite, Op. 1 (1766); 6 Sonate, Op. 2; 6 Partite, Op. 3; 3 Trios, Quartet, Musical trifles, and Concertos (1775).

Löschhorn, Albert, b. June 27, 1819, Berlin. Pupil (1837-39) of Ludwig Berger. Continued his studies with Kollitschgy, one of Berger's most experienced pupils, and in Harmony and Composition with Wilhelm Bach and Ed. Grell. 1851, he succeeded Kollitschgy as principal teacher at the Academical Institute for sacred music; 1847, he began to give, with the brothers Adolph and Julius Stahlknecht, highly successful Trio *Soirées*, which were continued for many years, and which offered an opportunity of exhibiting his admirable qualities as pianist, one of them being more particularly a beautiful, varied, and carefully graduated touch. In 1853 these excellent artists performed also with success in Russia. 1868, he received the title of Königl. Prof., and, 1889, the "Red Eagle" Order. He is a member of the Royal Society of Examining Judges. He is undoubtedly one of the most experienced educational composers of the present time, and the enumeration of his Studies is warranted:—

42 easy Studies, Op. 192; 21 melodious Studies, Op. 193; Studies for beginners, Op. 65; for more advanced, Op. 66; for advanced, Op. 67; characteristic Studies, Op. 118; 17 melodious Studies, Op. 194; 14 ditto, Op. 195; 12 ditto, Op. 196; Rhythmical Problems, Op. 197; melodious pieces for Study, Op. 186; Le trille, 14 Studies, Op. 165; Universal Studies, Op. 185; La vélocité, Op. 136; Scenes from Childhood, Op. 96 and Op. 100 (2 books each); melodious Studies, Op. 38; Studies for Children, Op. 181. Besides these he published Technical Studies, Octave School, Op. 176; School of Scales; 3 Instructive Sonatas, Op. 101. Solo pieces: "La belle Amazone," Op. 25; Tarantelle, Op. 133; A Vénise (barcarolle), Op. 162; Trois Mazurkas, Op. 163; Deux Valses, Op. 161; 4 elegant pieces, Op. 109.

Lövenskjold, Hermann Severin (Baron de), b. July 30, 1815, Norway; d. Dec. 5, 1870, Copenhagen. 1829, he went to Copenhagen, where he received his musical education. 1841, the King appointed him Kammermusiker.

Trio, Op. 2; Fantasias, Op. 3 and 5; Characteristic pieces, Op. 12; "Sogni d'Italia" (12 pieces); Rondos, &c.

Löw, Joseph, b. Jan. 23, 1834, Prague; d. there Oct., 1886. In 1854 he made a very successful tour through Moravia, Silesia, Galicia, and Buckowina. 1856, returned to Prague, where he established himself. Was a successful teacher and most industrious composer of light and popular drawing-room pieces, of which more than 450 were published. The best known are—
Jugend-Album, Op. 142; Soir de printemps, Op. 326; Deux Impromptus romantiques, Op. 187; Maiengruss, Op. 413; Allegro brillant for 2 Pf., Op. 325.

Löwe, Dr. Carl, b. Nov. 30, 1796, Löbejün (Cöthen); d. April 20, 1869, Kiel. Pupil of Türck (Halle). 1820, Cantor of St. Jacob's Church and Musical Director of the College at Stettin; he held these appointments for 46 years, when a stroke of apoplexy obliged him to retire. The University of Greifswald conferred on him the diploma of Hon. Doc. Phil. In his earlier years he wrote a good deal for the Pf.—
Sonatas, Op. 16, 33, 41, and 47; Evening Fantasia, Op. 11; "Mazeppa," tone-poem (after Byron), Op. 27; the "Brother of Mercy," tone-poem, Op. 28; Sonate élégiaque, Op. 32; "Spring," a tone-poem, Op. 47; Fantasia of the Alps, Op. 53; Biblical pictures, Op. 96; Gipsy Sonata, Op. 107; 4 Fantasias, Op. 137; Trio, Op. 12.

Logier, Johann Bernhard, b. Feb. 9, 1777, Cassel; d. July 27, 1846, Dublin. In 1805 he went to Dublin as flautist in an Irish regiment. When the regimental band was dissolved, he was appointed Organist at Westport (Ireland), where he invented the "Chiroplast," a device to regulate the position of the hands. 1816, he introduced his system of teaching several pupils at the same time—each playing on an instrument for her or himself. This system—a sort of wholesale instruction—found great favour, and he was invited by the Prussian Government to superintend the use of his Chiroplast and his new system as applied in the German schools. After some three years he returned to Ireland. His own compositions have no great merit (Concertos, Sonatas, &c.), but his books deserve much attention:
An explanation and description of the Royal patent *Chiroplast*, or hand-director for Pf. (1816); the First Companion to the Chiroplast (1818), which work treats of the "Unisono" playing; Logier's practical thorough bass (1819).

Louchet, Gustave, b. Oct. 4, 1840, Boulogne-sur-Mer. Pupil of Marmontel; resides at present in Paris. His short pieces, exhibiting a refined and elegant taste, are much in demand, more particularly—
6 pensées musicales, Op. 17; Improvisata, Op. 21; 3 Album leaflets, Op. 23, and the Valse caractéristique in A min., Op. 22.

Louis, Ferdinand (really Ludwig Friedrich Christian), Prince of Prussia (nephew of Frederic II.), b. Nov. 18, 1772, Friedrichsfeldt (Berlin); was killed Oct. 10, 1806, in the battle of Saalfeld. At an early age he showed very superior talent for Pf. playing and composing, and it seems that his tutors developed these talents to such a degree that they forgot to look after his general education and more particularly after the development of his moral character. His many romantic and erotic adventures and other escapades gave his family and himself many troubles; but, on the other hand, it cannot be denied that he redeemed these shortcomings by his wonderful gallantry and intrepidity as a soldier. His friendship with Dussek, who went (1800) to Berlin, is well known. That the Prince's talent was great is undeniable, for Beethoven, who made his acquaintance in 1796, said that he did not play like a Prince, but like a real musician. The Prince, on the other hand, was a warm admirer of Beethoven (who dedicated his Concerto in C min., Op. 37, to the Royal artist). A novel by Fanny Lewald, "Prince L. F. of Prussia," relates all the most noteworthy incidents of his life.
Quintet in C min., Op. 1; Quartet in E flat, Op. 5, and in F min., Op. 6; Trios, Op. 2, 3, and 10; Octet (Pf., Cl., 2 Horns, 2 Vla., and 2 V'cellos), Op. 12; Rondos with Orchestra; Larghetto, Op. 11; Notturno, Op. 8 (these two are with accompaniment of strings); Variations and Fugue, Op. 7.

Lübeck, Ernst, b. Aug. 24, 1829, The Hague (Holland); d. Sept. 17, 1876, Paris. Pupil of his father, he afterwards went to Paris. 1850-54, travelled in America; 1854, settled permanently in Paris, and gave chamber concerts with Lalo, Armingaud, and Jacquard. He was a highly popular teacher and much admired as a performer. His last years were darkened by deep melancholia, which necessitated his being confined in a private asylum. Only a few of his pieces were published.
Souvenir du Péron, Tarantelle, Berceuse, and Polonaise.

Lully, Jean Baptiste de, b. 1633, Florence; d. March 22, 1687, Paris. Founder of the French National Opera.

F

Lessons for the Harpsichord or Spinet, "Almands, Corants, Sarabands, Airs, Minuets, and Jiggs" (Daniel Wright, of London, printed, and sold by him). The genuineness of these lessons is doubtful.

*Lutter, Heinrich, b. March 18, 1854, Hanover. At first a pupil of C. Herner (Hanover), also enjoyed the advice and supervision of Dr. von Bülow. 1876-85, pupil of Liszt, in Weimar and Pesth. In the latter town R. Volkmann was his teacher for Composition. His excellent performances are everywhere cordially received and admired; and his visit to London gave him an opportunity of gaining the favourable opinion of a critical London audience.

Lysberg (really Bovy), Charles Samuel (known under the *nom de plume* of Lysberg), b. March 1, 1821, Geneva; d. there Feb. 15, 1873. At first he was educated in his native town, then went to Paris in order to take lessons from Chopin and from Delaire in Harmony. For some time Prof. at the Conserv. of Geneva. Many of his popular, pleasing, and, on the whole, correctly written pieces are to be found on the desks of lady amateurs. The greatest favourites are—

Sur l'Onde, Op. 94; Idylle, Op. 64; Menuet, Op. 60; Deux Nocturnes, Op. 29; La Napolitaine, Op. 26; Les Ondines, Op. 90.

M.

*MacDowell, Edward Alexander, b. Dec. 18, 1861, New York. Pupil of Desvernire and Madame Carreño (New York), Marmontel and Savard (Paris), Louis Ehlert, Joachim Raff, Carl Heymann and Liszt (Germany). He resides in Boston (Mass.), and is one of the foremost American artists of our time. Among his compositions, which deserve great attention, are—

Modern Suites, Op. 10 and 14; Concerto in A min., Op. 15; Concerto in D min.; Sonata tragica; and a considerable number of smaller pieces.

*Macfarren, Sir George Alexander, b. March 2, 1813, London; d. there Oct. 31, 1887. 1829, pupil at the R.A.M., under Charles Lucas, W. H. Holmes, and Cipriani Potter. 1834, became Prof., and, 1875, Principal of the R.A.M. 1875, Prof. of Music at Cambridge University. Knighted 1883. His published compositions are:

Quintet in G min. (for Strings and C.-Bass); Trio in E min.; Sonatas: No. 1 in E flat, No. 2 in A, No. 3 in G min.; Romanzas: 6 for Pf., and 5 for Pf. and Vln.; Sonata in B flat, for Pf. and Fl. (posthumous). *Unpublished compositions*: Concerto in C min. (with orchestra); 2 Sonatas (A and C) with Vln., and 7 solo Sonatas.

*Macfarren, Walter Cecil, b. Aug. 28, 1826, London. 1836-41, chorister at Westminster Abbey (under James Turle). 1842-46, student at the R.A.M., under W. H. Holmes, G. A. Macfarren, and Cipriani Potter. 1847, Associate; 1862, Fellow; from 1848, Prof. of Pf., and 1873-80, Conductor of the orchestra and choir at the R.A.M.

Concertstück in E (with orchestra); Concerto in B min. (unpublished); Trios (3) in C min., E min., and C sharp min. (unpublished);

Sonatas (2) in C sharp min. and A (unpublished); Sonatas (2) in F and D, with Vln.; Sonata in E min., with V'cello; Suites de Pièces (3); Caprices (4); Allegro appassionato in A min.; Allegro cantabile in B; Rondoletto (La Primavera); Rondinos (4); Polonaises (2) in D flat and G min.; Scherzos (2) in G and A min.; Toccata in G min.; Illustrations of Tennyson's Heroines (6); Tarantellas (5); Saltarella in A min.; Impromptus (3); Gavottes (5); Bourrées (4); Sarabandas (2); Valses (9); Mazurkas (5); Nocturnes (4); Songs; Berceuses (3); numerous Romanzas, Pastorales, Esquisses, &c.; 12 Studies (2 sets) in Style and Technique. *For 4 hands* L'Appassionata in G min., La Gracieuse (Rondo) in A, Andante and Bolero, Andante and Scherzo. Pianoforte Method, including 36 Original Progressive Studies. Editor of Mozart's, Bennett's, Beethoven's Sonatas, and of Popular Classics (180 numbers), &c.

*Mackenzie, Sir Alexander Campbell (Mus. Doc.), b. Aug. 22, 1847, Edinburgh. At first educated at Schwarzburg-Sondershausen, under Eduard Stein (Composition) and W. Ulrich (Vln.); afterwards at the R.A.M. under Charles Lucas (Composition), F. B. Jewson (Pf.), and Prosper Sainton (Vln.). Successor of Sir G. A. Macfarren as Principal of the R.A.M.; Conductor of the Philharmonic concerts. Mus. Doc. of the Universities of St. Andrew's and Cambridge. 1884, received the Hessian Gold Medal for Art and Science; and, 1893, the Cross of Merit, Coburg-Gotha. Knighted 1895.

Op. 13, 5 pieces; Op. 15, 3 Morceaux; Op. 20, Hymnus, Ritornello, Reminiscence, Chasse aux papillons, Rêverie, Dance; Op. 21, Rhapsodie écossaise; Op. 23, Scenes in the Scottish Highlands; Op. 24, Burns' Second Scotch Rhapsody; Op. 37, 6 pieces with Vln.; the same arranged for Pf. and V'cello; Quartet in E flat, with Vln., Vla., and V'cello; Intermezzo ("On the waters") for 4 hands.

Magnus, Désiré (really Magnus Deutz), b. June 13, 1828, Brussels; d. Jan., 1884, Paris. Pupil of Vollweiler (Heidelberg); later, at the Brussels Conserv., where he obtained the first prize. Gave concerts in England, Russia, Spain, &c. Settled in Paris as a teacher, composer, and reporter for several journals. Besides drawing-room pieces he also composed—
24 Studies for Velocity and Melody, Op. 190; and Grande Sonate, Op. 140. His Méthode élémentaire (1879) became very popular.

Mangin, Eugène Edouard, b. Dec. 9, 1837, Paris. Pupil of Marmontel at the Conserv., where he gained the second prize, 1853, and the first, 1857. 1872, he founded the Conserv. of Lyons.

Marcello, Benedetto, b. Aug. 1, 1686, Venice; d. July 24, 1739, Brescia. Pupil of Lotti and Gasparini.
Sonatas in C min., G min., F min., E flat, B flat, and A. Suites, Preludes, &c.

Marchand, Jean Louis, b. Feb. 2, 1669, Lyons; d. Feb. 17, 1732, Paris. Pupil of his father. 1697 or 1698, he went to Paris and was appointed Organist of the Jesuit Church. He was banished, 1717, owing to his bad behaviour and dissipated habits, and went to Dresden, where, in the same year, the well-known competition took place between him and Sebastian Bach. Some time after this event he was allowed to return to Paris, where he became the most fashionable teacher of the Clavecin.
Pièces de Clavecin, Paris (Ballard, 1705), and Deux Livres de pièces de Clavecin (1718).

Markull, Friedrich Wilhelm, b. Feb. 17, 1816, Reichenbach (near Elbing); d. April 30, 1887, Dantzig. Only in 1833 could he devote himself entirely to the study of music. First a pupil of his father (an organist), later of Kloss, and, 1833-35, of Fr. Schneider (Dessau). 1836, appointed principal Organist of the Marienkirche (Dantzig). He worked hard as a teacher, conductor, and composer; was Königl. Musik-Director and Conductor of a male choral society. His Pf. pieces testify to his being a thorough musician.
9 pieces, called "Auf der Reise," Op. 45, are particularly valuable. His arrangements of classical works are very good.

Marmontel, Antoine François, b. Jan. 18, 1816, Clermont-Ferrand (Puy de Dôme). Pupil at the Paris Conserv., under Zimmermann (Pf.) and Halévy and Le Sueur (Composition); gained, as early as 1832, the first prize. 1848, succeeded Zimmermann as Prof. at the Conserv., where, until quite lately, he was still working. Among his pupils were Guiraud, Paladilhe, Duvernoy, Jos. Wieniawski, Bizet, Dubois, and many others. For many years he was one of the authorities of France with respect to Pf. playing, and he received many distinctions (Legion of Honour, &c.). As a composer he was most successful in his educational works.
La première année de musique; 30 petites Etudes mélodiques, Op. 80; Etudes d'agilité et d'expression (24), Op. 9; (21), Op. 45; Ecole de mécanisme, Op. 105, 106, 107; 50 Etudes de Salon, Op. 108; L'Art de déchiffrer à quatre mains, Op. 111; Petite Grammaire populaire; Vade-mecum du professeur de Piano; L'Art classique et moderne du Piano (Advice for young Professors); Les Pianistes célèbres (Silhouettes, 1878).

Marpurg, Friedrich Wilhelm, b. Oct. 1, 1718, Seehausen (Altmark, Prussia); d. May 22, 1795, Berlin. 1746, went, as secretary of General Rothenburg, to Paris, where he made the acquaintance of Rameau and studied his system of music. After having returned to Germany (Berlin and Hamburg) he received a Royal appointment. His reputation is chiefly founded on his various theoretical works (on thorough bass, the fugue, historical and critical essays, elementary principles of musical theory, &c.) and less on his compositions.
6 Sonate per il Cembalo, 1756; Fughe e Capricci per il Cembalo, ded. to Eman. Bach, 1777; Die Kunst, das Clavier zu spielen, Vol. I., 1750, Vol. II., 1755 (3 editions published); Anleitung zum Clavierspielen, &c. (with 18 copper-plates), 1765; Clavierstücke für Anfänger und Geübtere (Pieces for beginners and for those more advanced), 3 parts, 1762-63.

Marschner, Heinrich (August), b. Aug. 16, 1795, Zittau (Saxony); d. Dec. 14, 1861, Hanover. Pupil of Schicht (Leipzig). After having been appointed teacher and conductor in Pressburg and Leipzig, he settled (1831) in Hanover as Hof-Capellmeister, where he worked for 28 years, and received (1859) his pension, with the title of General Musik-Director. His fame rests on his dramatic works; but as his Pf. compositions were in their time very popular, it is but right to mention them—
Grande Sonate, Op. 6; 4 Polonaises (4 mains), Op. 13; 3 Grandes Marches (4 mains), Op. 16; 3 Rondeaux agréables et progressives in C, G, and F, Op. 19-21; 3 Scherzi à 4 mains, Op. 28; Premier grand Trio, Op. 29; Esquisses caractéristiques, Op. 49; "La Belle Prude," Introduction and Rondo, Op. 57; Capriccio scherzando, Op. 59.

Martini, Padre Gian-Battista, b. April 25, 1706, Bologna, d. there, Oct. 3, 1784. Pupil of his father (Vln.), Padre

Predieri (Clavecin and Singing), and of Riccieri (Counterpoint). 1725, Organist of the Franciscan Church. Member of the Accademia dei Filarmonici (Bologna) and of the Arcadici (Rome).

> 12 Sonatas for Organ (Clavicembalo?), Amsterdam, 1738-1742. Sonate d'intavolatura per l'Organo e Cembalo (Op. 2), Bologna, 1747. New editions appeared in Clementi's "Practical Harmony" (4 Sonatas in Vol. II., 9 in Vol. IV.), and in Farrenc's "Trésor du Pianiste" (12 Sonatas).

Martucci, Giuseppe, b. Jan. 6, 1856, Capua. Son of a bandmaster, who gave him his first instruction. 1867-72, pupil at the Conserv. of Naples, of Cesi (Pf.), Carlo Costa (Harmony), and Paolo Serras and Lauro Rossi (Counterpoint). 1875, he visited London and Dublin; 1878, went to Paris, where he introduced several of his works with great success. 1880, appointed Prof. at the Naples Conserv., Director of the Società del Quartetto, and Conductor of the Orchestral Concerts. 1886, appointed Director of the Liceo Musicale of Bologna, which post he still holds.

> Sonata (prima), Op. 34; Fantasia for 2 Pf., Op. 32; Sonata with Vln., Op. 22; Trio in C, Op. 59 (which received the Milan prize, 1883); Capriccio di Concerto, Op. 24; Fugues, Op. 14, 18, and 28; Studio di Concerto, Op. 9; 7 Caprices, and about 20 smaller pieces; also Quintet with strings; 2 Concertos.

*Marx, Berthe, b. July 28, 1859, Paris. Daughter of a violoncellist. Showed most remarkable talent when only 3 years old. 1868, Auber (Director of the Conserv.) was so enchanted with her playing that he admitted her as a pupil without the usual preliminary examinations—a favour rarely accorded to students. First a pupil of Madame Retz. Gained the *solfège* and *harmonie* prizes and medals for Pf. playing. Then the (favourite and last) pupil of Henri Herz. Gained the first prize of the Conserv. when only 15. Has appeared in France and Belgium with great success. Since 1885 has played in association with Señor Sarasate at some 400 concerts in Continental towns and at 75 concerts in America. For the last 5 years has appeared both in London and in the provinces at Señor Sarasate's recitals. 1894, she married Otto Goldschmidt, secretary and accompanist to Señor Sarasate.

Marxsen, Eduard, b. July 23, 1806, Nienstädten (near Altona); d. Nov. 18, 1887, Altona. Pupil of Jacob Schmitt and Clasing (Hamburg), of Bocklet for Pf. and Seyfried for Composition (Vienna). After having finished his studies, he settled at Hamburg, receiving (1875) the title of Königl. Musik-Director. Among his pupils were Johannes Brahms, H. Böje, and Louis Bödecker (b. 1845 at Hamburg). He composed and published a considerable number of Pf. pieces, some of which enjoyed a certain popularity between 1840-50, but are now almost forgotten.

Mašek (Maschek), Vincent, b. April 5, 1755, Zwikovec (Bohemia); d. Nov. 15, 1831, Prague. Pupil of Franz Duschek (who must not be confused with Johann Ludwig Dussek) and Seeger. He was an excellent pianist and clever performer on the "Harmonika" (Harmonium). Mozart, when visiting Prague, spoke with decided approval of Maschek's musical abilities.

> Concertos, Sonatas, and several pieces for the Harmonika.

*Mason, Dr. William, b. Jan. 24, 1829, Boston; third son of Dr. Lowell Mason (one of the founders of the well-known harmonium manufactory, Mason and Hamlin). He played as early as 1846 at concerts; continued his studies in America till 1849, then went to Leipzig, where he entered the Conserv. and had lessons from Moscheles, Hauptmann, and Richter. After leaving Leipzig he went to Alex. Dreyschock (Prague) and spent part of the years 1853-4 in Weimar with Liszt, where H. von Bülow, C. Klindworth and Dionys Pruckner were his fellow pupils. 1853, he played twice in London; 1854, returned to America and gave Pf. recitals in Chicago and most of the larger cities. He settled eventually in New York, where he is a most successful, esteemed, and popular teacher. 1872, he received the honorary degree of Doctor of Music from Yale College. The following compositions are considered his best by the composer himself—

> Op. 4, Amitié pour moi; Op. 6, Silverspring; Op. 12, Ballade in B; Op. 13, Monody in B flat; Op. 20, Springdawn, Mazurka Caprice; Op 24, Rêverie poétique; Op. 34, Berceuse; Op. 39, Serenata; Op. 41, Scherzo. A Method for the Pf., by Mason and Hoadley; System for Beginners, &c., by Mason and Hoadley; Mason's Pf. Technics; Touch and Technic, in 4 parts, for artistic Pf. playing.

*Massart, Louise Aglaë (*née* Masson), b. June 10, 1827, Paris; d. there, July 26, 1887. Pupil of Madame Côche (1838) and of Louis Adam (1839) at the Conserv. 1875, appointed Prof. as successor of Madame Farrenc. Was highly esteemed for her excellent and

successful teaching. Madame Roger-Miclos and Mdlle. C. Kleeberg were among her pupils. With her husband, the eminent violinist, Lambert Joseph M. (1811-92), she composed—
Duets on themes from Weber's "Freischütz" and Rossini's "Comte Ory."

Massenet, Jules (Emile Frédéric), b. May 12, 1842, Montaud, near St. Etienne (Loire). Pupil at the Paris Conserv., of Laurent (Pf.), Reber (Harmony), and Ambroise Thomas (Composition). 1863, he received the Prix de Rome. He is a Membre de l'Institut, Officier de la Légion d'Honneur, and, since 1878, Prof. of Composition at the Paris Conserv. (as successor of Bazin). His best known and most popular pieces are—
Le Roman d'Arlequin; Aragonaise du "Cid"; Sarabande espagnole, du XVI. siècle; Improvisations, 20 pièces en 3 livres; 7 pièces de genre, Op. 10; Scènes de Bal, 7 morceaux à 4 mains, Op. 17; Scènes pittoresques; Scènes hongroises (2nd Suite).

*Mattei, Tito, b. May 24, 1841, Campobasso (near Naples). Pupil of his father, Alfonso M., Luigi Maggoni, Parisi, Ruta, Conti, and Thalberg. 1852 (when 11), was created "Professore dell' Accademia di Santa Cecilia" in Rome; later, "Membro" della Società dei Quiriti, Società Filarmonica di Firenze e Torino. He received a "Medaglia speciale d'oro" for playing before Pope Pius IX.; was named Pianist to the King of Italy, and received, besides other decorations, the Order of Knighthood of SS. Maurizio e Lazare. The most popular of his numerous compositions for Pf.—mostly intended for the drawing-room—is the well-known "Grande Valse." He has resided for some years in London.

*Matthay, Tobias Augustus, b. Feb. 19, 1858, Clapham (London). Pupil of Sterndale Bennett, Sullivan, and Prout for Composition, and of Dorrell and Walter C. Macfarren for Pf. 1871, he was elected to the first Sterndale Bennett Scholarship; gained, 1879, the annual medal and the "Reed" prize for a Piano Quartet; 1876-80, sub-Prof., and, 1880, Prof. at the R.A.M. Composer of a good deal of chamber music and a great number of solo pieces, of which the following have met with considerable success:
17 Variations on' an original theme; A Summer Day Dream; Moods of a Moment; A Waltz-Whim; Love Phases (3); Mono. themes (6); Scottish Dances (4); Lyrics (7).

Mattheson, Johann, born Sept. 28, 1681, Hamburg; d. there April 17, 1764. Pupil of Jacob Prätorius. 1697, he appeared as a tenor singer; 1699, as a composer, singer, and conductor (?) in his opera, "Die Plejaden." 1705, tutor to the English Ambassador's son, with whom he travelled. 1706, appointed Councillor of Legation, and, later, "Resident" (a kind of sub-Ambassador). 1715, Mus. Dir. and Canon (Canonicus) of the Hamburger Dom (Cathedral), which post he resigned (1728) on account of increasing deafness. His marvellous industry is not only shown in his highly important literary works, but also in the number of Operas (8), Oratorios (24), Cantatas, &c., that he composed.
Sonate pour le Clavecin, dédiée à qui la jouera le mieux, London, 1714; Monument-harmonique, 12 Suites pour le Clavecin, London, 1714 (a most important collection, which deserves entire re-publication). Die musikalische Fingersprache; Fugues (2 parts), 1735 and 1737; 9 Fughe per il Cembalo o l'Organo.

*Matthias (Mathias), Georges Amédée Saint-Clair, b. Oct. 14, 1826, Paris. Pupil of Kalkbrenner; later, for 4 years, of Chopin; also pupil at the Paris Conserv., under Halévy, for Composition. Was appointed Prof. (1862-87). Knight of the Legion of Honour, Commander (de numero) of the Spanish Order Isabella la Catholique, and the Saxe-Coburg medal for merit.
6 Trios for Pf., Vln., and V'cello, Op. 1, 15, 33, 36, 59, and 60; 5 morceaux symphoniques pour Pf., Vln., V'cello, Op. 30; Sonata for Pf. and Vln., Op. 68; Sonatas (Pf. solo) in B min., Op. 20; in F, Op. 35; Concerto, Op. 21; Second Concerto, Op. 57; Allegro appassionato, Op. 5; Allegro symphonique, Op. 51; 12 Pièces symphoniques, Op. 58; 10 Etudes de genre, Op. 10; Etudes de style et de mécanisme, Op. 28 (2 books). The most popular of his shorter pieces are: Nocturne et Barcarolle, Op. 3; Feuilles du printemps, Op. 8 and 17; 2ᵐᵉ Scherzo, Op. 63; 2 Pensées; Ballatina.

Mayer, Charles, b. March 21, 1799. Königsberg (Prussia); d. July 2, 1862, Dresden. His father, an excellent Cl. player, was for four years Capellmeister in St. Petersburg, then went to Moscow, where his wife taught Pf. and singing; she first instructed her highly-gifted son, but later entrusted his education to John Field, whose pupil he remained until 1814. He made his first tour in the same year, visiting Warsaw, Germany, Holland, and France with great success. 1819, he returned, being then at the height of his career as a performer and teacher, to St. Petersburg. 1845, he made a second journey, which embraced Stockholm (where he was elected Hon. Member of the Royal Academy of Music), Copenhagen.

(where the King appointed him Pianist to the Danish Court), Hamburg, Leipzig, and Vienna. In 1846, disinclined to return to the Russian capital, where Adolph Henselt had meanwhile come to the front, he settled in Dresden, and remained there till his death, working as a composer, performer, and teacher. Of his playing a contemporary says: " His style was that of the older Pf. school, much resembling that of John Field; his execution was exceedingly clear, delicate, even, and particularly brilliant in every technical detail." The same qualities distinguish his numerous and effective compositions, which are well and smoothly written.

Studies 6 Studies, Op. 31; 3 Grand Studies (No. 2, Tremolo; No. 3, Fsharp, Le ruisseau), Op. 61; Grand Studies (3), Op. 91; (3), Op. 92; 12 melodious Studies, Op. 93; 6 Etudes-Fantaisies, Op. 100; 12 Grand Studies (Für höhere Ausbildung), Op. 119; 6 melodious Studies, Op. 149; 40 Studies (4 books), Op. 168; La Vélocité, Op. 177; Ecole de la vélocité (24 Studies), Op. 200; 20 technical Studies, Op. 271; L'Art de délier les doigts, Op. 305; 25 easy Studies, Op. 340. *Other compositions:* Grand Concerto, Op. 70; Concerto Symphonique, Op. 89; Allegro de Concert, Op. 51; (2nd), Op. 60; Allegro di Bravura, Op. 102; Grande Fantaisie dramatique, Op. 54; **Concert Polonaise**, Op. 238; Valses Etudes, **Op.** 69, 71, 183, 116, **122**, †131, †133, 157; Toccata in E. *Educational Pieces:* Op. 121, Jugendblüthen (24); Op. 140, Immortelles (24); Op. 165, Flora (100); Op. 166, Mosaïque (24 romantic pieces); Op. 106, Myrthen (12).

Meglio, Vincenzo de, b. April 9, 1825, Naples. Pupil of Pasquale Mugnone; later of Francesco Lauza. He composed a considerable number of elegant and effective pieces.

Mehlig, Anna, b. July 11, 1846, Stuttgart. Pupil of Lebert, and, 1869, of Liszt. She is decidedly the most successful and best-known pupil of the "Stuttgart" School. 1869-70, she met with great success in America, and was on various occasions received with great favour in England. Since her marriage with a merchant (Falk) of Antwerp she has more or less retired from public life.

Méhul, Etienne Nicolas (not Henri), b. June 22, 1763, Givet (Ardennes); d. Oct. 18, 1817, Paris. Pupil of Wilhelm Hauser. Organist in the convent of Lavaldieu. 1778, he went to Paris. He is well-known as a dramatic composer.

3 Sonatas, Op. 1, for Pf. solo; 3 for Pf. and Vln.

Mendelssohn-Bartholdy (Jacob Ludwig), Felix, b. Feb. 3, 1809, Hamburg; d. Nov. 4, 1847, Leipzig. 1812, his father changed his residence and settled in Berlin. At first a pupil of his mother, later of Ludwig Berger (Pf.) and Zelter (Theory). 1818, he played for the first time in public; accompanied his father, 1816, to Paris, where he had lessons from Madame Bigot. 1829, he visited England for the first time, and paid further visits in 1832, 1833, 1837, 1840, 1842, 1844, and 1846. Mendelssohn's beautiful, intellectual, and thoroughly musical Pf. playing was everywhere listened to with rapture, and his improvisations were not less admired. He was Member of the Academy of Science (Berlin), Member of the "Ordre pour le mérite," and Hon. Doc. Phil. of the University of Leipzig (1836). 1843, he founded the Conserv. of Leipzig, in which he took an active part as a teacher. The King of Prussia conferred on him the title of Königlich preussischer General Musik-Director.

With Orchestra: Concertos: Op. 25, in G min. (1832); Op. 40, in D min. (1837); Capriccio in B min., Op. 22 (1832); Rondo brillant in E flat, Op. 29 (1834); Serenade and Allegro giojoso in B and D, Op. 43 (1838). *Chamber Music:* Sextuor for Pf., Vln., 2 Vla., V'cello, and C.-Bass, in D, Op. 110 (Posth.); Quartet for Pf., Vln., Vla., and V'cello, in C min , Op. 1 (1822); ditto, in F min., Op. 2 (1823); ditto, in B min., Op. 3 (1824). Trios for Pf., Vln., and V'cello, in D min., Op. 49 (1839); in C min., Op. 66 (1845). Sonatas for Pf. and Vln., in F min., Op. 4; for Pf. and V'cello (No. 1), in B flat, Op. 45 (1838); (No. 2), in D, Op. 58 (1843); Variations concertantes for Pf. and V'cello, in D, Op. 17 (1829); Song without words for Pf. and V'cello, in D, Op. 109 (Posth.). *Solo music:* Sonatas in E, Op. 6 (1826); in G min., Op. 105 (Posth.); in B flat, Op. 106 (Posth.). Capriccio in F sharp min., Op. 5 (1825); 7 Characteristic Pieces, Op. 7 (1824-28); Rondo capriccioso in E, Op. 14; Fantasia in E, Op. 15; 3 Caprices or Fantasias in A min., E min., and E, Op. 16 (1829); Fantasia in F sharp min., Op. 28 (1833); 3 Caprices in A min. (1834), E (1835), and B flat min. (1833), Op. 33. 6 Preludes and Fugues, Op. 35: No. 1, in E min., Prelude (1837), Fugue; No. 2, in D, Prelude (1836), Fugue (1837); No. 3, in B min., Prelude (1836), Fugue (1832); No. 4, in A flat, Prelude (1837), Fugue (1835); No. 5, in F min., Prelude (1836), Fugue, 1834; No. 6, in B flat, Prelude (1837), Fugue (1836). Variations sérieuses, in D min., Op. 54 (1841); 6 Christmas Pieces, Op. 72; Variations in E flat, Op. 82 (1841); ditto, in B flat, Op. 83 (1841); 3 Preludes, B flat, B min., and D, and 3 Studies, B flat min, F, and A min., Op. 104; Albumblatt in E min., Op. 117; Capriccio in E, Op. 118; Perpetuum mobile in C, Op. 119. Songs without words: Book I., Op. 19, E, A min., A, A, F sharp min., G min. (1830); Book II., Op. 30, E flat (1834), B flat min., E, B min. (1834), D (1833), F sharp min.; Book III., Op. 38, E flat, C min., E, A, A min. (1837), A flat ; Book IV., Op. 53, A flat, E flat, G min., F, A min. (1841), A (1841); Book V., Op. 62, G (1844), B flat (1843), E min. (1843), G (1843), A min.,

A (1842); Book VI., Op. 67, E flat (1844), F sharp min. (1839), B flat (1845), C (1843), B min. (1844), E; Book VII., Op. 85, F, A min. (1843), E flat, D (1845), A (1845), B flat (1841); Book VIII., Op. 102, E min., D, C, G min., A, C. Prelude (1841); Fugue in E min. (1827); Andante cantabile and Presto agitato (1838); Study, F min., and Scherzo, B min. (1836); Scherzo à Capriccio, F sharp min.; 2 Pieces, B flat and G min.; Gondoliera in A. *For 4 hands:* Andante and Variations in B flat, Op. 83 (1844?); Allegro brillante in A, Op. 92 (1841).

*Menter, Sophie, daughter of the excellent violoncellist, Joseph M. (1808-56); b. July 29, 1848, Munich, where she was at first a pupil of Schönchen; later, of L. Lebert (with Stark, founder of the Stuttgart Conserv.) and Niest. 1863, she appeared for the first time in public; 1867, she created an unusual *furore* in Frankfort o/M; in Leipzig; the same year, she made the acquaintance of Charles Tausig, who persuaded her to become his pupil in Berlin. 1869, she met Liszt in Vienna, who took the warmest interest in her career, encouraged and assisted her in every way, and often declared that " many call themselves my artistic children, but I recognise in Sophie Menter the only legitimate child of my muse." 1872, she married the famous violoncellist, Popper, which union was dissolved in 1886. The Prince of Hohenzollern appointed her Court Pianist; 1868, the University of Utrecht elected her Hon. Student, the King of Sweden bestowed a decoration on her, the Emperor of Austria appointed her Imperial Court Pianist, and the Conserv. of Prague gave her the title of "Hon. Prof." 1878, she accepted the post of Prof. at the Conserv. of St. Petersburg, but resigned in 1881. She is received with great enthusiasm wherever she appears. Her greatest merits are: never-failing clearness, accuracy and correctness of execution, nobility of feeling, tenderness and warmth of expression. Her technical execution baffles description. She resides at her castle Itter, in the Tyrol. Her most distinguished pupil is Wassily Sapellnikoff.

Mereaux, Jean Amédée le Froid de, b. 1803, Paris; d. April 25, 1874, Rouen. Pupil of his father and Reicha. 1835, he settled in Rouen, and was most successful and popular as a teacher. Here he composed 5 books of Grandes Etudes, which were approved by the musical section of the Institut de France, and used at the Paris Conserv. 1858, he was elected a Member of the Academy of Science, Rouen, and later Chevalier of the Legion of Honour. An excellent pianist, but best known as the editor of the valuable publication—
"Les Clavecinistes de 1637 à 1790. Œuvres choisies, classées dans leur ordre chronologique, revues, doigtées et accentuées avec les agréments et ornements du temps, traduits en toutes notes." (Paris, 1867.)

Merkel, Gustav Adolf, b. Nov. 12, 1827, Oberoderwitz, near Zittau; d. Oct. 29-30, 1885, Dresden. Pupil of Julius Otto (Counterpoint), Schneider (Organ), and Reissiger. R. Schumann also took great interest in his career. 1864, Hof-Organist, and, since 1861, Prof. at the Dresden Conserv.
Op. 81, Bagatelles (4); Op. 82, Tonblüthen (4); Op. 91, Haideröschen; Op. 92, Tarantelle; Op. 112, Polonaise; Op. 113, Impromptu; Op. 119, Reigen; Op. 120, Lenz und Liebe (5 pieces, †Nos. 1 and 5); Op. 121, Cantabile; Op. 125, 4 easy Sonatinas; Op. 126, 2 Sonatinas, Op. 136, 2 instructive Sonatinas; Op. 154, 2 Rondos; Op. 161, Lyrische Blätter (†Nos. 1 and 4); Op. 180, Skizzen; Op. 181, Miniatur bilder (3 pieces).

*Mertke, Eduard, b. June 17, 1833, Riga. Pupil of his father, later of S. v. Lutzau (Pf.) and Agthe (Theory). He performed in public when only in his tenth year. 1850, he went to St. Petersburg, where he was well received by A. Henselt and the violinist, Maurer, his concerts in St. Petersburg and Moscow meeting with undoubted success. 1853, he went to Leipzig and entered the Conserv. David, recognising his ability as a violinist, placed him among the first violinists in the Gewandhaus Concerts orchestra. He retained this post for six years. 1859, he made a tour as a pianist in Scandinavia. After his return to Leipzig he was appointed, 1860, Mus. Dir. at Wesserling (Alsace). When he left this small town he settled in Lucerne for four years. 1865 (Sept.), he went to Freiburg, but musical affairs being in a very unsettled state there, he gladly accepted the invitation of Vinzenz Lachner to establish himself as a teacher and performer in Mannheim. 1869, appointed Prof. at the Cologne Conserv., which post he still holds (1893). Taking great interest in educational matters, he published the valuable work—
Technical exercises for mechanism, ornamentation, and rhythm, and School of Octaves. He edited the Concerted Pieces of Mendelssohn, Weber, and Hummel, with a compressed score for second Pf. He also edited Chopin's works, and published paraphrases of Wagner's operas. 12 transcriptions of Songs by Schumann, Impromptus à la Valse on Songs by Schubert, " Ukrainische Melodien," &c. Composer of Op. 8, Suite in G min.; **Op. 7**, 4 pieces; Op. 23, Nocturne and Valse.

Meyer, Leopold von, b. Dec. 20, 1816, Baden (near Vienna); d. March 5-6, 1883, Dresden. Pupil of Czerny and Fischhof. His wonderfully graduated touch, delicacy, and elegance of performance created not only in Vienna, but also in Russia, America, &c., a great sensation. With regard to force he was unrivalled, without ever injuring his instrument. As a composer he is insignificant. His writings display a lamentable want of correctness, which, however, did not prevent his Waltzes and Polkas, when played by him, electrifying his audiences in all parts of the world. As a performer he was demonstrative to such a degree that the risible muscles of the audience were frequently called into activity. His specialty being light music and dances, it is intelligible that the classical style should be entirely opposed to his nature. His most popular compositions were:—

Op. 21, Nocturne; Op. 22, Machmudier, Air guerrier des Turcs; Op. 23, Bajazeth, Air national des Turcs; Op. 45, †Air bohémien russe; Op. 124, Air turque de Nedjies Pasha; Op. 180, Souvenir de Vienne, Valse; the †Grillen and †Pepita Polkas.

***Micheux, Georges,** b. 1805, Laibach (Illyria); d. Sept. 1, 1892, at the Château de Villeroy, belonging to his patroness, Countess de Vaucouleur. He received his musical education in Vienna, where he enjoyed the friendship of Franz Schubert. 1848, he settled in Paris, teaching and composing, but having to contend with many adversities. His best known compositions, mostly elegant and showy drawing-room pieces, are—

Echos de Hongrie, Op. 50; 6 Mélodies sympathiques, Op. 112.

Mihalovich, Edmund von, b. Sept. 13, 1842, Fericsaucze (Croatia). Studied at the College of Pesth, had lessons in harmony from Mosonyi (1814-70). 1865, went to Leipzig; was instructed in Composition by Hauptmann, and, later, by Bülow (Pf.), at Munich. His compositions belong to the New German School; his *Ballades* obtained a very considerable success. He resides at Pesth.

***Mikuli, Carl,** b. Oct. 22, 1821, Czernowitz (Bukowina), where he was first educated. 1839, he went to Vienna to study medicine; but his desire to become a musician was so great, and his talent for Pf. playing and Composition so decided, he finally devoted himself entirely to the study of music. 1844, he went to Paris, and became Chopin's pupil, while Reber instructed him in Composition. The political events of 1848 obliged him to leave Paris and to return to his native place. He then made several professional journeys through Russia, Roumania, and Galicia. His success in the latter country was so great that, in 1858, he was appointed Director of the Lemberg Conserv., which post he held until 1888, when he himself founded a music school which is attended by 172 pupils. 1889, the Emperor of Austria conferred on him the Order of Francis Joseph. He published an edition of Chopin's works (Leipzig: Kistner), for which he had the great privilege of using all the marks made by Chopin in Mikuli's copies. The preface to this edition is of great interest and undoubted importance with respect to Chopin's style of playing and method of teaching. Mikuli is an excellent pianist, and his compositions, although greatly influenced by his master, are of considerable merit and interest.

Op. 2, 3, 4, 10, and 11, Mazourkas; Op. 8, 2 Polonaises; Op. 9, 6 Pieces: 1, Prelude; 2, Agitato; 3, †Etude; 4, Lied; 5, Scherzino; 6, Reverie. Op. 12, Etude; Op. 13, 6 Danses allemandes; Op. 18, Valses; Op. 19, 2 Nocturnes; Op. 20, Valse; Op. 21, Ballade; Op. 21, 10 pieces (2 books); Op. 14, Meditation, and Op. 15, †Andante con Variazioni (both for 4 hands); Op. 22, Serenade for Pf. and Cl. Arrangements of orchestral parts for a second Pf. of Chopin's Op. 2, Variations; Op. 11, Concerto, No. 1; Op. 13, Grande Fantaisie; Op. 14, Krakowiak; Op. 21, Concerto, No. 2; Op. 22, Polonaise. The edition of the well-known Nocturne (Op. 9, No. 2, in E flat), with Chopin's authentic ornaments, is of great interest.

Mills, Sebastian Bach, b. March 13, 1838, Cirencester (Gloucestershire). At first a pupil of his father, later (1856-59) of Plaidy and Moscheles at the Conserv. of Leipzig. 1859, went to America, where his playing met with so much success that he resolved to settle in New York, where he is still one of the most popular and admired performers and, as a teacher, very successful. He published several effective pieces.

Mockwitz, Friedrich, b. March 5, 1785, Lauterbach near Stolpen (Saxony); d. 1849, Dresden. At first his parents desired him to study law, but soon yielded to his wish to devote himself to music. He settled in Dresden and was highly successful as a teacher. Since 1809 his name has become favourably known as an experienced arranger of overtures, symphonies, quintets, and quartets of the classical masters. His arrangements are practical, effective, and keep closely to the original text.

Moniuszko, Stanislaus, b. May 5, 1819, Ubiel, Minsk (an estate belonging to his father); d. June 4, 1872, Warsaw. Pupil of the organist Freyer, of Warsaw, and (1837-39) of Rungenhagen in Berlin. After struggling hard to earn a livelihood as a teacher, he became Organist in Wilna. Was afterwards appointed Conductor of the Opera, and lastly Prof. at the Conserv. at Warsaw. A Polonaise of his became generally known, and it may be mentioned that Tausig (Op. 2) composed a Fantasia on his Opera "Halka."

Montigny-Rémaury, Fanny Marceline Caroline, b. Jan. 22, 1843, Pamiers, Ariège. Pupil of Le Couppey. Excellent performer, who visited London on various occasions, where her performances met with as great a success as in Paris, where her name is well known.

Mortier de Fontaine (*see* Fontaine).

Moscheles, Ignaz, b. May 30, 1794, Prague; d. March 10, 1870, Leipzig. Pupil of Dionys Weber. He was able to play a Concerto of his own composition in public when only 14 years old. Soon after this first success he lost his father. With considerable reluctance his mother consented to send him to Vienna, where he was a pupil of Albrechtsberger and Salieri, whilst Beethoven took great interest in his progress. Sincere friendship connected him with Hummel and Meyerbeer, both at this time in Vienna. 1816, he undertook a professional tour to Munich, Dresden, and Leipzig. 1820, went to Paris, where he created a great *furore*. 1821, he settled in London; became a Director of the Philharmonic Society and Prof. at the R.A.M. Repeated journeys to the Continent brought him into contact with Mendelssohn, Schumann, and almost all the leading artists. Mendelssohn's devotion to Moscheles is as well known as Schumann's respect for his admirable qualities. When Mendelssohn founded the Leipzig Conserv. he was anxious to secure Moscheles as a teacher. The latter complied with his friend's wish, left London (1846), and settled in Leipzig, where he was actively working until a few days before his death. His pupils were very numerous, and came from every European and American town to profit by his sound and vast experience. His playing was very brilliant, full of fire and energy, and sharply rhythmicised. His compositions may be classified in two distinct categories—the popular and the educational. Of the first almost all the different works have been forgotten, whilst the second form a most important contribution to the classical literature of the Pf. His best works are—

Concerto (G min.), Op. 58; Concerto (C), Op. 87; Concerto Fantastique (B flat), Op. 90. Concertos less known are: Op. 45, 56, 64, 93, and 96; Souvenir d'Irlande, Op. 69; Sextuor for Pf., Vln., Fl., 2 Hns., V'cello, and C.-Bass, Op. 35; Sonata for Pf. and V'cello, Op. 121; Hommage à Händel (2 Pf.), Op. 92; Duo Concertante (2 Pf.) on Weber's " Preciosa " (with Mendelssohn), Op. 87b; Les Contrastes (2 Pf., 8 hands), Op. 115; Sonata in E flat (4 hands), Op. 47; Sonata Symphonique in B min. (4 hands), Op. 112; 24 Characteristic Studies, Op. 70; 12 Characteristic Studies, Op. 95; 50 Preludes, Op. 73; 4 Etudes de Concert, Op. 111; 2 Studies for the Beethoven Album, Op. 105; 2 Studies l'Ambition, l'Enjouement; Sonate Mélancolique, F sharp min., Op. 49; La Tenerezza, Rondo, Op. 52; Les Charmes de Paris, Op. 54; Cadenzas for Beethoven's Concertos. The works up to Op. 80 were published before 1830. His works reach the Opus number 142.

Moszkowski, Moritz, b. Aug. 23, 1854, Breslau where he received his first instruction. His father took him later to Dresden, where he entered the Conserv., and afterwards to Berlin, where he became a pupil of Kullak (Pf.) and Wüerst (Composition). 1873, he gave his first Concert, in which he created an unusual *furore* by his excellent, brilliant, technically finished, and elegant playing, and not less by the originality, freshness, and melodiousness of his compositions, which at once procured for the highly gifted young artist a rare popularity. His most celebrated compositions are—

Op. 5, Hommage à Schumann; Op. 15, 6 Pieces: †Serenade, Arabeske, Mazurka, Canon, Walzer, †Barcarole; Op. 17, 3 Pieces: Polonaise, †Minuet, and Walzer; Op. 18, 5 Pieces: Melodie, †Scherzino, †Etude, Marcia, Polonaise; Op. 24, 3 Concert Studies (†No. 2, Les vagues); Op. 27, Barcarole and †Tarantelle; Op. 28, 5 Miniatures; Op. 36, 8 Pieces: Pièce Rococo, Rêverie, †Expansion, †En automne, Air de Ballett, †Etincelles, Valse sentimentale, Pièce rustique; Op. 37, Caprice Espagnol; Op. 42, 3 Morceaux poétiques; Valse in A flat; Suite, Op. 50. *Duets:* †Op. 8, 5 Waltzes; †Op. 12, Spanish Dances; †Op. 21, Album Espagnol; †Op. 23, From foreign parts; Op. 25, German Rounds; Op. 33, 4 Duets (Kindermarsch, †Humoreske, †Tarantella, †Spinnerlied).

Mozart, Leopold, b. Nov. 14, 1719, Augsburg; d. May 28, 1787, Salzburg.

Son of a bookbinder. He devoted himself to music. 1743, became Hofmusikus to the Archbishop of Salzburg, and (1762) Vice-Capellmeister. He was one of the best instructed musicians of his time, and the excellent education he gave his great son testifies to his intelligence and commonsense.

> Der Morgen und der Abend, den Inwohnern der Hochfürstlichen Residenzstadt Salzburg melodisch und harmonisch angekündigt; oder 12 Musikstücke für das Clavier. Augsburg, 1759. (The Morning and Evening, 12 pieces for the Clavier. Augsburg, 1759). Musikalische Schlittenfahrt (Musical Sledge Drive). (Peters.)

Mozart, Wolfgang Amadeus (really Johannes Chrysostomus Wolfgang Gottlieb), b. Jan. 27, 1756, Salzburg; d. Dec. 5, 1791, Vienna. When only in his fourth year he received instruction from his father, Leopold M., and having reached his sixth year he made his first tour, with his sister, Anna Maria. In Munich, Vienna, (1763) in Paris and Brussels, and (1764) in London (see C. F. Pohl's "Mozart and Haydn in London") the young artists were received with the greatest enthusiasm. 1765, he left London for Holland, and returned (1766) viâ Paris to Salzburg. 1768, he went again to Vienna; returned (1769) to Salzburg; was appointed Concertmeister to the Archbishop, but left in the same year, and went with his father to Milan and Rome. In Rome the Pope conferred on him the Order of the Golden Spur. He was elected a Member of the Philharmonic Society of Bologna, and made there the acquaintance of Padre Martini, and of Sammartini at Milan and Valotti at Padua. 1771, he was again in Salzburg, but returned (1771-72) to Italy. In spite of his great success as an artist, his pecuniary circumstances were in a deplorable state, and when he returned to Salzburg he planned another tour, for which, however, the Archbishop refused his permission. Upon this, Mozart resigned his post, and went, accompanied by his mother, to Munich, Augsburg, Mannheim, and Paris. In Paris he lost his mother (1778); returned to Salzburg; was in Munich, 1781; and settled afterwards in Vienna, where the Emperor Joseph II. appointed him Imperial Capellmeister, which post he retained until his death. Mozart's Pf. compositions are works of the greatest beauty and importance. For gracefulness, sweetness of expression, never-ceasing euphony, he is unrivalled. Moreover, the study of his works is indispensable for all who would learn to play with fluency, steadiness, and natural expression. We find in his Pf. works an undeniable feeling for beauty and symmetry. Everything harsh and disconnected, all disorder, eccentricity, and rhapsodical excitement he regarded with antipathy. He did not care for mere technical playing. We observe everywhere the inclination to make the instrument sing; even in his most rapid passages he is harmonious and melodious. We recognise in his best Pf. works his innate sense for order, nature, and beauty—qualities which were predominant in his character.

Sonatas: In C, 4/4 (1777); in F, 3/4 (1777); †B flat, 2/4 (1777); E flat, 4/4 (1777); †G, 3/4 (1777); D, 4/4 (1777); †C, 4/4 (1778); †A min., 4/4 (1778); D, 4/4 (1778); C, 2/4 (1779); †A, 6/8 (1779); †F, 3/4 (1779); B flat, 4/4 (1779); †Cmin. (preceded by the Fantasia), 4/4 (1785); C (for beginners), 4/4 (1788); B flat, 3/4 (1789); †D, 6/8 (1789); †F, 4/4 (Allegro and Andante, 1788; Rondo, 1786). *For 4 hands:* Sonatas in G, 3/4 (1786); †B flat, 4/4 (1780); †D, 4/4 (1781); F, 3/4 (1786); C, 4/4 (1787); Fugue in G min., 4/4 (1782). *Fantasias:* In †C, 4/4, with a Fugue (1782); C min., 4/4 (1782); D min., 4/4 (1782); †C min., 4/4, followed by the Sonata (1785). *For 4 hands:* Fantasia, Adagio, 3/4, and Allegro, 4/4, in F min. and maj. (1790); †Fantasie in F min., 4/4 (1791). *Variations:* In G, 2/4 (1765); Willem von Nassau in D, 4/4 (1765); F, 2/4 (1768); Minuet de Fischer in C, 3/4 (1773); "Mio caro Adone" in G, 3/4 (1773); "Lison dormait" in C, 2/4 (1776); "Ah vous dirai-je, Mama," in C, 2/4 (1776); Mariage des Samnites in F, 4/4 (1780); "La belle Française" in E flat, 6/8 (1780); "Je suis Lindor" in E flat, 2/4 (1780); Salve tu Domine in F, 3/4 (1782); †"Unser dummer Pöbel meint" in G, 4/4 (1784); "Come un agnello" in A, 3/4 (1784); B flat, 4/4 (1786); Minuet de Duport in D, 3/4 (1789); †"Ein Weib ist das herrlichste" in F, 3/4 (1791). *For 4 hands* †Variations in G, 2/4 (1786). *For 2 Clavecins* Fugue in C min., 4/4 (1783); †Sonata in D, 4/4 (1784). *For 2 hands:* Rondo in D, 4/4 (1786); †A min., 6/8 (1787); in F, 2/4 (1791), originally written for a musical box; Suite in C, 4/4 (1782-83); Allegro, G min., 3/4 (1778); B flat, 4/4 (1782); †Adagio in B min., 4/4 (1788); †Gigue in G, 6/8 (1789). Minuets: In G, B flat, F, and D (1761-62); in D (1780); Waltz, B flat. *Sonatas with Vln.:* 4 (1763); 6 (1764); 6 (1765); 7 (1768); †Sonata in C, 4/4 (1778); †G, 3/4 (1778); E flat, 3/4 (1778); C, 4/4 (1778); †E min., 4/4 (1778); A, 6/8 (1778); †D, 4/4 (1778); †F, 4/4 (1781); F, 4/4 (1781); †B flat, 4/4 (1781); G, 2/4 (1781); E flat, 4/4 (1781); †A, 3/4 (1782); C, 4/4 (1782); C, 4/4 (1784); †B flat, 4/4 (1784); †E flat, 3/4 (1785); †A, 6/8 (1787); F, 4/4 (1788), for beginners. *Trios:* For Clavecin, Vln., and V'cello: In B flat, 3/4 (1776); D min., 4/4 (1783); G, 4/4 (1786); †E flat, 6/8 (1786). For Clavecin, Cl., and Vla.: In B flat, 4/4 (1786); E, 3/4 (1788); C, 4/4 (1788); G, 4/4 (1788). *Quartets and Quintets:* †G min., 4/4 (1785); †E flat, 4/4 (1786); E flat, 4/4, with Ob., Cl., Horn and Bssn. (1784). *Concertos:* In F, 4/4; B flat, 4/4; D, 4/4; G, 3/4 (1767);

D, 4/4 (1773); B flat, 4/4 (1776); C, 4/4 (1776); †E flat, 4/4 (1777); F, 3/4 (1782); A, 4/4 (1782); C, 4/4 (1782-83); E flat, 3/4 (1784); †B flat, 4/4 (1784); D, 4/4 (1784); G, 4/4 (1784); B flat, 4/4 (1784); F, 4/4 (1784); †D min., 4/4 (1785); †C, 4/4 (1785); †E flat, 4/4 (1785); †A, 4/4 (1785); |C min., 3/4 (1786); †C, 4/4 (1786); †D, 4/4 (1788); B flat, 4/4 (1791). For 2 Clavecins: E flat, 4/4 (1780). For 3 Clavecins: F, 4/4 (1776). 35 cadenzas for his Concertos.

Mozart, Wolfgang Amadeus (second son of the above), b. July 26, 1791, Vienna; d. July 29, 1844, Carlsbad (Bohemia). His early education was directed by Franz and Josepha Duschek and Prof. Franz Niemczek of Prague, intimate friends of his illustrious father. 1802, instructed by Andreas Streicher, in Vienna, published a Quartet and became, 1804, a pupil of Hummel, Vogler, and Albrechtsberger. 1804, he played at his own concert a Concerto in C (Op. 14) and Variations on the Minuet (Don Giovanni) of his own composition. 1811, he performed in Lemberg, was appointed teacher to the family of Count Baworowski. Was six years in Lemberg, then returned (playing in Warsaw, Königsberg, Danzig, Prague, Leipzig, &c.) to Vienna, where he remained till 1822, when he settled until 1838 in Lemberg, conducting the musical society and highly respected as a teacher 1838, he went again to Vienna, and remained there until June, 1844. His performances of his father's Concertos and Sonatas were remarkable for sincerity of feeling and correctness of execution. During the winter evenings (Tuesdays) of 1838-44, his two modestly furnished rooms were the meeting-place of the most celebrated musicians, poets, painters, &c., of Vienna, who listened to excellent quartet playing by Jansa, Durst, Zäch, and Borzaga.

Sonata in G, Op. 10; Concerto, Op. 25; Rondo favori in F; Variations, Op. 16 (Marche de Coriolan); Op. 20 (Russian air); and 4 other sets of variations.

Müller, August Eberhard, b. Dec. 13, 1767, Nordheim (Göttingen); d. Dec. 3, 1817, Weimar. Pupil of his father, an organist, later of Joh. Christoph Bach (ninth son of Seb. B.), who resided at Bückeburg. As his father had a numerous family he was obliged to begin earning his living when only 14 years old. His excellent performances on the clavecin and flute procured him a modest income and the friendship of many influential people. 1789, he settled in Magdeburg, and was appointed Organist of St. Ulrich's Church. 1792, visited Berlin, where he was cordially received by Marpurg, Fasch, and Reichardt, the latter recommending him for the post of Organist of the "Nicolai" Church at Leipzig. Here he soon became the friend and assistant of Joh. Adam Hiller and was, on Hiller's death (1804), unanimously elected Cantor of the Thomas School. 1807 and 1809, he taught the Princess of Saxe-Weimar, and was appointed Capellmeister (1810), retaining this appointment until his death. His works for clavecin (later piano) are of considerable importance—

Grands Caprices (6), Op. 29 (in †E min., †C, D flat, †C min., †B min., †G flat); ditto (3), Op. 31 (in A, †C, D min.); ditto (3), Op. 34 (in †F min., †G sharp min., E flat); ditto (3), Op. 41 (in D, D flat, †G min.); 3 Sonatas, Op. 7 (in A, E flat, and C); Concerto in E flat, Op. 21; Trio, and several other Sonatas; cadenzas for 8 Concertos by Mozart. *Educational works:* Pianoforte School (1804); the eighth edition was revised by C. Czerny. Small elementary book for pianists (new edition by C. Czerny).

Müller, Christian Heinrich, b. Oct. 10, 1734, Halberstadt; d. there Aug. 29, 1782, when Cathedral Organist. He was one of the first who wrote sonatas for 4 hands. Three of them were published at Dessau in 1783. Their somewhat curious title is:

"3 Sonaten für's Clavier als Doppelstücke, für 2 Personen mit vier Händen."

Müthel, Johann Gottfried, b. 1729, Möllin (Lauenburg); d. (date unknown), Riga. When only 17 years old, he was appointed Hof-Organist at Schwerin (Mecklenburg). After some years, received permission to become a pupil of Seb. Bach, in whose house he went to live. After Bach's death he went to Bach's son-in-law, Altnikol (Naumburg), and later to Emanuel Bach (Berlin). Returned to Schwerin for 2 years, and then became Director of an orchestra at Riga; he was also appointed Organist of the principal church there. Müthel was one of the most distinguished performers of his time on the organ and clavecin.

2 Concerti per il Cembalo, with Orchestra (Riga and Mitau, 1767); Duo for 2 Clavecins or Pfs. (Riga, 1771); 3 Sonate e 2 Ariosi, con 12 Variazioni (Nürnberg, Haffner).

Muffat, Georg, year of birth unknown; d. Feb. 23, 1704, Salzburg. He was for 6 years in Paris, where he made himself acquainted with Lully's style. Afterwards (up to 1675) Organist of the Strassburg Minster, which he resigned on account of the war. Went to Vienna and Rome, and was appointed (about 1690) Organist and Kammerdiener (butler) to the Archbishop of Salzburg and (1695) Capellmeister of the Court at Passau, where he also officiated as tutor to the pages. In this situation he remained until his death. The following work is of interest to clavecinists—

"Apparatus Musico Organisticus" (Augsburg, 1690). It contains 12 Toccatas, a Ciaccona, Passacaglia and Aria, and is dedicated to the Emperor Leopold I. (1640-1705). His son,

Muffat, August Gottlieb (Theophilus), b. April 25, 1690, Passau; d. Dec. 10, 1770, Vienna. Pupil of Fux, and, about 1727, Organist to the Imperial Austrian Court. His chief work is—

"Componimenti musicali per il Cembalo," ded. to the Emperor Charles VI. (1685-1740). The Court Library of Vienna possesses, in MS., Preludes, Fugues, Toccatas, old dances, a Partita in C, &c. Farrenc has published the entire work "Componimenti," &c., in his "Trésor du Pianiste."

Murschhauser, Franz Xaver Anton, b. (about) 1670, Zabern (Alsace); d. 1733. Munich. Pupil of J. Caspar Kerl until his death (1690). He succeeded him as Organist of the Frauen-Kirche.

Aria pastoralis variata in G (Pauer's "Alte Clavier-musik"). His works for organ are of considerable importance.

N.

Naegeli, Johann Georg, b. 1768, Zürich; d. there Dec. 26, 1836. He received his education at Berne, his native town, where he founded (1792) a music publishing business. 1803, he began to issue the "Répertoire des Clavecinistes," which consisted of works by Clementi, Cramer, Dussek, Steibelt, Beethoven, and others. It is well known that he was not over-conscientious in the publication of Beethoven's Sonatas, for—to cite only one instance—he added four bars towards the end of the first movement of the Sonata, Op. 31, No. 1, which alteration offended the great composer in the highest degree. Of his Pf. compositions only 12 Toccatas were published. One of the most popular of his songs is "Life let us cherish," of which the melody, according to the latest researches, belongs to the South of France. His literary productions are held in great respect in Switzerland, and it may be asserted that he alone, among his compatriots, influenced the progress of music in his country.

Napoleon (Napoleão), Arthur, b. March 6, 1843, Oporto. Pupil of his father (who was of German extraction) and of Charles Hallé. As early as 1845 he gave concerts, and created a great sensation. His compositions are popular and elegant. Since 1871 he has settled in Rio de Janeiro as a music-seller and agent of the foremost European Pf. manufacturers.

Naumann, Johann Gottlieb, b. April 17, 1741, Blasewitz, near Dresden; d. Oct. 23, 1801, Dresden. Pupil at the Kreuzschule, Dresden, but mostly self-taught. A rich Swedish musician, Weeström, heard him play Bach's pieces, and decided to take him as a companion to Italy; but, owing to unexpected bad treatment, Naumann parted from Weeström at Padua, and remained there alone, enjoying for three years Tartini's instruction in harmony; he also met Hasse. Tartini recommended him to Padre Martini, in Bologna, who gave him lessons in Counterpoint. 1764, the Princess Maria Antonia of Saxony, widow of the Palatine, offered him the post of Church Composer, and (1765) he was appointed Court Composer.

Concerto; Quartet, Op. 1; and 6 Sonatas, Op. 4.

Neate, Charles, b. March 28, 1784, London; d. March 30, 1877, Brighton. Pupil of John Field. Resided in London. Was highly respected as a teacher and promoter of the best interests of musical art.

A treatise on Fingering; Sonata in C min., Op. 2, published in Vienna.

Neefe, Christian Gottlob, b. Feb. 5, 1748, Chemnitz (Saxony); d. Jan. 26, 1798, Dessau. His youth was a very melancholy one; although his talent for music was evident, his father, a tailor, was too poor to cultivate it. 1769, he resolved to study law at the University of Leipzig, but at the same time occupied himself with the theoretical works of Marpurg and Emanuel Bach. Joh. Adam Hiller, taking great interest in the young musician, gave him good advice and recommended him (1776) as Conductor of the "Seiler" troupe, which played, till 1777, at Leipzig and Dresden. This company being dissolved in 1779, he went to Bonn as

Conductor of the "Grossmann-Hellmuth" company. Here he taught Beethoven. He remained there until 1796, but had—as the Palatine Max Franz was obliged to dissolve his princely establishment — to struggle hard to earn sufficient to keep himself and his family. His daughter, Louise, a clever singer, was engaged at the theatre of Dessau (1796) and her father was appointed Conductor. The death of his beloved wife accelerated his end. Neefe was not only an excellent musician, good composer, and admirable teacher, but also a man of sterling character and high intellectual capacities.

> Concerto for Clav. and Vln. (with orchestra); 12 Sonatas (Leipzig, 1772); 6 new Sonatas with Variations (1774); Fantasia; Variations; 6 Sonatas with Vln.

Neitzel, Dr. Otto, b. July 6, 1852, Falckenburg (Pomerania). Pupil at Kullak's "Neue Akademie der Tonkunst" (Berlin). Studied Philosophy and Art History at the Berlin University, and received, 1875, the diploma of Doc. Phil. After having resided for some time in Weimar and received advice from Liszt, he accompanied the singer, Madame Lucca, and the celebrated violinist, Sarasate, on their professional tours. Was appointed teacher at the Conserv. of Strassburg (Alsace), where he also conducted the Musical Society, and was for two years Capellmeister of the Strassburg theatre. 1881-85, was Prof. at the Imperial Conserv. of Moscow; went afterwards to Cologne to be teacher at the Conserv., which appointment he resigned, July, 1887, in order to act as musical reporter to the *Cologne Gazette*. He is an excellent pianist, and being well acquainted with piano literature his criticisms are full of interest and useful suggestions. At the present time he is again appearing as a public performer.

Neukomm, Sigismund, Chevalier de, b. July 10, 1778, Salzburg; d. April 3, 1858, Paris. Pupil of Michael Haydn (Salzburg) and (1798) of Joseph Haydn (Vienna). 1808, he published, by Joseph Haydn's advice, his first compositions, which were received with so much approval that both the Academies of St. Petersburg and of Stockholm elected him a Member. 1809, he went to St. Petersburg, and acted for some time as Capellmeister of the Imperial Opera; but this work not being sympathetic to his more earnest and refined taste, he subsequently went to Paris, where he enjoyed the friendship of Grétry, Cherubini, the great zoologist Cuvier, and other renowned persons. The Princess of Lothringen Vauvémont, who took a motherly interest in the young and highly-accomplished artist, introduced him to Talleyrand, who took so great a liking to him that he invited him to occupy apartments in his own house. 1814, accompanied Talleyrand to Vienna, where he composed a Requiem in memory of Louis XVI., for which Louis XVIII. made him a Chevalier of the Legion of Honour and conferred the rank of nobility on him. 1816, he accompanied the Duke of Luxemburg, the French Ambassador, to Rio de Janeiro (Brazil), where he remained until 1821, when he left with the Duke for Lisbon, but soon returned to Talleyrand in Paris. After many years of travelling in Holland, Belgium, Italy, and visits to London and the German capitals, he divided his time between Paris and London, staying in the latter city with his friend, Chevalier de Bunsen.

> Sonata, Op. 14; Sonata, "Le retour à la vie," Op. 40; Fantasia-Sonata; Elégie harmonique sur la mort de J. L. Dussek; ditto, sur la mort de la Princesse de Courland; L'amitié et l'amour; 2 Esquisses, 12 Valses, Caprices, Polonaises, and an Elegy on Chopin's death.

Neupert, Edmund, b. April 1, 1842, Christiania; d. June 22, 1888, New York. 1858, pupil at Kullak's Conserv. (Berlin); afterwards travelled in Germany, Sweden, and Norway, where his performances were greatly admired. 1868, he went to Copenhagen, where he was appointed successor of Rée (*see* this name). He went, later, to Moscow, but had to leave on account of the climate not agreeing with him. 1883, he settled in New York. Neupert was certainly one of the best Scandinavian artists.

> Characterstücke, Op. 21; Pieces, Op. 47; 24 Concert Studies, Op. 17; 24 Octave Studies, Op. 18; 24 Studies for technique and expression, Op. 19; 10 Poetical Studies, Op. 25 and 51; 4 characteristic pieces, Op. 45; 8 transcriptions of Studies by Cramer.

*****Neustedt**, Charles Frédéric, b. 1834, Saumur (Maine et Loire). Pupil of his father and Thalberg. "Officier de l'Instruction publique," one of the most popular teachers in Paris, and the Director of musical education in the convents. His compositions are effective, not too difficult, and enjoy considerable favour.

> Carillon de Louis XIV., Fête romaine, Gavotte du bon vieux temps; Menuet

d'enfants, Pavane, Gavotte favorite de Marie Antoinette, Pantomime, Minuetto dans le style ancien, Chanson des arciers.

Nichelmann, Christoph, b. Aug. 13, 1717, Treuenbriezen (Brandenburg); d. July 20, 1762, Berlin. At first instructed by Cantor Bubel and the organists, Schweinitz and Lippe; went (1730) to Leipzig, and entered the Thomas School, where Sebastian Bach taught him Composition and Friedemann Bach, Clavecin-playing. 1733, went to Hamburg, where he enjoyed the friendship of Keiser, Telemann, and Mattheson. 1738, he returned for a short visit to his native town, then went to Berlin, and was appointed Secretary to Count Barfuss. In Berlin he seized the opportunity of improving himself in Counterpoint under Quanz, and also attempted some vocal compositions. 1744, he intended to go to London, but went only as far as Hamburg, where he heard that he was appointed Kammermusikus and second Cembalist of the Opera in Berlin. He resigned these posts (1756) and lived there in retirement until his death.

Sei brevi Sonate da Cembalo, Op. 1 (1749); ditto, Op. 2 (1749); Clavecin pieces in Emanuel Bach's "Musikalisches Allerley" (1761-62); Sonaten and Fugen, edited by Emanuel Bach (1744); Concertos for Clavecin, with 2 Vln., Vla., and Bass.

*__Nicodé,__ Jean Louis, b. Aug. 12, 1853, Jersitz (Posen). At first instructed by his father and Hartkäs, then entered the "Neue Akademie der Tonkunst" (Berlin), where his teachers were Kullak (Pf.), Würst (Composition), and Kiel (Counterpoint and Composition). 1871-77, he taught at the above Academy; 1878-85, was teacher at the Conserv. of Dresden; 1885-89, Conductor of the Dresden Philharmonic concerts; previous to this, Director of the Berlin Monday Popular concerts. With the celebrated singer, Madame Artôt-Padilla, he gave concerts in Galicia and Roumania. He is Hon. Member of several important societies, and is held in great respect by his colleagues and the public. He is not only a very brilliant pianist, with command of an enormous technique, but also a highly distinguished composer, who in a very short time made himself a great reputation. His most popular works are—

Op. 6, Souvenir de Robert Schumann (6 pieces, I., II.); Op. 9, 2 Morceaux caractéristiques; Op. 13, Danses et Chansons Nationales Italiennes (Barcarole, Canzonetta, and †Tarantelle); Op. 18, Variations and Fugue; Op. 19, Sonata in F min.; Op. 21, 3 Studies (F sharp min., F, and †D min.); Op. 12, 2 Studies (Elfin dance); Op. 22, †Ein Liebesleben; Op. 28, ‡Walzer, ‡Burlesca, Scherzo. *Duets:* Op. 7, Miscellanées (Volkslied); Op. 19, †Valses Caprices; Op. 26, Eine Ball-Scene; Op. 29, ‡Bilder aus dem Süden (I., II., III.); Sonata for Pf. and V'cello in G; a second Pf. part for Chopin's Allegro de Concert, Op. 46.

Niedermeyer, Louis, b. April 27, 1802, Nyon, on the Lake of Geneva; d. March 14, 1861, Paris. Pupil of Moscheles (Pf.) and Förster (Theory) in Vienna; later of Fioravanti and Zingarelli in Rome. Greatly patronised by Rossini, he commenced by writing operas, which, however, were not successful; only two of his melodies—" Le Lac" and "Adieu donc, belle France"—became very popular. 1844, he received in Paris, where he had settled since 1823, the decoration of the Legion of Honour and an annual allowance of 5,000 francs for the continuation and improvement of the Society for Sacred Music, founded by Choron. He was an excellent teacher and accomplished musician.

Introduction, Variations, et Finale sur la dernière pensée de C. M. de Weber, Op. 5; Le Bal, Divertissement, Op. 15; Divertissement Espagnol, Op. 16; several other Fantasias and Variations on Italian opera airs are of small importance.

*__Norman,__ Ludwig, b. Aug. 28, 1831, Stockholm; d. there March 25, 1884. At an early age he showed great talent for music, and was patronised by Prince (now King) Oscar of Sweden, Jenny Lind, and the composer Lindblad. 1848, he was sent to Leipzig, and entered the Conserv. as a pupil of Moscheles (Pf.), Hauptmann and Rietz (Harmony and Composition). Almost all the eminent Leipzig authorities, including Robert Schumann, took great interest in his progress. 1857, he returned to Stockholm. Was appointed Prof. of Composition at the Royal Swedish Academy (1861), Conductor of the Royal Opera, and President of the Musical Academy. 1864, he married the celebrated violinist, Wilhelmine Neruda (now Lady Hallé). 1879, he retired on account of feeble health. It was then that King Oscar conferred on him the Orders of "Wasa" (Sweden) and "St. Olaf" (Norway), and likewise the title of Principal Capellmeister of the Swedish Court.

Op. 54, Concertstück (with Orchestra); Op. 3, Sonata in F, for Pf. and Vln.; Op. 28, Sonata in D, for Pf. and V'cello; Op. 32, Sonata in G min., for Pf. and Vla.; Op. 4, Trio in D, for Pf., Vln., and V'cello; Op.

10, Quartet in E, for Pf., Vln., Vla., and V'cello; Op. 1 and 2, †Characteristic pieces; Op. 5, 4 Fantasiestücke; Op. 7, 3 pieces for 4 hands; Op. 8, Capriccio on 2 Swedish melodies; Op. 9, †4 pieces; Op. 11, †Album leaves; Op. 12, †3 pieces in the form of Scherzos. His 30 transcriptions of Swedish national songs are written in excellent style.

*Noszkowski, Zygmunt von (Sigismund), b. May 2, 1846, Warsaw. 1864-67, pupil at the Warsaw Musical Institute. The Musical Society sent him (1873) to Berlin, where he studied with Kiel (Composition) and Oscar Raif (Pf.). After leaving Berlin he became Conductor of the Bodau Society, in Constance (Switzerland). 1881, appointed Director of the Musical Society and (1888) Prof. at the Conserv. of Warsaw.

Op. 24, Impressions, 4 pieces; Op. 27, Images, 6 Morceaux caractéristiques; Op. 31, Chansons et Danses cracoviennes; Op. 35, 3 pieces (conte d'hiver); Op. 36, Moments mélodiques (4 characteristic pieces); Op. 39, Petits rayons (4 pieces). *For 4 hands:* Op. 33, Mélodies Ruthéniennes (8 pieces); Op. 38, Mazury, Danses masoviennes.

Nottebohm, Martin Gustav, b. Nov. 12, 1817, Lüdenscheid (Westphalia); d. Oct. 30, 1882, Graz (Styria). 1838-39, pupil of Berger (Pf.) and Dehn (Composition) in Berlin; went (1840) to Leipzig, where he continued his studies under the superintendence of Mendelssohn and Schumann; settled (1846) in Vienna, where he had lessons from Sechter, and earned his livelihood as a teacher. The great merits of Nottebohm as an author are well known, and his works on Beethoven have been gratefully received by the musical public.

A Sketch Book of Beethoven (1865)—1855 is given as the date in Breitkopf and Härtel's Catalogue; Thematic Catalogue of Beethoven's Works (1868); Beethoveniana (1872); Neue Beethoveniana (1875); Beethoven's Studies (his studies with Haydn, Salieri, and Albrechtsberger, 1873); A Sketch Book of Beethoven from the year 1803; A Thematic Catalogue of Schubert's Works (1874); Mozartiana (1880). *Pf. Pieces:* Op. 1, Quartet for Pf., Vln., Vla., and V'cello; Op. 4, Trios; Op. 10, †Fliegende Blätter (6 pieces); Op. 11, 3 Caprices; Op. 13, 2 lyric pieces; Op. 14 and 15, Impromptus: La Séréna and La Contemplative; Op. 17, †Variations on an air by Seb. Bach for 4 hands.

Nowakowski, Joseph, b. 1805, Mniszck, near Radomsk (Poland); d. 1865, Warsaw. Pupil of Würfel and Elsner in Warsaw. He was an excellent pianist, who travelled a great deal and gained everywhere considerable success. After returning to Warsaw he was appointed Prof. at the Alexandra College, where he remained until his death. The most popular of his compositions (about 60) are—

Op. 14, Grande Polonaise pathétique; Op. 19 and 26, Mazurkas; Op. 25, 12 Grandes Etudes (dedicated to F. Chopin).

O.

Oesten, Theodor, b. Dec. 31, 1813, Berlin; d. there March 16, 1870. Pupil of Dreschker (Pf.), Rungenhagen, and Schneider (Composition). He was a most successful teacher, and his numerous educational compositions and arrangements found great favour. They are written in a correct, clear, and practical manner and are still much used.

Oginski, Count Michael Cleophas, b. Sept. 25, 1765, Guron, near Warsaw; d. Oct. 31, 1833, Florence. He became well known as the composer of 14 Polonaises. One called the "Death" Polonaise made the round of the world; popular fancy connected it with a romantic episode of his life, for it was said that Count Oginski, desperately in love with a lady who did not return his affection and married another gentleman, composed the Polonaise and committed suicide on the evening before her wedding. To make the incident more thrilling, it was reported that in a letter he had desired the Polonaise to be played during the wedding festivities. The sober facts are, however, that the "Death" Polonaise was composed in 1793, several years before the wedding in question, and that Oginski died thirty-eight years *after* the supposed tragedy. Besides the 14 Polonaises he published 3 Marches.

*O'Leary, Arthur, b. March 15, 1834, Tralee, County Kerry (Ireland). Pupil at the Leipzig Conserv. under Plaidy and Moscheles (Pf.), Hauptmann, Richter, and Rietz (Theory and Composition). Returning to London, he entered the R.A.M. and studied under Sterndale Bennett (Composition) and Cipriani Potter (Pf.). He is a Prof. at the R.A.M. and a most successful teacher.

Concerto in E min. (with Orchestra); †Theme in C min., with Variations (in 3 movements); Op. 2, 2 pieces; Op. 7, Im Gebirge, 3 characteristic pieces; †Toccata in F; Romanza in E flat min., and various smaller pieces.

Onslow, George, b. July 27, 1784, Clermont-Ferrand (Puy-de-Dôme); d. there Oct. 3, 1852. Grandson of Lord Onslow. Part of his youth was spent in London, where Hüllmandel, Dussek, and Cramer were his teachers. He returned later to his estate at Clermont, and used to play with some friends the best chamber music, taking the V'cello himself. It was there that he wrote a great number of works for string instruments.

34 Quintets; 36 Quartets; Sextet for Pf., Fl., Cl., Hn., Bssn., and C.-Bass, Op. 30; Sextet for Pf., with Strings, Op. 77bis; Quintets, Op. 70 and 76; Trios (3), A min., C, G min., Op. 3; Trios (3), E min., E flat, D; Trios: D min., Op. 20; C min., Op. 26; G, Op. 27. *Duos, with Vln.:* Sonatas (3), Op. 11; (3) Op. 16; Duo, Op. 15; and Op. 31. *Pf. Solo:* Sonata, C min., Op. 2; †Toccata, Op. 6; Variations, "Charmante Gabrielle"; Sonatas for 4 hands: †E min., Op. 7; †F min., Op. 22.

Ordenstein, Heinrich, b. Jan. 7, 1856, Offstein, near Worms. 1871-75, pupil at the Leipzig Conserv., under Reinecke, Jadassohn, Coccius, and Dr. Oscar Paul. 1881, teacher at the New Academy of Berlin. Founded (1884) the Conserv. at Carlsruhe (Baden), which now numbers about 400 pupils. The Grand Duke of Baden conferred on him the title of "Professor." He is the author of various essays on musical education.

*****Osborne,** George Alexander, b. Sept. 24, 1806, Limerick (Ireland); d. Nov. 17, 1893, London. He showed at an early age signs of uncommon musical talent. Went to Brussels, where Prince de Chimay took great interest in the young Irish musician, and allowed him to study the classical works in his library. He also made the acquaintance of Fétis, who gave him excellent advice. Prince de Chimay recommended him as teacher to the Crown Prince of the Netherlands, and the King conferred on him the Order of the "Crown of Oak." 1831, he went to Paris, formed a lasting friendship with Chopin and Berlioz, and took lessons from Pixis, and later from Kalkbrenner. 1848, he settled in London, where he had already been for artistic purposes in 1845. The abilities of the conscientious and experienced teacher, and his sterling qualities, procured him numbers of pupils and devoted friends; but seldom has an artist enjoyed so great and lasting a popularity and such sincere respect as fell to the lot of Osborne. He was a member of the Philharmonic Society, a Director of the R.A.M., and Vice-President of the London Trinity College.

Quartet; Sonata for Pf. and V'cello; Sextet for Pf., string and wind instruments; a great number of elegant and brilliant drawing-room pieces, of which "La Pluie des Perles," "A Summer's Eve," "Evening Dew," "Marche Militaire," and "Nouvelle Pluie de Perles" are the most popular. His Duo (with De Bériot) on Rossini's "William Tell" gave pleasure to numberless amateurs.

P.

Pachelbel, Johann, b. Sept. 1, 1653, Nürnberg; d. there March 3, 1706. Pupil of H. Schwemmer. After a short stay in Vienna, as assistant to J. C. Kerl (Organist of St. Stephen's), he went, 1675, to Eisenach, 1678 to Erfurt, 1690 to Stuttgart, 1692 to Gotha, and 1695 back to his native town as Organist of the Sebaldus Church. His compositions were mostly for the Organ; for the Clavecin he wrote—

A Ciacccona, with 13 variations; Fugues in E min. and C; and a Fughetta in C.

Pachelbel, Wilhelm Hieronymus, b. 1685, Nürnberg; date of death unknown. Either son or nephew of the above.

Musikalisches Vergnügen bestehend in einem Preludio, Fuga, und Fantasia for Organ or Clavecin. Nürnberg, 1725.

Pacher, Joseph Adalbert, b. March 28, 1816, Daubrowitz (Moravia); d. Sept. 2, 1871, Ischl. 1832, went to Vienna and became a pupil of Anton Halm; was successful as a public performer and teacher, and very industrious as a composer of educational and popular pieces.

Op. 29, Die Fundamente der Technik (I. and II.); Op. 11, 6 Octave Studies; Op. 50, 12 Etudes mélodiques; Op. 75, Der Pianist der guten Schule; Op. 9, La harpe; Op. 15, Elfenreigen; Op. 18, Grâce et Coquetterie; Op. 30, Papageno Caprice; Op. 53, Tendresse.

Pachmann, Wladimir von, b. July 27, 1848, Odessa. Pupil of his father, and,

1866, of Dachs in Vienna. He appeared in London for the first time in 1882; travelled in Austria, Germany, and Denmark, where the king conferred on him the Order of the "Danebrog." Went to America and, on his return, again gave concerts in England, where he is considered to be one of the best "Chopin" players.

Paderewski, Ignaz Ian, b. Nov. 6, 1859, Podolia. Pupil at the Warsaw Conserv., of Raguski for Harmony and Counterpoint, later of Urban and Wüerst (Berlin), and Theodor Leschetizki (Vienna). He was appointed Pf. teacher at the Conserv. of Strassburg (Alsace). For the last three years his performances have created a great and fully deserved sensation in Paris, England, and America. He is undoubtedly among the foremost performers of the present time.

Op. 1, Prelude and Minuet; Op. 6, Introduction et Toccata; Op. 5 and 9, Danses polonaises; Op. 10, Album de Mai, Scènes romantiques; Op. 11, Variations et Fugue; Op. 14, Humoresques de Concert, I.; †Menuet; Sarabande, Caprice; II.: Burlesque, Intermezzo pollaco, †Cracovienne fantastique; Op. 15, Dans le d·sert; Op. 16, Miscellanæ: †Légende, †Melodie, Thème varié, Nocturne; Op. 13, Sonate pour Pf. et Vln.; Op. 17, Concerto; Fantasia on Polish Airs, with orchestra.

Paër, Ferdinando, b. June 1, 1771, Parma; d. May 3, 1839, Paris. 1791, appointed Conductor in Venice; 1797, in Vienna; 1802-6, in Dresden; 1812-27, in Paris; 1831, became Membre de l'Académie; 1832, Director of the Royal Chapel.

3 Grandes Sonates pour Pf., Vln., et V'cello, B flat, A, and E flat; 6 Valses; Variations and Marches.

Paisiello, Giovanni, b. May 9, 1741, Tarento; d. June 5, 1816, Naples. Pupil of Durante. 1759, Assistant Teacher at the Naples Conserv.; 1776-84, at St. Petersburg; 1784-1802, Court Capellmeister at Naples; 1802-3, Conductor in Paris; but, after 1803, again in Naples.

Concertos (6), Quartets (12) with Strings; and 2 vols. of pieces for the Grand Duchess Marie of Russia.

Papendieck, Hermann, b. Jan. 16, 1832, Magdeburg. 1848-51, pupil of J. B. André (Berlin) for Pf. and Composition, and 1856 of Ernst Lübeck (Paris). 1858, he played for the first time in public (Paris, Berlin, &c.); 1855-70, was a teacher in Paris, then had to leave on account of the Franco-German war. A temporary engagement as teacher in Kullak's Academy kept him (1870-71) in Berlin; went afterwards to London, where he resides at present, a most successful teacher.

Capriccio, Op. 3 (which obtained first prize, the judges being Moscheles, Kullak, and Sechter); 12 Etudes mélodiques; Canzonetta, &c.

Paradies, Pietro Domenico, b. 1710, Naples; d. there 1792. Pupil of Porpora. He resided for the greater part of his life in London. Was an energetic teacher and also a dramatic composer.

12 Sonate di gravicembalo dedicate a sua Altezza Reale la Principessa Augusta. Printed for the author by Blundell (London, 1746). A second edition was published (1770) at Amsterdam.

Paradis (Paradies), Maria Theresia von, b. May 15, 1759, Vienna; d. there Feb. 1, 1824. She became blind in her third year (see Jahn, "Mozart"). Pupil of Kozeluch, Salieri, and Abbé Vogler. As godchild of the Empress Maria Theresia, she received a pension of 200 florins, and her beautiful playing and sweet voice won for her the favour of the Viennese. It is said that she was able to play 60 Concertos correctly and with exquisite taste; indeed, her memory seems to have been quite phenomenal. In Germany, Paris, and London she was received with great favour, and reaped not only plenty of laurels, but also considerable sums of money. She dictated her compositions note for note. A sincere friendship bound her to Leopold Mozart, and his illustrious son, W. A. M., composed a Concerto for her. Compositions published during her lifetime—

4 Sonatas, Amsterdam, 1778; 6 Sonatas, Op. 1, Paris, 1791; 6 Sonatas, Op. 2; An meine entfernten Lieben, Fantasia, 1786.

Parry, Charles Hubert Hastings, M.A.; Mus. Doc., Cantab (1883); Mus. Doc Oxon (1884); Choragus, Oxford University (1883); Mus. Doc., Dublin University; Prof. and Director (1894), Royal College of Music (London); b. Feb. 27, 1848, Bournemouth. Educated at Eton and Christ Church, Oxford, where he graduated Mus. Bac. in 1867 and B.A. in 1870. For a short time a pupil of Dr. (Sir) George Elvey, later of H. H. Pierson (Edgar Mannsfeldt) in Stuttgart, of Macfarren (Composition) and Dannreuther (Pf.) in London.

Sonnets and Songs without Words (3 books); Characterbilder; Grand Duo for 2 Pf. in E min.; Trio for Pf., Vln., and V'cello in E min.; Quartet for Pf. and Strings in A flat; Fantaisie Sonata for Pf. and Vln.; Sonata for Pf. and V'cello; another in A; Theme and Variations in D min.; Partita for Pf. and Vln. in D min.

Pasquini, Bernardo, b. 1637, Massa Valnevola (Toscana); d. Nov. 22, 1710,

Rome. Pupil of L. Vittori and A. Cesti, and teacher of Durante and Gasparini. Excellent performer. Little is known of his works for clavecin.

<small>Tóccata (Amsterdam, 1704); Sonata per gravicembalo, 1702; Sonata per gravicembalo, 1732 (MS., British Museum).</small>

Pasterwitz, Georg von, b. June 7, 1730, Burchhütten (Upper Austria); d. 1803 in the Monastery of Kremsmünster. Although he entered the Monastery of the Benedictines as early as 1744, he followed up his musical studies with rare energy, and enjoyed the friendship of Haydn, Mozart, Salieri, Albrechtsberger, and other celebrities. His compositions are but few, but they are written in the most correct and polished manner.

<small>8 Fughe secondo l'ordine de tuoni ecclesiastici per il clavicembalo; 8 Fughe secondo l'A, B, C, di musica per il clavicembalo, and 8 *Idem*, Op. 3 (Vienna).</small>

Pauer, Ernst, b. Dec. 21, 1826, Vienna. The only son of the Very Rev. Ernst P., Superintendent-General of the Protestant Churches of Austria, Director of the Theological Seminary, &c. He was educated by private tutors. Until 1839, pupil of Theodor Dirzka; 1839-44, of W. A. Mozart, jun. (Pf.), and Simon Sechter (Composition); 1845-47, pupil of Franz Lachner (Munich); 1847-51, Director of the Musical Societies of Mayence o/Rhine. He visited London in the spring of 1851; played at the Philharmonic and Musical Union concerts; returned to Germany (Frankfort o/M.) and then to London, Dec., 1851, in order to settle there. 1859, he succeeded Cipriani Potter as Prof. at the R.A.M.; 1861, began his historical performances of Clavecin and Pf. music in chronological order (3 series); 1862, was elected Juror of the International Exhibition for Austria and Germany, and commissioned to write the official report for the German Governments. 1867, principal Prof. at the National Training School, and, 1883, at the Royal College of Music. 1858, he received from the Grand Duke of Hesse the title of "Concertmeister"; 1861, the Austrian great gold medal for art and science; 1866, the patent as pianist to the Imperial and Royal Court of Austria; 1862,the Orders of the Prussian Crown and Albrecht of Saxony; 1863, of Francis Joseph (Austria), St. George and Michael of Bavaria, Houseorder of Coburg-Gotha; 1866, of Philip (Hesse); 1869, St. Stanislas of Russia and Crown of Italy. Hon. Member of the R.A.M. and of several other societies. His lectures on different musical subjects, delivered at the Royal and London Institutions, the South Kensington Museum, the Royal Institutions of Manchester, Liverpool, and other towns in the provinces (also in Ireland and Scotland) met with success.

<small>Author of the Primers: "The art of Pf. playing"; "Musical Forms"; "The beautiful in Music," which obtained popularity. The Historical publications—Alte Claviermusik (12 books); Alte Meister (65 numbers); Old English, Italian, French, and German composers—have been found useful. *Educational publications:* The New Gradus ad Parnassum (100 Studies of different composers); the Classical Companion (100 pieces); celebrated Concert Studies (50); Culture of the left hand (4 books). *Original Studies:* 24 easy and melodious Studies; 20 progressive Studies, 20 Rhythmical Sketches; Mozart Studies (12); the Culture of the Scale (24); Characteristic Studies for the left hand (12). *Educational pieces:* 4 Sonatinas; 6 National Sonatinas; **A** Child's Life; Suite facile; Suite for the left hand; 20 Musical Sketches; Musical Scrap-book (100). Composer of Quintet for Pf., Ob., Cl., Hn., Bssn., Op. 44 (also arranged as Quartet for Pf. and Strings); Sonata for Pf. and Vln.; Sonata for Pf. and V'cello; Solo Sonatas; Caprice, Op. 39, Passacaille, Op. 40; Valse de Concert, Cascade, Op. 37; Tarantelle, Op. 30; l'Adieu du Soldat, Op. 36, Caprice hongrois, Op. 58, &c. Editor of the Pf. Classics, Children's Classics (9), Pf. Library for study and amusement (10 books). Besides these he arranged Beethoven's and Schumann's Symphonies for 2 and 4 hands, 38 Overtures for ditto, and other classical pieces.</small>

Pauer, Max, b. Oct. 31, 1866, London. Son and pupil of the above. 1881-85, pupil of Vincenz Lachner (Composition); at the same time appointed Prof. at the Conserv. (Carlsruhe). 1887, appointed Prof. at the Conserv. (Cologne). He has taken extensive concert tours in Germany, Austria, Hungary, Russia, Holland, Belgium, &c. 1893, appointed Kammervirtuose to the Grand Duke of Hesse. Associate of the Royal College of Music.

<small>His arrangements of Mozart and Haydn's Symphonies for 2 and 4 hands, and his Album Classique for 4 hands (6 books) have given great satisfaction. Gavotte, Tarantelle à 4 mains, Rhapsody, Waltz, 7 pieces (4 hands), 3 pieces, Miniatures, &c.</small>

Paul, Dr. Oscar, b. April 8, 1836, Freiwaldau (Silesia). 1858, pupil of Plaidy and Richter. Studied theology at the University (Leipzig), became Doc. Phil.; was elected "Privat Docent" in 1866; 1869, Prof. at the Conserv., and, 1872, Prof. of Music at the University.

<small>Author of a "History of the Clavecin," of a "Handlexikon der Tonkunst" (2 vols.,</small>

1869-73), and Editor of Dr. Hauptmann's posthumous work, "Die Lehre von der Harmonik."

Paur, Emil, b. Aug 29, 1855, Czernowitz, Bukowina. Son of Franz P., a Conductor, who did not wish his son to devote himself to music. Emil went to Vienna and entered the Conserv. against the will and without the knowledge of his father, who thereupon disclaimed any further interest in his career. But when he heard that his son had received the first prize, a reconciliation took place. 1869, he obtained the appointment of violinist in the orchestra of the Vienna Imperial Opera, and, after some years, decided to become a conductor. In this capacity he was Capellmeister in Mannheim, afterwards in Leipzig, and, in 1893, accepted an appointment in Boston (U.S.). He is an excellent pianist as well as a good violinist.

Solo Sonata, Sonata for Pf. and Vln., and solo pieces.

Payer, Hieronymus, b. Feb. 15, 1787, Meidling (near Vienna); d. Sept., 1845, Wiedburg (near Vienna). His father, a poor schoolmaster, taught him the Vln., Organ, and to tune the Clavecin. With his modest savings he bought the works of Mattheson, Türck, Marpurg, and Kirnberger, and tried, with admirable perseverance, to further his career. 1800 (thirteen years old), he succeeded his father (who died that year) as organist, but resigned in 1816, when he was appointed Musical Director of the "New Theatre on the Wien" (a small river) in Vienna. 1818, he made a journey through Germany, became Capellmeister at Amsterdam, and went (1825) to Paris, where he was the first to perform in public on the Physharmonika (Harmonium). In Paris, and later in Vienna, he filled the post of Conductor of the Opera, and eventually retired to Wiedburg, near Vienna, where he died.

Concertino for Pf. and Orchestra, Op. 79; Variations for Pf. and Orchestra, Op. 71; Variations for Pf. and Quartet, Op. 30, 47, 88, 96, and 112; Trios for Pf., Vln., and V'cello; Sonatas; Rondos; Variations, &c., for 4 hands; Variations for Pf. solo.

Perabo, Ernst, b. Nov. 14, 1845, Wiesbaden. 1852, his parents settled in New York, where they remained for two years. The publisher, Wilhelm Scharfenberg (b. in Cassel), succeeded in finding the necessary means for sending the talented boy, first to Hamburg (1858), where he was instructed in the Educational Institute of Prof. Andresen, and, 1862, to Leipzig, where Wenzel and Moscheles, Papperitz, Hauptmann, Richter, and Reinecke were his teachers in the Conserv. 1865, he returned to New York, gave concerts in different towns of America, and settled in Boston, where he resides, an influential and successful pianist and teacher. Some of his compositions were published in America and Leipzig.

Pescetti, Giovanni Battista, b. 1704, Venice; d. there 1784. Pupil of Lotti. After 1726 he went to London. It is not known how long he remained in England.

9 Sonatas were published in London, 1739; they were also published in Haffner's "Raccolta Musicale" (Nürnberg).

Petersen, Dory (Burmeister), b. Aug. 1, 1860, Oldenburg. Pupil of Julius Leven, later (for seven years) of Liszt. She gave concerts in Italy, Hungary, Germany, Paris, and London. 1883, she married the pianist, Richard Burmeister, and, since 1887, has been Prof. at the Women's College of Baltimore.

Petersenn, Georg von, b. Sept. 1, 1849, Weimar (Livland). After finishing his studies at the University, he was a pupil at the Munich Conserv. 1875, appointed teacher at the Würzburg Music School. Afterwards took lessons from Bülow in Hanover. Received the title of "Professor," and, since 1884, has been Prof. at the Royal Hochschule of Berlin.

6 Studies in C, A flat, A min., E flat, C and F min., which are used in several German music schools.

Pflughaupt, Robert, b. Aug. 4, 1833, Berlin; d. June 12, 1871, Aix-la-Chapelle. Pupil of Dehn (Berlin); then of A. Henselt (St. Petersburg), where he married; and later of Liszt, at Weimar, where he resided from 1857 until 1862; afterwards in Aix-la-Chapelle. He left his money to the General German Musical Society, which used it for a "Beethoven" foundation.

Op. 1, Thème original et Variations; Op. 3, Petite Valse; Op. 6, Mazurka; Op. 9, Second Galop de Concert; Op. 11, Invitation à la Polka.

Pflughaupt, Sophie (née Stschepin), wife of the above, b. March 15, 1837, Dünaburg (Russia); d. Nov. 10, 1867, Aix-la-Chapelle. Pupil of Henselt and Liszt. Excellent pianist.

*****Pfeiffer,** Georges, b. Dec. 12, 1835, Versailles. Pupil of his mother, Clara P., who was a pupil of Kalkbrenner and Chopin. His instructors in Harmony and Composition were Maleden and Damcke. Excellent pianist. 1862, gave his first concert in Paris, introducing a Trio and other smaller pieces. He is one of the directors of Pleyel and Wolff's Pf. factory, and also Vice-President of the French Society of Composers, of which Saint-Saëns and Joncières were Presidents (1890-91 and 1892-93).

Concerto (No. 1), Op. 11; Concerto (No. 2), Op. 21; Trio, Op. 14; Sonatines, 1-3, Op. 59; Quartet for Pf. and Strings; Quintet for Pf. and Strings; 25 Etudes préparatoires à celles de Cramer, Op. 70; Mazurkas, Op. 35 and 88; Mélodies (I.-II.), Op. 105.

*Pierné, Gabriel, b. Aug. 16, 1863, Metz. Became in his eighth year (1871) a pupil at the Paris Conserv. 1879, first prize for Pf. playing (Marmontel's class); 1881, first prize for Counterpoint and Fugue; 1882, "Grand Prix de Rome" (Massenet's class); also first prize for Organ (teacher, César Franck); Member of the Jury for Competitions at the Conserv.

Fantaisie-Ballet (with Orchestra), Concerto in C min. (with Orchestra), Scherzo-Caprice (with Orchestra), Collection of 20 melodies, and several smaller pieces.

Pinto (really Sauters), George Frederic, b. Sept. 25, 1786, Lambeth (London); d. March 23, 1806, Little Chelsea. His education was directed by his grandmother, Mrs. Brent, who placed him under Salomon for Vln. When fifteen years old he gave concerts in London, Bath, Oxford, Cambridge, Winchester, and went afterwards with Salomon to Scotland, later to Paris, everywhere creating a great sensation. But his Clavecin playing was also wonderful, and his Sonata, dedicated to his friend John Field, testifies to his great faculties. Several of his contemporaries declare that he might have been a second Mozart if he had led a more regular life.

*Pirani, Eugenio de, b. Sept. 8, 1852, Ferrara. He studied at the College of Bologna and the Conserv. Rossini and passed excellent examinations. He intended to study law, but soon turned to the study of music instead. Dr. Kullak, of Berlin, wished to engage a competent teacher for the higher classes of his academy, and Pirani succeeded in getting the appointment. For ten years he worked there, and during that time he made concert tours through Germany, Russia, France, and Italy, and went several times to London, where he performed at St. James's Hall and the Albert Hall. He studied Counterpoint with Kiel. He is a successful author, and writes equally well in Italian and German. The King of Italy named him Officer of the Italian Crown, the King of Prussia, Knight of the Prussian Crown. He is also a Member of the Academies of Rome, Florence, Bologna, &c. He resides at Heidelberg. The following compositions enjoy considerable popularity:

Trios, Op. 24 and 48; Scena veneziana, with Orchestra (3 movements); Concert Studies, Op. 19 and 51; Fantasia, Op. 16; Serenade, Op. 16; Gavottes, Op. 25 and 34; Fughetta and Valse, Op. 30; Menuet, Op. 32, &c.

Pirkhert, Eduard, b. Oct. 14, 1817, Aussee (Styria); d. Feb. 27, 1881, Vienna. Pupil of Anton Halm and Czerny (Vienna). 1855, appointed Prof. at the Vienna Conserv. He was an excellent pianist, who fully deserved the admiration bestowed on his truly artistic performances.

Op. 3, 6 Etudes mélodiques; Op. 6, Thème original varié; Op. 9, 6 Mélodies; Op. 10, 12 Etudes de Salon.

Pixis, Johann Peter, b. 1788, Mannheim; d. Dec. 20, 1874, Baden-Baden. Pupil of his father, Fr. Wilh. P., an organist. Even in his ninth year he was an expert performer, and travelled in company with his elder brother, Fr. Wilh. P. (1786-1842), an excellent violinist; they obtained great success everywhere. 1803-8, he studied with perseverance in his native town, where he also taught; went (1809) to Paris, and settled there, 1825. After many journeys with his adopted daughter, Francilla P. (Göhringer), an excellent singer, he established himself (1840) in Baden-Baden, where he gave lessons, but no longer composed. Pixis was a performer of the school of Kalkbrenner and Herz—elegant, correct, and brilliant, but without deep feeling or enthusiasm. His compositions, some of which are not without merit, are scarcely known or played at the present time.

Concerto, Op. 100; Trios for Pf., Vln., and V'cello, Op. 75 and 87; Quartet with Strings, Op. 4; Sonatas with Vln., Fl., V'cello, Op. 14, 17, 24, 30, 35, &c.; Solo Sonatas, Op. 3, 10, and 185 (ded. to J. B. Cramer); Fantaisie militaire, Op. 121; Variations, Caprices, Polonaises, Valses, Rondos, Etudes en forme de Valses, &c.

Plachy, Wenzel, b. Sept. 4, 1785, Klopotowitz (Moravia); d. July 7, 1858, Prague. Pupil of his uncle, Anton P. 1811, he went to Vienna, obtained the appointment of Organist of the "Piaristen" Church, and was highly successful as a teacher. His educational compositions, practically and correctly written, are unpretentious, but pleasing and effective—

Elementary Studies, Op. 25; First Studies, Op. 79; Revue Musicale en 24 Etudes, Op. 101; Short and Practical Studies, Op. 110; Sonata, Op. 6; Rondeaux, Op. 2; 12 Preludes, Op. 97; Variations; and several collections of opera airs arranged as solo pieces.

Plaidy, Louis, b. Nov. 28, 1810, Wermsdorf (Saxony); d. March 3, 1874, Grimma (Saxony). Pupil of Agthe (Pf.) and Haase (Vln.) at Dresden. He first practised the Vln. as his principal instrument, but later the Pf., and studied with great attention the elementary and technical details. At the time of the opening of the Leipzig Conserv. (1842) Mendelssohn appointed him one of the Pf. teachers, and almost all English pianists who studied in Leipzig were his pupils, and recollect gratefully his patient and careful instruction. He retained this appointment until 1865, and afterwards became a private teacher. His well-known educational work, "Technical Studies," of which many editions were published, and a little pamphlet, "Der Clavierlehrer" (The Pf. Teacher), are so much respected they need no further notice. Plaidy was universally beloved for his simple, modest, but thoroughly reliable character, and his retirement proved a great loss for the Conserv.

Planté, François, b. March 2, 1839, Orthez (Basses-Pyrénées). Entered, in his tenth year (1849), Marmontel's class at the Paris Conserv.; obtained the first prize after seven months' tuition, and was selected by Alard and Franchomme as pianist for their Trio *Soirées*. 1853, he studied Thorough-Bass and Harmony with Bazin. He retired for ten years, then appeared as a most finished and brilliant performer, and was received by the public with great acclamation. His style is refined, graceful, elegant, his technique worked out with minuteness, his runs smooth and clear; but the whole is more fascinating for the amateur than for the musician, as the latter feels somewhat the absence of enthusiasm, grandeur, and what may be called the *feu sacré*. His transcriptions of classical pieces (Gluck, Mozart) are written with the greatest care. He is Chevalier de la Légion d'honneur.

Pleyel, Ignaz Joseph, b. June 1, 1757, Ruppersthal (near Vienna). The twenty-fourth child of a poor schoolmaster, whose wife, the daughter of an aristocratic family, was disinherited on account of her *mésalliance*. Died Nov. 14, 1831, at his estate, near Paris. He was patronised by several noble and highly influential persons. Amongst them was Count Erdödy, who first gave him Wanhal as a teacher, and later paid Joseph Haydn £100 a year for taking him as a pupil and boarder. He was five years with Haydn. 1777, the Count appointed him his Capellmeister, but allowed him to spend four years in Italy, so that he might make the acquaintance of the foremost Italian artists. 1781, he returned; 1783, he accepted the appointment of Assistant Capellmeister of the Strassburg Cathedral, where he was elected (1789) first Capellmeister. 1792, the Society of the "Professional Concerts," of London, invited him to come to England, where he composed and conducted some of his Symphonies. These concerts were in opposition to Salomon's, who had engaged Haydn in the same way. This rivalry did not interfere, however, with the friendship and mutual goodwill of master and pupil. 1795, Pleyel left London for Paris, where his elegant and light compositions were immensely popular. By degrees he became a thorough man of business. He established a music-publishing house, more or less for the publication of his own works, and somewhat later (1807) founded a Pf. manufactory, which still exists under the name of Pleyel, Wolff and Co. Later, he ceased to compose and retired to his estate near Paris.

Concertos; Trios (above 100, some of them being arrangements); many Sonatas for Pf. and Vln.; 6 great Solo Sonatas, Op. 15; easy Sonatas and Sonatinas; Variations; Rondos; Dances; †4 Rondeaux favoris; Sonatas for 4 hands. With Dussek he published a Method, of which another edition was published with the co-operation of Clementi.

Pleyel, Camille, b. Dec. 18, 1788 (1792?), Strassburg; d. May 4, 1855, Paris. Pupil of his father, I. J. P., and Dussek. 1824, he undertook, with Kalkbrenner, the direction of the Pf. manufactory founded by his father, and also continued the music-publishing business. He was Knight of the Legion of Honour. An excellent performer, of refined taste, he succeeded also in winning a certain success as a composer.

Quartet, Op. 3; 3 Trios, Op. 1; Sonatas with Vln.; and different solo pieces.

Pleyel, Marie Félicité Denise (*née* Moke), b. Sept. 4, 1811, Paris; d. March 30, 1875, St. Josse-ten-Noode (near Brussels). Pupil of Jacques Herz, Moscheles, and Kalkbrenner; also enjoyed the advice of Thalberg and Liszt. As Mdlle. Moke she was even in her fifteenth year one of the most excellent and distinguished of pianists, creating in Russia, Belgium, Austria, and Germany an unusual, but well-deserved sensation. 1848-72, Prof. at the Conserv. of Brussels.

Poisot, Charles Emile, b. July 7, 1822, Dijon. Pupil of Senart, Louis Adam, Stamaty, Thalberg, Leborne, and, 1844, of Halévy. 1868, he founded the Conserv. of Dijon, and is one of the foundation members of the Paris Society of Composers. He established also a Concert Society in his native town.

Duo for Pf. and Vln.; Trio (dedicated to Onslow); Fantaisie à 4 mains; Scherzo à 4 mains; Exercices de mécanisme.

Pollini, Francesco Giuseppe, b. 1763, Laibach (Illyria, Austria); d. Sept. 17, 1846, Milan. Instructed first in his native town, later in Vienna by Mozart, who dedicated to him a Rondo for Clavecin and Vln. 1793, he went to Milan, where, after having received instruction from Zingarelli, he became Prof. at the Conserv. He was a thoughtful and excellent performer, and was the first to use three staves, in order to distribute the melody between the two hands and to surround it with graceful figures (*see* his "Uno de '32 Esercizi in forma di Toccata," Op. 42).

Toccatas, Op. 31, 50, and 67; †Toccatina in G; 3 Sonatas, Op. 26; Caprices, Op. 28, 29; Rondo, Op. 43; Variations (6 books); †Divertimento pastorale, Op. 34; Method for Pf. playing.

Potter, Cipriani, b. Oct. 3, 1792, London; d. there Sept. 26, 1871. Pupil of his father, later of Wölfl (Pf.), Attwood, Crotch, and Callcott. 1818, went to Vienna, where he studied with Förster, and made Beethoven's acquaintance. 1822, appointed Prof. of Pf. at the R.A.M., London, and (1832) succeeded Crotch as Principal, which post he resigned (1859). He was an excellent linguist, a man of liberal judgment, an eminent teacher, and, as pianist, a performer of considerable merit. Well acquainted with Continental ideas about music, he was always anxious to draw the attention of his countrymen to foreign merit; at a time when Schumann's works were scarcely known in England, and almost ridiculed by those critics who did know them, Potter was aware of their great beauty, and loudly proclaimed his admiration; indeed, there has seldom been a man who filled his post with greater honour than he did. The following compositions, now scarcely known or used, deserve notice:

Sonata, Op. 3; 3 Toccatas in G, †B flat, and E, Op. 9; Pezzi di Bravura en forme d'Etudes, Op. 15 (I.-III.); Il Campiacente (Andante and Allegretto), Op. 16; †Etudes dans tous les tons majeurs et mineurs, Op. 19; Fantasia, Marcia e Trio, in E flat; †La Placidità, Divertimento in A; Rondeaux in F and C; Sextuor for Pf., Fl., Vln., Vla., V'cello, and C.-Bass, Op. 11; 3 Trios, Op. 12, in E flat, D, and B flat min.; Duo concertante for Pf. and Vln., Op. 14, in A; Duo for 2 Pf., Op. 6, in F; Introduction and Rondo (4 hands), Op. 8, in E flat.

Pradher (Pradère), Louis Barthélemi, b. Dec. 18, 1781, Paris; d. Oct., 1843, Gray (Haute Saône). Son of a violinist. Pupil of Gobert. 1797, he obtained, at the Paris Conserv., the second and (1798) the first prize for Pf.; 1802, he succeeded Hyacinthe Jadin as Prof. He was the teacher of Jacques and Henri Herz, Dubois, Lambert, and Rosellen. 1827, he left Paris and settled in Toulouse, and was appointed Director of the Conserv. He was an industrious composer.

Concerto in G; Trio, Op. 17; 5 Solo Sonatas, Op. 1, 2, 3, 13, and 16; Rondeau for 2 Pf.; Variations, &c.

*****Praeger, Ferdinand Christian Wilhelm**, b. Jan. 22, 1815, Leipzig; d. Sept. 2, 1891, London. Pupil of Hummel (Weimar) and Pape (Lübeck). For some time he resided at The Hague teaching, but settled (1834) in London, where he was a hard-working composer, teacher, critic, and author.

Lamentation, Elfenmärchen, Crépuscule, Rêve de Bonheur, Impromptu, Caprice, Moments joyeux, Flocons de Neige. A "Praeger Album" was published at Leipzig.

Preindl, Joseph, b. Jan. 30, 1758, Marbach (Lower Austria); d. Oct. 26, 1823, Vienna. Pupil of Albrechtsberger. 1780, Choirmaster of St. Peter's (Vienna) and (1809) Capellmeister of St. Stephen's.

2 Concertos; Sonatas, Variations, Fantasias, which enjoyed a brief popularity.

Prentice, Ridley, b. July 6, 1842, Paslow Hall, Essex. Pupil at the R.A.M., London, under George Alexander Macfarren (Composition) and Walter C. Macfarren (Pf.). Prof. at the London Guildhall School. Composer of several solo pieces.

Author of 6 books, entitled "The Musician," favourably received in England and America.

Proksch, Joseph, b. Aug. 4, 1794, Reichenberg (Bohemia); d. Dec. 20, 1864, Prague. Pupil of Kozeluch (Prague). When only in his thirteenth (seventeenth?) year he became totally blind, but pursued his studies with admirable perseverance. 1825, he left Prague for Berlin, where he became acquainted with the system of Logier; returned in the same year and opened a school in his native town, where instruction was given according to Logier's system. This undertaking met with great success. He then transferred the management of it to his brother, Anton, and opened on a larger scale a similar "Logier" school at Prague in 1835, no less successful than the first. He was an excellent teacher and was highly respected.

*Prosniz, Albert, b. Dec. 2, 1829, Prague. Pupil of Proksch and Tomaschek. For many years Prof. of Pf. and Musical History at the Vienna Conserv. He made his name favourably known by a—
Handbuch der Clavier Literatur (Vienna, 1884). A second volume, comprising the works of modern composers, has been promised.

Pruckner, Dionys, b. May 17, 1834, Munich. Pupil of Fried. Niest and (1852-56) of Liszt, in Weimar. 1856-58, he resided in Vienna; 1859, in Munich, and was appointed the same year Prof. at the Stuttgart Conserv. 1864, he received the diploma of Hof-Pianist and (1868) the title of Königl. Prof. From the King of Würtemberg he received the great gold medal for art and science on the riband of the "Crown" Order, the Order of Frederic, and the "Jubilee" medal. 1861, he founded, with the violinist, Singer, and the violoncellist, Goltermann, chamber-music evenings. He travelled in Germany and America, and also played in Paris. He is one of the best pianists of our time, the clearness, correctness, and rhythmical excellence of his playing have everywhere been admired. He is also a successful teacher.

Prudent (Beunie), Emile, b. Feb. 3, 1817, Angoulême; d. May 14, 1863, Paris. At an early age he lost his parents, and was adopted by a Pf. tuner. In the Paris Conserv. he was a pupil of Lecouppey and Zimmermann (Pf.) and Laurent (Harmony). He obtained the second prize, 1831, and the first, 1833. Thalberg, who came to Paris, 1836, made a deep impression on him, so that he studied with restless energy in order to reach the point at which his model had arrived. 1840, he surprised the Parisians by his excellent performances, and the critics declared that he stood between Thalberg and Döhler. His performances were loudly applauded in Germany, Belgium, England, and France. His compositions are neatly constructed, elegant, and full of nice detail, but they lack grandeur, poetry, and, above all, originality.
Op. 9, Andante; †Op. 11, L'hirondelle; Etude; Op. 12, La ronde de nuit; Op. 16, 6 Etudes de genre; Op. 30, †No. 1, La Berceuse, No. 5, Chanson Sicilienne; Op. 33, Farandole; Op. 40, Vilanelle; Op. 41, †Le Reveil des Fées; Op. 52, Sous les Palmiers; Op. 60, 6 Etudes de Salon; Op. 64, Le rêve d'Ariel; Trio; Concert Symphonique.

Purcell, Henry, b. (about) 1658, Westminster (London); d. there Nov. 21, 1695. Pupil of Cooke, Humfrey, and Blow.
10 Sonatas for the Harpsichord, (London, 1683); Lessons for the Harpsichord (London); "Musick's Handmaid," by Playford, 1689. See also Farrenc, "Trésor du Pianiste" (27 pieces), and Pauer, "Old English Composers."

Q.

*Quidant (Pierre Robert Joseph), Alfred, b. 1815, Lyons; d. Oct. 9, 1893, Paris. Pupil at the Paris Conserv. and of Liszt. Being a brilliant performer, who understood how to exhibit all the best qualities of an instrument, and who possessed the talent of improvising in an interesting manner, the firm of Erard (Paris) entrusted him with the task of playing on their instruments in all the Exhibitions, beginning with the first Paris Exhibition, 1834, and ending with that of 1889. The London Exhibition of 1851 especially offered him the opportunity of showing not only his accomplishments as a pianist, but also the excellent qualities of the Erard pianos. He has received Orders of Knighthood on different occasions.
"Mazeppa"; Royal Polka; Le Roulis; "Parles-moi"; La Châtaine; La Marche du Prince Impérial; Hymn, played before the English Queen in the Exhibition, 1851. *Educational works:* Gymnastique des Pianistes devenu célèbre; L'Ame du Piano, essai sur les deux Pédales.

R.

Rachmaninoff, Sergei Wassiliewitsch, b. 1873, Novgorod. Pupil at the Imperial Conserv. of Moscow, where Arenski (Theory) and Siloti (Pf.) were his teachers. Received (1891) the great gold medal.
Concerto, Op. 1; Morceaux de Fantaisie, Op. 3; Fantaisie pour 2 Pf., Op. 5; Trio élégiaque, Op. 9.

Raff, Joachim, b. May 27, 1822, Lachen, on the lake of Zürich; d. June 24/25, 1882, Frankfort o/M. Son of an organist, he was educated at Wiesenstetten (Würtemberg), and went to the Jesuit College of Schwytz; being too poor to attend a University, he became a teacher. His talent for composing showed itself at an early age, and several little pieces which he sent to Mendelssohn gained the latter's favour, and he recommended the young artist to Breitkopf and Härtel, so that Raff had the satisfaction of seeing his first works engraved and printed. They are Op. 2 to Op. 14; and among them is a Scherzo (Op. 3), 12 Romances en forme d'Etudes (Op. 8), and a Sonata and Fugue (Op. 14). These pieces were received with so much favour, he resolved to devote himself entirely to music. Liszt and Bülow both encouraged him, and played his compositions in public. Having tried unsuccessfully to get an appointment in Stuttgart, he followed Liszt (1850) to Weimar, where he remained until 1856, when he left for Wiesbaden, where he worked till 1877, and then accepted the Directorship of the newly-founded "Hoch" Conserv. of Frankfort o/M. This post he filled loyally until his death. Raff was not only an experienced composer, but also an excellent teacher. He was also one of the most thoroughly instructed of men—a splendid linguist, well acquainted with history, geography, and the natural sciences. This general knowledge brought him the flattering nickname of "the wandering Encyclopædia." His compositions (about 200 works are published) are very uneven; some of them are even trivial and shallow, others are manufactured to the order of the publishers, whilst others rank very high.

With Orchestra : Ode au printemps, Op. 76; Concerto in C min., Op. 185; Suite in E flat, Op. 200. *Chamber Music :* Quintet, Op. 107; Trios, Op. 102, 112, 155, and 158; Sonatas with Vln., Op. 73, 78, 128, 129, and 145; Suite with Vln., Op. 210. *Piano Solos—* Suites: in A min., Op. 69; in C, Op. 71; †in E min., Op. 72; in D min. and D, Op. 91; No. 3, Ländler in E flat, Op. 162; in G (Au soir, Rhapsodie, Idylle), Op. 163; †in B flat (Rigaudon and Tambourin), Op. 204; Aus der Adventzeit (8 pieces), Op. 216; 12 morceaux (Fleurette, Fabliau, Babillarde), Op. 75; 12 morceaux (No. 12, †Procida, Tarantelle), Op. 82; Elegy, Romance, Valse, Op. 22; Capriccio (imitation of Mendelssohn's Op. 14), Op. 64; Introduction and Allegro, Op. 87; †Messagers du printemps, Op. 55; Tanz-Capricen, Op. 54; Valse-Caprice, Op. 116; Valse in C, Op. 111; Impromptu Valse, Op. 94; †Polka de la Reine, Op. 95; Gavotte in A min., Op. 125; Bolero, Op. 111; Valse brillante, Op. 169; 30 Etudes progressives; †Etude de Salon, Op. 88; 2 Etudes mélodiques, Op. 130; Fantaisie-Polonaise, Op. 106; Cavatine, †La Fileuse, Op. 157; Nocturne, A flat, Op. 17; Vilanelle, Op. 89; Impromptu, Op. 196; Airs suisses, Op. 60; Chaconne (2 Pf. à 4 mains), Op. 150; Marche brillante à 4 mains, Op. 132.

Raif, Oscar, b. July 31, 1847, The Hague (Holland). Pupil of his father, Carl R., and Tausig (Berlin). 1875, named Königl. Prof. Teacher at the Hochschule, excellent pianist, and talented composer.
Concerto, Sonata for Pf. and Vln.

Rameau, Jean Philippe, b. Sept. 25, 1683, Dijon; d. Sept. 12, 1764, Paris. He was organist in Lille and Clermont, and went, 1721, to Paris, where Louis XV. conferred on him the title of "Compositeur de Cabinet."
Premier livre de pièces de Clavecin, Paris, 1706; 2me livre, 1721; 3me livre, 1731; Nouvelles Suites de pièces de Clavecin, avec des remarques sur les différents genres de musique; 3 Concertos pour Clavecin, Violon et Basse de Viole, 1741. Among the best known are the †Suite in A min.; 2 Gigues en rondeaux; †La tendre Plainte; †La Poule; †Les Niais de Sologne; †Le Rappel des Oiseaux; 2 Menuets; l'Egyptienne.

Rappoldi, Laura (*née* Kahrer), b. Jan. 14, 1853, Mistelbach, near Vienna. In her tenth year she received her first instruction in Pf. playing, and made such rapid progress that in 1864 she played before the Empress of Austria, who then defrayed the costs of her education at the Vienna Conserv., under Dachs (Pf.) and Dessoff (Composition). 1867, she received the first prize, and began her journeys through Germany, Russia, &c. Afterwards profited by the advice of Henselt, Liszt, and Bülow. 1874, she married the distinguished violinist Rappoldi, and resides with her husband in Dresden, where both are Profs. at the Royal Conserv.

Rasetti (Razetti), Amadeo, b. 1754, Turin; d. 1799, Paris. Pupil of the clavecinist Clément. He established himself (1781?) at Paris, where his compositions found many admirers and he himself found friends and pupils.
  Concert arabe, Op. 14; 4 Trios; Sonatas with Vln.; 6 Sonates dans les styles d'Eckard, Haydn, Clementi, Cramer, Steibelt, et Mozart (Op. 7).

Ratzenberger, Theodor, b. April 14, 1840, Grossbreitenbach (Thuringia); d. March 8, 1879, Wiesbaden. Pupil of Liszt (Pf.) and Cornelius (Composition). Court Pianist of Schwarzburg (Sondershausen). His technical execution and finished as well as refined performances were deservedly admired. 1864, appointed Prof. in Lausanne and (1868) in Düsseldorf. Only a few of his compositions — mostly drawing-room pieces — were published.

Ravina, Jean Henri, b. May 20, 1818, Bordeaux. Pupil at the Paris Conserv., where Zimmermann (Pf.) and Laurent (Theory) were his teachers. 1832, second, 1834, first prize for Pf. playing, and 1836, first prize for Harmony. He continued his studies with Reicha and Leborne. 1837, he left the Conserv. Afterwards he performed not only in France, but also in Russia (1858) and Spain (1871), and was received with great cordiality, the neatness, correctness, and elegance of his style being everywhere admired. 1861, made Chevalier de la Légion d'honneur. His pieces enjoy great popularity.
  Op. 14, 12 Etudes de style et de perfectionnement (I., II.); Op. 28, 25 Exercices Etudes (I., II.); Op. 50, 25 Etudes harmonieuses (I., II.); Op. 35, Simple histoire; †Op. 41, Douce Pensée; †Op. 55, Jour de Bonheur; Op. 62, Petit Bolero, †Confidence, Nocturne; Op. 71, Historiette; Op. 86, Câlinerie; Op. 78, 12 pièces intimes; Op. 13, †Nocturne in D flat.

Reber (Napoléon), Henri, b. Sept. 23, 1807 (Fétis, Oct. 21), at Mühlhausen (Alsace); d. Nov. 24, 1880, Paris. Pupil at the Paris Conserv. under Reicha and Lesueur. 1862, succeeded Halévy as Prof. of Composition. 1853, elected Membre de l'Académie des Beaux-Arts; 1854, Chevalier de la Légion d'honneur.
  Op. 8, Trio; 2nd Trio; Op. 34, 6th Trio; Op. 36, Bagatelles (30); Op. 13, 2nd Suite; Valses for Pf., and some for Pf. and Vln.

*Redon, Ernest, b. June 15, 1835, New Orleans. Pupil of Schad (Pf.) and Schaffner (Harmony) at Bordeaux, where he now resides.
  "Hommage à Schumann," "Reflets d'Orient," "Chants créoles" (4).

*Rée, Anton, b. Oct. 5, 1820, Aarhus, Jütland; d. Dec. 20, 1886, Copenhagen. In his fifteenth year (1835) he went to Hamburg and was a pupil of Jacques Schmitt and Carl Krebs. 1839, he went to Vienna, and met with great success as a pianist; 1841, he was in Paris, became a pupil of Chopin, and also enjoyed the advice of Kalkbrenner. 1842, he settled in Copenhagen, where he worked as a teacher and as a reporter for the best German papers. Among his pupils were Aug. Winding, F. Hartvigson, and Mdlle. Th. Sanne. His compositions are mostly written for educational purposes. A book, "Musikhistorike Momenter," and the exercises, "Bitrag tie Klaverspiltets Teknik," are well known in Denmark.
  Sonatine, Op. 9; 3 Danses caractéristiques, Op. 17; Cadenzas to Mozart's Concertos in C and D min., and Beethoven's in C min.

Rehberg, Willy, b. Sept. 2, 1863, Morges (Switzerland). Son and pupil of the music teacher and organist, Friedrich R. Later he went to the Zürich Music School and then to Leipzig, where he entered the Conserv. He was appointed teacher there in 1884. 1890, Principal Prof. at the Music School of Geneva. He is an excellent performer and his compositions evince taste and elegance. The Duke of Altenburg gave him the title of "Court Pianist."
  Op. 2, 3 Characteristic Pieces: Menuet, Chanson d'amour, and Gavotte; Op. 4, 2 Etudes de Concert; Op. 3, Sonata in G min.; Op. 10, Sonata in D for Pf. and Vln.

Reicha, Anton, b. Feb. 27, 1770, Prague; d. May 28, 1836, Paris. Pupil of his uncle, Joseph R. 1794, went to Hamburg; 1799, to Paris. 1802-8, he resided in Vienna, where he was in friendly intimacy with Beethoven, Haydn, Albrechtsberger, and Salieri. 1808, he returned to Paris; 1818, appointed Prof. of Composition at the Conserv. (as successor to Méhul); 1835, he succeeded Boieldieu as "Membre de l'Académie." He was also Chevalier de la Légion d'honneur.
  Quartet, with wind instruments; Trios; Sonatas with Vln.; Solo Sonatas, Op. 40, 43, and 46; 36 Fugues, according to a new system; 6 Fugues, Op. 81; L'Art de varier, 57 Variations, Op. 57; Etudes et Exercices, Op. 31; Etudes dans le genre fugue, Op. 97.

Reinecke, Carl (Heinrich Carsten), b. June 23, 1824, Altona. Pupil of his father. 1843, in Leipzig, where he enjoyed Mendelssohn and Schumann's friendship and advice; 1846, Court Pianist to the King of Denmark; 1848-49, he resided at Leipzig, afterwards at Bremen; 1851, appointed Pf. Prof. at the Cologne Conserv.; 1854, Musik Director at Barmen; 1859, in a similar position at Breslau; 1860, appointed Prof. at the Leipzig Conserv. and Conductor of the Gewandhaus Concerts, which appointment he still holds. Among his pupils were many well-known and celebrated names, such as Max Bruch, J. Brambach, Arnold Krug, E. Rudorff, Arthur Sullivan, Svendsen, Edvard Grieg, Hans Huber, Ernst Perabo, Otto Klauwell, and Hugo Riemann for Composition; L. Maas, James Kwast, August Winding, Rafael Joseffi, the ladies Schirmacher and Jeanne Becker for Pf. His merits have often been recognised. The King of Saxony gave him the title of Royal Prof., the Leipzig University conferred on him the diploma of Doc. Phil., *hon. causâ*, he is Hon. Member of many societies, and many sovereigns bestowed high Orders on him. He is a prolific composer, as the following list will show—

> Concertos (with Orchestra), Op. 72 and 120; Quintet; Quartet; Trios (6); Sonatas for Pf. and V'cello (2); Sonatas for Pf. and Vln. (4); Fantasia for Pf. and Vln., Op. 160; Sonatas for 2 and 4 hands; Sonatinas, Op. 47 (3); Op. 98 (3); Op. 127a (6); Op. 136 (6); Fantasia in the form of a Sonata, Op. 15; Romanzas (3), Op. 28; Serenade, Op. 48; Old and New Dances (4), Op. 57; Märchen-Vorspiele à 4 mains, Op. 99; Maiden's Songs (10), Op. 88; Fantasiestücke (10), Op. 17; Serious and gay (12), Op. 145; Aus der Jugendzeit (8), Op. 106; †Ein neues Notenbuch für kleine Leute, Op. 107; 24 Studies, Op. 121; 4 pieces, Op. 129 (†No. 3); 4 characteristic pieces, Op. 13 (Nos. 1 and 4); Nocturne, Op. 69; 6 pieces, Op. 123 (Nos. 1, 5, and 6); †Ballade, Op. 20; Hausmusik (1-18), Op. 77; Variations on an Air of Händel, Op. 84; Duos for 2 Pf., †Op. 66 ("Manfred"); ditto, "La belle Griselidis," Op. 94.

*****Reinhold,** Hugo, b. March 3, 1854, Vienna. Pupil at the Conserv. under Schenner and Epstein (Pf.), Bruckner (Harmony), Dessoff (Composition). Since 1874, when he left the Conserv., he has devoted his time entirely to composition. Excellent pianist.

> Suite, with Orchestra, Op. 7 (received the Beethoven Priz*)*; Sonata for Pf. and Vln.; 2 Serenades for Pf. and Vln.; Bagatelles (5), Op. 12; †Intermezzo, Op. 14; Jugend-Album (10), Op. 27; Impromptus (3), Op. 28.

*****Reisenauer,** Alfred, b. Nov. 1, 1863, Königsberg (Prussia). Pupil of Louis Köhler and Liszt. Appeared for the first time at Cardinal Hohenlohe's palace (Tivoli, Rome) with Liszt. 1881, he gave concerts in London and Leipzig; 1881-82, he studied at the University of Leipzig. Since 1882 has made journeys in Austria, Sweden, Norway, Denmark, Germany, Russia, Siberia, Central Asia, &c. Eminent pianist.

Reissiger, Carl Gottlieb, b. Jan. 31, 1798, Belzig, near Wittenberg; d. Nov. 7, 1869, Dresden. 1811, pupil, at the Leipzig Thomas School, of Schicht; 1822, of Winter (Munich); 1826, engaged to organise a Conserv. at The Hague (Holland), but eventually engaged as Capellmeister in Dresden. His compositions enjoyed popularity with amateurs, and his Quartets, and particularly his Trios, were for a long time favourite pieces. The valse, generally called "Weber's last idea," is by Reissiger.

> Quartets: Op. 29, in A min.; Op. 70, in C min.; Op. 108, in E flat; Op. 138, in E flat; Op. 141, in E flat. Trios (15): Op. 33, 40, 56, 75, 77, 85, 97, 103, 115, 125, 137, 150, 158, 167. Sonatas with Vln.: Op. 45, 94, 102; with V'cello: Op. 102, 152; Sonatas (3); Sonatas, for 4 hands (2); Rondeaux, Op. 27 (4 hands), Op. 37, 39; Valses, Op. 49; Danses modernes et brillantes (12), Op. 38; (12), Op. 46.

Remmert, Martha, b. Sept. 13, 1854, in the village Gross-schwein, near Glogau. Pupil of Kullak, later of Tausig and Liszt. She is considered one of the best pianists of the present time.

Rendano, Alfonso, b. April 5, 1853, Carolei, near Cosenza (Calabria). Pupil at the Conserv. of Naples, later of Thalberg, and (1871) at the Leipzig Conserv. During his visit to London he played with great success at the Philharmonic Society and Musical Union Concerts. He resides in Italy, where his works (mostly drawing-room pieces) are published.

Rheinberger, Joseph Gabriel, b. March 17, 1839, Vaduz, Liechtenstein (on the Swiss frontier). 1851-54, pupil at the Royal Music School of Munich, where he settled; 1859, appointed Prof.; 1867, Royal Prof. and Inspector of the same school; 1877, Königl. Capellmeister of the Hofkirche. Member of the Bavarian Maximilian Order for art and science, Knight of several other Orders, and Member of the Royal Academy of Prussia.

> Concerto in A flat, Op. 94; †Quintet, Op. 115; †Quartet in E flat, Op. 38; Trios (2): †No. 2, Op. 112; Sonatas for Pf. and Vln.:

No. 2 in E flat, Op 105; Solo Sonatas: Sonata Symphonique, Op. 47; Sonata. D flat, Op. 99; **Sonata**, E flat, Op. 115; Toccatas, Op. †12, 101, 104, †115; Preludes (24), in the form of Studies, Op. 14; Etude, Op. 101; 6 Morceaux Fugués, Op. 39; ditto, Op. 68; Etudes (3), Op. 6; †Humoresques (4), Op. 28; †From Italy (3), Op. 29; †2 Morceaux, Op. 45, †1 petits Morceaux de Concert, Op. 5; †Waldmärchen, Op. 8; Theme with 61 Variations, Op. 61; Tarantelle, Rhapsody, and Rondoletto, Op. 53; †Capriccio, Menuet, and Fugue for the left hand, Op. 113; En vacances, 4 pieces for 4 hands, Op. 72; †Tarantelle, Op. 13.

Riccius, August Ferdinand, b. Feb. 26, 1819, Bernstadt, near Herrnhut (Silesia); d. July 4, 1886, Carlsbad. Until his fourteenth year he was instructed by Schönfeld; attended (1833) the college of Zittau; 1840, studied theology at the Leipzig University, but then resolved to devote himself to music. 1849, appointed Director of the Euterpe concerts; 1855, Conductor of the Leipzig and (1864) of the Hamburg Opera.

Sonate mélancolique, Op. 16; 4 easy characteristic pieces, Op. 2; 5 melodious pieces (†No. 4), Op. 25; A Christmas gift for the house (12 pieces), with descriptions and verses; 2 Marches à 4 mains, Op. 21; Allegro appassionato à 4 mains, Op. 41.

*Richards, Brinley, b. Nov. 13, 1817, Carmarthen (Wales); d. May 1, 1885, London. His father, an organist, was his first teacher. Although intended to study medicine, his talent for music was so pronounced that he entered the R.A.M., London, where he received (1835-37) the King's Scholarship. He soon gained distinction by his excellent reading and performance of classical Pf. music. After a visit to Paris, where he met Chopin, he was appointed Prof. at the R.A.M. His compositions, written in a fluent, light, pleasing, and practical style, became very popular. His Andante con moto, Caprice in F min., and some others prove that he studied composition in an exhaustive manner. As a teacher he was sincerely beloved by his pupils and respected by his colleagues for his upright, frank, and excellent character. He belonged to the staff of the Guildhall School until his too early death. His name will be perpetuated by the composition of the beautiful National Anthem, "God bless the Prince of Wales" (produced for the first time on Feb. 14, 1863).

Richter, Ernst Friedrich, b. Oct. 24, 1808, Gross-Schönau, near Leipzig; d. April 9, 1879, Leipzig. Pupil of Weinlig. 1843, appointed Prof. at the Leipzig Conserv.; 1868, Musical Director and Cantor of the Thomas School; also Musical Director of the University. Received the title of Königl. Prof.

Op. 7, 3 Romanzas; Op. 21, 3 Preludes and Fugues; Op 26, Sonata with Vln. (A min.); Op. 27, Sonata (C sharp min.); Op. 30, 4 characteristic pieces; Op. 31,'4 pieces; Op. 33, Sonata (E flat); Op. 34, Variations on an original air for 4 hands.

Ricordi, Giulio, b. 1835, Milan. He received an excellent musical education, and is the present proprietor of the well-known firm Ricordi, of Milan. His compositions—Studies, Fantasias, &c.—show considerable talent, while the pieces published under the *nom de plume* of *Burgmein* are finished with much care and possess decided elegance and refinement.

Rie, Bernhard (Bernard-Rie), b. Oct. 25, 1839, Prague. Up to 1856 pupil of Alex. Dreyschock. He resides in Paris.

25 Etudes spéciales and 25 Etudes d'agilité, Op. 37; "La belle Batelière," and a Tarantella.

Riemann, Dr. Hugo, b. July 18, 1849, Grossmehla, near Sondershausen. Pupil of Frankenberger (Theory), Barthel and Ratzenberger (Pf.). 1865-68, he studied at the Convent School of Rossleben, later at the University of Berlin. 1870-71, he had to serve in the army, and then resolved to devote himself entirely to music. For this purpose he became a pupil at the Leipzig Conserv.; became (1873) Doc. Phil. of the University of Göttingen. For several years Conductor at Bielefeld, he went (1878) to Leipzig as "Privat Dozent" of the University; 1880, as teacher to Bromberg; 1881, to Hamburg as one of the principal teachers at the Conserv.; 1890, appointed Prof. at Sondershausen; and at present is similarly occupied at Wiesbaden. He edited, with remarks and directions for phrasing, Mozart and Beethoven's Sonatas, Schubert's Impromptus, Bach's Inventions and 48 Preludes and Fugues, and Clementi and Kuhlau's Sonatinas.

Theoretical Works: Catechism of musical instruments; ditto of musical history; ditto of Pf. playing; Analysis of Bach's 48 Preludes and Fugues; Dynamik und Agogik (method of musical phrasing); On phrasing in the elementary instruction; Dictionary of Music (4th edition, 1893). *Pf. Compositions*: Sonata; 6 Sonatinas, Op. 43; Sonatina for 4 hands, Op. 49; Sonata with Vln.; Elementar-Schule; Technical and other Studies, Op. 40 and 41; 5 Pieces, Op. 21; Romanza in F sharp, Op. 7.

Ries, Ferdinand, b. Nov. 29, 1784, Bonn on the Rhine; d. Jan. 13, 1838, Frankfort o/M. 1800-4, Beethoven's pupil at Vienna. Left Vienna 1805, went, *via* Coblenz, to Paris, where he remained for two years, leaving afterwards for Russia. 1813, he arrived in London, where he succeeded admirably as a teacher, composer, and performer; 1830, he left London and settled in Frankfort o/M. He was an industrious composer, but only a very few of his works were able to withstand the influence of time and altered fashion, and are thus almost completely forgotten. The following is only an approximate list of his Pf. works:—

Concertos: Op. 42 in E flat; †Op. 55 in C sharp min.; Op. 115 in C min.; Op. 120 (Pastoral) in D; Op. 123 in C; Farewell Concerto, Op. 132, in A min.; Op. 151, "Salut au Rhin," in A flat; Op. 177 in G. *Chamber Music*: Op. 25, Septuor in E flat; Op. 100, Sextet in C; Op. 142, Sextet; Op. 128, Octet; Op. 74, Quintet in B min.; Quartets, Op. 13, 16, 141; Trios, Op. 2, 28, 63, 95, and 143; 24 Sonatas with Vln.; 3 Sonatinas with Vln. *Solo Music:* 52 Sonatas; 15 Fantasias; Rondos; Variations; Ballades †Studies, Op. 31; 40 Preludes, Op. 60, &c.

Rietz, Dr. Julius, b. Dec. 28, 1812, Berlin; d. Sept. 12, 1877, Dresden. Pupil of Romberg and Ganz. 1834, Conductor at Düsseldorf; 1847, Capellmeister of the Leipzig Theatre; 1848, Conductor of the Gewandhaus Concerts; 1854, having given up the post of Capellmeister, he devoted himself entirely to the Gewandhaus Concerts and accepted the appointment of Prof. at the Conserv.; 1859, the Leipzig University conferred upon him the diploma of Doc. Phil., *hon. causâ;* 1860, he succeeded Reissiger as Königl. Hof-Capellmeister of the Dresden Opera, and was elected Director of the Royal Conserv.; 1874, the King of Saxony gave him the title of "General Musik Director."

Sonata in A min., Op. 17; Sonata with Vln.; Sonata with Fl.; Scherzo capriccioso, Op. 5; Arrangements of Haydn's Symphonies, Mendelssohn's Overtures, Marches, &c.

Rimbault, Edward Francis, LL.D., London, Doc. Phil., *hon. causâ*, Göttingen, b. June 13, 1816, London; d. there Sept. 26, 1876. Pupil of his father and Wesley, he was, as early as 1832, Organist in Soho; founded (1841), with E. Taylor and William Chappell, the Musical Antiquarian Society; edited the book "Parthenia"; published (1860) "The Pianoforte, its origin, progress, and construction." He was very industrious in arranging operas, oratorios, and in writing a great number of educational works.

Rimsky-Korsakow, Nicolaus Andrejewitch, b. 1844, Tichwin (Russia). An officer of the Navy, he studied music only as an amateur, and had mostly to depend upon self-instruction; but thanks to his perseverance and admirable energy he was (1871) appointed Prof. of Composition at the Conserv. of St. Petersburg, and succeeded Balakirew as Director of the Free Music School.

Op. 10, Valse, Intermezzo, Scherzo, Nocturne; Prélude et Fugue; 6 Variations sur le thème B-A-C-H; Op. 11, 4 Morceaux; Berceuse; Tarantella; Menuetto; Carillon; Fugue grotesque. The last 5 pieces are introduced in the collection "Bigarrures."

Rinaldi, Giovanni, b. 1840, Reggio (Emilia). Biographical details are entirely wanting.

Fantasias, Sketches, Novellettes, Nocturnes, and Barcarolles.

Rinck, Johann Christian Heinrich, b. Feb. 18, 1770, Elgersburg (Thuringia); d. Aug. 7, 1846, Darmstadt. 1786-89, pupil of Kittel (Erfurt); 1790, organist at Giessen; 1805, at Darmstadt; 1813, Hof-Organist; 1845, Doc. Phil., *hon. causâ*, of the University of Giessen. Excellent organist and teacher.

Trios: Sonates pour Pf., Vln., et V'cello, Op. 32 (3), and one in E flat; Sonatas with V'cello; also for 4 hands; Preludes, Op. 25; Two-part exercises (30), Op. 67; Exercises for beginners for 2 and 4 hands (I., II.), Op. 60.

Riotte, Philipp Jacob, b. Aug. 16, 1776, Trier; d. Aug. 20, 1856, Vienna. He was for several years conductor of the opera at Prague, afterwards in the same capacity at Vienna. In his time he enjoyed great popularity in Austria as a composer for the Pf.

Concertos, Op. 8 and 15; Concerto for 2 Pfs.; Trios, in F and E flat, Op. 9; Sonatas with Vln. (7); Solo Sonatas (13); Variations (12 sets); Rondos (6). His best known work is "The Battle of Leipzig," a characteristic tone-picture, of which there were several editions.

*****Risler, Edouard**, b. Feb. 23, 1873, Baden-Baden (of French parents). Pupil at the Paris Conserv. of L. Diémer (Pf.). 1889, he received the first prize and travelled in Germany, profiting by the advice of Eugen d'Albert. His performances in London were very successful.

Ritter, Théodore (Bennet), b. April 5, 1841, near Paris; d. April 6, 1886, Paris. Pupil of Liszt. Excellent pianist and a talented composer. Of his elegant, brilliant, and effective pieces, one became a great favourite—"Les Courriers."

*Röckel, Joseph Leopold, b. April 11, 1838, London. Pupil of Eisenhofer (Würzburg) and Götze (Weimar) for Composition, and of his father and brother, Eduard R., for Pf. For many years has lived at Clifton (Bristol) and is highly respected as an excellent teacher.

Air au Dauphin; Allegretto pastorale; "Gwendoline" (Idyl and Dance of the Sylphs). For his operatic Fantasias and easier pieces he uses the pseudonym "Edouard Dorn."

Röder, Martin, b. April 7, 1851, Berlin. 1870-72, pupil at the Hochschule; then he received an appointment in Milan. Since 1880 he has resided at Berlin as a teacher of singing.

Trio in F min.; "Aus meinem Skizzenbuch" (2 books, each containing 6 pieces).

Röntgen, Julius, b. May 9, 1855, Leipzig. Pupil at the Conserv., where Hauptmann, Richter, and Reinecke were his teachers. Since 1878 he has resided at Amsterdam as Prof. of the Music School. He is an excellent pianist and a talented composer.

Sonata with Vln.; Sonata with V'cello; Solo Sonatas; Op. 5, a Cycle of Pf. pieces; Op. 6, Ballade; Op. 7, Suite (4 movements); Op. 8, Fantasia; Op. 12, Julklapp (a Christmas piece); Op. 16, Introduction, Scherzo, Intermezzo, and Finale.

*Roger-Miclos, Marie, b. May 1, 1862, Toulouse. 1873, she became a pupil at the Paris Conserv. of Madame Massart. After having gained (1877) the first prize, she was appointed Prof. 1891, and obtained the (for a lady) rare distinction of being made Officier de l'Instruction publique. She is one of the most distinguished pianists of the present time, and has several times been heard and admired in London.

Rohde, Eduard, b. 1828, Halle a/S.; d. March 25, 1883, Berlin. Among the modern educational composers he is certainly one of the best; his pieces are throughout solidly constructed, correctly and practically written, and their melodiousness and ingratiating qualities have made his name well known.

Sonatinas; Feuilles volantes, Op. 36, &c.

Rolle, Johann Heinrich, b. Dec. 23, 1718, Quedlinburg; d. Dec. 29, 1785, Magdeburg. Pupil of his father, an organist. Studied (1736) at the Leipzig University; went afterwards to Berlin as member of the Royal Orchestra; remained there till 1746, when he was appointed Organist at the principal church of Magdeburg, and, after the death of his father (1752). Musik-Director of the town.

3 Concertos, Op. 1 (Berlin); Sonatas (Leipzig); and shorter pieces, to be found in Em. Bach's "Musikalisches Vielerley und Allerley" (1760-62).

*Rollfuss, Bernhard, b. July 21, 1837, Göritzhain (Saxony). Pupil of Friedrich Wieck and Blassmann (Pf.), and of Julius Otto (Composition), of Dresden; later of Hauptmann and Julius Rietz (Leipzig). 1863-75, he played at his Chamber Music Concerts (Dresden). Founded (1875) a musical academy for ladies and an elementary school, in which sixteen experienced teachers are giving lessons. The King of Saxony conferred on him the title of Königl. Prof.

Melodious Finger Exercises; Studies, Op. 12 and Op. 25 (to strengthen the fourth and fifth fingers); Drawing-room pieces, combined with Scale exercises; Op. 23, Nocturne; Op. 24, Scherzo; Op. 26, Andante cantabile; Op. 27, Intermezzo; Op. 30, Prelude, Romanza, and Novellette.

Rosellen, Henri, b. Oct. 13, 1811, Paris; d. there March 20, 1876. Pupil at the Conserv., where his teachers were Pradher and Zimmermann for Pf., Dourlen, Fétis, and Halévy for Composition. After having left the Conserv. he took lessons from Henri Herz (1835). Highly successful as a teacher and extraordinarily popular as a composer of easy, practically written, and agreeably sounding drawing-room pieces.

Trio, Op. 82, in F; 25 Etudes de moyenne force, Op. 133, which ought to precede the 12 Etudes brillantes, Op. 60; Manuel des Pianistes, Op. 116; Nocturne et Tarantelle, Op. 92; †Rêverie in G; 3 Rêveries, Op. 28; 76 Fantaisies on operatic airs; 11 Rondos; and many sets of Variations.

*Rosenhain, Jacob (Jacques), b. Dec. 2, 1813, Mannheim; d. March 21, 1894, Baden-Baden. Pupil of Jacob Schmitt (at that time residing in Mannheim) and of Schnyder von Wartensee, in Frankfort o/M. 1837, he went to London, where he gave a concert, and performed at one of the Philharmonic Society concerts. In the autumn (1837) he went to Paris, where he remained until 1870, when the Franco-German War obliged him to reside at Baden-Baden, where he had a villa. He was a hard-working teacher and composer, and had received decorations from Holland, France, Spain, Portugal, and Baden, and was elected Hon. Member of the St. Cecilia Society of Rome.

Quartet for Pf. and Strings, Op. 1; Trios, Op. 2, 32, 50, and 80; Sonatas for Pf. and V'cello, Op. 38 and †53; Concertino, Op. 5; †Concerto, Op. 73; 12 Etudes caractéristiques, Op. 17 (†No. 2, Sérénade du Pêcheur; †No. 5, Danse des Sylphes); 24 Etudes mélodiques, Op. 20 (Introduction to those of Cramer); Sonata in F min., Op. 41; †Sonate symphonique, F min., Op. 70; Sonata in D min., Op. 74. Mélodies caractéristiques: I., Op. 25 (†Chant montagnard); II., Op. 31; III., Op. 37 (†Chants orientaux); IV., Op. 45 (†Calabraise et Ballade); V., Op. 67 (Chanson slave); VI., Op. 68 (Barcarolle); VII., Op. 82 (Berceuse). Historiettes, Op. 97; †Rêveries, Op. 26; Scène dramatique, Op. 30.

Rosenthal, Moriz, b. Dec. 18, 1862, Lemberg. Pupil (1873) of Mikuli, with whom he played, when only a child, Chopin's Rondo in C for 2 Pf. 1875, his parents settled in Vienna, where he studied with Rafael Joseffy. 1876, he gave a successful concert in Vienna, and his parents then went with him to Belgrade and Bucharest, where the youth of fourteen was named Pianist to the Roumanian Court. In the same year (1876) he was introduced to Liszt, who invited him to accompany him to Weimar. 1878, after having been in Weimar, he went to Paris and St. Petersburg, where he created a great sensation. In order to follow up his general studies he attended (for twenty months) the Staats-Gymnasium in Vienna, passed his "maturity" examination, and went to the University lectures of Zimmermann, Brentano, and Hanslick; in spite of this—with him an earnest and serious occupation—he continued his Pf. studies with the greatest energy. After six years' retirement he reappeared (1882) in Vienna, and his marvellous performances were received with the utmost enthusiasm. Since then his reputation has increased in a wonderful degree, and in Berlin, Dresden, Cologne—indeed, everywhere — he has astonished and bewildered the most experienced musicians by his unrivalled technique, and earned the most phrenetic expressions of approval from crowded audiences. His playing is distinguished principally by his enormous virtuosity. It is not only his astonishing technique, but his marvellous endurance, which is really phenomenal, and puts into shade everything that has yet been known. The results of his technical studies are laid down in the work lately published.

School of modern Pf. Virtuosity: "Technical Studies for the highest degree of development." By Moriz Rosenthal and Ludvig Schytte.

Rosetti, Franz Anton, b. 1750, Leitmeritz, Bohemia—where he was called Roester; d. June 30, 1792, Ludwigslust. His parents intended him to become a priest, and he took (1769) the first vow as lay-priest: but as he wished to devote himself entirely to music he went to Rome and obtained a dispensation. He was for some time conductor of the band of Prince Wallerstein, but received (1789) the appointment of Hof-Capellmeister at Schwerin. 1792, the King Frederic William III. of Prussia invited him to Berlin, where he conducted an oratorio of his own composition.

Concerto; Trios; Sonatas for Pf., Vln., and V'cello (6), Op. 1; (3), Op. 2; 3 Divertissements.

Rubinstein, Anton Gregorowitsch, b. Nov. 30, 1830, Wechwotynecz, Bessarabia (this date was given by himself); d. Nov. 20, 1894, Peterhof, near St. Petersburg. Showed at a very early age extraordinary talent for music, and was first instructed by his mother. His parents taking up their abode in Moscow, where the father established a pencil manufactory, Anton's musical education was entrusted to Villoing, who was the only master of the great artist. When he was ten years old Villoing took his pupil to Paris, where he introduced him to Liszt and Chopin; both were so struck with the boy's eminent talent that they (particularly Liszt) strongly advised that he should be taken to Germany for further education. From Paris, master and pupil went to Holland, England, Scandinavia, Germany, and finally to Moscow. In all these countries the young artist gave Concerts with the greatest possible success. On their return (1843), Anton's younger brother, Nicolaus, also highly gifted, was just seven years old, so the mother decided to take both boys to Berlin, where Anton, on the recommendation of Meyerbeer, became a pupil of Prof. Dehn. All the Berlin musicians took great interest in the career of the genial youth, and Mendelssohn also felt the sincerest sympathy for him. 1846, the mother was obliged to return (with her youngest son Nicolaus) to Moscow, owing to the illness of her husband, whilst Anton remained in Berlin, only leaving for a short tour in Hungary with the eminent flautist, Heindl. Owing to political events, he returned (1848) to Russia, where he found a generous patron in the

Grand Duchess Helena (Princess of Würtemberg); 1852, advised and assisted by the Grand Duchess and Count Wielhorski, he again went to Germany, where he found publishers for his numerous works. After having given Concerts in Paris and London he returned (1858) to St. Petersburg, was appointed Pianist to the Court and Conductor of the concerts. 1859, he accepted the direction of the Russian Musical Society; founded, 1862, the Imperial Conserv., and became its Director. 1867-70, he travelled through Europe, giving concerts, and being received with the greatest enthusiasm. 1872-73, he was on a tour in America. After 1867 he had no fixed appointment, but, 1887, after Davidoff's death, he again undertook the direction of the St. Petersburg Conserv., which he relinquished shortly before his death. He possessed one of the noblest characters imaginable, and was an artist in the full sense of the word— free from any envy or jealousy, a generous and liberal colleague, full of veneration for all that is good and grand, entirely devoid of vanity, or of the desire to put himself forward; was indifferent to praise, and, in spite of his enormous successes, retained a simplicity and modesty rarely to be found. The Czar of Russia conferred on him the Vladimir Order, with the rank of nobility, and appointed him Imperial Director-General of Music, with the rank of Imperial Councillor and the title of "Excellency"; the French Republic named him Officer of the Legion of Honour; he was also a Member of the "Ordre pour le Mérite," the highest possible distinction an artist can receive in Germany, and nearly all the European Sovereigns decorated him. He was an Hon. Member of learned and musical societies, including the Royal Academy of Prussia—in fact, he received the greatest rewards which an artist can receive. Rubinstein was a serious and earnest artist. His book, "Music and its Masters," testifies to his thorough knowledge of musical history, and many of his articles in musical papers are full of original, correct, and excellent ideas. At the same time he was one of the greatest of all pianists past and present, his execution was marvellous, his touch possessing all imaginable qualities and gradations of tone and expression. In his readings greater importance was attached to the general musical contents than to minute technical details—the emotional at times overweighting the intellectual. Everything played by him appeared to the listener an intelligible musical speech. Even when not coinciding with our own opinions, his playing never lacked the charm of conviction and originality.

Concertos: No. 1, E min., Op. 25; No. 2, in F, Op. 35; †No. 3, in G, Op. 45; †No. 4, in D min., Op. 70; †No. 5, in E flat, Op. 94; Fantaisie in C, Op. 84; Caprice Russe, Op. 102; Concertstück, Op. 113. *Chamber Music:* Octet, Op. 9, in D, for Pf., Vln., Vla., V'cello, Double Bass, Fl., Cl., Hn.; Quintet in F, with wind instruments, Op. 55; Quintet with strings, in G min., Op. 99; Quartet in C, Op. 66. Trios: No. 1, in F; No. 2, G min., Op. 15; †No. 3, in B flat, Op. 52; No. 4, in A, Op. 85; No. 5, in C min., Op. 108. Sonatas with Vln.: No. 1, in G, Op. 13; No. 2, A min., Op. 19; No. 3, in B min., Op. 98; 3 Morceaux, Op. 11; Sonata with Vla. in F min., Op. 49. Sonatas with V'cello: †No. 1, in D, Op. 18; No. 2, in G, Op. 39. *For 4 hands:* (2 Pf.) Fantaisie in F, Op. 73; (Pf.) Character-Bilder (6), Op. 50; Sonata in D, Op. 89; †Bal Costumé, Suite, &c., Op. 103. *Solo Music:* Sonatas: No. 1, in E, Op. 12; No 2, in C min., Op. 20; No. 3, in F, Op. 41; No. 4, in A min., Op. 100. 2 Mélodies, Op. 3; 3 Pieces: Polonaise, †Cracovienne, Mazurka, Op. 5; Kammenoi Ostrow (24), Op. 10; Le Bal (10 pieces): †Polka Mazurka, †Polonaise), Op. 14; 3 Morceaux (No. 3, Serenade), Op. 16; 3 Caprices (No. 3), Op. 21; †6 Etudes, Op. 23; 6 Préludes, Op. 24; 2 pieces (†No. 1), Op. 26; 2 pieces (No. 1, Barcarolle), Op. 30; (6) Soirées à St. Petersbourg (No. 3); 6 Morceaux (No. 1, Mélancolie in G min.), Op. 51; 5 Morceaux (†Nos. 2 and 3), Op. 69; Album de Peterhof (†Nos. 2 and 5), Op. 75; Fantaisies in E min., Op. 77; in C, Op. 84; 6 Etudes, Op. 81; †Etude in C (No. 1); †in E flat (No. 3); †Valse Caprice; †Barcarolle, No. 4, in G; Miscellanées (Book 1-9); †Romanza in E flat; †Melody in F.

Rubinstein, Nicolaus, b. June 2, 1835, Moscow; d. March 23, 1881, Paris. Pupil of Villoing, Kullak, and Dehn. For some time it was thought that he possessed greater talent for Composition than his brother Anton, but this supposition was not realised. 1859, he founded the Russian Musical Society of Moscow, which Society opened (1864) the Conserv., of which Nicolaus was the Director until his death. 1878, he conducted, during the French Exhibition, three "Russian" concerts in the Trocadero, which were so successful that he gave a fourth, at which he also appeared as a pianist. His brother, Anton, declared Nicolaus to be the better performer, but this opinion was not shared by the general public. His playing was full of fire and impetuosity, and he particularly excelled in the performance of his brother's compositions. Only a few of his pieces were published, but these are original and full of taste and elegance.

Op. 11, Mazurka, No. 1, †Mazurka, No. 2; Op. 13, †Bolero; Op. 14, †Tarantelle; Op. 15, Polka; Op. 16, †Valse de Salon; Op. 17, Polonaise, Scène de Bal; Deux feuilles d'Album.

Rudolph, Johann Joseph Rainer, Archduke of Austria, Cardinal, Prince-Bishop of Ollmütz, youngest son of the Emperor Leopold II., b. Jan. 8, 1788, Florence; d. July 24, 1831, Baden, near Vienna. Pupil and friend of Beethoven, who dedicated the following important works to his Imperial pupil:

Concerto, No. 4, in G, Op. 58; No. 5, in E flat, Op. 73; Sonata, "Les Adieux, l'Absence, et le Retour," in E flat, Op. 81a; Pf. score of the opera "Fidelio," Op. 72b; Sonata with Vln., in G, Op. 96; Sonata in B flat, Op. 106; Trio in B flat, Op. 97; Missa solennis, Op. 123; Fugue for Strings, Op. 133; and several smaller pieces.

The Archduke's own published compositions were—

Sonata for Pf. and Cl., Op. 2; and a theme given by Beethoven, varied 40 times.

Rudorff, Ernst Friedrich Carl (son of the Prof. and Privy Councillor (Geheimrath), Dr. Adolph R.), b. Jan. 18, 1840, Berlin. At first a pupil of Bargiel (Pf.), he passed his "Abiturienten" Examination, and intended to inscribe his name as student at the University, but left (1859) for Leipzig, where he entered the Conserv., and studied under Plaidy and Moscheles (Pf.) and J. Rietz (Composition), taking, later, private lessons from Hauptmann and Reinecke. 1865, appointed Prof. at the Cologne Conserv., and (1869) Principal Prof. at the Hochschule (Berlin). Among his pupils the most distinguished are Natalie Janotha and Bernhard Stavenhagen. For ten years he was Conductor of the Stern Choral Society. He received the Prussian Order of the Red Eagle and the Order of "Christ" of Portugal, and is a Member of the Royal Academy of Prussia.

Variations for 2 Pfs., Op. 1; 6 pieces for 4 hands, Op. 4.

Rüfer, Philippe Barthélemy, b. June 7, 1844, Liège, where his father, a German, was appointed Prof. at the Conserv. Pupil at the Conserv.; 1867, Musik-Director at Essen; settled (1871) at Berlin, where he was teacher at the Stern Conserv., and then at the Scharwenka Conserv. As a composer he made his name favourably known by—

Sonata with Vln., Op. 1; Phantasiestücke for 4 hands, Op. 10; and solo pieces, Op. 14, 21, and 22; Op. 24, Scherzo; Op. 26, Scherzo; Op. 27, 6 pieces; Op. 34, Trio (Bolero).

*****Rummel**, Franz, b. Jan. 11, 1853, London. Pupil of Louis Brassin (Brussels). 1872, gained the first prize; 1877-78, he made a tour, with Minnie Hauck and Ole Bull, through Holland; 1878, made his first, 1886, his second journey to America; 1884-85, teacher first in Kullak's, then in Stern's Academy (Berlin). 1889, the Kings of Sweden and Denmark conferred Orders on him. His excellent playing has everywhere been received with great favour. He resides at New York.

Rust, Friedrich Wilhelm, b. July 6, 1739, Dessau; d. there Feb. 28, 1796. He studied law at the Leipzig University until 1762, but then devoted himself to music. Pupil of Höckh (Vln.); 1763, of Franz Benda (Composition). Prince Leopold III. of Anhalt-Dessau took Rust with him to Italy (1765-66), and appointed him (1775) Hof-Musik-Director. Rust was really a violinist, but his compositions for the Clavecin deserve recognition.

6 Sonatas; 24 Variations on a Song by Schulz (1782); Allegretto grazioso with Variations (1797); Grande Sonate (posthumous). His grandson, Wilhelm Rust, has lately published two Sonatas (B flat min. and F sharp min.) by his grandfather.

Ruthardt, Adolph, b. Feb. 9, 1849, Stuttgart. 1864-68, pupil at the Conserv., where his teachers were Lebert and Speidel (Pf.), Faisst and Stark (Composition). After having finished his studies he went to Geneva, and remained there eighteen years (1886) actively promoting the classical and modern German music. 1886, appointed Prof. at the Leipzig Conserv.

Sonata for 2 Pfs., Op. 31; Trio pastorale for Pf., Ob., and Vla., Op. 34; Schritt für Schritt (12 pieces for 4 hands), Op. 27; Menuet, Op. 4; Romanza, A flat, Op. 6; 6 Morceaux de genre, Op. 11; 2 Preludes and Fugues, Op. 15; Sérénade du Nord, Op. 16; Introduction et Scène du Bal, Op. 24; 6 Valses, Op. 21. Editor of the new edition of Eschmann's "Guide."

Rutini, Giovanni Maria, b. 1730, Florence; d. there, 1797. Pupil at the Onofrio Conserv., of Naples. After having travelled through Germany, he resided for several years at Prague. 1786, he returned to Italy and was first appointed Capellmeister by the Duke of Modena, and then by the Grand Duke Leopold of Toscana.

6 Sonatas, Op. 1; (6), Op. 2; (6), Op. 12; Sonata in C (Haffner's Raccolta); Sonatas for Clavecin and Vln., Op. 10 and 11.

S.

Sacchini, Antonio Maria Gasparo, b. July 23, 1734, Puzzuoli (Naples); d. Oct. 7, 1786, Paris. Pupil of Durante. Operatic composer. For the Clavecin he composed—
  12 Sonatas with Vln., Op. 3 and 4 (Paris and London).

Sachs, Julius, b. 1830, Meiningen; d. Dec. 28, 1887, Frankfort o/M. Pupil of Eduard Rosenhain (Pf.) and Kessler (Composition), of Frankfort o/M. (not J. C. Kessler, of Lemberg). Excellent pianist and a talented composer.
  Suite, Op. 40, F sharp min.; 3 pieces, Op. 4; Berceuse, Op. 51.

Saetta, Vincenzo, b. 1836, Naples. Pupil of Staffa and Mercadante. He devoted his talent almost exclusively to teaching. He published the esteemed book—
  "La Scienza estetica" and the well-written "Theoretical and Practical Piano Method."

Saint-Saëns, Camille (Charles), b. Oct. 9, 1835, Paris. Pupil at the Conserv. of Stamaty (Pf.), Maleden (Theory), Benoist (Organ), and Halévy, Reber, and Gounod (Composition). 1855, Organist of St. Merry; 1858, of the Madeleine, which appointment he resigned in order to devote himself entirely to Composition. He is not only an original composer, but also a most distinguished pianist and organist; indeed, a most accomplished musician all round, such as we seldom meet with. His country conferred the highest honours upon him—viz., the Legion of Honour and the Membership of the Academy, whilst the University of Cambridge made him (June 13, 1893) Mus. Doc., *hon. causâ*.
  Concertos: No. 1, D min., Op. 17; †No. 2, G min., Op. 22; No. 3, E flat, Op. 29; †No. 4, C min., Op. 44. Quintet, Op. 14; Quartet, Op. 41; Trio, Op. 18; Suite for Pf. and V'cello, Op. 16; Sonata with V'cello, Op. 32; Berceuse, Op. 38; Romanza with Vln., Op. 48; †6 Etudes, Op. 52; Gavottes, Op. 23 and 65; Mazurkas, Op. 21, 24, and 66; Allegro appassionato, Op. 70; Marche héroïque, Op. 34; †Variations for 2 Pf., Op. 35; Polonaise for 2 Pf., Op. 77; Marche à 4 mains, Op. 25; Fueillet d'Album, Op. 81; Album (6 pieces), Op. 72.

*****Salaman**, Charles Kensington, b. March 3, 1814, London. Pupil at the R.A.M., and afterwards private pupil of Charles Neate. His first public performance took place in 1828, after which he left for Paris, and took lessons from Henri Herz. 1833-37, he gave annual concerts in London; 1846-48, he resided in Rome, where he was made Hon. Member of the St. Cecilia Society and Hon. Member of the Philharmonic Academy; 1855, he began his lectures on the history of the Pf.; 1858, was one of the founders of the Musical Society of London, of which he was Hon. Secretary until 1865. Several of his numerous compositions for Pf. have met with great favour, and have been performed in public.
  Toccata; Saltarello; Prelude and Gavotte; Rondo alla Giga; Remembrance (Capriccio); Capriccio in E flat; Nocturnes; Twilight Thoughts and Tranquillity; La Vivacità (Scherzo); Joy (Impromptu); 12 Voluntaries; 6 characteristic melodies; Crépuscule; Rêverie, &c.

Sandt, Max van de, b. Oct. 18, 1863, Rotterdam. Pupil of his father (Pf.), Th. Verhey (Theory), and Gernsheim (Composition). After having successfully performed in his own country, he gave concerts in Cologne (1884), and studied for two years with Liszt (Weimar). He travelled through Germany, Austria, Switzerland, France, &c., everywhere with great success. 1889, appointed Prof. at the Stern Academy of Berlin, in succession to the late Dr. Hans Bischoff.

*****Sapellnikoff**, Wassily, b. Oct. 21, 1868, Odessa. His musical education began in his seventh year, when his father, an eminent violinist, gave him Vln. lessons, and soon after his mother instructed him on the Pf. His next Pf. teacher was Franz Kessler (Odessa). In his eleventh year he gave a concert, appearing as a pianist and violinist. He continued to study both instruments with equal industry, until, in his fourteenth year, Anton Rubinstein decided that the Pf. ought to be his principal instrument; on Rubinstein's recommendation the town of Odessa gave him a scholarship, which enabled him to study for five years at the St. Petersburg Conserv., under Louis Brassin, and later, after Brassin's death, under Sophie Menter. 1888, he gave, in Hamburg, before a critical German audience, an excellent performance of Tschaïkowsky's Concerto in B flat, under the composer's direction. He is well known to the London public.

Sarti, Giuseppe, b. Dec. 1, 1729, Faenza, d. July 28, 1802, Berlin. Pupil of Padre Martini (Bologna). 1769, he was in London, where he published 3 (6?) Sonatas for the Harpsichord, and Sonatas with Vln., Op. 1 and 2.

Satter, Gustav, b. Feb. 12, 1832, Vienna. His father desired him to study medicine, but Gustav's undeniable talent for music, particularly for Pf. playing, made him concur with the son's wish to devote himself entirely to music. He undertook a tour in America; resided (1863) at Vienna, later at Dresden, Hanover, Gothenburg, Stockholm, and is at present in America.
Op. 104, Sonata in E; Op. 107, in G min.; Op. 157, in E; Op. 158, 6 grand Studies; Op. 162, 6 Studies; Valses de Concert: No. 1, A min., Op. 111; No. 2, in G flat, Op. 113; No. 3, in B min., Op. 114; No. 4, in E, Op. 117; Saltarello, Op. 147.

*****Sauer, Emil,** b. Oct. 8, 1862, Hamburg. Pupil of his mother; 1879-81, of Nicolaus Rubinstein (Moscow); and, 1884-85, of Liszt (Weimar). Since 1882 he has made highly successful journeys through Germany, Austria, Roumania, Russia (three times), Denmark, Sweden, Spain, Italy, and England. He is considered one of the best pianists of the present time.
Suite moderne (5 movements); Aus lichten Tagen (5 pieces); Concert Study; Romance sans paroles; Valse de Concert.

Scarlatti, Domenico, son of Aless. S. (1659-1725), b. 1685 (1683?), Naples; d. 1757, Madrid (according to Padre Sacchi, at Naples). Pupil of his father and Gasparini (Rome). 1709, he met Händel at Cardinal Ottoboni's in Rome. Of his playing at that time Thomas Roseingrave relates: "After a pupil of Gasparini's had sung one of his cantatas, which the composer himself accompanied, an earnest young man, dressed in dark clothes with a black wig, came from a corner and began playing. I thought ten hundred devils had taken possession of the instrument, for never had I conceived such execution or effect possible. The playing of this young man surpassed anything I could ever have imagined." 1715, appointed Maëstro di Capella of St. Peter's, in succession to Baj; 1719, Maëstro al Cembalo of the Italian Opera, London; 1721 (not 1716), the King of Portugal appointed him teacher to the Princesses at Lisbon; and when, in 1729, Princess Magdalena Theresia married the Crown Prince of Spain (1746, became King Ferdinand VI.) he followed her to Madrid (having been decorated with the Order of San Giacomo), where he remained till 1754, when he retired with a pension, and died at Madrid; but, according to a report in the *Gazetta Musicale di Napoli* (15/9/1838), he returned (1754) to Naples, where he died in a state of great poverty. He was a prolific composer—the Abbé Santini possessed no less than 349 of his pieces, and declared his collection not complete. New editions of his pieces were published by Czerny (200), Farrenc (130), Breitkopf and Härtel (60), Pauer (50), Banck (30), &c. The following is Schumann's opinion: "Scarlatti has much that is excellent, and that distinguishes him among his contemporaries. The mailed order (if we may say so) of a Seb. Bach's flow of ideas is not to be found in Scarlatti: he is far more shallow, rhapsodical, and superficial, and so quick in making and unmaking complications that it is difficult to follow him. His style is—for his time — short, piquant, and pleasing; but although his works hold so important a place in musical literature, we confess that there is much in them that cannot now please us." ("Schumann," II., 91.)

Schachner, Rudolph, b. Dec. 31, 1821, Munich. At first a pupil of Madame de Fladt, who also taught A. Henselt; 1837-38, of J. B. Cramer, at that time in Munich; had lessons in Composition from Caspar Ett. 1842, he went to Vienna, where he played in public with considerable success. A few years later he visited Paris, where he had the rare opportunity of playing a Concerto of his own composition at a Conserv. concert, for which performance he received a gold medal. Returning to Germany, he was kindly received by Mendelssohn (Leipzig), who invited him to play at the Gewandhaus Concerts. 1853, he went to London, and remained there for a number of years, without appearing much in public. At present he resides in Vienna.
Concerto, Op. 6; Poésies musicales, Op. 8 and 9; Romance variée, Op. 11; Ombres et Rayons (6 books), Op. 13 and 17; La chasse, Op. 12; Phantasiestück, Op. 15.

Schad, Joseph, b. March 6, 1812, Steinach (Bavaria); d. July 4, 1879, Bordeaux. At first a pupil at the Würzburg Conserv.; later of Aloys Schmitt (Frankfort o/M.). 1834, organist, teacher, and conductor at Morges (Canton Vaud); later Prof. at the Conserv. of Geneva, and, since 1847, one of the most successful teachers of Bordeaux. His compositions are melodious, practically written, and popular.

Le Soupir, Op. 19; La Gracieuse (Valse), Op. 22; †La Rose des Alpes, Op. 38; †Fleur des Alpes, Op. 39; Tarentelle, Op. 55.

Schaeffer, Dr. Julius, b. Sept. 28, 1823, Krevese, near Osterburg (Prussia). First studied philosophy and theology. Friendly intercourse with Rob. Franz strengthened his love for music, but circumstances obliged him to accept for two years an appointment as tutor in Jassy (Moldavia). Through Franz he became acquainted with Schumann, Mendelssohn, and Gade, and, following their advice, he resolved to devote himself entirely to music. 1850, he took lessons from Dehn (Berlin), and (1855) was appointed Musik-Director of Schwerin, where he founded the well known "Schloss Kirchenchor." 1860, named Musik-Director of the Breslau University and Conductor of the Sing-Academie; 1861, he received the diploma of Königl. Musik-Director; 1878, that of Prof.; 1872, the University conferred on him the degree of Doc. Phil., *hon. causâ*.

Op. 1, Fantasiestücke; Op. 2, Fantasie Variationen; Op. 4, Polonaise in A min.; Op. 7, Barcarolle; Op. 8, Notturno.

Scharwenka (Ludwig), Philipp, b. Feb. 16, 1847, Samter (Posen), where his father was a builder. 1859, the family moved to Posen, where he completed his studies at the "Gymnasium"; went with his parents to Berlin (1865). Here he entered Kullak's Academy as a pupil of Kullak (Pf.) and Wüerst (Composition), taking also private lessons from Dorn. 1870, appointed teacher of composition at Kullak's Academy, he is now (1893) director of the Klindworth-Scharwenka Conserv. (Berlin). His educational compositions are of great value, and his larger works are highly respected.

Op. 34, Aus der Jugendzeit; Op. 18, Miscellen; Op. 31, Humoresken (3); Op. 33, Album polonaise; Op. 54, Festklänge für die Jugend; Op. 36, Bergfahrt (6); Op. 59, Scherzo; Op. 64 and 68, Kinderspiele (8 pieces, 2 series); Op. 60, Seestücke (6); Op. 65, Romantische Episoden; Op. 72, Von vergangenen Tagen (5); Op. 61, Sonata in A, No. 1; No. 2, in F sharp min.; Op. 85, Rhapsidieen; Op. 55, Divertissements (10); Op. 27, Feuilles d'Album (5); Op. 32, In bunter Reihe (6); Op. 46, Momens musicaux (4); Op. 47, Capriccio in D min.; Op. 26, Morceaux de Fantaisie (5). *Duets:* Op. 21, Tanz-Suite; Op. 23, Wedding March, Valse, and Evening Music; Op. 30, All' Ongarese and Valse; Op. 38, Polish Dances; Op. 54, Songs and Dances; Op. 57, Stimmungsbilder; Op. 50, Herbstbilder, Op. 75, Dance-Scenes (5); Op. 91, Scherzi (3).

Scharwenka (Franz), Xaver, b. Jan. 6, 1850, Samter (Posen). His education was the same as that of his brother Philipp, only he gave greater attention to the study of the Pf. Kullak and Wüerst were also his teachers. His excellent performances, as well as his spirited, bright, and melodious compositions, soon gained the attention of the musical public, not only of Berlin, but of other German towns. 1868-74, was teacher at Kullak's Academy. 1881, he opened the "Scharwenka" Conserv., which, after his departure for America, was directed by his brother, and was lately (1893) amalgamated with Klindworth's Academy. Xaver S. is decidedly one of the most talented pianists and composers of the present time, and some of his pieces are universally known.

Concertos: No. 1, in B flat min., Op. 35; No. 2, in C min., Op. 56; Quartet for Pf. and strings; Trios: No. 1, Op. 1; No. 2, Op. (?); Sonata with Vln., Op. 2; Sonata with V'cello, Op. (?); Solo Sonatas (2): No. 1, in C sharp min., Op. 6; Studies and Preludes (6), Op. 27 (†No. 3, Staccato Study); Im Freien (5), Op. 38 (No. 5, All' Ongarese); †Waltzes, Op. 44; †Theme and Variations, Op. 48; †Album (6), Op. 43 (†No. 6); Polish Dances, Op. 13, 9, 29, 34, 58 (21 numbers: †Nos. 1, 4, 5, 13, 15).

Scheuenstuhl, Michael, b. March 3, 1705, Guttenstetten, near Bayreuth; d. (?) Hof (Saxony). Some of his works are remarkable for their quaint titles.

"Gemüths- und Ohrenergötzende Clavier-Uebung, bestehend in 6 leichten nach heutigem Gout gesetzten Galanterie-Partien, meistens für Frauenzimmer componirt." 2 Theile. Nürnberg. (An ear and soul-pleasing Clavecin-Study, consisting of 6 easy fancy parts, composed in the taste of the day, mostly for ladies.) "Die beschäftigte Muse Clio, 3 Galanterie Suiten." (The busy Muse Clio, 3 Fancy Suites.) Clavier Sonate, 1736, and Clavier Concerte (2), 1738.

Schiffmacher, Joseph, b. 1827, Eschau, near Strassburg. Pupil of Reber, Rosenhain, Prudent, Thalberg, Haberbier, and others. He resides at Paris. His compositions are mostly short, elegant, and effective.

Morceaux de Salon.

*****Schirmacher, Dora,** b. Sept. 1, 1862, Liverpool. Pupil of her father, later of E. F. Wenzel and Reinecke of Leipzig, where she gained the "Mendelssohn" prize. Her performances at the Leipzig Gewandhaus, Quartet and Euterpe concerts were received with great favour; not less successful were her appearances in Frankfort o/M.

(Museum), Wiesbaden, Amsterdam (Felix meritis), Dresden, Berlin, Cologne, and other large German towns. She obtained also much praise for her playing at the Popular and Crystal Palace concerts (London), Philharmonic concerts (Liverpool), Hallé's concerts (Manchester), and concerts in numerous other English towns.

Suite, Valse Caprice, Sonata, Tone-pictures, Evening Song, Serenade, &c., published on Rubinstein's recommendation at Hamburg.

Schlösser, Adolph, b. Feb. 1, 1830, Darmstadt. Pupil of his father, Louis S. After having performed with decided success in Germany, he settled (1854) in England, where he is Prof. at the R.A.M., and was also elected Hon. Member. Knight of the Portuguese Order of Christ.

Quartet (with strings), Trio, Studies, †Suite in D min., and a considerable number of shorter solo pieces. He edited several examples of older Clavecin music.

Schlottmann, Ludwig, b. Nov. 12, 1826, Berlin. Pupil of Taubert (Pf.) and Dehn (Composition). He holds no public appointment, but is much occupied in careful, practical, and highly successful teaching. 1875, he received the title of Königl. Musik-Director.

Op. 8, Trois Capricettes; Op. 11, Polonaise de Concert; Op. 19, Andantino and Variations; Op. 22, †Jugendspiegel (6).

Schmitt, Aloys (sen.), b. Aug. 26, 1789, Erlenbach o/M. (Bavaria); d. July 25, 1866, Frankfort o/M. Pupil of his father, later of A. André at Offenbach o/M. From 1816 he resided, with few exceptions, in Frankfort o/M. as a highly influential and successful teacher. 1820, he went for some time to Berlin, and (1825-29) was at Hanover as Court Pianist to the Duke of Cumberland. His name is particularly well known by his educational works, which made the round of the world.

Studies, Op. 16, 55, 62 (Rhapsodies), 67, and 115; Method of Pf. playing, Op. 114; Sonatinas and Rondos, and Concertos, Sonatas, and Variations, which are less known.

Schmitt, Jacob (Jacques), younger brother and pupil of the above, b. Nov. 2, 1803, Obernburg (Bavaria); d. June, 1853, Hamburg. He settled in Hamburg, where he was an active teacher, pianist, and composer. Of his compositions (about 370), his Sonatinas are decidedly the most popular for their practical style, clearness, and melodiousness.

Sonatina in B flat, Op. 29; †3 Sonatines faciles et progressives, Op. 83; Sonatine, Op. 84; †6 Sonatines, Op. 207; Sonatine in A, Op. 248; †2 Sonatinas in F, Op. 249. His "Musikalisches Schatzkästlein" (Musical Treasure-box), Op. 325 (133 short pieces), is of great value. His Rondos—La Coquette, Op. 113; Rondo militaire, Op. 88; and l'Elégant, Op. 250—and his Nocturnes (14)—especially "Tendre reproche," Op. 123—have met with great favour. For 4 hands: Sonatinas, Op. 65, Op. 31, 49, 118, and 208.

Schmitt, Georg Aloys, son of A. S. (see above), b. Feb. 2, 1827, Hanover. Pupil of his father and of Vollweiler (Heidelberg). He travelled as a pianist with great success in Germany, Belgium, and France; visited also London, Algiers, &c. After having filled the post of Capellmeister of the Opera at Aix-la-Chapelle and Würzburg, he was appointed (1857) Hof-Capellmeister at Schwerin. Among his pupils was Emma Brandes (see this name). Several of his solo pieces met with considerable favour.

*Schmitt, Hans, b. Jan. 14, 1835, Koken (Bohemia). Was at first, as oboe-player, a pupil at the Prague Conserv. 1851, became a member of the orchestra of Bucharest; 1856, of the Court Orchestra of Vienna; and (1867) of the Imperial Theatre and Royal Opera Orchestra; 1860-62, he enjoyed the tuition of Dachs (Pf.), at the Vienna Conserv.; became teacher, later Prof. there. Author of many educational works.

His graduating classification of Stephen Heller's Studies, his essays on the use of the Pedal (1875), progressive order of educational material, and the basis of Pf. technique; 120 short pieces for tuition; a School edition of Clementi's "Gradus," and several other publications were received with great approbation. Compositions: Characteristic solo pieces, and Duets for Pf. and Vln.

Schneider, Dr. Friedrich Johann Christian, b. Jan. 3, 1786, Altwaltersdorf, near Zittau; d. Nov. 23, 1853, Dessau. Pupil of his father, Gottlieb S., who was originally a weaver. Friedrich attended (1798) the Zittau College (Gymnasium), and, 1805, the University of Leipzig; 1807, appointed Organist of the Pauliner Church; later, of the Thomas Church; 1821, called to Dessau, where he officiated as Hof-Capellmeister, and opened (1829) a Music School, which obtained a great reputation. Until the opening of the Leipzig Conserv., the Dessau School was considered the principal school of Germany. Although as a composer he was more occupied with sacred works (Oratorios, Masses, Psalms), he was also an industrious writer for the Pf.

Quartets: for Pf. and Strings, Op. 24, in E flat; Op. 34 in F; Op. 36 in C min. Trios: Op. 10 in B flat; Op. 38 in E flat. Duo with Vln., Op. 31. Sonatas for 4 hands: Op. 2

in E flat; Op. 8 in A; Op. 13, 29, and 78 in B flat. *Solo Sonatas:* 3 Sonatas, Op. 1; ditto, Op. 3, 5, 6, 14, 20 (2), 21, 26, 27, 30, 37, 40; †Sonata di Bravura, Op. 76 and 80.

Schobert (Schubart)—his christian name is unknown—b. 1730, Strassburg; d. 1768, Paris. There are no details about his education. He was appointed Organist in Versailles, but dismissed on account of his negligence. 1760, the Prince de Conti employed him as his Clavecinist. The following compositions (which are not without interest) were published:

6 Concertos; 6 Symphonies for Clavecin and 2 Hn.; 3 Sonatas for Clavecin and 3 string instruments; 16 Sonatas for Clavecin and Vln.; 8 Solo Sonatas for Clavecin. A complete collection of his works, Op. 1-17, was published in London for the benefit of his son.

*Schönberger, Benno, b. Sept. 12, 1863, Vienna. Pupil at the Vienna Conserv., of Anton Door, Bruckner (Counterpoint), and Robert Volkmann (Composition); later, pupil of Liszt, at Buda Pesth and Rome. His public performances began in Vienna (1874), he then travelled through the greater part of Europe, until 1880; 1888, he visited England for the first time. In Valencia and Madrid he was given the title of Hon. Prof., and also received decorations from Spain, Italy, Servia, and Roumania.

3 Sonatas, Phantasiestücke, Novelletten, Bolero, Polonaise, &c.

*Scholtz, Hermann, b. June 9, 1845, Breslau. Pupil of Brosig. 1865, went to Leipzig, where he continued his studies with C. Riedel (Counterpoint) and L. Plaidy (Pf.). On Liszt's advice he went (1867) to Munich, where he became a pupil of Bülow in the Royal Music School, receiving at the same time lessons from Rheinberger in Composition; 1870-75, was teacher in the same school; 1875, he settled in Dresden, where (1880) the King of Saxony conferred on him the title of "Court Pianist." He is one of the foremost pianists of the present time, an admirable teacher, careful editor, and refined composer. His edition of Chopin's complete works is well known and very reliable.

Trio in F min., Op. 51; Sonata in G min., Op. 44; 5 books of Variations; Traumbilder, Op. 22; Stimmungsbilder, Op. 60; Ballade, Op. 66; Passacaglia in D min., Op. 73; 5 Collections of lyric pieces (†Albumblätter).

*Scholz, Bernhard, b. March 30, 1835, Mayence o/Rhine. Pupil of E. Pauer, at that time (1847-51) Musik-Director of the Choral Societies, and, later, of Dehn (Berlin). 1856-57, he was teacher of Counterpoint at the Conserv. of Munich; 1857-58, Capellmeister at Zürich; 1858-59, at Nürnberg; 1859-65, Hof-Capellmeister at Hanover; 1865-66, Director of the Cherubini Society of Florence; 1866-71, he resided at Berlin; 1871-83, Conductor of the Orchestral Society of Breslau; 1883, appointed Director of the Hoch Conserv. of Frankfort o/M. He received the Hanoverian Order of the Guelphs, the title of Königl. Prof., and the University of Breslau conferred on him the diploma of Doc. Phil., *hon. causâ.*

Op. 3 and 55, Sonatas for Pf. and Vln.; Op. 5, Sonata for Pf. and V'cello; Op 25, Quintet; Op. 41, Sonatinas; Op. 24, Valses à 4 mains; Op. 31, 6 Duets for Pf. and Vln.; Op. 57, Concerto; Op. 35, Capriccio (with Orchestra).

Schröter, Johann Samuel, b. 1750, Warsaw; d. Nov. 1, 1788, London. 1767, he began his tours through Holland and other countries. 1774, he went to London, where at first he had great difficulty in gaining a livelihood, until Joh. Christ. Bach became acquainted with his compositions and recommended him to the publisher, Napier (?). His works soon obtained public favour, and his playing was greatly admired. "He plays in a very elegant and masterly style; his *Cadenzas* are well imagined, and if his *penchant* was not rather to play rapidly than *al core*, he would excel on the Pf." (A. B. C. Dario, p. 44). It is said that he was one of the first who understood how to treat the newly-introduced Pf. with due effect. The Prince of Wales gave him the title of Chamber-Musician.

6 Sonatas for Pf., Op. 1; 3 Quintets for Pf., 2 Vln., Alto, and Bass; 6 Trios, Op. 2; 6 Concertos, Op. 3; 3 ditto (Berlin); 3 ditto; Op. 5; 6 ditto, Op. 6 (Paris); and 2 Trios, Op. 9 (1787).

Schubert, Franz (Peter) (son of a poor schoolmaster), b. Jan. 31, 1797, District Lichtenthal (Vienna); d. Nov. 19, 1828, Vienna. He was one of nineteen children. At first a pupil of his father (on the Vln.), his pretty voice obtained for him a place in the Imperial Chapel and a scholarship in the Imperial "Convikt" (a college subsidised by Government). His teachers were Ruc'ziszka and Salieri (thorough bass). 1813, he left the Imperial School, became assistant to his father, and taught in the elementary classes of the Lichtenthal School until 1817. His friend, Schober, assisted him in every way, and he received (during the summer months, 1818-1824) the appointment of music teacher in the family of Count Esterházy, in Zelesz (Hungary). Unsuccessful in obtaining fixed appointments, he was obliged to gain his livelihood as a composer; however, the sums he received for his splendid and immortal works appear to have been—viewing them from our present state of payment for new works—quite ludicrous. Like Mozart, Schubert had during his whole life to fight against adversity. Although he never performed in public on the Pf., his works are a proof that he was a consummate master of the instrument.

Quintet for Pf., Vln., Vla., V'cello, and C.-Bass, Op. 114 (1819); Trios: No. 1 in B flat, Op. 99 (1827); No. 2 in E flat, Op. 100 (1827); Adagio and Rondo concertant in F (1816); Nocturne in E flat, Op. 148 (appeared 1844). For *Pf. and Vln.*: Sonata in A, Op. 162 (1817); 3 Sonatinas (in D, A min., and G min.), Op. 137 (1816); Rondeau brillant in B min., Op. 70 (1826); Fantasia in C, Op. 159 (1828). For *Pf. and Fl.*: Introduction and Variations, Op. 160 (1824); Arpeggione (a small harp) Sonata in A min. (1824). For *4 hands*: Grand Duo in C, Op. 140 (1824); Fantasia in F min., Op. 103 (1829); Sonata in B flat, Op. 30 (1824); Rondo in A, Op. 107 (1828); Andantino varié et Rondeau militaire, Op. 84 (1826); Rondeau, "Notre amitié est invariable," in D, Op. 138 (1835); Divertissement à la Hongroise in G min., Op. 54 (1824); Divertissement in the form of a March in E min., Op. 63 (1826); Lebensstürme, characteristic Allegro in A min., Op. 144 (1828); Characteristic Marches (2), Op. 121 (1830); Grande Marche héroïque, A min., Op. 66 (1825 or 1826); 3 Marches héroïques, Op. 27 (1815, 1816, 1824); 3 Marches militaires, Op. 51 (1826); 6 Grandes Marches, Op. 40 (1826); Marche funèbre, C min., Op. 55; Kindermarsch (1827); 4 Polonaises, Op. 75 (1827); 6 Polonaises, Op. 61 (1828); Overture in F, Op. 34 (1825); in C, Op. 170 (Italian style, 1817); in D (1817); Fugue in E min., Op. 152 (1828); Variations in E min., Op. 10 (1821); in A flat (original theme), Op. 35 (1824); in C (theme by Hérold), Op. 82 (1827). For *Pf. solo*: Sonatas in A min., Op. 42 (1825); in D, Op. 53 (1825?); in G (Fantasia, Andante, Menuetto, and Allegretto), Op. 78 (1826); Sonata in A, Op. 120 (1825?); in E flat, Op. 122 (1817); in A min., Op. 143 (1823); in B, Op. 147 (1817); in A min., Op 164 (1817); 3 (posth.) Sonatas in C min., A, and B flat (1828). Variations (Waltz by Diabelli), 1821; 13 Variations (theme by Hüttenbrenner), 1817; Adagio in E (1818); †Adagio and Rondo in E, Op. 145 (1817?); Allegretto in C min. (1827); †3 Clavierstücke (Nos. 1 and 2, 1828; No. 3, before 1828); 5 Clavierstücke (1843); †4 Impromptus, Op. 90 (1828); †4 Impromptus, Op. 142 (1838); †Moments musicaux, Op. 94 (1828); †Fantasia in C, Op. 15 (1820); 2 Scherzi (1817); 12 Ländler, Op. 171 (1823); German Dances and Ecossaises, Op. 33 (1823-24); Hommage aux belles Viennoises, Op. 67 (1826); Galopp and Ecossaisen, Op. 49 (1826); Grazer Walzer and Galopp (1827); First Valses, Op. 9 (1816-21); Last Valses, Op. 127 (1824); Valses nobles, Op. 77 (1827); Valses sentimentales, Op. 50 (1826); Valses, Ländler, Ecossaises, Op. 18 (1816-21); 20 Ländler (1824); 12 German Dances and 5 Ecossaises (1817); March in E (1840); Relic (unfinished Sonata), 1825.

*Schütt, Eduard, b. Oct. 10, 1856, St. Petersburg. At first a pupil at the Conserv.; later of E. F. Richter and Jadassohn in Leipzig, and of Theodor Leschetizki in Vienna. 1882-87, Conductor of the Academical Wagner Society in Vienna. As pianist, he travelled with great success in Germany and Russia. Several of his compositions are included in the repertory of the most celebrated pianists of the present time. 1889-91, was in Paris, but since 1891 has lived in Vienna.

Op. 7, Concerto (G min.), Op. 8, †5 pieces; Op. 9, †Variations for 2 Pfs.; Op. 12, Quartet (F); Op. 3, Lose Blätter (1-12); Op. 15, 3 Morceaux (†Idylle); Op. 16: 1, †Etude mignonne; 2, †Valse mignonne; Op. 19, Scènes de Bal (†Valse lente, †Rococo); Op. 25, Bluettes en forme de Valse; Op. 26, Sonata with Vln.; Op. 27, Trio (C min.); Op. 28, 3 Morceaux (†Scherzino); Op. 29, Thème varié et Fugato; Op. 32, 2 Morceaux; Op. 35, †Preludes (8); Op. 36, Poèsies d'Automne.

*Schulhoff, Julius, b. Aug. 2, 1825, Prague. His first Pf. teacher was Kisch, then J. Tedesco, and in Theory and Composition, W. Tomaschek. 1842, he went, *via* Dresden, Weimar, and Leipzig to Paris, where he performed with great success. On Chopin's advice, he gave (1845) his first public concert in Paris, and his elegant, brilliant, and graceful performance, and melodious, rhythmical, and agreeable compositions at once took hold of the Parisian public. Not less striking was his success in London. During the winter, 1850-51, he gave concerts in Warsaw, St. Petersburg, and Moscow; and 1852-53, in South Russia (Odessa, Crimea, Kieff, Charkow, &c.). After residing for many years in Dresden, he settled permanently in Berlin. Some of his compositions became exceedingly popular Their chief merit lies in melodiousness, correct writing, practicability of execution, and total absence of triviality.

Op. 5, Mazurkas; Op. 8, 3 Impromptus (†No. 2); Op. 13, Etudes de Concert (No. 6, Le Trille), †Op. 11, 19, †28, Nocturnes; Op. 17, †Galop di Bravura; Op. 20, Valse in D flat; Op. 23 (No. 2); Op. 27 (No. 3); Op. 36 (No. 2), Idylles; Op. 30, †Souvenir de Varsovie; Op. 35, L'Ondine; Op. 39, †Souvenir de Kieff; Op. 42, †Aubade; Op. 45, Chants d'amitié (No. 1); Op. 49, 2 Romances sans paroles; Op. 53, †6 Morceaux de musique intime (Nos. 4 and 6).

Schulz-Schwerin, Carl, b. Jan. 3, 1845, Schwerin. 1862-65, pupil at the Stern

Conserv. of Berlin, where Bülow, Geyer, Stern, and Weitzmann were his teachers. After finishing his studies, appointed principal teacher of Pf. at the Conserv. of Stettin; later, Conductor of the Musical Society of Stargard (Pomerania). Since 1885 has resided in Berlin. He published a considerable number of solo pieces, and arranged for orchestra several celebrated Pf. pieces, among them Mendelssohn's Rondo Capriccioso, Op. 14.

Schumann, Georg Alfred, b. Oct. 25, 1866, Königstein (Saxony). Pupil of Baumfelder (Dresden), and, 1882-87, at the Leipzig Conserv., where Jadassohn, Reinecke, and Zwintscher were his teachers. After finishing his studies he received the "Beethoven" prize.

<small>Concerto with Orchestra, Quintet, Trio, several pieces for 4 hands, and solo pieces, of which the "Traumbilder" are the best known.</small>

Schumann, Gustav, b. March 15, 1815, Holdenstedt; d. Aug. 16, 1889, Berlin, where he resided as a teacher and composer. The following are his best known works:

<small>Op. 2, Characteristic pieces; Op. 9, Impromptu; Op. 10, 3 Fairy Tales (†No. 3); Op. 11, Tarantelle; Op. 12, Valse brillante; Op. 18, Scènes de Bal (Valse); Op. 19, Caprice. Most of his pieces have been revised and edited by Adolph Henselt.</small>

Schumann, Robert, b. June 8, 1810, Zwickau (Saxony); d. July 29, 1856, Endenich, near Bonn o/Rhine. His father, a bookseller, encouraged his musical studies (at first directed by the Baccalaureus Kuntzsch), and wrote to C. M. von Weber, asking him to undertake his son's education: this plan was not realised, and the father dying (1826), the mother insisted upon her son's attending the Leipzig University to study law. This study proved unsympathetic to his poetically-inclined nature, and, having spent a happy year in Heidelberg, where he attended the musical meetings in Prof. Thibaut's house, he returned to Leipzig, where Fr. Wieck examined him and advised him to devote himself entirely to music. He began (1830) his regular studies under Wieck (Pf.) and Dorn (Composition). In his eagerness to obtain the independent working of his fingers, he disabled his second (German fingering) finger entirely, and so was obliged to discontinue the career of a virtuoso. 1834, he founded, with his friends Julius Knorr, L. Schunke, and his teacher Wieck, the *Neue Zeitschrift für Musik*. 1835-44, he conducted alone this interesting journal, for which he wrote many instructive, poetic, æsthetic, fanciful, and thoroughly original articles and essays, thus procuring for the journal a unique position in musical history. The articles on Mendelssohn, Beethoven, Chopin, Schubert, Bach, &c., have never been rivalled with regard to purity, elevated and romantic tendency. 1838, he went to Vienna; 1839, returned to Leipzig; 1840, received from the University of Jena the diploma of Doc. Phil., *hon. causâ*, and married, in the same year, Clara Wieck. 1843, Mendelssohn made him a Prof. at the newly-founded Conserv.; but this work did not prove attractive to his rather musing and self-absorbed disposition, and he resigned the following year. He made a journey with his wife to St. Petersburg, and on his return settled at Dresden. 1850-53, Conductor of the Choral Society of Düsseldorf. Signs of deep melancholia, which had already appeared in 1833 and 1845, now showed themselves more frequently, and (1854) it was necessary to entrust him to the care of Dr. Richartz, of Endenich, near Bonn. The characteristics of Schumann's music are the union of the most fiery passion, the most sincere feeling, and the tenderest thoughtfulness, with a most refined and minutely finished execution. His sentiment is everywhere sustained by strong intellectuality, and his feeling is the outcome of a high moral soul. The words spoken at his grave, by his friend Ferdinand Hiller, give a correct description of his character: "Thou hast been a *genuine* artist, and what is implied therein of powerful, incorruptible will, of devoted activity, of persistent courage—is not known to many! And thou wert good and kind to others, and *just*, as far as it is permitted that any mortal being should be. Thy melodies glow with the gracefulness of a noble soul—they shine with the warmth of a loving heart. Quietly listening to the melodious waves of thine own soul, and to all the wonderful harmonies that dwelt there, like flowers on the bottom of a deep sea, thou wouldst never give way to a frivolous vanity, which tempts an artist's soul too often with seductive chords and melodies; thou didst not lend an ear to them; perhaps they sought thee not, knowing that it was useless." The surest monument an artist can possess should be that his works are beloved and esteemed by his brethren. There is no doubt that the memory of Schumann is held sacred by everyone who loves the art and knows how to value the high principles which he possessed. The following is a complete list of Schumann's works for Pf.:

Concerto in A min., Op. 54 (1841-45); Concertstück in G, Op. 92 (1849); Concert Allegro in D min., Op. 134; Quintet in E flat, Op. 44 (1842); Quartet in E flat, Op. 47 (1842). Trios: In D min., Op. 63 (1847); in F, Op. 80 (1847); in G min., Op. 110 (1851). Sonatas for Pf. and Vln.: In A min., Op. 105 (1851); in D min., Op. 121 (1851). Fantasiestücke for Pf., Vln., and V'cello, Op. 88 (1842); 3 Romanzas for Pf. and Ob., Op. 94 (1849); Fantasiestücke for Cl. and Pf., Op. 73 (1849); 5 easy pieces in a popular manner for Pf. and V'cello, Op. 102 (1849); Märchenbilder for Pf. and Vla., Op. 113 (1851); Märchenerzählung for Cl., Vla., and Pf., Op. 132 (1853 ?); Sonata in F sharp min., Op. 11 (1835); Grande Sonate (Concert sans Orchestre) in F min., Op. 14 (1836); Sonata in G min., Op. 22 (1833 and 1838); Fantaisie in C, Op. 17 (1836); Allegro in B min., Op. 8 (1831); Études symphoniques in C sharp min., Op. 13 (1834); Studien nach Capricen von Paganini, Op. 3 (1832); Études de concert d'après des Caprices de Paganini, Op. 10 (1833); Variations (Abegg), Op. 1 (1830); Intermezzi, Op. 4 (1832); Papillons, Op. 2 (1829 and 1831); Carnaval, Op. 9 (1834 and 1835); Fantasiestücke (8), Op. 12 (1837); Davidsbündlertänze (18), Op. 6 (1837); Kreisleriana, Op. 16 (1838); Novelletten (8), Op. 21 (1838); Nachtstücke (4), Op. 23 (1839); Faschingsschwank aus Wien in B flat, Op. 26 (1839); Scherzo, Gigue, Romanze, and Fughette, Op. 32 (1838); Humoreske in B flat, Op. 20 (1839); 3 Romanzen, Op. 28 (1839); Studies for the Pedal Pf., Op. 56 (1845); Sketches for the Pedal Pf., Op. 58 (1845); 4 Fugues, Op. 72 (1845); 6 Fugues on the name of Bach, Op. 60 (1845); 4 Marches, Op. 76 (1849); 7 Fughettas, Op. 126 (1853); Waldscenen, Op. 82 (1848 and 1849); Arabeske in C, Op. 18 (1839); Blumenstück in A flat, Op. 19 (1839); Toccata in C, Op. 7 (1830-33); Impromptus in C, Op. 5 (1833); Bunte Blätter, Op. 99 (1836, 1838, 1841); Albumblätter, Op. 124 (from 1842 till 1845); 5 Fantasiestücke, Op. 111 (1851); Scenes from Childhood, Op. 15 (1838); Album for the young, Op. 68 (1848); Gesänge der Frühe, Op. 133 (1853 ?); 3 Sonatas for the young, Op. 118 (1853). For 4 hands: Bilder aus Osten, Op. 66 (1848); Children's pieces, Op. 85 (1849); Ball-Scenen, Op. 109 (1851); Andante and Variations (2 Pf.), Op. 46 (1843); Kinderball, Op. 130 (1853).

Schumann (née Wieck), Clara Josephine, wife of Robert S., b. Sept. 13, 1819, Leipzig. Daughter of Fr. Wieck. Showed very early extraordinary talent for music, and more particularly for Pf. playing. In her tenth year she performed for the first time in public, and when thirteen made a tour with her father. Her performances of Beethoven's Sonatas, Bach's Fugues, and Chopin's and Henselt's pieces created everywhere a great sensation. Combined with a thoroughly correct execution were womanly tenderness and sincere feeling, which struck a sympathetic chord in the breasts of numberless hearers. But it was only in 1837, when she was betrothed to Robert S., that, owing to the influence of his genial, romantic, and poetic nature, she fully realised the profound meaning and imperishable beauty of the classical composers' works. This influence awakened in her a conception of the art hitherto unknown to any lady pianist. Her appearances in Holland, Austria, Paris, and Germany were greeted with the utmost enthusiasm; and admiration for her artistic performances was enhanced by hearty affection, evoked by her touching devotion to her husband during the last years of his life. The English public—at all times strongly influenced by the critics' judgments, which were at first, from personal reasons, cold and unfavourable—learned by degrees to value, esteem, and at last venerate the rare talents and merits of the celebrated artist, thus making her annual visits to England veritable epochs. 1878-92, principal Pf. Prof. at the Hoch Conserv. of Frankfort o/M., and then worked as a private teacher. Amongst many different distinctions may be named the great gold medal for Art and Science (Prussia) and the title of "Pianist to the Imperial and Royal Court of Austria." The best known of her compositions are:

Op. 7, Concerto; Op. 10, Scherzo; Op. 14, Second Scherzo; Op. 15, 4 Pièces fugitives; Op. 16, 3 Preludes and Fugues; Op. 17, Trio in G min.; Op. 20, Variations on a theme of Robert Schumann; Op. 21, 3 Romanzas; Op. 22, 3 Romanzas with Vln.

Schunke, Carl, b. 1801, Magdeburg; d. (by his own hand) Dec. 16, 1839, Paris. At first a pupil of his father, Michael S. (1780-1821), later of Ferd. Ries, whom he followed to England. 1828, he went to Paris, where his elegant playing was received with so much favour that he was appointed Pianist to the Queen and obtained the Légion d'Honneur. Unfortunately a stroke of apoplexy robbed him of the power of speech, and, despairing of ever getting better, he threw himself out of the window and was killed. He was a popular composer, but most of his pieces are brilliant transcriptions of operatic airs and other popular melodies. The collection, "Le Pensionnat" (1-24), was, in its time, much liked.

Schunke, Ludwig, son of Gottfried S. (1777-1840), b. Dec. 21, 1810, Cassel; d. Dec. 7, 1834, Leipzig. When only in his tenth year he played Mozart and Hummel's Concertos with ease, and was very successful when he appeared (1824) in Vienna and Munich. In the same year he went to Paris to study with Kalkbrenner (Pf.) and Reicha (Composition). 1830, he went to Stuttgart; 1832, again to Vienna; later, to Prague, Dresden, and Leipzig. In Leipzig he made the acquaintance of Robert Schumann, for whom he had the warmest friendship and affection, which was heartily reciprocated (Schumann's Toccata, Op. 7, is dedicated to him). He became one of the collaborators of the *Neue Zeitschrift*. He delighted everyone by his beautiful, expressive, and intellectual performances.
> Op. 3, Variations; Op. 9, Caprice; Op. 10, second Capriccio; Op. 13, Characteristic pieces; Op. 14, Variations. *See* Robert Schumann's remarks in his "Gesammelte Schriften," Vol. I., pp. 92, 325; Vol. II., pp. 56, 277.

Schwalm, Robert, b. Dec. 6, 1845, Erfurt. Pupil of Pflughaupt, later, at the Leipzig Conserv., where Wenzel, Moscheles (Pf.), and Reinecke (Composition) were his teachers. 1870-75, was a teacher at Elbing, and conductor of several musical societies. He is now Königl. Musik-Director and Prof., and resides at Königsberg (Prussia).
> Excellent Studies, and Editor of the valuable collection, "Classische Hausmusik," Op. 10.

*****Schwarz,** Max, b. Dec. 1, 1856, Hanover. Pupil of Franz Bendel, Hans von Bülow, and F. Liszt. 1880-83, teacher at the Hoch Conserv. of Frankfort o/M.; since 1885, Director of the Raff Conserv. in the same town. Excellent pianist, and a much respected teacher.

*****Schweizer,** Otto, b. May 26, 1846, Zürich. 1857, his mother and stepfather moved to Rudolstadt a/S. Pupil of his stepfather. 1863, went to Winterthur, where he enjoyed the advice of H. Götz and Theodor Kirchner; 1867, pupil at the Leipzig Conserv., where Wenzel and Moscheles (Pf.), E. W. Richter and Oscar Paul (Theory) were his teachers. Since 1870, he has resided in Edinburgh, but is also Prof. of Pf. at the Athenæum School of Music, Glasgow.

> Suite in C min.; Polonaise brillante; Romantic Studies (3); Morceaux populaires (3), Op. 37; Suite, No. 2 (1-6); Sonata in A flat min.; Sonata for Pf. and V'cello, Op. 28.

*****Schytte,** Ludvig, b. April 28, 1848, Aarhus, Jütland (Denmark). He studied chemistry at first, but devoted himself from his twenty-second year (1870) to music. Pupil of Rée, later of Neupert (Pf.) and of W. Niels Gade (Composition), at Copenhagen. 1884-85, resided in Berlin. Since 1885, teacher of the highest class in Horak's Music Academy of Vienna. Some of his compositions enjoy considerable popularity.
> Characterstücke, Op. 12; Naturstimmungen, Op. 22; Concerto, Op. 28 (performed with great success by M. Rosenthal); Pantomimes, à 4 mains, Op. 30 (a great favourite of Liszt); Danish Melodies, Op. 35; Swedish Songs and Dances (4 hands), Op. 52; Sonata, Op. 53; Bojarentänze (4 hands), Op. 61; Studies, &c. With M. Rosenthal he published a Method for the higher development of Pf. playing (*see* Rosenthal).

Sechter, Simon, b. Oct. 11, 1788, Friedberg (Bohemia); d. Sept. 10, 1867, Vienna. Pupil of Kozeluch and Hartmann (Vienna). 1811, teacher of music in the College of the Blind; later, Member of the Imperial Chapel and Organist to the Imperial Court; 1851, Prof. of Harmony and Composition at the Conserv. He was Harmony teacher of Thalberg, Döhler, Henselt, Vieuxtemps, Berens, Bruckner, Rufinatscha, and other distinguished musicians. Although most of his works were written for the organ, he also published several interesting—with regard to scholarship—pieces for the Pf.
> Dances in Counterpoint, Op. 13; Fugue on Haydn's hymn, "God preserve the Emperor"; 12 contrapuntal pieces, Op. 62; Prose and Music, Op. 76. Very amusing are 24 Fugues for 4 hands on the most popular national and operatic airs, Op. 55 (4 books).

Seeling, Hans, b. 1828, Prague; d. there May 26, 1862. On account of feeble health he went (1852) to Italy; 1856, to Constantinople, Syria, and Greece; 1857, returned to Italy; 1859, was in Paris; then resided until his death in Germany. He was an excellent pianist, possessed a masterly technique, and his style was particularly admired for sincere feeling and natural expression, combined with great elegance and refinement.
> †Loreley (Lurline), Op. 2; Nocturnes, Op. 2 and 12; Idyl, Op. 6; 2 Poems, Op. 7; †12 Concert Studies, Op. 10; Memoirs of an Artist, Op. 13 (1-10).

*****Seifert,** Uso, b. Feb. 9, 1852, Römhild (Thuringia). Pupil at the Dresden

Conserv., where Dr. Wüllner, G. Merkel, A. Blassmann, and Nicodé were his teachers. He resides at Dresden; is Prof. at the Conserv. and Organist of the Reformed Church.

Op. 2, Capriccietto; Op. 3, Valse Impromptu; Op. 8, Polacca graziosa; Op. 15, Grand Study, "Ohne Rast, ohne Ruh"; 2 Christmas pieces; and Op. 18, Polonaise (D min.). Method of Pf. playing. Editor of Leuckart's "Salon-Album" (2nd vol.) and of many educational works.

*Seiss, Isidor, b. Dec. 23, 1840, Dresden. Pupil of Fr. Wieck and L. Niedermeyer (Pf.), Julius Otto and C. Riccius (Harmony and Composition); later of M Hauptmann at Leipzig. 1861, appointed Pf. Prof. at the Conserv. of Cologne, where he still works. 1878, he received the title of Königl. Prof.; 1892, the Order of the Prussian Crown. His performances of classical works (more particularly of Mozart's) are justly admired, whilst his reputation as a careful and successful teacher is well recognised.

Op. 8, Sonatinas; Op. 10, Bravura Studies; Op. 11, Toccata; Op. 12, Preludes; Op. 7 and 9, Clavierstücke; †Transcriptions of Beethoven's Contredanses et Danses allemandes.

Seydelmann, Franz, b. Oct. 8, 1748, Dresden; d. there Oct. 23, 1806. Pupil of his father; later of Weber (*not* C. M. von W.) and Naumann. At the expense of the Palatine he was sent to Italy. He returned 1770, was appointed "Kurfürstlich Sächsischer Kirchencomponist," and (1787) Capellmeister. He was in his time a very popular composer, who contributed a great deal towards the literature of Clavecin music.

3 Sonatas for Clavecin and Vln., Op. 3; 7 ditto; 6 Sonatas for 4 hands; 1 ditto; 6 Sonatas for Clavecin and Flute; 3 Solo Sonatas; and a Sonata for 2 Clavecins. Gerber mentions also 6 Duet Sonatas, Op. 1 (1781), and 3 Sonatas (1787).

Sgambati, Giovanni (Commendatore), b. May 18 (28?), 1843, Rome. Son of a lawyer. Pupil of Barberi, Natalucci, and Aldega. As a performer, his progress was so extraordinary that Liszt took great interest in his musical education. His excellent performances were applauded not only in Italy, but also in England, Germany, Denmark, and Russia. Since 1877 principal Prof. of Pf. at the newly founded Liceo di Santa Cecilia of Rome. He has received several decorations, and is a *persona grata* at the Italian Court.

Quintets, Op. 4 (F min.) and Op. 5 (G min.); Concerto, Op. 15 (G min.); Prelude and Fugue, Op. 6; 2 Études de Concert, Op. 10;
Fogli Volanti, Op. 12 (1-8); †Gavotte, Op. 14; 4 pieces, Op. 18; 3 Notturni, Op. 20; Suite in B, Op. 21 (1-5).

*Sharpe, Herbert Francis, b. March 1, 1861, Halifax (Yorkshire). 1876, gained a scholarship at the National Training School (London), where J. F. Barnett was his teacher. 1884, appointed teacher at the Royal College of Music.

Deux Caprices brillantes, Op. 6; Variations for 2 Pf., Op. 46; Suite in C, Op. 58; and 3 Symphonic pieces for 4 hands, Op. 59.

*Sherwood, William H., b. Jan. 31, 1854, Lyons (New York). At first a pupil of his father, the Rev. L. H. S. (founder of the Lyons Musical Academy), afterwards of Ed. Heimburger, Pychowski, and William Mason, of New York (*see* this name). Went to Berlin, studied with Th. Kullak and Deppe, and later with Liszt (Weimar); for Theory, Counterpoint, and Composition was under Dr. Weitzmann, C. Doppler, R. Wüerst (Berlin), and Richter (Leipzig). During his stay in Germany he played with great success in Hamburg, Leipzig (Gewandhaus), Bremen, Cassel, Berlin (at Court), Weimar, &c. Returning to America, he made his *début* at the "Centennial," at Philadelphia (1876), and made his name known in all the principal towns of the United States and Canada. He is one of the founders of the American College of Musicians, also a member of the Music Teachers' National Association and member of the Societies of Boston, New York, and Chicago. He resides at Chicago and is Director of the Pf. department of the Conserv. there.

Op. 5, Suite (5); Op. 6, 2 Mazurkas; Op. 7, Scherzo; Op. 8, Romanza appassionata; Op. 9, Scherzo Caprice; Op. 10, Gipsy Dance; Op. 12, Allegro patetico; Op. 13, Medea; Op. 14, Suite (5). Besides these works, he edited a goodly number of compositions by different masters.

*Siboni, Erik Anton Valdemar, b, Aug. 26, 1828, Copenhagen. Pupil of J. P. E. Hartmann; 1847, pupil of Moscheles and Hauptmann (Leipzig); after 1850, resided in Vienna, then until 1865 in Copenhagen, as a teacher and composer, and now teaches in the Music Academy of Soröe (near Copenhagen).

Quartet, Op. 10; Impromptus (3); Caprice; Ablum leaves (6); Ballad and Cradle Song; Scherzo; Phantasiestücke (3); Sonates faciles (2); 2 Sonatines for 4 hands; Concerto (D min.), Op. 64; Quartet, Op. 61, &c.

Siemers, Carl Heinrich August, b. May 7, 1819, Goldenstedt (Oldenburg); d. Nov. 30, 1876, Dresden. Pupil of K. Arnold, at Münster (Westphalia);

1839, of Seyfried (Vienna). 1845, he went to Hamburg; 1855, to Manchester, as Organist of the German Church. 1864, he settled in Dresden, where he was a highly successful teacher. Several of his compositions (on Hungarian airs, &c.) enjoyed at one time considerable popularity.

*Silas, Edward, b. Aug. 22, 1827, Amsterdam. 1837, appeared for the first time as a pianist in Amsterdam. Pupil of Grua (Harmony) at Mannheim; 1839, of Louis Lacombe (Frankfort o/M.); 1842, of Kalkbrenner (Paris); he entered later the Conserv., where Benoist (Organ) and Halévy (Fugue and Studies for Opera-writing) were his teachers. He received two gold medals and (1849) the first prize for Organ. 1850, he settled in England. 1866, he received the first prize, consisting of a gold medal and 1,000 francs, from the Assemblée Générale des Catholiques en Belgique, for the composition of a Mass. There were seventy-six competitors from twelve different nations. He is Prof. at the Guildhall School and London Academy of Music. Among his many compositions for Pf., the following deserve particular mention—

10 Romances sans paroles, Books I. and II.; †Amaranth; Sonata, Op. 10; Caprice in F; †Gavotte, Passepied, and Courante; Persian Serenade, Op. 44; a great number of Impromptus, Nocturnes, Mazurkas, Bourrées, Valses, Gavottes (7), Romanzas, Barcarolles, &c. Among his greater compositions are 4 Trios (in C min., A, C, and D); a Trio for Pf., Cl., and V'cello; 6 Duets for 4 hands, Op. 23; and a Concerto (performed at the Crystal Palace, London).

*Siloti, Alexander von, b. Oct. 10, 1863, Charkow. At first a pupil of his father. 1873, he went to Moscow, where he entered the Conserv., and was taught by Zwereff; later (1876-81), by Nicolaus Rubinstein (Pf.) and Tschaikowsky (Theory). He received a diploma and the gold medal. 1883, he went to Liszt (Weimar); 1887-90, Prof. at the Moscow Conserv. Since 1890 he has lived in Paris. He belongs to the foremost pianists of the day, and has earned many laurels in Germany, Belgium, England, and France.

*Sinding, Christian, b. Jan. 11, 1856, Köngsberg (Norway). He studied in Dresden and Munich, and in Leipzig with Reinecke, and settled as organist and teacher in Christiania, but does not hold any official appointment.

Romanza and Suite for Pf. and Vln.; Pf. Quintets (2); Concerto (1890); Sonata for Pf. and Vln.; Variations for 2 Pf., 4 hands; Buch der Lieder, &c.

*Sjögren (Johann Gustav), Emil, b. June 15 (16?), 1853, Stockholm. First an assistant in a music warehouse; later, pupil at the Conserv. 1879-80, he had lessons in Counterpoint from Kiel and in organ playing from Haupt, of Berlin. Since 1890, Organist of the Johannes Church (Stockholm).

Op. 15, Novelletten; Op. 20, Stemninger (Stimmungsbilder) (8); †" Erotikon " (5); Op. 24, Sonatas for Pf. and Vln. (E min.); Op. 27, 2 Fantasiestücke for Pf. and Vln.

*Slivinski, Joseph von, b. Dec. 15, 1865, Warsaw. Pupil at the Warsaw Conserv., under Strobel; afterwards went to Vienna, where he was pupil of Th. Leschetizki for four years, and later of Anton Rubinstein (St. Petersburg). His merits as an excellent and refined pianist are well known. He has not published his compositions.

Sloper, Lindsay, b. June 14, 1826, London, d. there July 3, 1887. Pupil of Moscheles, on whose advice he went (1840) to Germany. Studied under Aloys Schmitt (Frankfort), and, later, with C. Vollweiler (Heidelberg). For several years he resided in Paris, where he formed a sincere friendship with Stephen Heller, to whom he dedicated 24 Studies (Op. 3). Leaving Paris, he settled in London, where he soon became popular as a teacher and much admired as a performer. 1880, appointed Pf. Prof. at the Guildhall School. His compositions are elegant, ably written, and well constructed.

Smetana, Friedrich, b. March 2, 1824, Leitomischl (Bohemia); d. May 12, 1884, Prague. Pupil of Proksch (Prague); later, for a short time, of Liszt (Weimar). He opened a music school at Prague; married the pianist, Katharine Kolár, and (1856) was appointed Conductor of the Musical Society of Gothenburg (Sweden). His wife succumbed to the climate and died (1860). 1861, he gave concerts in Sweden, and returned afterwards to Prague. 1866-74, Conductor of the Opera (Prague); then resigned because he had entirely lost the faculty of hearing. He was essentially a national (Czechish) composer, and presents his works in a thoroughly national dress.

Trio, Bohemian National Dances, 16 Morceaux caractéristiques, and Album Leaves.

*Smith, Sydney, b. July 14, 1839, Dorchester; d. March 3, 1889, London. His father, a Prof. of music, was his first teacher. 1855-58, pupil at the Leipzig Conserv., under Plaidy and

Moscheles (Pf.), Hauptmann, Richter, and Papperitz (Harmony and Composition), and Grützmacher (V'cello). 1859, he settled in London, where he was highly successful as a teacher, and even more so as a composer of light, pleasing, popular, and practically-written pieces, of which some became very generally known.

Sorge, Georg Andreas, b. March 29, 1703, Mellenbach (Schwarzburg); d. April 4, 1778, Lobenstein, while Hof- und Stadt-Organist, which post he had held since his nineteenth year (1722). His reputation chiefly rests on his theoretical and scientific works, of which he published a great number.

<small>6 Sonatas, Op. 1 (1738); 6 Sonatinas; Wohl-gewürzte Klangspeisen, bestehend in 6 Clavier Parthien; Sonatas, composed according to modern taste; 6 Symphonies for the Clavecin; 12 Minuets with Vln.; Toccata per omnem circulum xxiv. modorum for Clavecin.</small>

***Sormann, Alfred,** b. May 16, 1861, Dantzig. 1879-84, pupil at the Hochschule (Berlin), where Rudorff, Barth, Spitta, and Bargiel were his teachers; 1885, he went to Liszt; 1886, he appeared in public and gave successful concerts at most of the principal German towns; 1889, the Grand Duke of Mecklenburg-Strelitz named him Pianist to the Court, and bestowed upon him the Golden Cross of the Mecklenburg Order. He is considered to be one of the foremost pianists of the present time.

<small>Trio, Concerto in C min., and several smaller works.</small>

Sowinsky, Albert Czyli Wojcech, b. 1803 (?), Ladyzyn (Ukraine); d. March 5, 1880, Paris. Pupil of Czerny, Leidersdorf, and Seyfried at Vienna. Author of the biographical work "Les musiciens polonais et slaves anciens et modernes." He was an excellent pianist and composer.

<small>Grandes Etudes de Concert, Op. 60; Tarantelle, Op. 67; Sicilienne, Op. 70; †Berceuse, Op. 73.</small>

Speidel, Wilhelm, b. Sept. 3, 1826, Ulm. Pupil of Ignaz Lachner, Wanner, and Kuhe, at Munich. 1846-48, teacher at Thann (Alsace); 1848-54, at Munich; 1855-57, Musik-Director at Ulm; founded later, with Lebert Stark and Faisst, the Music School at Stuttgart, where he was working until 1874, when he opened the "Künstler und Dilettantenschule für Clavier" on his own account. His talents as a teacher are unquestionable, and his Institute proved a great rival to the older school. For twenty-eight years Conductor of the Society "Liederkranz." The King of Würtemberg named him Königl. Prof. and Knight of the Frederic Order; whilst the King of Prussia decorated him with the Order of the Red Eagle. He is Hon. Member of many musical societies. His excellent, correct, and brilliant performances were much admired, while his compositions are very popular.

<small>Trios; Sonata with V'cello (D min.); Concert Solo, Op. 4; 3 Morceaux de genre, Op. 32; Saltarello, Op. 20; Pictures from the Highlands; Short scenes, &c.</small>

***Spindler, Fritz,** b. Nov. 24, 1817, Wurzbach, near Lobenstein. Pupil of the organist, W. Ioch. 1831, he attended the College at Schleiz, to prepare for the study of theology; but his desire to study music was so great that his parents gave way to it. Pupil of Fr. Schneider, of Dessau. 1841, he settled in Dresden, where he soon became a favourite teacher. His compositions are of moderate difficulty, melodious, well-constructed, and practically-written. Several of his trifles have become universally known; but although his popular pieces were more admired than his more serious works, he continued to write Symphonies (Op. 60 and 150), and never ceased following up his studies. The following are some of his best-known works:—

<small>Op. 5, "Frisches Grün"; Op. 6, Wellenspiel; Op. 7, Under the Window; Op. 140, Husarenritt; Op. 116, Le Carillon; Op. 66, Butterflies; Op. 171, Forest Hermitage; Op. 113, Murmuring of the Waves. Sonatines, Op. 290, 294, and 157; Sonatines for 4 hands, Op. 136; 3 easy Trios for Pf., Vln., and V'cello, Op. 305; Concerto in D min., Op. 260; Trio, Op. 154; Quartet, Op. 108; Quintet for Pf., Ob., Cl., Hn., and Bssn., Op. 360; Sonata for Pf. and Hn., Op. 347.</small>

Stadler, Abbé Maximilian, b. Aug. 4, 1748, Melk (Lower Austria); d. Nov. 8, 1833, Vienna. Son of a baker. Was educated in the Jesuits' College, Vienna; 1772, entered the Benedict Monastery in Melk; 1786, became Abbot at Lilienfeld; 1789, at Kremsmünster; and then resided in Vienna, being an intimate friend of both Haydn and Mozart. His compositions were mostly Masses, Psalms, and Requiems.

<small>Sonata (1799), 2 Sonatas and a Fugue, 6 Sonatinas (1796), Fugues, and a Fugue on the name of Franz Schubert ("Too soon lost"). He also finished the Fugue in G min. for 4 hands, by W. A. Mozart.</small>

Stamaty, Camille Marie, b. March 23, 1811, Rome; d. April 19, 1870, Paris. 1831, pupil of Kalkbrenner (Pf.),

Benoit and Reicha (Organ and Composition). 1835, he gave, with unusual success, his first concert in Paris; was chosen by Kalkbrenner as assistant, but became so great a favourite with his pupils that he over-exerted himself, and, 1836, went for a short rest to Leipzig, where Mendelssohn took great interest in his playing and compositions. On his return to Paris he gave concerts with the singer Delsarte, and introduced the Parisians to the works of Bach, Beethoven, and Mozart. 1846, he lost his mother and retired to Rome for a year. Returning to Paris, he worked incessantly until his death. Among his most celebrated pupils were Gottschalk and Saint-Saëns. He was a most excellent teacher, and his merits were not only recognised by his colleagues, but also by the Government, which conferred on him (1862) the Légion d'honneur. His educational works are of decided merit.

> Etudes progressives, Op. 37; 25 Etudes pour petites mains, Op. 38; Chant et mécanisme, 20 Etudes, Op. 39; 24 Etudes de perfectionnement, Op. 46; Chant et mécanisme, 12 Etudes à 4 mains; 12 Etudes pittoresques, Op. 21; 6 Etudes caractéristiques sur Oberon de Weber, Op. 33; Le Rhythme des doigts à l'aide du metronome, Op. 36; Concerto, Op. 2; Solo Sonatas, Op. 8 and 14; Trio, Op. 12, Variations, Op. 5 and 19.

Stanford, Charles Villiers, b. Sept. 30, 1852, Dublin. Pupil of A. O'Leary and Sir Robert Stewart; matriculated at Queen's College, Cambridge, as choral scholar. 1873, succeeded Dr. Hopkins as Organist of Trinity College; 1874, graduated there in classical honours; was appointed Conductor of the Cambridge University Musical Society; 1874-76, he continued his studies of Composition with Reinecke (Leipzig) and Kiel (Berlin); 1877, he received the degree of M.A.; 1883, of Mus. Doc., *hon. causâ*, from the University of Oxford; 1885, he succeeded Otto Goldschmidt as Conductor of the Bach Choir; 1887, elected Prof. of Music at Cambridge University; 1883, Prof. of Composition at the Royal College of Music, London.

> Suite and Toccata, Op. 2 and 3; Sonata for Pf. and V'cello, Op. 9; Sonata with Vln., Op. 11; 3 Intermezzi with Vln., Op. 13; Trio in E flat, Op. 35; Quintet for Pf. and Strings, Op. 25; Sonata for Pf. and V'cello (No. 2), Op. 39; Characteristic Pieces, Op. 42 (MS.).

Stark, Dr. Ludwig, b. June 19, 1831, Munich; d. March 22, 1884, Stuttgart. Pupil of Ignaz and Franz Lachner. Resided for some time in Paris. 1856, he founded, with Dr. Faisst, Lebert, Brachmann, and Speidel, the well-known Stuttgart Music School, where he taught harmony, score-reading, and history of music. 1861, was in Weimar, enjoying the advice of Liszt; 1873, he travelled in Italy to continue his studies. His principal work was "The Great Method of Pf. playing," which was translated into French and English. As to his editions (with phrasing, fingering, and terms of expression) of classical works, there exists a great and serious difference of opinion.

*Stavenhagen, Bernhard, b. Nov. 24, 1862, Greiz (Principality of Reuss). Pupil of Rudorff at the Hochschule and of Kiel at the Meisterschule (Berlin). Gained the "Mendelssohn" prize of the Hochschule. 1885, he went to Liszt (Weimar), whose favourite pupil he became, and with whom he remained until Liszt's death, 1886. He settled in Weimar, where he assembles, after Liszt's fashion, a considerable number of pupils. On his journeys through Austria, Hungary, France, Holland, England, &c., he gained most enthusiastic receptions and acclamations, due to his excellent performances, representing all the best qualities of his illustrious teacher and friend, Liszt. 1890, the Grand Duke of Saxe-Weimar named him Pianist to the Court, and, 1892, he conferred on him the "Knighthood of the White Falcon." Of his compositions, only about six short pieces were published.

Steffan, Joseph Anton, b. March 14, 1726, Kopidluo (Bohemia); d. (?) at Vienna. Pupil of Wagenseil (Vienna). He remained in Vienna, and was appointed teacher of the Clavecin to the Archduchess Marie Antoinette (who became the wife of the unfortunate Louis XVI. of France).

> 6 Divertimenti per il Cembalo, Op. 1 (1756); 6 Sonate, Op. 2; 6 Sonate, Op. 3; 40 Preludi per diversi tuoni, 1762; a collection of German songs for the Clavecin (1778-81); 25 Variations on a Bohemian air (1802).

Steibelt, Daniel, b. 1765, Berlin; d. Sept. 20, 1823, St. Petersburg. Son of a Clavecin-maker. Pupil of Kirnberger. Endowed with great talent, he created a sensation by his excellent, brilliant, and fascinating performances; but was everywhere disliked for his dissipated and extravagant habits, which often bordered on dishonesty. 1789, he began his tours; 1790, appeared at

Paris, where his publisher, Boyer, succeeded in procuring him numbers of pupils; 1808, was obliged to leave Paris to escape numerous creditors. He went to St. Petersburg and succeeded Boieldieu as Conductor of the Imperial Opera. Most of his compositions are now entirely forgotten, and it is not necessary to enumerate them all.

29 Solo Sonatas and Sonatinas; 37 Sonatas with Vln.; 4 Trios; 5 Concertos, of which No. 3, in E (Op. 35), contains the well-known "Storm" Rondo; 15 Rondeaux; 18 Fantasias; 6 Bacchanales; †50 Studies, Op.78; 12 Studies from his "Method," and many Variations. A Duo for 2 Pf., the Elegy on the Death of Prince Soltykoff, and a Rondo, "Le Berger et son troupeau," in B flat, enjoyed considerable popularity.

Stein, Nanette, b. Jan. 2, 1760, Augsburg; d. Jan. 16, 1833, Vienna. Wife of Johann Andreas Streicher, whom she married (1793). Highly talented performer, about whom W. A. Mozart wrote a very amusing letter (Augsburg, Oct. 23, 1777). Until her marriage she assisted her father, Georg Andreas Stein (1728-92), who was a pupil of Silbermann, in the manufacture of clavecins. After 1793 she settled in Vienna, and with her husband established the firm "Nanette Streicher geb. Stein." Being an excellent pianist, who, before performing in public, tuned the Pf. herself, and a very kind and generous woman, her house became the meeting-place of all the most celebrated composers and performers. She reckoned Beethoven amongst her truest and most faithful friends, and he was always deeply grateful for the care she took of his (sometimes unsettled) household.

Steinkühler, Emil, b. May 12, 1824, Düsseldorf; d. Nov. 21, 1872, Ghent. Pupil of his father, who taught him the Vln. and Pf. He profited much by Mendelssohn's advice when in Düsseldorf. 1840, he went to Frankfort o/M. and became a pupil of Aloys Schmitt. 1845, he visited Paris and settled afterwards in Lille, where he remained until the French war began (1870).

Trio, Op. 35; Duos for Pf. and V'cello, Op. 12 and 50; †18 Etudes mélodiques, Op. 58.

***Stephens**, Charles Edward, b. March 18, 1821, London; d. there July 19, 1892. Pupil of J. M. Rost and Cipriani Potter (Pf.), of Rost, Smith, and Blagrove (Vln.), and J. A. Hamilton (Harmony and Composition). 1850, an Associate, and, 1857, a Member of the Philharmonic Society; 1865, Fellow of the College of Organists; 1870, Hon. Member of the R.A.M.; 1874, original member of the Musical Association; and 1880-92, Hon. Treasurer of the Philharmonic Society.

Quartet with Strings, Op. 2; Trio, Op. 1; Duo concertant for 2 Pfs., Op. 4; Sonata, Op. 8; Duo brillant for 4 hands, Op. 19, and several shorter pieces.

Sterkel, Abbé Johann Franz Xaver, b. Dec. 3, 1750, Würzburg; d. there Oct. 21, 1817. Pupil of Kette and Weissmandel. He made such rapid progress that, in spite of his vocation as a priest, the Palatine sent him to Italy, where his brilliant performances were cordially received. 1778, before his journey to Italy, he was appointed Clavecinist and Chaplain to the Palatine of Mayence, who was residing at Aschaffenburg. 1805, Capellmeister at Ratisbon (Regensburg), but, owing to political events, he returned (1813) to Würzburg, where he died. In a letter, dated Nov. 26, 1777, Mozart speaks rather unfavourably about Sterkel's playing: ". . . came Sterkel. He played five Sonatas with Vln., but so fast that one could not understand it; it was neither distinct nor in time."

6 Concertos; about 30 Trios; many Duets; 7 Solo Sonatas shorter pieces, including the once popular "Rondo comique"; and Sonatas for 4 hands.

***Sternberg**, Constantin (Ivanovitch Edler von), b. July 9, 1852, St. Petersburg. Pupil of Moscheles and Kullak (Pf.), Reinecke and Wüerst (Composition). 1871, Hof-Capellmeister of the Strelitz Opera; 1876, Court Pianist (Strelitz). Travelled through the whole of Europe, and settled finally in Philadelphia (U.S.).

Op. 9, Hochzeits-Polonaise; Op. 22, Al Fresco, 10 pieces; Op. 24, 3 pieces; Op. 38, Concert-Polonaise; Op. 48, Italian Scenes (4); Op. 50, 3 pieces (No. 2, Historiette; No. 3, Staccatella); Op. 57, Chasseresse; Op. 58, Passepied; Trios, &c.

Stiehl, Heinrich Franz Daniel, b. Aug. 5, 1829, Lübeck; d. May 1, 1886, Reval. Pupil of Lobe at the Leipzig Conserv. 1853-56, Organist of St. Peter's Church and Conductor of the Choral Society of St. Petersburg. For artistic purposes, travelled afterwards in Germany, Italy, and England, and (1874-78) was Conductor of the St. Cecilia Society of Belfast; 1878-80, he resided at Hastings as a teacher, but afterwards accepted the post of Organist of St. Olai and the direction of the Choral Society in Reval. He was an excellent musician, brilliant performer, and talented composer.

Trios (3); **Sonata** with V'cello; several Sonatas with Vln.; 5 Fantasiestücke, Op. 58; "In lonely hours" (4 pieces), Op. 75; 4 Musical Portraits, Op. 166, &c.

*Stojowski, Sigismond, b. May 2, 1870, Strelce (Poland). Pupil of L. Zelenski (Cracow). 1887, he went to Paris; completed his education at the Sorbonne, and continued his musical studies at the Conserv., under Diémer (Pf.) and Léo Delibes (Composition). Since then he has studied with I. Paderewski. 1889, he received the first prize both for playing and composition; 1891, he gave an orchestral concert in Paris, at which he introduced a Concerto of his own composition. His appearance in London was highly successful, and the musical public follows his career with great attention. His published pieces are very graceful, elegant, and effective.

Streabbog (*see* Gobbaerts).

Streicher, Johann Andreas, b. Dec. 13, 1761, Stuttgart; d. May 25, 1833, Vienna. He was a fellow student of Schiller at the "Carlsschule" and assisted him in his flight from that institution. 1793, he married Nanette Stein and established with her a Pf. manufactory at Vienna He was a good and well-instructed musician, a devoted friend of Beethoven, and the teacher of Mozart's son and many other pianists—in short, one of the most influential men in the Austrian capital.

Strelezki, Anton (*nom de plume* of an English composer), b. Dec. 5, 1859, Croydon. 1876, pupil at the Leipzig Conserv., later of Madame Schumann.

The following are the most popular of his pieces:
Valsette; Menuet à l'antique (E flat); Sérénade espagnole; Jagdstück; Tarantelle (D min.); Valse-Souvenir.

Székely, Imre (Emeric), b. May 8, 1823, Malyfolva (Hungary). Was educated at Buda-Pesth; travelled in 1846, and gave concerts in Paris and London. 1852, established himself as a successful teacher and popular performer in Buda-Pesth.
Compositions de Salon, Op. 20-27; 30 Hungarian Fantasias on National Airs ("Magyar Abránd's).

*Szumowska, Antoinette, b. Feb. 22, 1868, Lublin (Poland), the daughter of a Prof. of the Lublin College, who was banished to Siberia. After his return from exile, he settled at Warsaw, where his daughter worked at her musical studies under Strobel and Michalowski. Later she went to Paris and studied with Paderewski. Her performances in London, the provinces, and Paris met with great approbation.

Szymanowska, Marie (*née* Wolowska), b. 1790, Poland; d. 1831, St. Petersburg. Pupil of John Field at Moscow. 1815-30, she resided at Warsaw, where she appeared with eminent success. With the same success she played at Leipzig, Vienna, Berlin, Hamburg, and St. Petersburg, where she was appointed Pianist to the Court, and was much respected as a teacher. Schumann speaks very approvingly of her "Studies"; and her 24 Mazurkas, as well as the Nocturne, "Le Murmure," all of which testify to considerable talent.

T.

Talexy, Adrien, b. 1820, Paris; d. there Feb., 1881. He composed a great number of light and popular pieces.
20 Etudes expressives, Op. 80; and a Méthode élémentaire et progressive de Piano.

Tappert, Wilhelm, b. Feb. 19, 1830, Ober-Thomaswaldau near Bunzlau (Silesia). 1856, pupil of Kullak and Dehn (Berlin). After finishing his studies, he lived until 1866 at Glogau, but then settled permanently at Berlin as a teacher of Pf. and Theory, and as a reporter to the *Kleines Journal* and the *Neue Berliner Musikzeitung*.
50 Studies for the left hand, and Album-leaves, Op. 11.

Taubert, Ernst Eduard, b. Sept. 25, 1838, Regenwalde (Pomerania). Studied Theology and Philology, but then resolved to devote himself to music. Pupil of Dietrich (Bonn) and Kiel (Berlin). At present Prof. at the Stern Conserv. of Berlin, and reporter to the *Post* Journal. He is a distinguished composer, and the following works deserve particular mention:
Op. 8, Suite (5 pieces) for 4 hands; Op. 9, 4 easy pieces for 4 hands; Op. 10, Novelletten; Op. 13, Humoreske; Op. 27, Concert-Walzer; Op. 28, 6 Arabesques; Op. 30, Polonaise; and Op. 33, Waltzes for 4 hands.

Taubert, Wilhelm (Carl Gottfried), b. March 23, 1811, Berlin; d. there Jan. 7,

1891. At first a pupil of Neithardt, later (with Mendelssohn) of Ludwig Berger (Pf.). Studied composition under Bernhard Klein. Worked for several years as a teacher; 1831, he became Conductor of the Court Concerts; 1842, Hof-Capellmeister of the Royal Opera, which appointment he held (from 1869 as first Hof-Capellmeister) until 1870. From 1875 till a few years before his death he was Chairman of the musical section of the Royal Academy of Arts. As a pianist he was unrivalled in his performances of older music, and his style was much admired for exquisite refinement, fine graduations of tone, irreproachable part-playing, absolute correctness, clearness, and tender expression. All these qualities are represented in his Pf. works.

Quartet in E flat, Op. 19; Trio in F, Op. 32; Duets (with Vln.), Op. 1 and 15; Sonatas, Op. 4, 20, 21 (2), and 35; Sonatinas, Op. 44; †6 Scherzi, Op. 8; 6 Impromptus, Op. 14; †An die Geliebte (8); Concerto, Op. 18; Camera obscura; †12 Etudes de Concert, Op. 40; †La Campanella, Op. 41a; Grâce et Bravour, Op. 41b; †La Nayade, Op. 49; Silvana, Op. 60; †Jugendparadies, Op. 84.

Tausch, Julius, b. April 15, 1827, Dessau, where he was a pupil of Fr. Schneider. 1844-46, attended the Leipzig Conserv.; 1853, acted temporarily instead of Schumann as Conductor of the musical societies of Düsseldorf, and, 1855, succeeded him. He is an eminent pianist and a clever composer.

Fantasiestücke, Sonata with Vln., &c.

Tausig, Carl (son of Aloys T., who died 1885), b. Nov. 4, 1841, Warsaw; d. July 17, 1871, Leipzig. Pupil of his father (who was a pupil of Thalberg), and later of Liszt. His technical execution was stupendous, and he overcame, with the greatest ease, the most difficult and complicated intricacies; indeed, his technique was not only irreproachable, but infallible. He owed his marvellous dexterity entirely to his systematic and persevering study of technical figures of all kinds, which resulted in an independence of the fingers never before attained. These remarkable finger-exercises have been published by his friend Ehrlich, and are used by every pianist and in every music school. Tausig edited a selection from Clementi's "Gradus ad Parnassum," and added to the various studies a mode of fingering which appears at times almost tantalising, but tends to improve the strength and flexibility of the hands. Besides a few original compositions (Etudes de Concert, &c.), he transcribed, with more or less success—

5 Sonatas by Domenico Scarlatti, Schubert's Military March, Hungarian Gipsy Melodies, Weber's Invitation to the Dance, Wagner's "Walkürenritt," †Siegmund's Liebeslied, from the "Walküre"; Bach's Organ Toccata and Fugue in D min., some of Strauss's Valses, as "Nouveaux Soirées de Vienne"; and a Fantasia on themes of "Halka," by the Polish composer Moniuszko (1819-1872).

*Taylor, Franklin, b. Feb. 5, 1843, Birmingham. Pupil of the late C. E. Flavell (who was a pupil of Aloys Schmitt) and of J. Bedsmore, late Organist of Lichfield Cathedral. 1859, went to Leipzig, entered the Conserv., and studied with Plaidy and Moscheles (Pf.), E. F. Richter and Hauptmann (Theory). After leaving Leipzig he spent a winter in Paris. He appeared for the first time in London (Crystal Palace) in 1865. 1876, appointed Pf. Prof. at the National Training School, and, 1883, at the Royal College of Music (also a Member of the Board). From 1891-94, one of the Directors of the Philharmonic Society; also Member of the Associated Board of the R.A.M. and Royal College of Music for Local Examinations (established 1889). He translated three of Richter's theoretical works, wrote a Primer of Pf. playing (translated into German), a Pf. tutor for beginners, and many articles on technical matters in Grove's "Dictionary of Music." Since 1883 he has given up playing in public.

Tedesco, Ignaz (Amadeus), b. 1817, Prague; d. Nov. 13, 1882, Odessa. Pupil of his father and Triebensee, later of W. Tomaschek, who also instructed him in Composition. In Vienna, and on his travels through Germany and Russia, he met with great success. For several years he resided at Odessa, where he had a great number of pupils. Afterwards went to Hamburg and Oldenburg (where he was named Pianist to the Court) and visited England. His playing was exceedingly elegant and brilliant, although his execution was not nearly so great and dazzling as that at present expected from pianists. His compositions are light and popular, and his transcriptions of celebrated airs and classical movements are conscientiously written.

Telemann, Georg Philipp (contemporary and great friend of Seb. Bach), one of the most prolific composers that ever existed, b. March 14, 1681, Magdeburg; d. June 25, 1767, Hamburg. His father, a clergyman, superintended his first studies. 1700, he attended the University of Leipzig; 1704, appointed Organist of the Neukirche. Before this he had had to write every fortnight a new work for the Thomas Church, where Kuhnau was Cantor. He founded the historically interesting Collegium Musicum. 1708, he accepted an appointment at Eisenach; 1712, named Music Director of St. Catharine's Church, Frankfort o/M.; and 1721, Musical Director of the town of Hamburg, where he remained until his death.

> Fantaisies pour le Clavecin, 3 douzaines; 6 Sonatinas, 1718; 20 short Fugues, 1731; 6 Concertos and 6 Suites for Clavecin, Fl., V'cello concertante; 6 Overtures, French, Polish, and Italian.

Tellefsen, Thomas Dyke Acland, b. Nov. 26, 1823, Drontheim (Norway); d. Oct., 1874, Paris. Although he showed decided musical talent, his parents wished him to become a clergyman, and he studied for this calling until his nineteenth year, when the desire to devote himself entirely to music (particularly the Pf.) became so strong that he went to Paris to take lessons from Chopin, to whom he proved a most devoted friend. After the outbreak of the French war (1870), he resided for some time in London. He was an excellent performer, who combined elegance and gracefulness with poetic expression. In his compositions the national element is everywhere apparent, but never dominates over the forms and dogmas of the art. He was a Knight of the "Seraphine" Order of Norway.

> 2 Concertos, Trio, Sonata for Pf. and Vln., Sonata with V'cello, Duets for Pf. and Vln., and a considerable number of Nocturnes, Mazourkas, Valses, &c.

Ten Brink, Jules (or Brink, Jules ten), b. Nov., 1838, Amsterdam. Pupil of Heinze, later of A. Dupont (Brussels) and E. F. Richter (Leipzig). 1860-68, Music Conductor at Lyons, but settled (1868) in Paris, where several of his compositions were favourably received.

> Op. 8, six pièces à 4 mains.

Thalberg, Sigismund (son of Prince Joseph Dietrichstein and the Baroness Wetzlar), b. Jan. 7, 1812, Geneva; d. April 27, 1871, Naples. Pupil of Sechter for Composition and of Mittag, first Bssn. player of the Imperial Opera at Vienna, for Pf. He never was a pupil of Hummel, as asserted by some of his biographers. In his fifteenth year he was already a very clever performer, and created a great sensation in private circles. 1830, he undertook his first journey to Germany, where he quickly made a lasting reputation; 1835, he went for the first time to Paris, and carried everything before him; 1836, he competed with Liszt, but as their style was an entirely different one, it was impossible to declare who was the greater performer. On the one hand, Liszt, genial, poetic, impetuous, and grasping everything with an iron hand; on the other, Thalberg, cool, collected, aristocratic, never losing sight of his principal object—to create an effect—it was not possible to compare them. 1836-55, he travelled through the whole of Europe, everywhere received with enthusiastic admiration; 1855, he went to Brazil; 1856, to N. America; 1858, he retired for some years to Naples, where he took great interest in cultivating wines; 1862, he went again to Paris and London; and, 1863, for a second time to Brazil. He was pianist to the Emperor of Austria and the King of Saxony, and decorated by most of the European Sovereigns and the Emperor of Brazil. The chief qualities of his playing were absolute correctness, clearness, and smoothness, faultless phrasing, polished execution, and most admirable graduations of tone. His careful use of the pedal was a study for every pianist, and his touch, from the softest to the loudest, was, without exception, full and round. But his style lacked warmth and spontaneity of feeling, and his posture and manner before the instrument were so quiet and motionless that the listener, although experiencing a feeling of comfort and reliance, could never be stirred up to a state of frenzy, as was often the case when listening to Liszt's playing. With regard to his innovation of dividing the melody in the middle of the Pf. between the two hands, so as to give the full bass and rich accompaniment to the left, whilst the right hand surrounds the melody with runs, broken chords, figures in octaves—it has to be observed that this decidedly striking method had already been used by Eli Parish-Alvars, a famous harpist, and was imitated not only by a number of pianists, but also by such a composer as Mendelssohn, who, in his second Concerto, Op. 40 (first movement), employs it with excellent effect.

I

Op. 5, Concerto in F min.; †Op. 15, Caprice in E min.; Op. 19, Caprice in E flat; Op. 16, 2 Nocturnes; †Op. 21, 3 Nocturnes; †Op. 26, 12 Studies; Op. 28, Nocturne in E; Op. 31, Scherzo; †Op. 32, Andante; Op. 35, Nocturne (F sharp); Op. 36, †La Cadence, †Study in E flat; †Op. 38, Romance et Etude in A; †Op. 41, 3 Romances; †Op. 45, Thème original et Etude in A min.; Op. 56, Sonata in C min.; †Op. 60, Barcarolle; †Op. 64, Les Capricieuses, Valses; Op. 65, Tarantelle. *Operatic Fantasias:* †Op. 20, Huguenots; †Op. 33, Moïse; Op. 40, Donna del Lago; Op. 51, Semiramide; Op 52, Muette de Portici; †Op. 66, L'Elisir d'amore; Op. 67, Don Pasquale.

Thern, Willi, b. June 22, 1847, Ofen,
Thern, Louis, b. Dec. 18, 1848, Pesth, sons of Carl T. (1817-86). Received their first instruction from their father, but studied (1864-65) with Moscheles and Reinecke in Leipzig. Both are excellent pianists and musicians, who won particular distinction by their wonderful *ensemble* playing, the evenness and exactitude of which has never before been attained. They reside and are popular as teachers in Vienna.

Thomé, François Lucien Joseph (Francis), b. Oct. 18, 1850, Port Louis, Mauritius. Entered (1866) the Paris Conserv. and studied with Marmontel (Pf.) and Duprato (Harmony). His elegant and graceful compositions have become very popular.

Simple aveu, Op. 25; Menuet dans le style ancien, Op. 68; Sous la feuillée, Op. 29; Papillons bleus, Op. 59; Coquetterie, Illusion, Op. 60; 3 Valses, Op. 36; Agitato, Op. 50; Les Lutins, Op. 69.

Thurner, Theodor, b. Dec. 13, 1833, Pfaffersheim, Upper Rhine; d. May 20, 1893, Marseilles. 1846, pupil at the Paris Conserv., under Zimmermann and Alkan (Pf.) and Bazin (Composition). 1849, gained the first prize; 1850, he established himself at Toulon; 1864-74, at Marseilles as Prof. of the Conserv. His Trio-Soirées were highly successful—indeed, he was an influential agent in the interest of classical music.

6 Romances sans paroles, Barcarolle, †Tarantelle, †Sarah la baigneuse, 2 Valses dans le style de Chopin, and Etude-Toccata.

Tietz, Hermann, b. March 8, 1844, District Driesen (Frankfort o/Oder). 1859-63, he studied chemistry, but then resolved to make music the aim of his life; 1865, pupil of Kullak (Berlin), who appointed him (1866) teacher of the junior classes of his Academy; 1868, he went to Gotha, founded a Musical Society and (1880) the Conserv. Was named (1869) Pianist to the Court and (1888) Prof.

Timanof, Vera, b. Feb. 18, 1855, Ufa (Russia). Pupil of Ludwig Nowitzky. Played in her ninth year in public. 1866, was, for a short time, a pupil of Rubinstein (St. Petersburg); afterwards, for two and a half years, of Tausig (Berlin). Returned to St. Petersburg; resided (1871) in Prague; 1872, at Vienna; and went almost every year to Weimar, in order to profit by Liszt's advice. She is one of the foremost lady pianists of the present time.

Tinel, Edgar, b. March 27, 1854, Sinay (Belgium). Pupil at the Brussels Conserv., where he was instructed by Brassin (Pf.), Kufferath and Gevaert (Theory and Composition). He published several pieces at Brussels, but his fame rests principally on his sacred works.

Tinto, Michele, b. Feb. 10, 1822, Aversa (Caserta). 1831, pupil at the Conserv. of Naples, where Zingarelli, Lanza, and Nacciarone were his teachers. His pieces only appeared in Italy.

Tischer, Johann Nicolaus, b. 1707, Böhlen (Schwarzburg); d. 1766, Schmalkalden. Pupil of the organist, Rauche; later of Graf. 1731, Organist of the principal church at Schmalkalden. The titles of his several works are highly amusing:

The pleased ear and the refreshed intellect, in six elegant Partitas for the ladies' instruction; 1, 2, and 3. Divertissement musical consistant en 3 Suites. Agreeable Clavecin fruits, consisting of 6 short Suites, for the service of beginners, but more especially of children. Musical twins, in 2 concerts of the same key (major and minor) for the Clavecin; first fruit in C and C min., second fruit in D and D min., &c., up to A and A min.; last and easy concert as a finale of the musical twins; Part No. 7. A lamenting Kyrie and rejoicing Hallelujah, or harmonious joy for the heart, represented in 2 Concertos in C and C min., in which the sentiment of several added passages in writing is a little expressed by pleasant melodies and well-applied modulations (Nürnberg).

Tofano, Gustave, b. Dec. 22, 1844, Naples. Pupil of Castrucci (Pisa), Domenico Caldi (Turin), and Stefano Golinelli (Bologna). 1872, appointed Prof. at the Liceo (Bologna). He is considered one of the foremost Italian pianists of the present time.

Tomaschek, Wenzel, b. April 17, 1774, Skutsch (Bohemia); d. April 3, 1850, Prague. 1787, he entered and was educated in the Monastery of Iglau, but had generally to pursue his musical studies by himself, with the aid of the works of Marpurg, Kirnberger,

Mattheson, &c. Later he attended the Prague University as a student of the law, but found a generous patron in the person of his pupil, Count Georg Bucquoy, who, by providing sufficient means, enabled him to devote himself entirely to music. He was a successful teacher, and among his pupils were Kittl, A. Dreyschock, J. Schulhoff, I. Tedesco, W. Kuhe, S. Goldschmidt, Worzischek, Würfel, and others. His compositions somewhat crude and unsympathetic, are but little known, but offer good material for teaching.

Sonatas, Op. 14, 15, 21, 48; Sonata in B, without opus number; Eclogues (6), Op. 35; (6), Op. 47; (6), Op. 51; (6), Op. 63; (6), Op. 66; and (6), Op. 83; Rhapsodies (6), Op. 40; (6), Op. 41; 3 Ditirambi, Op. 65; Allegri capricciosi di Bravura (3), Op. 52; and (3), Op. 84.

*Tours, Berthold, b. Dec. 17, 1838, Rotterdam. Pupil of Verhulst (Amsterdam), Fétis (Brussels), Julius Rietz and E. F. Richter (Leipzig). Settled, about 1863, in London. Composer of small (exceedingly well-written) pieces, among which the "Juvenile Album" deserves particular mention. He arranged, in a very efficient manner, Gounod's sacred works, "The Redemption" and "Mors et Vita," and is the careful editor of various albums.

Tschaïkowsky, Peter Iljitsch, b. Dec. 25, 1840, Wotkinsk (Government Wiåtka, Russia); d. Nov. 6, 1893, St. Petersburg. He studied law and entered the service of the Government, but soon after the foundation of the St. Petersburg Conserv. by A. Rubinstein he became a pupil, and, 1866-77, Prof. of Composition. He resided in Russia, Paris, Italy, and Switzerland. He was considered one of the most typical composers of Russia, and some of his works have attracted great attention. June 13, 1893, the University of Cambridge conferred on him the hon. degree of Mus. Doc.

Op. 23, Concerto, No. 1, in B flat min.; Op. 44, Concerto, No. 2; Op. 56, Fantasia with Orchestra; Op. 50, Trio; Op. 2, †Souvenir de Hapsal (3 pieces); Op. 5, Romance; Op. 9, 3 Morceaux; Op. 10, 2 Morceaux; Op. 19, 6 Morceaux; Op. 37, Sonata; Op. 37a, The Seasons (12 characteristic pieces); Op. 39, Kinder-Album (24 pieces); Op. 40, †12 Morceaux; Op. 51, 6 Morceaux; Op. 72, 18 Morceaux. All other pieces are arrangements of orchestral or chamber music.

Türck (Türk), Daniel Gottlieb, b. Aug. 10, 1756 (1751?), Claussnitz, near Chemnitz (Saxony); d. Aug. 26, 1813, Halle. At first a pupil of his father, later of Homilius (Dresden); 1772, of Adam Hiller (Leipzig), who became his warm and faithful friend. 1776, Hiller procured him the appointment of organist and teacher at the Protestant College of Halle; 1779, he received another appointment as organist in Halle; 1808, the University made him Prof. and conferred on him the degree of Doc. Phil., *hon. causâ*. His literary works are very important, and his works for Clavecin proved very useful.

Method for teachers and learners (1789); 60 Exercises (Handstücke) for beginners; 30 Sonatas in 5 collections (1789, 1793, 1798); 120 easy pieces for 4 hands (4 books).

Tyson-Wolff, Dr. Gustav, b. April 12, 1840, Berlin. Pupil of A. Löschhorn (Pf.); 1862, pupil at the Leipzig Conserv., where Plaidy, Moscheles, Hauptmann, Richter, and Reinecke were his teachers. From 1866 he resided for several years in Bradford (Yorkshire), where he established a music school and arranged concerts for chamber music. Received from the Archbishop of Canterbury the diploma of Mus. Doc., *hon. causâ*. 1884, he returned to Germany, and has resided since 1886 in Berlin as a teacher of Composition, Theory, and Pf. The following compositions deserve notice:

Op. 17, Trio; Op. 19, 32 Etudes; Op. 26, 36 Morceaux mélodiques; Op. 11, 2 Sonatinas; Op. 12, 2 Sonatinas; Op. 4, 2 Morceaux caractéristiques à 4 mains; Op. 5, Barcarolle; Op. 25, "Für kleine Leute"; Op. 27, "In the Woods."

U.

Uhl, Edmund, b. Oct. 25, 1853, Prague. Pupil at the Leipzig Conserv., where Richter, Reinecke, Jadassohn, and Wenzel were his teachers. Received, 1878, the "Helbig" prize. At present he resides in Wiesbaden and is Prof. at the Freudenberg Music School.
<small>Trios, Sonata for Pf. and V'cello, Variations, and several smaller pieces.</small>

Ulrich, Hugo, b. Nov. 26, 1827, Oppeln (Silesia); d. May 23, 1872, Berlin. He was a richly-gifted artist, a thorough musician, and gave promise of becoming a distinguished composer. Pupil of Mosewius (Breslau) and (1846) of Dehn (Berlin). 1859-63, Prof. of Composition at the Stern Academy (Berlin). Being very poor he had to earn his livelihood by working as a corrector and arranger for the publishers. Only a Trio of his own composition was published, but his name will be gratefully remembered for his most excellent arrangements of Beethoven's Symphonies (for 4 hands), works of Schubert, &c.

Urbach, Carl Friedrich, b. Sept. 26, 1833, Burg (Magdeburg). He made himself favourably known by a Method of Pf. playing (which received a "prize") and a second practical Pf. school. Since 1857 he has been a teacher at Egeln (Province Magdeburg).
<small>Sonatinas, Studies, and various short pieces.</small>

*****Urspruch, Anton,** b. Feb. 17, 1850, Frankfort o/M. Pupil of Wallenstein (Pf.) and Ignaz Lachner (Composition), later of Liszt and J. Raff.
<small>Quintet; Sonata for Pf. and Vln.; Sonata for Pf. and V'cello; 5 Fantasiestücke, Op. 2; Sonata for 4 hands; Concerto; Trio; Variations and Fugue on a theme of Seb. Bach, for 2 Pf., &c.</small>

V.

Van den Gheyn, Matthias, b. April 7, 1721, Tirlemont (Belgium); d. June 22, 1785, Louvain. Probably a pupil of the Abbé Raick (Louvain). 1741, he received the appointment of Organist of St. Peter's (Louvain). He was the foremost Carilloneur of his time, and every Sunday, for forty years, charmed the people of the town, who used to crowd into the adjacent streets in order to admire his excellent performances. His works for Clavecin were published by Xavier van Elewyck, who also wrote his biography.
<small>12 petites Sonates, 6 Divertissements; and a collection of Preludes, Rondos, and Fugues, &c., 2 vols. (Schott and Co., Brussels).</small>

Van der Does, Charles, b. March 6, 1817, Amsterdam; d. Jan. 30, 1878, The Hague. At first instructed in his native town; afterwards a pupil of Rummel (Wiesbaden). On his return to Holland, the King named him Pianist to the Court, and the Dowager Queen conferred on him the Orders of the Crown of Oak and the Lion of the Netherlands. He was Prof. at the Royal School (Hague) and Inspector of the Dutch Music Schools. According to various reports, he was an excellent pianist.

Van Elewyck, Chevalier Xavier Victor, b. April 24, 1825, Ixelles-les-Bruxelles; d. April 28, 1880, Louvain. Pupil of Boutmy (Pf.) and Bosselet (Harmony). He attended the Louvain University, became Secretary and finally President of the Louvain Music Academy, founded the Society of St. Cecilia, and took the greatest interest in everything which could promote the progress of music in Belgium. His chief merit consists in the publication of Van den Gheyn's works, which were, up to the time of Elewyck's researches, entirely unknown. The Kings of Belgium and Holland showed their appreciation by conferring on him high classes of their Orders. He was also a Member of the St. Cecilia Society (Rome) and of many other learned academies.

Verger, Virginie du (*née* Morel), b. 1799, Metz; d. 1870, at the Château du Verger, her husband's property—a Lieut.-Colonel of the Staff—whom she married in 1829. 1814, she became a pupil at the Paris Conserv., was patronised by Méhul, and received important and useful advice from Clementi; for some time she was also a pupil of

Hummel. The Duchesse de Berry named her "Pianiste." Other details are wanting.

Viènot, Edouard, b. 1825, Paris (?). Composed a great number of popular light pieces of considerable brilliancy. The only information to be got from his principal publisher is that he was an officer in the Cuirassiers, and dated his letters from different garrison towns, but that lately the correspondence has entirely ceased.

> Etudes, Galop, Carillon, Berceuse, Gelées blanches, Barcarolle, Op. 23; Mazurka russe, and Galop des Guides.

Vierling, Georg, b. Sept. 5, 1820, Frankenthal (Palatinate). Pupil of Neeb (Frankfort o/M.) and Rinck (Darmstadt). 1842-45, he studied Composition with A. B. Marx (Berlin); 1847, Organist at Frankfort o/Oder; 1852-53, Conductor of the Choral Societies (Mayence on the Rhine); settled, 1853, at Berlin, where he received (1859) the title of "Königl. Musik-Director." He is an experienced composer, whose works have met with considerable success.

> Capriccio with Orchestra, Trio, Fantasiestücke for Pf. and V'cello; Fantasia for Pf. and Vln., Sonata, Op. 44; Valse Caprice, Op. 43; 3 Impromptus, Op. 53, &c.

Vilbac (Alphonse Charles), Renaud de, b. June 3, 1829, Montpellier; d. March 19, 1884, Paris. Pupil at the Paris Conserv., where Lemoine, Halévy, and Benoit were his teachers. 1844, he received the Grand Prix de Rome and went to Italy; 1856, Organist of St. Eugène (Paris). Excellent performer and a popular composer of easy, pleasant, melodious, and practically written pieces.

> 3 Morceaux de Salon, Op. 23 (†No. 3, Corricolo); 3 Caprices, Op. 25 (†No. 2, Della Notte; †No. 3, La Ziza); Les Amazones, Galop; Duos à 4 mains on Donna del Lago, Op. 19; †Elisir d'amore, Op. 24. The collection: Beautés des Opéras (Rossini, Weber, Donizetti, Gounod, Wagner, Halévy); Method of Pf. playing.

Villoing, Alexander, b. (information wanting), St. Petersburg; d. there Sept., 1878. His fame rests on being the sole teacher of Anton and Nicolaus Rubinstein, and on having written the excellent book "l'Ecole Pratique du Piano," in which the system on which he instructed the famous brothers is explained. He is the composer of a Concerto and of some shorter pieces.

Viole, Rudolph, b. May 10, 1815, Schochwitz (Mansfeld); d. Dec. 7, 1867, Berlin, where he resided. A careful and industrious teacher, but little known, until he became a pupil of Liszt, who warmly recommended his compositions. Since 1857, contributor to the *Neue Zeitschrift für Musik*.

> 11 Sonatas, Op. 1 and 21-30; "Die musikalische Gartenlaube," 100 Studies, Polonaise, Ballade, Caprice héroïque, Poésies lyriques.

Vogler, Abbé Georg Joseph, b. June 15, 1749, Würzburg; d. May 6, 1814, Darmstadt. For a very short time pupil of Padre Martini (Bologna) and Valotti (Padua). Ordained a priest in Rome; received the title of "Protonotar," the dignity of Papal Chamberlain, and the Order of the "Golden Spur"; he was also elected a Member of the Arcadians. 1775, at Mannheim, where he established a music school; 1781, at Munich; 1783, in Paris; 1786, in Stockholm, from whence he returned (1799) to Germany. 1807, appointed Hof-Capellmeister at Darmstadt, where he established a school, at which C. M. von Weber, Meyerbeer, and Gänsbacher were the most distinguished pupils. Many of his contemporaries declared him to be a charlatan; it is certain that he understood how to make the most of his talents.

> Concertos (he called them Symphonies), Quartet, "The matrimonial quarrel," Sonata with accompaniment of strings; Polymelos ou caractères de musique de différentes nations, 6 Sonatas for 2 Pf., Variations, Preludes.

Vogt, Johann (Jean), b. Jan. 17, 1823, Gross-Tintz, near Liegnitz; d. July 31, 1888, Berlin. Educated at the Seminary of Bunzlau. 1845, went to Berlin, where Wilhelm Bach and Grell were his teachers; later to Breslau, where Hesse and Seidel instructed him. Henselt advised him to go to St. Petersburg, and he settled there in 1850. 1855, he made tours through Germany, England, France; 1857, to Leipzig, Vienna, Berlin, &c.; 1861, he established himself at Dresden; 1865-71, was a teacher at the Stern Academy (Berlin); then lived for two years in New York; afterwards returned to Berlin.

> Pf. Quartets and Trios; Prelude and Fugue for 2 Pf., Op. 18; Prelude and Toccata, Op. 19; Preludes and Fugues (3 books), Op. 20; 12 Grandes Etudes, Op. 26; Valse brillante, Op. 39; 3 Impromptus, Op. 69; Salonstücke (6), Op. 73.

Volkmann (Friedrich), Robert, b. April 6, 1815, Lommatzsch (Saxony); d. Oct. 29/30, 1883, Pesth. At first a pupil of his father (a Cantor); afterwards of Anacker (Freiberg) and K. F. Becker (Leipzig). During his sojourn at Leipzig, Robert Schumann had great influence on the development of his talent, and it may be asserted that there is considerable affinity of character in Schumann's and Volkmann's compositions. 1839, music teacher at Prague; 1842, working in Pesth; 1854-58, he lived in Vienna, but returned to Pesth, and was appointed teacher of composition at the National Music School. His compositions are throughout noble and distinguished, his melodies are interesting and fascinating, his harmonisation euphonious and without any harshness. His contributions to the literature of the Pf. are very valuable.

> 2 Trios, Op. 3 and 5; Allegretto capriccioso for Pf. and Vln., Op. 15; Rhapsody for Pf. and Vln., Op. 31; Concertstück with Orchestra, Op. 42; Solo Sonata, Op. 12; Variations on a theme of Händel for 2 Pf., Op. 26. Shorter pieces are: †"Grandmother's Songs," Op. 39; Morning, noon, evening, and night; Op. 60 and 61, Sonatinas; †Op. 21, Visegrád; †Op. 23, Wanderskizzen; Op. 22, 4 Marches; Op. 20, Hungarian Melodies. *For 4 hands:* "Musical Picture-Book," Hungarian Sketches, and 3 Marches.

Vollweiler, Carl, b. 1813, Offenbach o/M.; d. Jan. 27, 1848, Heidelberg.

Pupil of his father. He lived for several years at St. Petersburg, but returned during the last years of his short life to Germany (Heidelberg).

> Trios, Op. 2 and 15; a "prize" Sonata, Op. 3; Lyric Studies, Op. 9 and 10; 6 Etudes mélodiques, Op. 4. He also published Fantasias on operatic airs.

Voss, Charles, b. Sept. 20, 1815, Schmarsow, near Demmin (Pomerania); d. August 28/29, 1882, Verona. 1846, went to Paris, and soon made himself a name as an elegant performer and careful teacher; remained there until 1860, when he varied the places of his residence. The number of his Fantasias, Transcriptions, Paraphrases, easy and more difficult arrangements of operatic, national, and lyric music is very great. The style of his pieces (effective without being difficult) became so popular that his works were eagerly bought by German, French, English, Russian, and Italian publishers, thus tempting the otherwise talented author to devote his time to mere trifles, lightly written and heavily paid.

W.

*****Wachs,** Paul, b. Sept. 19, 1851, Paris. Pupil at the Conserv., where Victor Massé, Marmontel, César Franck, and Duprato were his teachers. 1872, he gained the first prize for Organ. His pieces, generally short, elegant, graceful, and piquant, quickly gained considerable popularity.

> "Tiens, c'est gentil!" Valse des Myrtes; Capricante; "Aujourd'hui, autrefois," Valse interrompue.

Wagenseil, Georg Christoph, b. Jan. 15, 1715, Vienna; d. there March 1, 1777. Pupil of Fux (author of the "Gradus ad Parnassum"). Teacher to the Empress Maria Theresia and her children, with whom he was a decided favourite. He composed a considerable number of works, written in a formal, conventional, and somewhat empty style.

> Suavis artificiose elaboratus concentus musicus continens VI. parthias selectas ad clavicembalum compositas, 1740; 6 Sonatas, Op. 1; 4 Symphonies for Clavecin with strings, Op. 4; 30 Suites; 27 Concertos; Divertissement for 2 Clavecins; Quartets; Trios; Sonatas with Vln.; "The bells of the Vatican at Rome," for Clavecin.

*****Waley,** Simon, b. Aug. 23, 1827, London; d. there Dec. 30, 1875. Pupil of Moscheles (Pf.), W. Horsley (Harmony), later of Sterndale Bennett and B. Molique. Although an amateur, his endeavour to do his best in music warrants his name being included in this book. He was an expert and brilliant performer, and his composition show sound and conscientious learning. 1852-60, he was an active member of the Amateur Musical Society, of which Henry Leslie was conductor, and his house was a meeting-place for artists, who met with the kindest reception from him and his family.

> Concerto, with Orchestra, Op. 16; Trios, Op. 15 and 20.

Wallace, William Vincent, b. July 1, 1814, Waterford (Ireland); d. Oct. 12, 1865, Touraine (Pyrenées). Pupil of his father. From his eighteenth year he travelled a great deal, visiting Australia, New Zealand, India, South America, the United States, and Mexico. 1841-42, he conducted the Opera in Mexico; 1843-53, he resided in New York, afterwards in England; 1863-65, in Paris. He had great facility in writing, his melodies having a popular character; his style resembles that of the later works of Henri Herz, and might be called "gushing." His most popular pieces are—

La Gondola, Op. 18; 3 Nocturnes, Op. 20; Nocturne mélodique, Op. 30; Mélodie irlandaise, Op. 53; Valse brillante de Salon; Tarantelle; Andante and Variations; †" Music murmuring in the trees."

*Wallenstein, Martin, b. July 22, 1843, Frankfort o/M. Pupil of his father, later of A. Dreyschock (Prague), Hauptmann and Rietz (Leipzig). His performances have been greatly admired, but he excels more particularly in refinement of taste and in working out in detail the ornamental part, &c. He received the title of Königl. Musik-Director and is Pianist to the Hessian Court.

Concerto, D min.; Studies; Solo pieces.

Wanhal (Vanhall), Johann Baptist, b. May 12, 1739, Neu - Nechanitz (Bohemia); d. Aug. 26, 1813, Vienna. Being the son of a peasant he had to teach himself, until Countess Schaffgotsch took him to Venice, introduced him in the best families, and afforded him the opportunity of profiting by excellent masters. Later he went to Vienna, where he married and lived in comfortable circumstances until a temporary mental disease—originating in religious scruples—interfered with his composing in his usual industrious manner. Getting better, he re-commenced to compose, although Haydn, Mozart, and Beethoven's creations put his former reputation into the shade. In his day he was the favourite composer of amateurs. The following (partial) list may give an idea of the number of his compositions:—

2 Concertos; 8 Concerts faciles; 8 Quartets; many Trios; Sonatas with Vln., Fl., Cl., Guitar; 6 Solo Sonatas (congratulatory Sonatas); Sonate militaire; "The Battle of Würzburg," Sonata; "The Battle of Trafalgar," Sonata; many Sonatinas; 70 books of Variations; †12 Sonatinas; short and easy pieces (of which many editions were published).

Weber, Carl Maria (Friedrich Ernst), Baron von, b. Dec. 18, 1786, Eutin (Oldenburg); d. June 5, 1826, London. At first a pupil of his step-brother, Fritz; 1796, of Heuschkel (Hildburghausen); 1797, of Michael Haydn (Salzburg); 1798-1800, of Kalcher (Theory); 1801, for the second time a pupil of Michael Haydn; 1802, at Hamburg; 1803, at Augsburg and Vienna, where Joseph Haydn declined to take him as a pupil; 1803, had lessons from Abbé Vogler; 1804, Capellmeister at Breslau; 1806, Musical Director of the Prince Eugen of Würtemberg's orchestra at Carlsruhe (Silesia). After having resided for some time at Stuttgart, he was appointed (1813) Capellmeister at Prague and (1816) Hof-Capellmeister of the German Opera at Dresden. He was a most excellent pianist—original, impetuous, tender, romantic, and fascinating. His hands were so large, he could strike twelve notes (duodecime) with ease. His Pf. works contain, consequently, a much wider distribution of chords than had hitherto been known; and it was this innovation which created an extraordinary sensation, and connects his Pf. works more closely with the present style of writing, with that of Beethoven and others. It may be asserted that he brought effects of orchestral instruments like the Fl., Cl., Vln., Bssn., and V'cello within the domain of the keyed instrument. Although the style of his Sonatas is sometimes rather fragmentary, disjointed, and rhapsodic, these defects are in themselves so charming and fascinating that they appear, in their decided originality, so many merits.

Concertos: No. 1 in C, Op. 11; No. 2 in E flat, Op. 32; Concertstück in F min., Op. 79. Sonatas No. 1 in C, Op. 24 (1812); No. 2 in A flat, Op. 39 (1816); No. 3 in D min., Op. 49 (1816); No. 4 in E min., Op. 70 (1822). Trio for Pf., Fl., and V'cello in E flat, Op. 63; Quartet for Pf. and Strings in E flat; Duo for Pf. and Cl. in E flat, Op. 48. Duets with Vln.: No. 1 in F, No. 2 in G, No. 3 in D min., No. 4 in E flat, No. 5 in A, No. 6 in C. Variations: (6) on an original theme in C, Op. 2; (8) on "Castor and Pollux" in F, Op. 5; (6) on "Samori" in B flat, Op. 61, (7) on †" Vien qua Dorina bella" in C, Op. 7; (7) on an original (?) theme in F, Op. 9; (9) on a Norwegian theme in D min., Op. 22; (7) on "Silvana" in E flat, Op. 33; (7) on "Joseph" (Méhul) in C, Op. 28; (9) on "Schöne Minka" in C min., Op. 40. Momento capriccioso in B flat (1808); Polonaise in E flat, Op. 21 (1808); Rondo brillante in E flat, Op. 62 (1819); Aufforderung zum Tanze in D flat, Op. 65 (1819); Polacca brillante in E, Op. 72 (1819); 6 favourite Waltzes (1812); Original Waltz (1815); 12 Allemandes, Op. 4 (1801); 6 Ecossaises (1802). For 4 hands: 6 petites pièces faciles, Op. 3; (6) Op. 10; (8) Op. 60.

Wehle, Carl, b. March 17, 1825, Prague; d. June 3, 1883, Paris. Pupil of Moscheles (Leipzig) and Kullak (Berlin). His journeys extended to Asia, America, Africa, Australia, New Zealand. 1853, he settled in Paris. He was a brilliant and excellent pianist, who understood how to combine a popular manner of playing with a firm musical foundation. In a pleasant manner he related the events of his journeys in the *Leipziger Signale*.

Fête bohémienne; "Marche cosaque"; †" Berceuse javanaise"; "Un songe à Vaucluse"; 2 Sonatas, Op. 38 and 58; Suite, Op. 86.

Weitzmann, Carl Friedrich, b. Aug. 18, 1808, Berlin; d. there Nov. 7, 1880. Pupil of Hauptmann and Spohr. 1832, Director at Riga, 1836, at St. Petersburg; 1846, in London and Paris; he settled (1848) at Berlin as a teacher of Composition and author; 1863, he wrote a history of Pf. playing and literature, which was supplemented (1880) by a history of the Pf.

<small>Valses nobles, pieces for 2 and 4 hands, Riddles (Canons) for 4 hands, and not less than 1,800 Preludes and Modulations, of which the first book is called "Classical," the second "Romantic."</small>

Wenzel, Ernst (Ferdinand), b. Jan. 25, 1808, Waldorf, near Löbau (Saxony); d. Aug. 16, 1880, Kösen (District Merseburg). He attended the University of Leipzig, where he studied Philosophy. As a pupil of Fr. Wieck (Pf.) he formed an intimate friendship with Schumann. 1843, was appointed by Mendelssohn teacher of Pf. at the Conserv., which post he filled with uninterrupted success. Almost all English pianists who studied in Leipzig were pupils and also devoted friends of the highly intelligent, witty, and somewhat eccentric little man. His critical remarks were caustic and sharp, but correct, and uttered in a manner which could not offend.

Wermann, Friedrich Oscar, b. April 30, 1840, Neichen, near Trebsen (Saxony). Pupil of J. Otto, Krägen, Fr. Wieck (Dresden); later at the Leipzig Conserv. Was Conductor at Wesserling; later Prof. of the Seminary of Neufchâtel; 1868, appointment in Dresden; 1876, Organist and Cantor of the "Kreuzschule" and Musik-Director of the three principal Protestant churches (Dresden). His educational works are of great merit.

<small>24 easy melodious studies, Op. 6; 10 easy characteristic pieces for playing in a small circle, Op. 7; 6 easy characteristic pieces, Op. 8; (3) Leaves of Recollection, Op. 9.</small>

Werner, August, b. 1841, St. Petersburg. Son of Swiss parents. He received his instruction in Germany, and has resided for many years in Geneva as Prof. and Member of the Committee of the Conserv.

<small>Etudes (10), Op. 18; ditto (6), Op. 34; 2 Idylles, Op. 37; Nocturne à 4 mains, Op. 25; Marche hongroise, Op. 23, &c.</small>

Wesley, Samuel, b. Feb. 24, 1766, Bristol; d. there Oct. 11, 1837. For detailed biography *see* Grove's "Dictionary," Vol. iv., pp. 445-47.

<small>8 Harpsichord Lessons (1777), 11 Sonatas, 2 Sonatinas, 16 Rondos (mostly on popular airs), 7 sets of Variations, Preludes, Polacca in G, Grand Fugue, 4 Marches, Trio for 3 Pf., 4 Waltzes.</small>

Wesley, Samuel Sebastian, b. Aug. 14, 1810, London; d. April 19, 1876, Gloucester. Educated at the Bluecoat School; 1824, Chorister at the Chapel Royal; 1827, Organist, St. James's Church, Hampstead Road; 1829, at Camberwell; 1832, Organist of Hereford Cathedral; 1835, at Exeter; 1842, at Leeds Parish Church; before 1842, Mus. Doc., Oxon; 1849, Organist of Winchester Cathedral; 1865, until his death, Organist of Gloucester Cathedral.

<small>Air and Variations, March in C min., Rondo in C.</small>

***Westlake,** Frederick, b. Feb. 25, 1840, Romsey, Hampshire. 1855, he entered the R.A.M. (London), and was taught by the brothers Macfarren, but profited also by the advice of Sterndale Bennett, Charles Lucas, and Dorrell. 1863, appointed Prof. there, and is still one of their most experienced, careful, and successful teachers. Member of the Associated Board for Local and School Examinations.

<small>Duo concertante for Pf. and V'cello; 9 Episodes; a Fugue in Octaves. He is also editor of the valuable collection, "Lyra studentium."</small>

Weyse, Christoph Ernst Friedrich, b. March 5, 1774, Copenhagen; d. there Oct. 4, 1842. His first teacher was his grandfather, J. A. P. Schulz (1747-1800). Under his superintendence he published his first work, Allegri di bravura per il Clavicembalo del Signor Weyse publicate per i maestri di Capella Schulze e Reichardt (1796). He was an excellent teacher, who was proud of being able to call the distinguished Danish composer, Gade, his pupil.

<small>4 Sonatas; Studies (much respected by Schumann); several Allegri di bravura, Op. 50; and some included in the Répertoire des Clavecinistes.</small>

Widor, Charles Marie, b. Feb. 24, 1845, Lyons. The son of an Alsatian, whose family came originally from Hungary. Pupil of Fétis (Brussels) and Rossini (Paris). His organ performances were so much admired in Lyons and other French towns that he was appointed (1869) Organist of St. Sulpice in Paris.

<small>Concerto in F min. (1876); Trio, Op. 19; Quintet, Op. 7; Serenade for Pf., Fl., Vln., V'cello, and Harmonium, Op. 10; Suite Polonaise, Op. 51; Dans les Bois (5), Op. 44; Valse en Ré bémol, Op. 11, I.; Chant d'Avril, Aubade; †Marche Américaine, Op. 31, XI.; 6 Morceaux de Salon, Op. 15; l'Orientale, Scherzo, Op. 8.</small>

Wieck, Clara (*see* Schumann).

Wieck, Friedrich, b. Aug. 18, 1785, Pretzvch, near Torgau; d. Oct. 7, 1873, Loschwitz, near Dresden. After having completed his studies in the College of Torgau, he attended the University of Wittenberg, in order to study Theology, but his desire to become a musician was so great that he preferred to accept situations as private tutor in the families of Baron Seckendorf (Querfurt) and Madame von Levezow, so as to have sufficient time to study music. He established a Pf. manufactory and circulating library of music in Leipzig, and was also a teacher. He was twice married —Clara, Alwin, and Gustav were his first wife's children, and Marie, his second wife's child. Foremost among his pupils were his daughter Clara, Robert Schumann, H. von Bülow, Anton Krause, Fritz Spindler, J. Seiss, Rollfuss, and G. Merkel (*see* these names). He published several Essays on musical education, and 2 books of Studies.

*Wieck, Marie, b. Jan. 17, 1835, Leipzig. Pupil of her father (*see* above). Showed at an early age signs of considerable talent, and played as early as 1843 at concerts (Dresden). 1858, the Prince of Hohenzollern named her "Pianist to the Court." She gave many concerts in the principal towns of Germany, Sweden, &c., and appeared also with great success in London. At present she conducts at Dresden a school for Pf. playing, after the principles of her late father.

Wiedeburg, Michael Johann Friedrich, b. 1735, Halle, a/d/Saale; d. about 1790. Organist at Norden (East Frisia). He wrote one of the earliest Methods of Clavecin playing under the quaint title of

"The self-instructing Clavecinist, or clear and easy instruction in Clavecin playing" (first part, 1765; second part, 1767; third part, 1775). Also additional contributions to the self-instructing Clavecinist, or twice 24 easy and 24 more difficult Preludes, 1776. He also published Musical Card-playing for Clavecinists (first game, 1788).

Wiel-Lange, Frederick Johannes, b. Jan. 20, 1849, Viskinge (Seeland). 1874, Licentiate of Theology of the University of Copenhagen, and entered the Conserv. the same year as pupil of Gade and Hartmann, who took such warm interest in his rare talent that they soon promoted him to a Professorship. 1877, he married the pianist, Minna Fries (b. Aarhus), whose delicate health obliged him to reside in the country. At present he is clergyman at Broost, a small town near d'Oester-Svenstrup (Jutland). His Pf. works are, so to speak, musical illustrations of Andersen's fairy tales:—

Skovblomster (3 pieces), Ved Löwfald (4), I Skumringen (6). Besides these he published: "Récits d'aventures," five short pieces, Stimmungsbilder (2).

Wieniawski, Joseph, b. May 23, 1837, Lublin. 1847, entered the Paris Conserv. under Zimmermann, Marmontel, and Alkan (Pf.), and Le Couppey (Harmony); 1850, he returned to Russia, and gave concerts with his brother, Henri W. (the famous violinist); 1855-58, in Germany, studied with Liszt in Weimar; and, 1856, with Marx, in Berlin. After this he returned to Paris; left, 1867, for Moscow, where he was appointed Prof. at the Conserv.; went later to Warsaw as Director of the Musical Society, resided there for some years, and then settled in Brussels. He is a most excellent performer, able to satisfy all the high demands of the present time. He possesses a marvellous technique, noble and refined expression, and musicianly feeling. He received decorations from Russia, Persia, Holland, &c. 1875-78, was member of the Jury for the public examinations of the Paris Conserv., and Hon. Member of the Lemberg Society. He invented the Piano à double clavier renversé (exhibited at the Paris Exhibition of 1878).

Concerto, Op. 20; Trio, Op. 40; Sonata, Op. 22; Sonata with Vln., Op. 24; Sonata with V'cello, Op. 26; Fantasia for 2 Pf., Op. 42. Studies: Romance Etude, Op. 10; Etudes de Concert, Op. 33 and 36; †24 Etudes, Op. 44; Polonaises, Op. 13, 21, 27, 48. Valses: †Op. 3, 7, 18, 30, 46; †Mazurkas, Op. 23; Fantaisie et Fugue, Op. 25, and a good many shorter pieces.

Willmers, Rudolph, b. Oct. 31, 1821, Berlin; d. (insane) Aug. 24, 1878, Vienna. Pupil of Hummel (Weimar) and Fr. Schneider (Dessau). For some time he taught at the Stern Academy (Berlin), but afterwards resided in Vienna, where the Emperor named him Imperial and Royal pianist, and where he was highly respected. His specialty was a most perfect shake; indeed, the great beauty of a shake— its swelling and diminishing—and the wonderful evenness in the performance of the so-called "Trillerketten" had never been exhibited before with such supreme mastery as by him. But his technique was equally remarkable in all other points. His compositions, although well-constructed, are somewhat dry and uninteresting; the wonderful way in which they were performed, however, made these blemishes appear less.

†Sehnsucht am Meere, Op. 8; Un jour d'été en Norvège, Op. 27; 2 Études de Concert (†No. 1, La Pompa di Festa), Op. 28; 6 Études, Op. 1; Sérénade érotique (left hand), Op. 5; La Sylphide, Op. 49; Northern National Songs, Op. 29 (†No. 1); †Trillerkeiten, Op. 69; Tarantella giocosa, Op. 35.

*Wilm, Nikolai von, b. March 4, 1834, Riga (Livland). His first studies were superintended by his father, an accomplished amateur, later by Weller, Marx, Markus, and Willmans (Riga). 1851-56, pupil at the Leipzig Conserv., under Hauptmann, Richter, Rietz, Plaidy, &c. After leaving Leipzig he travelled, but accepted (1857-58) the post of second Conductor of the Riga Opera; 1858, went to St. Petersburg, where, on the recommendation of Henselt, he received the post of teacher at the Imperial Institute, "Nicolai"; 1875, he went to Dresden, but has lived since 1878 at Wiesbaden. His compositions enjoy a great reputation and begin to be very popular.

For Pf. and Vln.: Sonatas, Op. 83 and 92; Suite, Op. 88 and 95. *For Pf. and V'cello*: Sonata, Op. 111. *For 2 Pf.*: Prelude and Sarabande, Op. 62; Theme and Variations, Op. 64; Waltzes, Op. 72. *For 4 hands*: †Reisebilder aus Schlesien, Op. 18; Suites, †25, †30, †44, †53, and 100; Suite of Waltzes, Op. 86, 90, 93; Calendarium (4 books), Op. 39. *Solo Pieces*: 10 Characteristic pieces, Op. 24; People and times in the mirror of their dances, †Op. 31 (5 books); Fantasia, Op. 68; Theme and Variations, Op. 89; Valse brillante, Op. 13 (No. 2); Valse Impromptu, Op. 45; In the Russian village, Op. 37 (No. 2); and several collections of pieces.

Wilms, Jan Willem, b. March 30, 1772, Witzhelden (Province Berg); d. July 19, 1847, Amsterdam. Pupil of his father, an organist. Influential teacher at Amsterdam, where he was elected Member of the Academy of Holland and Hon. Member of the society "Toonkunst." His playing was much admired and he was universally respected for his admirable qualities.

Concertos, Quartets, Trios, Sonatas with Vln., Sonatas for 4 hands, Grand Sonata (1793), †Sonatinas (Op. 16), "The Battle of Waterloo."

*Winding, August (Henrik), b. March 24, 1835, Taaro, Isle of Laaland (Denmark). Pupil of his father, Reinecke, and Rée (Copenhagen); also of A. Dreyschock (Prague) and Niels W. Gade (Copenhagen). Director and Prof. of the Copenhagen Conserv. and Knight of the Order of Danebrog. He is a highly talented and original composer, whose works deserve close acquaintance in order to be fully appreciated.

Concerto, Op. 16; Concert Allegro, Op. 29; Quartet, Op. 17; †10 Clavierstücke in form of Studies, Op. 18; Preludes in all keys, Op. 26; Sonatas for Pf. and Vln., Op. 5 and 35; Studies, Op. 25; Duets (for 4 hands), Op. 32, I. and II., †Contrasts (2 Books); Phantasiestücke for Pf., Vln., or Cl., Op. 19; Reisebilder, Op. 3; Genrebilder, Op. 15; Ländliche-Scenen (10); Valses (3); Humoreske; Toccata, Op. 34, &c.

*Wingham, Thomas, b. Jan. 5, 1846, London; d. there March 24, 1893. Pupil of Sterndale Bennett (R.A.M.). He was a highly-successful teacher, and warmly appreciated by his colleagues for his simplicity, amiability, and thoroughness.

Barcarolle (F min.), Concert-Capriccio, Elegy on the death of Sterndale Bennett, and several other smaller pieces.

*Winkler, Louis, b. Sept. 1, 1813, Brunswick; d. there Sept. 16, 1885. He was organist of one of the principal churches, a successful teacher, and his name is favourably known by his excellent arrangements of classical works (notably those of Beethoven) for Pf. (2 hands).

Winterberger, Alexander, b. Aug. 14, 1834, Weimar. 1848-49, pupil at the Leipzig Conserv.; later of Liszt. 1861, he went to Vienna; 1869, he succeeded A. Dreyschock as Prof. at the St. Petersburg Conserv. Since 1872 has resided at Leipzig. He is considered one of the best pianists of the present time.

Alinen-Dances (Valses, Mazurkas, Menuets, &c.), Op. 20; 3 pieces, Op. 25; Concert-Study and Valse Caprice, Op. 27; Concert-Adagio, Op. 63; 23 instructive and characteristic pieces, Op. 72; 2 Sonatinas, Op. 93.

Wittasek, Johann Nepomuk August, b. Feb. 22, 1770, Horzin (Bohemia); d. Dec. 7, 1839, Prague. At first a pupil of his father (a schoolmaster); afterwards Princess Lobkowitz made him a pupil of Franz Duschek (Clavecin) and Kozeluch (Composition), Prague. 1814, appointed Organist of the "Domkirche"; 1826, Director of the Organ School. His performances of classical Concertos (notably Mozart's) were greatly admired, and Mozart himself expressed his gratification at hearing his playing. As a composer he was less known.

Concerto, Sonatas with Vln., Favourite pieces (3 books), †Rondeaux, Romanza — all of them now completely forgotten, but in their time popular in Prague society.

*Witte, Georg Henri, b. Nov 16, 1843, Utrecht. Son of a well-known organ builder. 1859-62, pupil at the Royal Music School at The Hague, where

Van der Does (Pf.), Lübeck (Vln.), and Nicolai (Organ and Theory) were his teachers; 1862-65, pupil at the Leipzig Conserv., under Plaidy and Moscheles (Pf.), Hauptmann (Counterpoint), and Reinecke (Composition). 1865-67, taught in Leipzig; 1867-70, teacher in Alsace; 1871, appointed Director of the Musical Society of Essen (Westphalia). Received (1882) the title of Königl. Musik-Director.

Quartet with Strings, Op. 5; Sonata with V'cello, Op. 15, and 3 pieces with V'cello, Op. 14 (these obtained a prize); Waltzes, Op. 1, 3, 7 (à 4 mains); 4 Impromptus, Op. 4; Sonatina à 4 mains, Op. 8; 2 characteristic pieces, Op. 13.

Wölfl (Wölffl, Woelfl), Joseph (at one time an admired composer and rival (?) of Beethoven), b. 1772, Salzburg; d. May 11, 1812, London. Pupil of Leopold Mozart and Michael Haydn (Salzburg). Created a great sensation with his improvisations, which by some connoisseurs (?) were preferred to those of Mozart and Beethoven. 1792-94, he resided at Warsaw; 1794-98, at Vienna; 1801, went to Paris. A few years later he travelled with Elmenreich, an actor of very doubtful character, who tempted him to become his associate in dishonest card-playing, which, being detected, they were obliged to leave Brussels in great haste, and seek refuge in London; there he found himself ignored, where before he had received a splendid reception. Although he appeared again in public he had lost his former popularity. The events of his last years are shrouded in mystery. It is said that he died in a state of great poverty in a suburb of London.

6 Concertos, Op. 20, 26, 32, †Op. 43; Concerto militaire, Op. 49 (Coucou); Le Calme and a Concerto da camera; 18 Trios; 30 Duos with Vln. Sonatas Op. 1 (3); Op. 6 (3, dedicated to Beethoven); Op. 15 (3, dedicated to Prince Louis Ferdinand); †Op. 41, Non plus ultra; †Op. 50, Le diable à quatre; Sonatas (2) in C min.; 14 books of Variations; Rondeaux; Fantasias; Sonatas for 4 hands; Sonata for 2 Pf.; Méthode de Piano (with 100 Studies), Op. 56; 24 Préludes.

Wohlfahrt, Heinrich, a highly respected educational composer and practical teacher, b. Dec. 16, 1797, Kössnitz, near Apolda; d May 9, 1883, Connewitz, near Leipzig. He attended the Seminary at Weimar, where Häser was his teacher; had several appointments as private teacher and Cantor in small towns of Thuringia, until he retired to Jena. 1867, settled at Leipzig.

Method for children (about 30 editions); the First Tuition, Op. 50; Der Klavier-freund (36 Studies for children); Kleine Leute, Op. 86; 3 Sonatas for children; instructive pieces, Op. 74; Anthologic method of Pf. playing, Op. 47, &c.

Wolf, Ernst Wilhelm, b. 1735, Grossbehringen, near Gotha; d. Dec. 7, 1792, Weimar. 1755, he attended the University of Jena, but then decided to devote himself to music. 1761, appointed teacher to the Duchess of Weimar; 1786, Hof-Capellmeister. He published essays, descriptions of artistic journeys, &c.

7 Concertos; 4 Quintets for Pf., Fl., Vln., Vla., and V'cello; 7 books of 6 Sonatas each, and other Sonatas (4 with *affection*).

Wolff, Edouard, b. Sept. 15, 1816, Warsaw; d. Oct. 16, 1880, Paris. Pupil of Zawadski (Pf.) at Warsaw, and (1828) of Würfel at Vienna. After his return to Warsaw, he had lessons in Harmony from Elsner (Chopin's teacher); 1835, went to Paris, where he remained until his death, with the exception of some journeys to Germany, the provincial towns of France, and the Danubian principalities. He was an admirable performer, a well educated musician, and a favourite teacher. His compositions are influenced by the genius of his friend and countryman, Chopin.

24 Etudes, Op. 20; †24 nouvelles Etudes, Op. 50; l'Art de l'expression; 24 Etudes faciles, Op. 90; l'Art de l'exécution; 24 Improvisations en forme d'études, Op. 100; l'Art de chanter sur le Pf., 48 Etudes, Op. 189; La Favorite, Valse, Op. 63; Chansons polonaises originales, Op. 139; Tarantelle, Op. 148; †Chansons bacchiques, Op. 164 and 186.

Wollenhaupt, Heinrich Adolph, b. Sept. 27, 1827, Schkeuditz (district Merseburg); d. Sept. 18, 1863, New York. Pupil at the Leipzig Conserv. 1845, he went to New York, where he was admired for his excellent playing and pleasant, popular compositions; and warmly beloved for his admirable qualities as son, brother, and friend. It is but seldom that the loss of a young and talented artist is so sincerely deplored as was the case with him. In his compositions there is much natural, spontaneous feeling, and a great deal of rhythmical charm.

Marches militaires, †Op. 19 and 31; Valses styriennes, †Op. 27 and 47; Nocturne, Op. 32; Galop di Bravura, Op. 24; Improvisation, Op. 30; †Scherzo brillante, Op. 72; and Valse héroïque in E flat.

Worzischek (Johann), Hugo, b. May 11, 1791, Wamberg (Bohemia); d. Nov. 19, 1825, Vienna. He was—after receiving elementary tuition from his father, a schoolmaster—a pupil of W. Tomaschek (Prague). He went to

Vienna to obtain a State appointment, but his love of music was so great he finally devoted himself entirely to it, and was fortunate enough to receive the post of Organist at the Imperial Chapel. He was a richly-gifted composer, and a general favourite in the musical circles of Vienna.

12 Rhapsodies, Op. 1; Variations: la Sentinelle, Op. 6; 3 Impromptus, Op. 7; Fantaisie, Op. 12; †Rondeau Espagnol, Op. 17; Grande Sonate, Op. 20; and several other smaller works.

Wouters (François), Adolphe, b. May 28, 1841, Brussels, where he was a pupil at the Conserv. Since 1871, Prof. there, and conducts the class for ladies. His edition of classical works, "Répertoire du Conservatoire de Bruxelles," is considered a standard work, and his technical Studies are much used in Belgium.

*****Woycke**, Eugen (Adelbert), b. June 19, 1843, Dantzig. 1864-67, pupil at the Leipzig Conserv. under Plaidy and Moscheles (Pf.), Hauptmann (Composition); also Reinecke (Pf.) and E. F. Richter (Harmony, Counterpoint, and Fugue). After leaving Leipzig he settled in Edinburgh, where he is a teacher.

Sonatas: "Dramatique," "Romantique," "Poétique," "Capricieuse," "Héroïque," "Fantastique," and "Sentimentale"—the last two are with Vln.; 8 Novellettes, Op. 41; 6 characteristic pieces, Op. 42; "Au Rouet," Op. 23; "L'Oisillon," Op. 35; and Andante (D flat), Op. 19.

Wraniczky (Wranitzky), Paul, b. Dec. 30, 1756, Neureisch (Moravia); d. Sept. 28, 1808, Vienna. Received his musical education, first in a monastery near his native place, later at Iglau and Olmütz. 1776, he went to Vienna and entered the Seminary so as to study Theology, but his qualities as a violinist were so remarkable he was elected Musik-Director. He continued his studies of composition in Vienna with the Swedish composer, Joseph Kraus. With every year his productivity became greater, and his music being that of a regular "Viennese" composer—cheerful, light, for a short time fascinating—he soon became the favourite musician of the Austrian capital. Amongst other operatic works he wrote the music to the Ballet "Das Waldmädchen," the Russian dance of which Beethoven took as theme for his charming Variations in A.

Sonatas, some of them with Vln.; 3 Trios, Op. 21; and †La Chasse, with accompaniment of wind instruments.

*****Wrigley**, John, b. Sept. 29, 1830, Ashton-under-Lyne. 1849, entered the R.A.M. (London), where he received (1852) excellent testimonials from the principal Professors; 1853, named A.R.A.M., and, 1887, F.R.A.M. His useful work as a teacher is acknowledged by all who profited by it. He resides at Manchester.

2 Sonatas, Allegro de Concert, Tarantella, Presto scherzando, Waltz, and the "Sprites' Frolic."

Wüllner, Dr. Franz, b. Jan. 28, 1832, Münster (Westphalia). Pupil of A. Schindler (Beethoven's friend) and Ferdinand Kessler (1793-1856), of Frankfort o/M (must not be confused with Joseph Chr. K., of Lemberg); later of Grell and Dehn (Berlin). 1854, appointed Prof. at the Royal Munich School; 1858-65, Conductor of the Musical Societies of Aix-la-Chapelle. After 1865, he returned to Munich as Principal of the vocal classes of the Music School; 1870, Director and Prof. of the Royal Academy (formerly School) of Munich and Conductor of the Opera; 1877, appointed Director of the Conserv. (Dresden), Hof-Capellmeister; and Conductor of the Catholic Church choir and orchestra; 1884, Principal of the Conserv. of Cologne; Conductor of the Gürzenich concerts and the Town Orchestra, Member of the Royal Academy of Arts (Berlin); Doc. Phil., *hon. causâ*, of the University of Munich; Knight of several Orders, &c.

Solo Sonatas: Op 6 (D min.) and Op. 10 (E); Trio (D), Op. 9; Sonata with Vln. (E min.), Op. 30; Variations on themes of Bach, Op. 23; Schubert, Op. 39 (with V'cello); on an original air, Op. 19; and several Duets for 4 hands, Op. 11 and Op. 27.

Würfel, Wilhelm, b. 1791, Planian (Bohemia); d. April 22, 1852, Vienna. At first instructed by his mother, he had later to depend entirely on his own exertions. Chopin, when in Vienna, met Würfel, and spoke with gratitude of the assistance he gave in arranging his concert. 1815, appointed teacher at Warsaw; returned to Vienna, and received (1826) the post of Sub-Conductor of the Opera. He was an admirable pianist and a highly successful teacher.

Concerto, Op. 28; Allegro and Rondo caractéristique; Fantaisie, Op. 45; Rondeaux; Variations, &c.; "Wellington's Victory"; Op. 13, for 4 hands.

*****Wurm**, Marie, b. May 18, 1860, Southampton. Pupil at the Stuttgart

Music School, under Dr. Stark (Harmony) and D. Pruckner (Pf.). 1878-80, pupil of Madame Mehlig, Mary Krebs, I. Wieniawski, F. Taylor, and Madame Montigny-Rémaury; 1880, of Madame Schumann and Dr. Joachim Raff (Frankfort o/M). 1884, she gained the Mendelssohn Scholarship, and became a pupil of Sir Arthur Sullivan, Dr. V. Stanford, and Dr. F. Bridge; 1886, of Dr. Reinecke (Leipzig).

Tanzweisen, 4 hands; Valse de concert; Barcarolle; Gavotte and Pastorale (by Reinecke), arranged for 2 Pf.; Concerto; Sonata; Sonata for Pf. and Vln.; Sonata for Pf. and V'cello; Prelude and Fugue for 2 Pf. Ballades for 2 Pf. are still in MS.

Wylde, Henry, Mus. Doc., b. 1822, Hertfordshire; d. March 13, 1890, London. Pupil of Cipriani Potter. 1852, Director of the New Philharmonic Society; 1863, Prof. at Gresham College; established (1867) the London Academy of Music. Among his numerous pupils was John Francis Barnett.

Concertos, Sonatas, Rhapsodies, Fantasias, &c.

Z.

*Zabalza, Don Dámaso, b. Dec. 11, 1833, Irurita (Province Navarra); d. Feb. 25, 1894, Madrid. Pupil of Don Casimiro Sagabeta, later of D. Luis Vidaola and of D. Mariano Garcia (Harmony). Settled (1858) at Madrid, where he made himself known by giving successful concerts; soon after appointed assistant teacher at the Conserv. He received the Cross of Charles III. and various Academical honours.

Sonatinas, Studies (adopted by the schools of Paris, Madrid, Barcelona, and Milan).

Zarembski (Zaremski), Jules de, b. Feb. 28, 1854, Zitomir (Russian Poland); d. there Aug., 1885. Pupil of Dachs (Vienna), later of Liszt (Weimar), who warmly recommended his studies and procured for him the appointment of Prof. at the Conserv. of Brussels, which he held for five years. Returning for a holiday to his native place, he suddenly died, only thirty-one years old. His compositions are original, quaint, and full of national colour.

Op. 23, A travers Pologne (6); Op. 27, Etrennes (6); Op. 26, Sérénade espagnole; †Op. 7, Trois Études de Concert; Op. 18, Ballade; Op. 20, Sérénade burlesque; Op. 22, Berceuse in A.

*Zarzycki, Alexander, b. Feb. 21, 1834, Lemberg (Austrian Poland). Received his first musical education in Lemberg; 1856-61, he resided at Paris, taking lessons in Theory from Henri Reber; played with eminent success in concerts, visited (giving concerts) Germany, Austria, and Poland. 1870, he undertook the direction of the Musical Society of Warsaw; 1879, appointed Director of the Conserv. His merits as a brilliant pianist were everywhere warmly admired, and his effective compositions deserve recognition.

Op. 7, Grande Polonaise (with Orchestra); Op. 17, Concerto (with Orchestra); Op. 37, Suite Polonaise (with Orchestra); Op. 34, 3 Morceaux; Op. 18, Grande Valse; Op. 19 and †Op. 20, Mazurkas; Op. 24, Serenade and Valse Impromptu; †Op. 10, 2 Nocturnes.

*Zichy, Giza, Count, b. July 22, 1849, Sztára (Hungary). From his childhood devoted to music and studied the Pf. with rare industry, but had the misfortune to lose his right arm in 1866 (when seventeen years old); in spite of this calamity he threw his whole energy into the study of playing with the left hand only, and reached so wonderful a degree of facility and technical perfection that his performances were received with bewildered astonishment and phrenetic acclamations. All critics unite in describing his playing as unrivalled and wholly unique. His teachers were Mayrberger, Volkmann, and Liszt (Pesth). He was Director (Intendant) of the Royal and National Opera of Pesth.

Collection of Studies and Pieces for the left hand (Paris).

Zimmermann, Agnes, b. July 5, 1847, Cologne o/Rhine. Went at an early age to London, where she was a pupil at the R.A.M. of Cipriani Potter, and later of Pauer (Pf.), of Dr. Steggall and George Macfarren (Composition). She twice obtained (1860 and 1862) the King's Scholarship, received the silver medal two years in succession and did full honour to the R.A.M. Her merits as a pianist were often recognised and praised by the audiences at the Crystal Palace and the Popular concerts, as well as in Germany and the English Provinces. At her own concerts she provided excellent programmes, and showed every year continued progress. Trio, Op. 19; 3 Sonatas for Pf. and Vln., Op. 16, 21, and 23, Suite, Op. 22; 2 pieces, Op. 18; and a number of shorter pieces. Editor of Beethoven and Mozart's Sonatas and of pieces by Schumann.

Zimmermann, Pierre Joseph Guillaume, b. March 19, 1785, Paris; d. there Nov., 1853. 1798, entered the Conserv. as pupil of Boieldieu, Rey, Catel, and Cherubini. 1816, appointed Prof. and continued working until 1848, when he received the Legion of Honour and his pension. Amongst his most celebrated pupils were Alkan, Prudent, Marmontel, Ravina, Lacombe, and A. Thomas.
Encyclopédie du Pianiste; 24 Etudes, Op. 21; 2 Concertos (with Orchestra); Sonata, Op. 5; a great number of Variations, and several Rondeaux.

*Zwintscher, Bruno, b. May 15, 1838, Ziegenhain, near Meissen (Saxony), son of a clergyman. For two years pupil of Julius Otto (Dresden); 1856-59, at the Leipzig Conserv., where Plaidy and Moscheles (Pf.), E. F. Richter, Hauptmann, and Rietz (Harmony and Composition) were his teachers. 1875, appointed Prof. there.
"Technical School," "School of Ornaments," with a supplement about the "Metronome and its use."

PIANO MAKERS.

B.

Babcock, Alpheus, established (1829) in Philadelphia, the inventor (1825, in Boston) of the complete metal frame, with hitchpin plate, in one casting (Babcock's iron ring); it was applied to square pianos. In 1830, he took out another patent for "cross-stringing." The business was afterwards carried on in Boston, Mass.

*Bacon, Francis, late Raven and Bacon, of New York. The history of this house is as follows: 1789, Jan. 10, I. Jacob Astor, of 81, Queen Street, had for sale imported pianos from the best makers in London; 1802, Astor retired, and was succeeded by John and William Raff, 127, Broadway, N.Y.; 1815, they were succeeded by William Dubois, 126, Broadway; 1836, the firm became Dubois and Bacon, and (1841) Bacon and Raven; 1856, by the death of the senior Bacon, the firm became Raven and Bacon; 1871, Bacon and Karr; they were succeeded (1880) by Francis Bacon. "Bacon" pianos were manufactured as early as 1789. 1876, the highest awards were granted at Philadelphia; 1856, by the Franklin Institute of the State of Pennsylvania, by the Metropolitan Mechanics' Institute (N.Y.), and (1893) by the Columbian Exposition, Chicago. The firm produces squares, uprights, and grands.

*Baldwin, D. H., and Co., of Cincinatti, Ohio, U.S. Founded (1863) as retail and wholesale dealers. The factory (of uprights) was started 1891. The firm is composed of D. H. Baldwin, Lucien Walsin, A. A. van Buren, George W. Armstrong, jun., and Clarence Wulsin. "The factory of The Baldwin Piano Co. is planned on the best modern models, and there are added to these many new ideas that individualize the plant and give it a certain distinctive character."

*Bechstein, Carl, of Berlin, founder of the celebrated firm, manufacturer to the German Emperor, the Empress Frederick, Queen of England, Duke of Saxe-Coburg and Gotha, &c., was born June 1, 1826, at Gotha. He worked in several factories; 1848-52, was manager of Perau's piano business (Berlin); studied also in London, in Paris (Pape and Kriegelstein), and began with very modest means, in 1856, his present great and highly influential business. Almost all continental pianists use the Bechstein instruments for their public performances, and the beauty of their tone, elasticity of touch, and excellent mechanism have obtained for them universal favour. The instruments are made in Berlin in three distinct factories, in which above 500 workmen are employed, producing about 3,500 instruments per year, the greater number being grand pianos. The factory furnishes five styles of grands and four styles of uprights. Bechstein is assisted by his three sons, who take active parts in different departments. The King of Prussia decorated him, and named him Counsellor of Commerce; other European Sovereigns also decorated him, and the Guild of German musical instrument makers elected him chairman.

*Becker, Jacob, of St. Petersburg, founder of the firm, was born in Neustadt a/d/Haardt; d. 1884, St. Petersburg. Received diplomas as "Fournisseur de S.M. l'Empereur" (Russia), and of the Emperor of Austria, King of Denmark, the Grand Dukes Vladimir, Constantin, and Nicolai, of Russia. After his retirement from the business (1871), Michael Bietepage became the proprietor; he is hereditary hon. citizen of St. Petersburg, Commander of the St. Stanislas Order, &c. The firm's specialty is grand pianos.

Behning and Son, of New York. (1864, Behning and Klix; 1873, Behning and Diehl; 1880, Behning and Son.) Henry Behning (b. in Hanover) served his apprenticeship in the factories of

Gercke and Helmholtz (must not be confused with the eminent scientist of the same name); arrived (1856) in New York, entered the factory of Lighte, Newton and Bradbury, and remained there until 1857. 1864, he started business with Klix, continued (1873) with Diehl, and, after the latter's retirement, with his own son Henry (b. Nov. 26, 1859, Bridgeport, Conn.). Another son, Albert (b. 1866), is in charge of the book-keeping, and the youngest son, Gustav (b. 1868), superintends the factory. The firm's chief patents are a "compensating agraffe" (1874), "sounding-board extension for uprights" (1882), and "concave name-board" (1875). A new bijou instrument, the "General Tom Thumb" piano, has been added to their various kinds of instruments.

Behr Brothers, of New York (Henry, b. 1848, and Edward, both b. in Hamburg). They founded their business in 1881. 1889, they took out patents for their "hammer compensating lever" in grand piano actions and for their "new stringing device." The firm was joined by Siegfried Hansing, from Bückeburg, Germany (b. June 12, 1842), who arrived (1884) in America. At present the business is a close corporation: Henry and Edward Behr, Emil Hartzig, Charles L. Burchard, and Siegfried Hansing.

Bent, R. M., and Co., of New York. The firm was founded (1868) by Richard M. Bent (b. 1834, New York, of English parents) and James F. Beames (d. Dec., 1889). Patents were taken out by R. M. Bent for "detachable arms and key bottom," for "bushed tuning-pins in full iron-frame," and for "practice pedal or muffler."

*Biese, Wilhelm, of Berlin, manufacturer to the Prussian Court, b. April 20, 1823, Rathenow, near Potsdam. He served his apprenticeship with Schulz, and Günther (of Magdeburg), Eck (of Cologne), Kisting and Stöcker (of Berlin). He founded the firm in Berlin (1851). Has now 120 workmen, and turns out about 800 instruments (uprights) per year. In 1893 the 15,000th instrument left the workshop. Gold medals: Stettin, 1865; Cassel, 1870; Moscow, 1872; Berlin, 1879; Melbourne, 1880; Nürnberg, 1882, &c. The firm is well known and greatly respected.

*Billberg, C. H., of Göteborg (Gothenburg), Sweden. The business was founded 1868. After his death, William Nilsson become proprietor (1886). The factory makes pianinos and grands (see J. G. Malmsjö), and received fifteen medals and diplomas. Gold medal, 1872, at Moscow; silver medal, 1891, Gothenburg.

*Blüthner, Julius Ferdinand, b. March 11, 1824, Falkenhain, near Merseburg. Piano manufactory at Leipzig. He founded the firm (Nov. 7, 1853) with three workmen. 1856, he introduced a new mechanism and the "symmetrical" pianos, and (about 1873) the far-famed "Aliquot" system. The business flourished so much that in 1880 (scarcely seventeen years after its foundation) the 15,000th, and, in 1882, the 20,000th instrument was sold. 1,800 pianinos and 1,200 grands are made per year. The factory is worked by two steam-engines and covers an area of 24,250 square metres; branch establishments in London, Berlin, Hamburg, and other towns. The following are the medals and diplomas received: Gold medals and first prizes—Merseburg, 1865; Paris (first prize), 1867; Chemnitz, 1867; Cassel (1867, centennial medal); Philadelphia, 1876; Puebla, 1880; Sydney, 1879 (2); Melbourne, 1881 (2) and 1889. Diplomas of honour—Vienna, 1873; Brunswick (as Juror), 1877; Amsterdam, 1883; Teplitz (as Juror), 1884. Personal decorations: Knight of the Order of Saxe-Coburg-Ernestine House, the Danebrog, Albrecht of Saxony, Griffin of Mecklenburg-Schwerin; gold medal with the crown, Saxe-Altenburg; gold medal of the Royal Italian "Bellini" Club of Catania; patent of manufacturer to the Kings of Saxony and Greece; Counsellor of Commerce, &c. The excellence of his instruments is everywhere acknowledged and appreciated.

Boardman and Gray, of Albany, U.S. The firm was founded (1835) by William Boardman (b. 1800, Albany; d. 1881), James Gray (b. 1815, New York), and Hazelton (see this name), the latter working in the business. 1850, Gray went with several instruments to England, and introduced his patented "Dolce Campana," insulated iron-rim and frame, and the corrugated sounding-board. 1877, his son, William, was admitted as partner.

*Bösendorfer, Ludwig, of Vienna, b. April 10, 1835. The firm was founded (1828) by his father, Ignaz Bösendorfer (b. 1795, d. 1859, Vienna), a pupil of

Brodmann, who soon succeeded in making his name known and respected. After his death his son, Ludwig, introduced great improvements, and adapted the construction of his pianos more to American and English principles, while adhering to the so-called Vienna mechanism. His concert grands, however, are made with the English action. He introduced the "Piano Imperial" (compass, 8 octaves). The firm received the highest medals and several diplomas, but exhibits now as *hors concours*. Received the patent as Kaiserl Königl.-Hof und Kammer Pianoforte Fabrik. Ludwig was decorated with the Golden Cross of Merit with the Crown, and received the title of Imperial Counsellor of Commerce. 1872, he opened a concert-room, in which nearly all the chamber concerts are given. The beauty of his pianos, their elastic touch, excellent treble, sonorous bass, and singing quality of the middle registers is recognised by all the pianists who perform in the Austrian capital and provincial towns. He is well known as a generous and liberal patron of young and striving artists.

*Boisselot, fils et Cie, of Marseilles. This eminent firm was founded (1828) by Jean Louis Boisselot (b. 1788) and his son, Louis (b. 1810, d. 1850), as Boisselot et fils. It was continued by the son Xavier. Since 1865, it has been Boisselot, fils et Cie., and is under the direction of Jean Louis's grandson, Marie Louis Franz (b. 1845). 1844, the firm received the patent as "Fournisseur du Roi"; 1838, as "Fournisseur de l'Institut"; 1855, the Cross of the Légion d'honneur. Gold medals, 1844 and 1849, Paris; silver medals, 1834 and 1839; medal of the first class, 1859, Paris; prize medal, 1862, London; diplomas and medals at the "Expositions régionales." The firm patented pianos with "pedal tonale," "Clediharmonique à queue," &c. The factory is worked by steam, and the instruments are greatly esteemed.

*Bord, A., et Cie., of Paris. This well-known factory was founded (1840) by Jean Denis Antoine Bord (b. 1814, d. March 4, 1888, Paris). The firm employs 300 workmen (up to 1893 had made 84,000 instruments, mostly pianinos), uses steam power in the chief factory at St. Ouen (Seine), and makes ten instruments per day. Bord was Knight of the Legion of Honour, member of the Jury at Paris (1878), Rouen, and Bordeaux. Gold medal, Lyons, 1872; Melbourne, 1880; Bordeaux, 1882; Amsterdam, 1883; Rouen, 1884; Paris, 1889; prize medal, London, 1862.

Bosert and Schomar., of Philadelphia. (*See* Schomaker and Co.)

*Bretschneider, Alexander, of Leipzig. Founded 1833, by Ludwig Alexander Bretschneider (b. 1806, Gera; d. 1870, Leipzig). He was succeeded by his son, Robert. The firm makes grands and uprights, and enjoys a good reputation for solidity of construction, evenness of tone, and elasticity of touch.

Briggs and Co., of Boston, Mass. C. C. Briggs entered (1854) the business of Emerson, soon became foreman, contributed materially to the improvement of the Emerson pianos (*see* Emerson), and, entering (1861) into partnership with George M. Guild (*see* this name), founded the firm Guild and Co. After some years he entered into business with his son, C. C. Briggs, jun. Briggs and Co. were among the first to develop the resources of the upright in America for general use.

*Brinsmead, John, and Sons, of London. Founded (1837) by John Brinsmead, in Charlotte Street, Fitzroy Square; moved from there to Tottenham Court Road, and eventually to Kentish Town; the warehouse is in Wigmore Street, Cavendish Square. The firm turns out about 2,000 instruments per year, and patented a perfect check repeater. Has exhibited in European and Colonial towns, and received many medals and diplomas. The principal of the firm was decorated with the Legion of Honour (1878) and a Portuguese Order (1883). His son, Edgar, is the author of a "History of the Piano." Medals: London, 1862, 1884, 1885; Paris, 1867, 1870, 1874, 1878; Jamaica, 1891; Edinburgh, 1890; Barcelona, 1888; Calcutta, 1884; New Zealand, 1882; Melbourne, 1881; Naples, 1886, &c.

*Broadwood, John, and Sons. Warehouses: 33, Great Pulteney Street; 9, Golden Square; and Bridle Lane, London. Manufactory: Horseferry Road, Wood Wharf, Grosvenor Road, Westminster. Founded (1732) at Great Pulteney Street, by Burkat Shudi (Burkhard Tschudi). Shudi (b. 1702, d. 1773), harpsichord maker, took

K

John Broadwood (b. 1732, d. 1812) into partnership (known as Shudi and Broadwood) in 1770. Shudi's patent for the Venetian swell in harpsichords (No. 947, 1769) was for an invention subsequently transferred to the organ. After Shudi's demise John Broadwood continued the business with Shudi's son, Burkat—an arrangement which lasted about nine years, and then left John Broadwood sole proprietor. After the elder Shudi's death, John Broadwood devoted himself to the improvement of the newly introduced pianoforte. His patent (No. 1379, 1783) was for the invention of the loud and soft pedals, and an entire remodelling of the square piano. About 1788 he divided the belly bridge, the lower section to carry the bass strings. As he did not patent this invention, it was at once universally adopted. 1795, he took his son, James Shudi (b. 1772, d. 1851) into partnership, and the firm became John Broadwood and Son; 1808, by the admission of another son, Thomas, the firm became Broadwood and Sons. The most important invention introduced by James and Thomas Broadwood was the metal string plate, first applied in 1822, and patented in combination with metal bars (No. 5,485) in 1827. 1834, Henry Fowler Broadwood (b. 1811, d. 1893) joined the firm, and for more than fifty years was the leading partner. 1847, he invented the grand piano in a complete iron frame, combined with a diagonal bar. Averse to patents, he took no steps to protect this or any improvement effected during his control, with the exception of an iron pin-piece and screw tuning-pins (No. 1,283, 1862). 1843, Walter Stewart Broadwood and Thomas Broadwood, jun., became partners; 1857, George Thomas Rose, Fr. Rose, and, until 1861, John Reid; 1881, Henry John Tschudi Broadwood; 1883, Geo. Daniel Rose; 1890, James Henry Tschudi Broadwood; and (1894) W C. Dobbs, grandson of H. F. Broadwood and, in direct descent, of the sixth generation, counting from Shudi. The last four, with Fr. Rose, form the present firm (1895). Recent patents are (No. 1,231, 1888) for a steel frame piano without bars, taken out by H. J. Tschudi Broadwood, and (No. 7,665, provisionally, 1893) for an improvement in the repetition grand action, by G. D. Rose. The medals awarded to the firm in connection with Exhibitions are dated 1851, 1862; Paris, 1867 (first gold medal for England); and in the last important piano competition, which took place at the Inventions Exhibition, 1885, a gold medal, and, in addition, the further honour of the gold medal of the Society of Arts. A gold medal was also received from the Tasmanian Exhibition, 1892. From 1740, and, it may be, earlier, this house has had the patronage of the English Court. It is the oldest pianoforte business in the world, and is probably the oldest existing in England of any kind still located in the original premises.

[Besides the great merits this firm may honourably claim as manufacturers, there is another, and not the least, which they could not themselves advert to, but may be justly added; and that is the most generous manner in which they have assisted some of the foremost English musicians to pursue their studies in Germany, and have found opportunities for removing otherwise almost insuperable difficulties for young artists in the early days of their career.]

Brown and Hallett, of Boston, Mass., established 1835. Edwin Brown took out patents for several important improvements. (See Hallett, Davis & Co.)

Brown, Simpson & Co., of Worcester, Mass. Founded Aug. 10, 1883, by Theodor Brown (b. Oct. 2, 1860, Malden, Mass.). The specialty of their instruments is "first-class in every respect." A gold medal was granted at New England Fair, 1889.

*Browne, Justin, piano manufacturer, London; b. Dec. 21, 1838, London. He served his apprenticeship with Messrs. Ennever and Son, and was subsequently with Messrs. Broadwood and Sons, and Erard. He started his own business in 1864, and is now in the first rank of English piano makers. The secret of his success was the introduction of a new iron frame, which was registered under the number of 32,924. His uprights are built on exactly the same lines as horizontal grand pianos, and thus stand equally well in tune; they combine all the improvements which produce delicacy and responsiveness of touch, perfection of repetition, &c. During the last thirty years above 16,000 instruments have been sold in the home and foreign markets. Prize medal, London, 1885; gold medal, Liverpool, 1886; highest award, New Zealand Exhibition, 1890. These are the only exhibitions where his instruments were shown. Vice-President of the **Musical Trades Asso**ciation, and elected by the London Chamber of Arbitration as Arbitrator to settle disputes in connection with the music trade and profession.

C.

***Challen and Son**, of London. Founded (1804) by Thomas Butcher, who retired (1830) and was succeeded by William Challen (associated with him since 1816). He died 1861, having retired in favour of his son, C. Challen. 1862, C. Challen entered into partnership with the publishers, Duff and Hodgson; after the death of Duff (1863) and Hodgson (1873), C. H. Challen was admitted as partner, the style of the firm being altered to Challen and Son. Their upright pianos enjoy a well-merited and extensive reputation. Among many medals received in 1862, 1877, 1881, 1885, 1886, is the "Medaille d'honneur" awarded at the Paris Exhibition, 1878. One of their specialties is the "Dulcephone," or piano tone moderator.

***Chappell & Co.**, of London (warehouse, 53, New Bond Street; factory, Belmont Street, Chalk Farm Road, N.W.). The firm commenced 1861 and has, up to the present time (1893), made upwards of 30,000 instruments. Thomas Chappell, as head of the firm, takes great interest in the improvement of the instruments and the enlargement of this successful business. The specialties are "Student's Piano" (five octaves), school pianinos, cottage oblique, overstrung and horizontal grand pianos, the Eolian piano (a combination of piano and harmonium), and yacht pianinos with folding keyboard. The latest improvement is the "upright grand." Since 1862, the firm has received nine medals.

***Chickering and Sons**, of Boston and New York. This far-famed factory was founded in April, 1823, by Jonas Chickering (b. April 5, 1798, Mason, New Hampshire; d. Dec. 8, 1853). At present, Geo. H. Chickering is president; Henry Saltonstall, vice-president; and C. H. W. Foster, treasurer of the very extensive business. At first Jonas Chickering only made square pianos; these were succeeded (1830) by uprights, and (1840) by grands. Of square pianos three different kinds are made, of uprights the same number, and of grand pianos the firm makes small parlour grands, semi-grands, and full concert grands. Up to March, 1894, 84,000 instruments had been sold. Medals were obtained—1876 (gold), Paris; 1875 (first grand gold), Santiago de Chili; 1876 (gold), Philadelphia; 1883, Cork; 1884, London, Crystal Palace; three first gold medals at exhibitions in the United States during 1884. "In all a total of 128 first medals and awards." Cross of the Legion of Honour, 1867 (Paris). The factory, in Tremont Street, Boston, has about five acres of floor space. The beauty and solidity of the instruments have been acknowledged by the most celebrated artists of the present time.

***Collard and Collard**, of London. The founders of this celebrated firm were the publishers, Longman and Broderip, located, since 1767, at 26, Cheapside, London. They were joined (1798-1800) by Muzio Clementi, who invested part of his money in the factory, and succeeded by degrees, in company with F. W. and W. P. Collard, in gaining a lasting reputation for their instruments. 1798-1800, the firm was Clementi and Co. Clementi did not possess any practical knowledge of piano construction, but suggested all possible advantageous points for the performer, whilst F. W. Collard took out (as early as 1811) patents for important improvements. After the retirement of Clementi, the firm became Collard and Collard. On the decease of F. W. Collard and the retirement of F. W. Collard, jun. (1859), Charles Lukey Collard, who was left sole remaining partner, determined to remove the headquarters of the firm to the West-End (Grosvenor Street), when an enormous expansion of trade followed. Charles L. Collard died at his Bournemouth residence (Ravensworth) on Dec. 9, 1891. The names of the present partners are William Stuartson Collard, John Clementi Collard, and Cecil Collard. The world-wide fame which the Collard and Collard pianos have obtained through their solidity of construction, extraordinary durability, brightness and sweetness of tone, is so great as to need no further comment.

Conover Brothers, of Kansas City and New York (J. Frank Conover, b. Jan. 31, 1843, and George H. Conover, b. June 20, 1844). The firm was established (1870) in Kansas and (1880) in New York. The Kansas business was sold in Jan., 1889. Patents have been taken out since 1878: 1884, for a "duplex bridge with auxiliary vibrators," According to reports, the accuracy of which cannot be vouched for, the business was given up in 1893.

*Cramer and Co., of London. The business was started (1865) by George Wood, in connection with the well-known music warehouse established (1824) in Regent Street. Specialties are pianettes, uprights, and grands, also table and yacht pianos. Silver medal, 1885, in London.

Cristofori, Bartolommeo di Francesco (b. 1651; d. 1731), a harpsichord maker, of Padua, afterwards of Florence, in the service of Prince Ferdinand dei Medici, and, at last, of the Grand Duke; the inventor of the pianoforte. In 1709, Cristofori had made four pianofortes, three being of the usual harpsichord or grand form, the other not described. Two grand pianos by him are still existing in Florence, dated respectively 1720 and 1726. The action of these instruments is complete, with escapement, check, and damper.

D.

Decker Brothers, of New York (David and Johann Jacob, both born in Germany). "They have, from 1862 to 1890, kept well in the front rank," and are known and esteemed for their intelligence, self-confidence, practical skill, and sympathy with musical art. David retired several years ago. The firm has taken out five patents.

Decker and Son, of New York. Founded by Myron A. Decker (b. 1823, Manchester, Ontario, C. of New York), who arrived (1844) in New York; "served four years' apprenticeship in the shop of Van Winckle"; accepted (1849) an offer to go to Albany, to the firm of Boardman and Gray; started (1856) his own business in Albany, and opened (1864) his house in New York. Since 1875 his son, Frank C. Decker (b. 1858), has been partner. The firm enjoys great popularity, and the Decker pianos have a ready sale.

*Dörner, F., and Son, of Stuttgart. The firm was founded by Fr. Dörner (b. 1806, Stuttgart; d. there Jan. 21, 1882) in 1830, and soon obtained the patronage of his countrymen, and, later, of the public of other countries. The firm obtained twelve first medals, the patent as manufacturers to the Court of Würtemberg and to H.R.H. the Prince of Hohenzollern, and the principal was decorated with the "Friedrich" Order. Their pianinos and grands are solidly constructed, and possess all the most important improvements of recent date.

*Duysen, Jes Lewe, of Berlin, b. Aug. 1, 1821, Flensburg. He served his apprenticeship in the factory of Hansen (Flensburg). 1860, he established himself at Berlin, and was soon successful, the construction, tone, touch, and solidity of his instruments being much admired. The factory turns out 250 pianinos and 200 grands per year. Manufacturer to the German Emperor and Grand Duke of Saxe-Weimar; Counsellor of Commerce; Knight of the Prussian Crown and of a Tunisian Order. First medal: Vienna, 1873; Santiago, 1875; Utrecht, 1876; Berlin, 1879.

E.

*Eavestaff, W. G., and Sons, of London. The factory was founded by William Eavestaff (1823) and carried on, since 1851, by his son, William G. Eavestaff. The specialty of their uprights is full and rich tone, excellent repetition, and evenness of registers. 1855, the firm introduced entire cast-iron frames. The Eavestaff pianinos belong to the best manufactured in England.

*Eck and Lefébvre (late of Cologne). This, for a short time (1840-44), celebrated and valued firm, was founded by Jacob Eck (b. 1804), who was joined by Lefébvre. Without any fault of theirs, the business had to be liquidated, and Eck retired to Zürich, where he died about 1849.

Emerson Piano Company, of Boston, Mass. Founded (1849) by William P. Emerson. 1854, C. C. Briggs (see this name) entered the shop, became foreman at once, and contributed materially towards the reputation of the company. Briggs left (1861), and joined G. M. Guild in the establishment of the firm M. Guild and Co.

Erard, of Paris and London. This world-wide known firm was founded by Sebastian Erard (Erhard), b. April 5, 1752, Strassburg; d. Aug. 5, 1831, at his château, near Passy, Paris. About 1772 he established himself with his brother, Jean Baptiste, in the Rue de Bourbon (Paris). The branch establishment in London was opened 1786, and the firm obtained both in England and France a great reputation and permanent success. 1821, the highly important repetition action was invented. After Sebastian Erard's death the business passed into the hands of his nephew, Pierre Erard (b. 1796, d. Aug. 18, 1855), who published (1834) "Perfectionnement apportés dans le mécanisme du piano par les Erard depuis l'origine de cet instrument jusqu'à l'exposition de 1834." Pierre was succeeded by the nephew of his wife, Pierre Schäffer (d. 1878), and the proprietor of the business is now Comte de Franqueville. The London manufactory has been discontinued since 1890. The Erard firm has been connected with all the foremost pianists (Chopin excepted) of our time. Piano maker to H.M. Queen Victoria, the Prince and Princess of Wales, the Queens of Spain and Belgium. Only Council medal, London, 1851; Grand Prix de Paris, 1889; gold medal, Paris, 1819, 1823, 1827, 1834, 1839, 1844, 1851, 1855, 1878; and medals (2), Sydney, 1879; Melbourne (3), 1880; Kimberley, 1892.

Estey Piano, The, formerly known as "Arion" piano, manufactured by Simpson and Co., which is now the "Estey" Company (New York). The manager is at present Stephen Brambach (brother of the celebrated composer of Bonn on the Rhine), whilst another brother, Carl, also entered the business. R. Proddow and J. B. Simpson are the principals.

F.

*Fischer, J. and C., of New York. This firm, at first established in Naples (Italy), was started (1840) in New York by John N. and Charles S. Fischer, both born in Naples. They manufacture grand and upright pianos, and have received, among other medals, those of the Exhibitions at Montreal, 1881; New Orleans, 1885; and Chicago, 1893.

G.

Gale, A. H., and Co., of New York (*see* New York Piano Co.). Their pianos were familiar features of the American trade for upward of thirty years; but the firm disappeared about 1870.

Geib, John, probably a German, was a square pianoforte maker in London, and is known to have made such instruments for Longman and Broderip, in Cheapside. His claim to permanent record rests upon his having invented the "hopper," a form of escapement lever that was employed in square and upright pianos for many years. He patented this invention in 1786. He transferred his business to New York, John and Adam Geib appearing as piano makers in the directory of that city in 1807. He appears to have died before 1809, but the name has been carried on in different American firms until a recent date.

*Graf, Conrad, of Vienna, b. Nov. 17, 1782, Riedlingen (Würtemberg); d. March 18, 1851, Vienna. At first a cabinet maker. 1799, had to serve in the Voluntary Rifle Corps of Vienna; 1802, he entered the business of Schelkle (Vienna) as a workman, and developed such remarkable talent for mechanical works that, in 1804, he was able to establish himself as piano maker. Being a man of great energy, perseverance, and industry, he has succeeded in gaining, since 1830, a great reputation for his pianos, which were used by Thalberg, Liszt, Döhler, Willmers, Sophie Bohrer, and other eminent performers. On the occasion of the marriage of Clara Wieck with Robert Schumann, Graf presented the bride with an excellent piano of his manufacture, which Robert Schumann liked so much that he used it until his death, after which it came into the possession of Johannes Brahms, who presented it to the Museum of the "Gesellschaft der Musikfreunde" (Vienna). Graf received the patent as manufacturer to the Imperial and Royal Court of Austria, and several gold medals. The great reputation of the "Vienna" pianos rests principally on those made by Streicher and Graf, and, in later years, by Bösendorfer.

Guild, George M., of Boston, Mass. The pianos made since 1861 (*see* Briggs) "are well known for their modest price."

H.

*Hagspiel and Co., of Dresden. Founded (1851) by Gustav Hagspiel (b. 1820, d. 1879), and is at present under the direction of his son, Oscar (b. 1852). The specialty is the so-called "semi-grand." These instruments have obtained considerable fame, and brought to the firm medals—Dresden, 1871 and 1875; Chemnitz, 1867; Vienna, 1873; San Jago, 1875; Graz, 1880; and London, 1884. The King of Saxony named him manufacturer to the Court.

Haines Brothers. Napoleon J. Haines (b. 1824, London) and Francis W. Haines (d. Sept. 18, 1887), of New York. The brothers worked from 1839 in the shop of the New York Piano Manufacturing Company, and started business on their own account in 1851. The firm soon gained a foremost place. Since 1870 they have directed their chief attention to the manufacture of uprights, and have left off making square pianos.

Hallet, Davis and Co., of Boston, Mass.; followed the firm of Brown and Hallet (*see* this firm), under the direction of Russell Hallet and George Davis. The latter died in 1879, when the firm was changed into Hallet and Allen.

Hallet and Allen (later, Hallet and Cumston) 1839, Cumston took out a patent for a damper improvement in squares.

*Hals Brothers, of Christiania (Norway). Manufacturers to the King of Sweden and Norway. The firm was established on Nov. 3, 1847, by the brothers Karl and Petter Hals. The latter died 1871, and Karl carried on the business alone (b. April 27, 1822) on the family estate,

Willberg, near Christiania. His sons, Thor and Sigurd, entered later as partners. The firm employs 100 workmen; produces 10 to 12 instruments per week—concert grands, semi-grands, and uprights. A music warehouse is connected with the manufactory; and in the adjoining concert-room (holding 600 persons) the principal concerts of native and foreign artists are given. The principal is Commander of the St. Olaf Order (Norway), Danebrog (Denmark), and Knight of the Legion of Honour; also gold medalist of King Oscar II. Medals received: London, 1862; Stockholm, 1866; Paris, 1867, 1878, and 1880; Drammen, 1873; Christiania, 1874 and 1880; Melbourne, 1888.

Hardman, Peck and Co., of New York. Founded, 1842, by Hugh Hardman; later, the firm consisted of John Hardman (son of Hugh Hardman, who retired) and Leopold Peck. John Hardman died Nov. 10, 1889, but the name of the firm remains unaltered. Among the patented improvements used are a "key frame support" and a "harp stop."

Hawkins, John Isaac, an Englishman, who, by the way, invented ever-pointed pencils, has the great merit of having invented the modern upright pianoforte, with the strings descending below the keyboard and the bottom of the instrument resting upon the floor. Before his, upright pianos were either grand or square pianos turned up on end, and resting upon a stand or framed support. He patented his invention for a "portable grand," as he called it, at Philadelphia, U.S.A., where he was living at the time, in Feb., 1800, and in the same year he patented it in London, through his father, Isaac Hawkins. The specification contains a bundle of inventions, some of which have since been developed with important results. Hawkins's "portable grand" is the modern cottage piano, but with the instrument independent of the case, in an iron frame, and the wrest-plank resting upon a metal support. It has an equal length of string throughout, tuning by mechanical screws, and a system of iron rods at the back to resist the tension; also metal supports to the action, which, in its principle, anticipated Wornum's famous action; finally, a folding keyboard and a "volte subito," or leaf-turner. Other ideas in his patent are not carried out in the specimen Messrs. Broadwood possess. One was coiled strings in the bass, to do away with tension; another a *sostenente*, to be attained by a rapid reiteration of the hammer blow. He introduced this *sostenente* by means of a ring-bow mechanism in an instrument he called the "claviol," resembling a cabinet piano, in a concert at Philadelphia, June 21, 1802. He removed to Bordentown, New Jersey, and, in 1813, went to England to exhibit his inventions, which had been, however, to a certain extent, already appropriated. He subsequently became a prominent member of the Institution of Civil Engineers. The years of his birth and death do not appear to be recorded.

Hazelton Brothers, of New York. The firm was founded by Henry Hazelton (b. 1816, New York). 1831, he served seven years' apprenticeship in the factory of Dubois and Stodart. May 19, 1838, he went, in company with James A. Gray and other young piano makers, to Albany, and entered the business of William G. Boardman; but soon after he engaged in the manufacture of the "Hazelton" pianos, having as partners A. G. Lyon and Talbot. 1841, he removed to New York, and associated (1850) with his brothers Frederick and John, when the name of the firm became Hazelton Brothers. They build grands, squares, and uprights, the excellence of which has won a high reputation for the makers.

*Herz, Henri, of Paris. This celebrated manufactory was founded 1825, and obtained, after a comparatively short time, a European reputation. The fine, rich tone, evenness of registers, and excellence of touch were everywhere admired, and won for their grands and uprights the following distinctions:—Gold medals: Paris, 1844, 1878. Medals of honour: Paris, 1855; Oporto, 1865; Melbourne, 1880, 1881, 1889; London, 1862. Diplomas of honour: Metz and Nantes, 1861; Bordeaux, 1865; Amsterdam, 1869; Paris, 1875. *Hors concours:* Paris, 1867; Lyons, 1872. 1864, he received the patent as "Fournisseur de l'Impératrice des Français." (For other distinctions, *see* Henri Herz.) Up to the present (1893) 33,500 instruments have been sold. After Herz's death (Jan. 5, 1888) the business was continued by Amédée Thibout et Cie. Thibout is "Officier de l'Académie."

*Hopkinson, J. and J., of London. Founded by John Hopkinson, b. Dec. 5, 1811, Chatham; d. April 4, 1886, Criccieth (North Wales). 1835, he began to make pianos at Leeds, but, taking his brother James into partnership, moved (1846) to London, and opened warerooms in Soho Square, employing six workmen and two apprentices. 1851, he took out a patent for a repetition and tremolo action on an entirely new principle. 1853, a new factory was built in Diana Place, Euston Road, but destroyed by fire in 1856: during the rebuilding of the factory, the warerooms were removed to 235, Regent Street, where the business was carried on for twenty-six years. James Hopkinson, who had, till 1856, managed the business at Leeds, came to London, leaving another brother, Thomas Barker Hopkinson, as his successor at Leeds. 1866, a new factory was built at Fitzroy Road, Primrose Hill. 1869, John Hopkinson retired, and two sons of James Hopkinson (John and James) were (1874) admitted as partners. The warerooms were moved to 95, New Bond Street. 1883, James Hopkinson (sen.) retired, and William Wood, a trusted superintendent of the business, was taken as partner. The firm received the following medals:—1851, prize medal, London; 1855, gold medal, Paris; 1862, prize medal, London; first class medals were gained at Wakefield, Dublin, and York (1885 and 1886), Dublin and Leeds (1872 and 1875). Only gold medal for England, 1878, Paris; prize medal, York, 1879; Edinburgh, 1886; gold medal, London, 1885, and Melbourne, 1888. The warerooms are at present (1892) at 34-36, Margaret Street, Cavendish Square, London.

*Hornung and Möller, of Copenhagen, manufacturers to the Danish Court. The manufactory was founded (1827) by Conrad Christian Hornung, b. July 1, 1801, Skjelsbor, Island of Seeland (Denmark), who transferred it (1851) to his former assistant, Hans Petter Möller (b. May, 1802, Copenhagen). It was still called Hornung and Möller. 1842, the firm introduced the entire cast-iron frame. The factory is worked by steam aud employs about 100 workmen. The excellence of the instruments is generally acknowledged.

*Hüni and Hübert, of Zürich. This once highly successful firm was founded by Hüni, a native of Switzerland, and Hübert, a German; their successors were the brothers Bourry from Alsace. After a conflagration in 1885, which destroyed the factory, the business was given up. The pianos exhibited (1862) in London showed extreme solidity and general beauty and excellence of tone and touch.

I.

*Ibach, Rudolf Johann, of Barmen, Schwelm, and Cologne. This celebrated firm was founded (1794) by Johannes Adolph Ibach (b. 1766, Barmen; d. there 1848); he was succeeded by his eldest son, Rudolf (1804-63), who was succeeded by his eldest son, Rudolf (1843-92), who was succeeded on his death by his sons. Manufacturers to the King of Prussia, Duke of Meiningen, &c. The beauty and solidity of their grand pianos, uprights and school instruments are well known, and won diplomas and medals of the highest class in the Exhibitions of Düsseldorf, Aix-la-Chapelle, London, Altona, Dresden, Vienna, Philadelphia, Melbourne, and Sydney. Branch establishments in London, Berlin, and Cologne.

*Irmler, sen., J. G., of Leipzig. The business was founded (1818), by Joh. Christian Gottlieb Irmler, b. Feb. 11, 1790, Grumbach, near Dresden; d. 1857, Leipzig. His successors were his sons, Otto and Oswald, and his grandson, Emil Irmler. Manufacturers to the Grand Duke of Mecklenburg-Schwerin. The excellence of their pianos was recognised by several medals and diplomas, and (1842) a gold medal for special merit from the King of Saxony.

Ivers, Pond and Co., of Boston, Mass. The business was started (1872) by William H. Ivers, a graduate of the Chickering Factory (Boston). Since 1872 he has patented many improvements.

J.

James and Holstrom, of New York. This successful firm was founded in 1873, and, according to Spillane, the historian of the American piano, their instruments have come to be known as reliable in every sense. They have a good musical connection.

K.

*Kaim und Sohn (formerly Kaim and Günther), of Kirchheim and Teck, near Stuttgart; founded, 1819, by Franz Kaim. Their grand pianos, uprights, and square pianos for hot climates received medals wherever they were exhibited. The firm holds appointments to the Kings of Bavaria and Würtemberg and other princely houses. Branch establishments in Munich, Augsburg, and Stuttgart, whilst their instruments are sold in London (84, New Bond Street).

Kaps, Ernst, of Dresden, manufacturer to the Court of Saxony, b. Dec. 6, 1826, Döbeln (Saxony); d. Feb., 1887, Dresden. After having visited the best factories of Copenhagen, Stockholm, Paris, Italy, and London, and worked in several of them, he established himself (1859) in Dresden, and succeeded after a short time in getting many orders for his (now well-known) short grands. He patented a "Resonator Patent Flügel," a "Pianino mit Ton-Reflektor," and advertised the "Piano a pittura" and the "Resonator Mascagni Flügel." He was succeeded by his sons.

Keller Brothers and Blight Co., The, of Bridgeport, Ct. The firm was founded by Joseph Keller (b. Sept., 1856, New York) in 1882. The specialty of the firm is upright pianos, for which they have received several State Fair medals.

Kirkman and Son. This firm was founded by Jacob Kirchmann (the *c* has been dropped and the *h* altered into *k* in the present century) in the neighbourhood of Golden Square, London, before 1740, and is one of the two oldest houses in the pianoforte trade now existing.

> Whereas Mr. Hermann Tabel, late of Swallow Street, the famous Harpsichord maker, dead, hath left several fine Harpsichords to be disposed of by Mr. Kirckman, his late Foreman; this is to acquaint the Curious, that the said Harpsichords, which are the finest he ever made, are to be seen at the said Mr. Kirckman's, the corner of Pulteney Court in Cambridge Street, over against Silver Street, near Golden Square.—*Daily Gazetteer*, May 8, 1739.

According to the parish books of St. James's, he rented a house in Great Pulteney Street East, on the opposite side of the way to his rival, Shudi, from June, 1739, to the end of 1749. The rate book of 1750 is not forthcoming, and in the next year he had gone elsewhere. Jacob Kirckman acquired a great reputation as a maker of spinets and harpsichords; in the time of Dr. Burney his business was carried on at the sign of "The King's Arms" (now No. 19, Broad Street, Soho), which testifies to the patronage he was honoured with from George II. and George III. He married the widow of his former master, Tabel, a harpsichord maker in Swallow Street, Piccadilly, and having no children by this marriage, he ultimately took (about 1770) his nephew, Abraham Kirkman, into partnership with him. He died, according to Burney, about 1778. Towards the end of the century a Joseph Kirkman owned the business alone. There is a harpsichord of his make existing dated 1798. The Kirkmans began to make pianofortes as early as 1774, and the development of the instrument, in their hands, followed on similar lines to those adopted by their contemporaries. The second Joseph Kirkman (who died, aged eighty-seven, in 1877) became the head of an important pianoforte business, which was much advanced by his second son, Henry, who, however, pre-deceased him.

*After 1877 it was continued for his eldest son, Joseph, and, since 1883, has been controlled by his grandson, Henry Reece, representing the fifth generation of the same family. Kirkmans removed from Broad Street to No. 3, Soho Square, in 1820, and, in 1893, to George Street, Hanover Square, premises formerly the well-known Edwards Hotel. The manufactory has been at Hammersmith since 1866. Two of Kirkman's patents deserve notice:—(1) For the use of wrought steel tension bars and wrestplank for horizontal grand pianos, taken out in 1870, and renewed in 1877; and (2) the "Melo" attachment for grand pianos, an Italian invention bought by them in 1875 (relinquished in 1882). Influenced by the German school of pianoforte making, they early adopted the "overstrung" system, but, after careful trial, abandoned it. They, however, aim at a compromise between the German and English systems, and also use the Herz-Erard action in their grand pianos. In exhibitions, the Kirkman firm has been awarded a silver medal in 1851 and a prize medal in 1862, the medal of progress at Vienna in 1873, and a gold medal at the Inventions Exhibition, 1885.

Knabe, William, of Baltimore, b. 1803, Kreuzburg, district Oppeln (Prussia); d. 1864, Baltimore. On his arrival in America he worked in Hartye's factory, and then started a business (1839) with Henry Gaehle. The partnership was dissolved in 1854. 1860, the great excellence of the Knabe pianos was generally recognised and willingly acknowledged. He was succeeded by his sons, William (1841-1889) and Ernest, and a relative, Charles Keidel.

*Knake, Gebrüder, of Münster, Westphalia. The firm was founded (1808) at Heiden (Westphalia), by Joh. Bernhard Knake (b. July 18, 1774, Heiden; d. there Aug. 10, 1856). After 1840 the factory removed to Münster, where it is carried on by J. B. Knake's son and grandsons. The excellence of their small grands and uprights has been acknowledged for many years, and the firm is decidedly successful. Medals were received in London, 1862; Paris, 1867; and Barcelona, 1888.

*Knauss, Söhne, of Coblenz o/Rhine (proprietors, Emil and Rudolph Knauss). The manufactory was founded 1821. Received the Government gold medal and patent as manufacturer to the German Emperor. The factory is worked by steam, and turns out 1,600 uprights and short grands (cross-stringed). The firm has an agency in London.

Krakauer Brothers, of New York. The business was started in 1878. Krakauer, sen., was once a teacher of music of some note. He arrived (1853) with his family in New York. The son, Daniel, is an experienced pianist.

*Kranich and Bach, of New York. Established (1864) by Helmuth Kranich and Jacques Bach (both b. 1833, in Germany). The specialties of their instruments are: styles of cases, patent action rack, patent spiral temperature spring, patent sounding-board, patent dampers, and patent music or note rack; also patent grand action ("the best used") and sustaining pedal. Medals were received at Philadelphia, 1876; Boston Mechanics' Fair, 1887; Piedmont Exposition and Atalanta Government, 1891 and 1892; and World's Fair, Chicago, 1893.

*Kriegelstein & Co., of Paris. Founded (1831) by Jean Georges Kriegelstein (b. 1801, Riquewihr, Upper Rhine; d. Nov. 20, 1865, Paris). He established himself with Arnaud, and received, as early as 1834, medals for great improvements: in square pianos for hammers striking from above; 1839, for a grand piano with improved dampers; 1841, for introducing "agraffes de précision pour faciliter l'accord"; 1844, for a simplified "double échappement," &c. 1842, he invented a Mignon pianino of only $42\frac{1}{4}$ inches height, which created general admiration, and was the theme of great praise in the London Exhibition of 1862. It is an elegant and delightful instrument, rich in tone and even in the registers. 1858, he transferred the business to his son, Charles (b. Dec. 16, 1839, Paris). The firm makes ten different pianos. Silver medals: 1834, 1839, 1867, 1878 (Paris); gold medals: 1844, 1849, 1855, 1875 (Paris); Bordeaux, 1859, 1865, 1882; Hâvre, 1868; Altona, 1869; Antwerp, 1885. Prize medal, 1862, London; 1876, Philadelphia; Médaille unique, 1893, Chicago, *hors concours*; 1872, Lyons, diplomé d'honneur. The wellmerited reputation of his instruments is based upon their extreme solidity and rich tone.

*Kroeger, Henry, and Sons, of New York. Founded by Henry Kroeger (b. Nov. 1, 1827, Hamburg). Associated with him were his sons, Henry (b. May 24, 1859, New York; d. there Aug. 17, 1890) and Otto (b. March 25, 1863, New York). Henry, sen., served his apprenticeship (1847-55) in Hamburg. He arrived (1855) in New York, and was employed in the factory of Steinway and Sons. The firm's principal patents relate to a Capo d'astro (1866) and an acoustic patent for a method of sounding-board adjustment. The business is a very thriving one.

*Kurtzmann, C., and Co., of Buffalo, New York. Founded (1848) by Christian Kurtzmann (now deceased), and is at present directed by L. S. Kurtzmann and A. Geòger. They make upright pianos (high grade), employing 150 workmen in a large factory (corner of Niagara Street and Penn Avenue). "They ship to all parts of the United States, and have an established reputation for first-class work."

L.

Lindemann, William, and Sons, of New York. Founded (1835) by William Lindemann (b. in Dresden; d. Dec. 24, 1875, N. York), who was succeeded by his son, Henry (b. Aug. 3, 1838, New York). The firm exhibited (1847), in the Mechanics' Institute, a square which met with great approval. 1860, they took out a patent for the "Cycloid" piano, in some respects a precursor of the bijou grand. "They have always aimed at making instruments of an artistic grade, and their efforts have deservedly won emphatic recognition at the hands of the musical press and impartial connoisseurs."

*Lipp, Richard and John, of Stuttgart. Founded 1831, and makes concert and drawing-room grands, horizontal Mignon instruments, and uprights. The excellence of their pianos was recognised by awards of sixteen medals, several diplomas, the patent as manufacturers to the Court of Würtemberg, and the gold medal for art and science.

Loud, Thomas, an English pianoforte maker, who followed Hawkins in making the modern upright pianos with the strings descending below the keyboard. 1802, he patented in London an upright piano with a "diagonal," since called oblique, scale of stringing, portability being "the leading intention and feature." This instrument anticipated William Southwell's vertical "cabinet" piano of 1807. Loud settled in New York about 1816, and died there in 1834. A firm in Philadelphia, styled Loud Brothers, was, according to Daniel Spillane, in 1824, the most extensive for pianos in the United States.

M.

*Malmsjö, J. G., of Göteborg (Gothenburg (Sweden). Founded, Dec., 1843, by Johan Gustav Malmsjö (b. Jan. 14, 1815, Lund, South Sweden; d. Sept. 13, 1891, Göteborg); he served his apprenticeship with Marschall, of Copenhagen. For several years he was one of the magistrates (Stadtrath) of Göteborg, and greatly respected for his many excellent qualities. The manufacture is now the greatest and most important of Sweden, and the only one which makes grand pianos. Up to 1893, when the firm celebrated its fifty years jubilee, 5,600 instruments had been sold; latterly, about 135 pianos have been made per year, concert and semi-grands, larger and smaller pianinos. Manufacturer to the Swedish Court. First prizes at the Exhibitions of Stockholm, 1851, 1866; Göteborg, 1860, 1871; London, 1862; Paris, 1867; Copenhagen, 1872 and 1880; Malmö, 1865 and 1881; Karlsbad (Sweden), 1862; Vienna, 1873; Philadelphia, 1875, &c. (total, nineteen first prizes). 1891, a special prize of honour was awarded in Göteborg. After Malmsjö's death, his son-in-law, Vilhelm Seydel, was appointed Director.

*Mand, Carl, of Coblenz, manufacturer to the Prussian Court. The business was started in 1835, and is eminently successful. The excellence of the instruments (grand pianos and uprights) has been recognised by medals conferred—1880, in Düsseldorf: (2), 1881, Melbourne; 1883, Amsterdam; 1885, Antwerp; 1886, Coblenz; 1888, Brussels; and 1889 (2), Cologne. Many of the leading artists have testified their approval of the beauty of tone, elasticity of touch, and decided solidity of construction.

*Martin et Cie, of Toulouse. Founded (1810) by Jean Bapt. Martin, the specialty of the firm being grand pianos. The firm received twenty-five gold medals and several diplomas, and (with Boisselot, of Marseilles) is decidedly the foremost provincial factory of France.

Mason and Hamlin, of Boston, Mass., started their piano business in 1883, and introduced a patented system of stringing and tuning, which, although sceptically received by the American piano makers, has been retained with success by the firm.

Matashek (Mataschek), Frederic, and Co., of New Haven, Connecticut. Fr. Matashek (b. June 9, 1814, Mannheim o/Rhine) went (1848) to America, having studied in the principal factories of Germany, Austria, Russia, and Paris (Pape). 1855, associated with Spencer Driggs; he dissolved partnership in 1870, and started on his own account the firm Matashek and Co. His patents for inventions are numerous.

*Mayer, J., and Co., of Munich. Founded, Oct. 18, 1833, by Joh. Jacob Mayer (b. March 23, 1805, Altenburg, Würtemberg), and is at present the foremost piano factory of Bavaria. Medals were received—1876 (Munich); 1881 (Melbourne); 1882 (Nürnberg); 1883 (Amsterdam); 1884 (London); 1888 (Barcelona and Munich). 1876, the Bavarian King named Mayer manufacturer to the Court, and (1893) the Prince Luitpold conferred the same distinction on him. Specialties are grands (overstrung) and pianinos. The present principal and proprietor of the business is F. Schmidt, son-in-law of Mayer.

Mehlin and Sons, of New York—Paul Mehlin (b. Feb. 28, 1837, Stuttgart) and his sons, Paul and Charles. Paul, sen., served his apprenticeship in the factory of Fr. Dörner (see this name); went (1854) to New York, where he was employed in the factories of Raven and Bacon, Light and Bradbury, E. Gabler and Brother (1865), with whom he remained for sixteen years. 1881, he started his own business. Among his most important improvements are his grand plate and scale for uprights (1889), hammer scale (1885), and his touch-regulator (1887). In all, the firm took out twelve patents.

Meyer, Conrad, of Philadelphia. C. Meyer (b. Marburg, Hesse-Cassel) went (1819) to Baltimore, where he was an apprentice in the factory of Jos. Hiskey. About 1830 he established himself in Philadelphia. Great differences of opinion exist about his being the first to introduce the full iron plate, and some judges maintain that the priority of this invention belongs to Babcock (see this name). One of Meyer's pianos was exhibited (1878) in Paris, where it attracted considerable attention.

Miller, Henry F., and Sons, of Boston, Mass. The founder of the firm was born Sept. 4, 1825, Providence, and died Aug. 14, 1884, Wakefield, Mass. He first intended to become a pianist and organist, but later studied piano making, and joined the firm of Brown and Allen (Boston). Having worked for five years with Emerson, he started (1862) his own business, being associated with N. M. Lowe and J. H. Gibson. After a comparatively short time, he became sole proprietor, and at present his five sons represent the very successful and greatly respected firm.

N.

*Neumeyer, F., of Berlin, manufacturer of grand pianos and uprights. The firm was founded (1861) by F. Neumeyer (b. April 4, 1837, Eilhausen, Waldeck) and employs 150 workmen; up to 1893 had sold about 19,300 instruments. The factory is worked with steam and turns out about 1,200 instruments per year. Branch establishment in London.

Newman and Brothers, of Baltimore. 1850-60, the firm was, with those of Charles M. Stieff and J. T. Stoddard, highly respected in Baltimore. Founded (1850) by Joseph Newman, who, after 1853, was associated with W. R. Talbot, took out a patent for improvement in sounding-boards. Talbot died 1884, after having assisted to bring the firm into greater repute.

New York Piano Manufacturing Co., The, began business between 1837-38. Haines Brothers were apprentices in the Company, which was started by some twenty of the best workmen of Nunns and Clark. The firm soon changed into that of A. H. Gale & Co.

Nunns and Clark, of New York (1838). *See* Nunns, Robert and William.

Nunns, Robert and William, of New York, arrived (1821) from England and started (1824) in business. 1831, a patent was granted them for a square action; they had already bought (1827) the "scale" of Charles S. Sackmeister. 1833, they admitted John Clark as partner, the firm's style then being Robert Nunns, Clark and Co. William Nunns withdrew from the business and began a factory of his own, later associated with J. and C. Fisher. 1851, Nunns and Clark purchased the hammer covering invention, patented by Rudolf Kreter, and greatly improved by Alfred Dolge.

P.

Pape (Johann), Heinrich, of Paris (b. July 1, 1789, Sarsted, Hanover; d. Feb. 2, 1875, Paris). He was one of the most prolific inventors of recent times. After having visited England in 1811, he went to Paris; assisted Ignaz Pleyel (*see* this name) in the formation of his factory; started his own establishment in 1815, and produced almost every year something new, without, however, obtaining a lasting success or influence by his decidedly interesting innovations. An exhaustive account of his inventions and innovations is to be found in "Notice de M. H. Pape" (Benard, Paris, 1862). He received the Legion of Honour and other French distinctions. *See* Grove's Dictionary, Vol. II., page 647.

Peck and Son, of New York. They opened their business in 1851. Since 1878 the firm has made great strides, and now enjoys general confidence.

*****Pleyel, Wolff and Co.,** of Paris. Founded by the composer, Ignaz Pleyel (pupil of Jos. Haydn). 1824, his son, Camille (husband of the celebrated pianist, Marie Pleyel, *née* Moke), succeeded him as principal, and was much assisted by Kalkbrenner. Camille, who died May 4, 1855, was succeeded by Auguste Wolff (principal from 1855 until his death in Feb., 1887), who brought out the "Pedalier" and "Clavier transpositeur." Since 1887, Gustave Lyon has been Director of the firm, now formed into a company. Under his direction were introduced: La Pédale harmonique; Balance digitale (Taffanel-Pleyel); le Molliphone and le Durcisseur. The firm makes pianinos, semi-grands, and concert grands; employs 600 workmen. 1889, their 100,000th instrument was sold. Distinctions and rewards: 1810, Ignaz Pleyel was made manufacturer to the King of Westphalia; 1827, Louis Philippe, Duc d'Orleans, conferred the title of "Fabricant de Piano à queue"; 1829, King Charles X. conferred the title of "Fournisseur de sa Majesté"; 1831, King Louis Philippe conferred the same title. Gold medals: 1827, 1834, 1839, 1844, 1855, 1878 (all from Paris); 1861, Metz; 1875, Chili; 1881, Milan. The firm was *hors concours*, 1849 and 1867, Paris; 1872, Lyons; 1873, Vienna; 1883, Amsterdam; 1887, Toulouse; 1887, Hâvre; 1888, Brussels; 1888, Melbourne and Copenhagen. Grand Prix, 1889, Paris. Diplomas of honour: 1861, Metz; 1875, Blois; 1885, Antwerp. 1834, Camille Pleyel, Knight of the Legion of Honour; 1862, Auguste Wolff, Knight of the Legion of Honour. Gustave Lyon received the Belgian Order of Leopold, Legion of Honour and Danebrog. Branch establishments in London, Brussels, and Moscow.

*****Pohlmann and Sons,** of Halifax, Yorkshire. Founded (1786) by Johannes Pohlmann, who was, it is believed, the maker of the first pianofortes constructed in England. The firm in Halifax was opened (1823) by Henry Pohlmann, the firm being Pohlmann and Pohlmann, later Pohlmann and Son. The present principal is Frederick Pohlmann. The firm possesses a great number of valuable patents and has received nine medals.

R.

Rachals and Co., of Hamburg. This well-known firm was established by Matthias Ferd. Rachals (b. June 4, 1801, Milan; d. Sept. 6, 1866, Hamburg). He worked (1821) as apprentice with Brix (St. Petersburg); 1827, with Sachsossky (Cassel); 1828-31, with Wagner (Hamburg). 1832, he established (with *one* workman) his own factory, and had the satisfaction of selling (1845) his 1,000th instrument. His son, Adolph Ferd. Rachals, who studied in the principal factories of North America, succeeded (1866) his greatly esteemed father. The firm makes grands, obliques, and squares. Among their specialties is a piano packed in four cases à 80-90, or in six cases à 60 kilos weight. The Jury of the Chicago Exhibition (1893) published a highly flattering report about the tone and action of these pianos, and the ingenuity of facilitating transport, which was declared "an entirely new feature."

Raven and Bacon, of New York. On the death of George Bacon (1856), his son, Francis, became a partner until 1871, when the partnership was dissolved, and Karr took his place; but retired in 1880, whereupon Francis re-entered the firm. "Their instruments are well spoken of" (*see* Francis Bacon).

Ritmüller, W., and Sohn, of Göttingen. Established (1795) by Andreas Georg Ritmüller. His son, Wilhelm, succeeded him, and was joined by his sons, Wilhelm and Martin, the firm being W. Ritmüller and Sons. When the elder son left (in 1860) it was altered to W. Ritmüller and Son. Another son became partner of W. Ritmüller, sen., and was, until 1891, sole proprietor. Since 1891, the business has belonged to Bernhard Schröder. For their grand pianos and uprights twelve medals and diplomas were received in Germany and (1884 and 1885) in London. The instruments are solidly constructed and enjoy a merited and considerable popularity.

Römhildt, L., of Weimar. The business was founded by Ludwig Römhildt (b. Sept. 7, 1817, Elsterberg, Saxony; d Feb. 20, 1864, Weimar). He was succeeded by his son, Ludwig (b. April 28, 1849, Weimar; d. there May 31, 1890). Up to 1855 only squares were built, and, owing to bad health, Römhildt almost entirely gave up piano making, devoting himself to selling other makers' instruments; but when the son took the business (1869) he began to make instruments, and had the satisfaction of selling, up to 1880, 500 pianos, which number was increased, in 1883, to 1,000. After the death of Ludwig Römhildt, jun., his cousin, Theodor Vetterling, became director of the manufactory, in which 100 workmen are employed. Ten to eleven pianinos are finished per week. The firm received ten gold medals, and possesses testimonials from the most celebrated artists. The instruments are sent to all parts of the world and enjoy a most excellent reputation.

Rönisch, Carl, of Dresden (b. 1814, Goldberg, Silesia; d. July 21, 1894, Blasewitz, near Dresden) He founded (1845) his factory, which grew rapidly into large dimensions. He was the first to build short grands in Dresden. Up to 1892, 20,000 of his instruments had been sold; 300 workmen are employed, and the business is steadily increasing. He was manufacturer to the Court of Saxony, Royal Counsellor of Commerce, Knight of several orders, and the recipient of first-class medals. The yearly production is 1,500 instruments.

Rogers and Son, of London (60, Berners Street). Founded (1843) by George Rogers. Turns out: 1. Cupola steel frame, allowing great freedom and richness of tone. 2. Stud-top bridges, helping to give clearness and penetration of tone. 3. Sound-boards of large size and great reflecting freedom, given them in the adaptation of the strengthening ribs or bars. 4. Front escapement check-action, combining great delicacy and power in the touch and perfection of repetition. 5. Over-stringing, so as to obtain the greatest length of string. They are now building horizontal grands.

Rosenkranz, Ernst, of Dresden. The firm was founded 1797. Has received fifteen prize medals, and produces grand pianos of different sizes and pianinos with the usual and "Janko" keyboards. Their smallest horizontal instruments enjoy great favour.

S.

*Scheel, Carl, b. Feb., 1812, Cassel; d. there Jan. 25, 1892. Son of a poor cabinet maker. After having served his apprenticeship with his father, he left (1832) his native town, after old German fashion, with knapsack on back, and walked to Frankfort o/M., where he served for nine months as assistant in the business of the cabinet maker, Wulff. Being very fond of music, he turned his attention to the manufacture of pianos, and went to Darmstadt, where he was (1833-37) assistant of the piano maker, Vierheller. He then proceeded on foot to Strassburg, as his modest means only allowed him to take from there the "Diligence" to Paris, where, being an excellent tuner, he soon found employment. Erard's firm detected the great gifts of the young German and (1837-46) employed him as a workman. A few years after his entrance, he was promoted to the responsible post of "Chef d'atelier." 1845, when on a visit to Cassel, he determined to start a business on his own account, and began at Easter, 1846, to build his first pianino. Soon the remarkable excellence of his instruments became known and (1854) he was able to move to a much bigger house. 1859, his factory was burnt down; but his great energy and general assistance from his townsmen enabled him to conquer all obstacles, and, with even greater success than before, he enlarged his factory. 1877, the Crown Prince of Prussia (Emperor Frederick) named him manufacturer to the Court, 1880, his son, Carl Heinrich, and (1888) his son, Fritz, were admitted partners. The solidity and general excellence of the "Scheel" pianinos are proverbial, and in Germany and adjoining countries are unconditionally recognised.

Schiedmayer, of Stuttgart. This firm was started (1854) by Julius and Paul Schiedmayer, for the manufacture of harmoniums; 1860, for that of pianinos also; and, somewhat later, of grand pianos. Julius Schiedmayer died Jan., 1878, and the firm now consists of Paul Schiedmayer and his son-in-law, Oscar Förster. Their instruments enjoy a good reputation and are, like those of Schiedmayer and Söhne, well known in England. The firm holds the patents of manufacturers to the Queen of England, the German Emperor, and the Kings of Würtemberg and Italy. Julius Schiedmayer acted as juror at the Exhibitions of London (1862), Paris (1867), Vienna (1873), Philadelphia (1876), Stettin (1865), and received for his services as such Orders of Knighthood from Austria, Italy, Würtemberg, &c. Paul Schiedmayer acted as juror in the Exhibitions of Zürich (1883) and Antwerp (1885).

*Schiedmayer und Söhne, of Stuttgart. Founded (1781) by Johann David Schiedmayer, at that time in Erlangen. The business was continued by his son, Johann Lorenz (b. Dec. 2, 1786, Erlangen; d. March, 1860, Stuttgart). 1809, he associated himself with Dieudonné (d. 1825), afterwards remained sole proprietor till 1845, when his sons entered the firm. These were Adolph (b. 1819, d. Oct. 17, 1890) and Hermann (b. 1820), the firm now being Schiedmayer und Söhne. 1842, the firm began to make pianinos. 1854, the King of Würtemberg conferred on it the great gold medal for art and science, whilst a gold prize medal was received at the London Exhibition (1851) and in Munich (1854); 1873, diploma of honour at the Vienna Exhibition, and (1881) the same distinction at Stuttgart. 1881, the eldest member of the firm, Adolph Schiedmayer, received the title of "Counsellor of Commerce," whilst the patents of Court manufacturers to the Kings of Würtemberg and Roumania were obtained (1877 and 1888). After the death of Hermann Schiedmayer, jun. (1891), his brother, Adolph (b. 1847), became the principal of the house. In all, the firm received six diplomas, nineteen medals, and took out six patents. It is the oldest firm in Würtemberg.

Schomaker (Schumacher) & Co., of Philadelphia. Founded (1838) as Bosert and Schomaker (Schumacher, b. 1800 in Germany; d. 1875, Philadelphia). Bosert retired (1842), when the firm took its present name. 1846, the business was formed into a stock company in Philadelphia, U.S.A., with Colonel H. W. Gray (b. 1830, Ephrata, Lancaster County) and H. S. Schomaker, jun., as principal officer and secretary. The chief specialty of the firm is the use of electro-plated piano strings in gold (patented 1876). A similar patent was taken out (1851) by H. J. Newton, of New York, and (1862) by Martin Miller. Colonel Gray admits that coating strings had been tried previously, but not "wrapped strings."

*Schröder, C. M. (piano manufactory at St. Petersburg). Founded by Johann Fr. Schröder (b. 1785, Stralsund; d. 1852, St. Petersburg); succeeded by his son, Michael (b. 1828, St. Petersburg; d. there 1889); succeeded by the present head of the firm, Carl Nicolai Schröder (b. 1862, St. Petersburg). In order to recognise the importance of the firm (then seventy-five years old), the Czar conferred on C. N. Schröder, in 1893, the title of "Manufacturrath." The grand pianos are made in six, the uprights in three, different sizes. The grands are built after the American system, seven and one-third octaves, repetition action, &c. The firm employs 250 workmen and turns out 1,000 instruments per year. Gold medals: Moscow, 1872; Paris, 1878; London, 1885. Silver medals: St. Petersburg, 1839; Moscow, 1865. Hon. diplomas: St. Petersburg, 1861; Cassel, 1870; Antwerp, 1885; Chicago, 1893. Medal for progress: Vienna, 1873. Orders of knighthood: Francis Joseph (Austria); Legion of Honour (France); Leopold (Belgium); Imperial Eagle (Russia); St. Stanislas (Class III.), St. Anna (Class III., 1877, Class II., 1883), Vladimir (Class IV). Manufacturer to the Emperors of Russia, Austria, Germany, and the Kings of Denmark and Bavaria.

*Schwechten, G., of Berlin, manufacturer to the Court. Founded 1854, and employs at present 120 workmen. The specialty is uprights, of which (1893) not less than 22,000 have been sold. Medals have been awarded in London, Paris, Vienna, Philadelphia, Melbourne, &c.

*Schweighofer, J. M., und Söhne, of Vienna. Founded (1792) by Michael Schweighofer (b. about 1765, in Bavaria; d. 1809, Vienna); succeeded by his widow, and, 1832, by his son, Johann Michael (d. 1852); the business was then left to the latter's sons, Carl and Johann. The excellent qualities of their grands (three models) and pianinos have been generally acknowledged. The firm received many medals and diplomas, and, at the date of the centenary of the foundation (1892), the Emperor of Austria conferred on the senior partner the title of Imperial Councillor and the Golden Cross of Merit with the Crown, whilst the Vienna magistrate declared the brothers " tax freie bürger " (tax-exempted citizens). The firm was also honoured with the patent as manufacturers to the Imperial and Royal Court of Austria.

*Shoninger (Schöninger ?), B., and Co., of New Haven. Founded March (1850) by B. Schöninger (b. 1828, in Bavaria). "Their piano has many special improvements and patents; is especially adapted to withstand all climatic changes; is of the greatest durability." Medals awarded by: New England State Agricultural Society, 1868; Philadelphia, 1876; Paris, 1878; Rotterdam, 1883; New York State Fair, 1886; also many State Fairs. The firm has warerooms in Chicago and New York.

Silbermann, Gottfried, originally an organ builder (b. 1683, d. 1753), of Kleinbobritzsch, near Frauenstein, Saxony; settled at Freiberg, 1709, and subsequently Dresden. As early as 1726 he submitted two pianofortes to the judgment of J. S. Bach. About 1746 he supplied pianofortes to Frederick the Great, three of which are still preserved at Potsdam, in the Stadtschloss, Sans Souci, and the Neues Palais. Mr. A. J. Hipkins's examination of these instruments in 1881 proved them to be built upon Cristofori's model. Silbermann has the credit of being the earliest German pianoforte maker. His instruments, from the specimens above-mentioned, were undoubtedly good.

Sohmer and Co., of New York. The founder and principal of the firm is Hugo Sohmer (b. 1846, in the Black Forest, Baden). He received a classical education, studied piano playing as well as piano making, and went (1862) to America, where he worked as apprentice in the factory of Schütze and Ludolf, of New York; paid, 1868, a temporary visit to Germany, where he studied piano making from the European point of view; returned, 1870, to New York and opened, in 1872, his business, with Joseph Kuder as partner, the new firm being successors to J. H. Börnhäft, who in his turn had succeeded the old house of Marschall and Mittauer. Kuder is a native of Bohemia. 1876, the Centennial Exhibition authorities awarded high honours to the firm. 1883, an additional factory was taken and was enlarged in 1886. The firm has taken out fifty-one patents. The Sohmer "pianissimo" pedal is an improved attachment for producing refined and artistic piano effects, and is used in combination with the ordinary soft pedal. Their pianos are held in high respect.

*Sprecher-Wirth, Theodor (formerly Sprecher and Sons), of Zürich. Founded (1847) by Christian Sprecher (b. 1810). Makes grand and upright instruments. Received fifteen diplomas and first medals, and is the principal firm of Switzerland.

Steck, G., and Co., of New York. The founder of the firm, George Steck (b. July 19, 1829, Cassel), was apprenticed in the factory of Carl Scheel (see this name). 1853, he arrived in New York, and "worked for four years in the best shops," until he started (1857) his own business. 1865, he opened the "Steck Hall." 1884, the business was formed into a company (Rob. C. Kammerer, Fr. Dietz, and Nembach). Popular nicknames of his instruments are "The Little Giant" (upright) and "The Steck Baby Grand." His pianette, a novel instrument, is said to "weigh only 178 pounds, and is considered to have a grand future before it."

Stein, Johann Andreas, of Augsburg (b. 1728, Heidesheim (Palatinate); d. Feb. 29, 1792, Augsburg). Pupil of Silbermann. 1758, he was in Paris, and remained there for some years. On his return he settled as an organ builder in Augsburg, and began also to make pianos, introducing several important improvements, about which Mozart speaks in a letter (Oct., 1777) to his mother. Stein is really the founder of the Vienna School of pianoforte making, and if not the absolute inventor, certainly the improver of a mechanism, generally called the "Vienna mechanism." He introduced the "genouillière," or knee-pedal for raising the dampers. In one of his pianos, described by Gerber, he applied the Saitenharmonica (1789), a pedal shifting the keyboard, and thus carrying the hammers from three strings to one (*una corda*). He called this instrument the "Spinettchen." He had two sons and a daughter—Matthæus Andreas, Friedrich, and Maria Anna, generally called Nanette (see Streicher). Matthæus Andreas (b. Dec. 12, 1776, Augsburg; d. May 6, 1842, Vienna) succeeded, with his sister, to the business of his father, accompanied her to Vienna, and established himself there in 1802; his son, Karl Andreas (b. Sept. 4, 1797, Vienna; d. there Aug. 28, 1863), was his pupil in piano making, but distinguished himself also as a pianist and composer. He devoted, however, his chief energies to the factory, took out a patent in 1829, and was made Manufacturer to the Court in 1844. He published a book "On the Playing, Tuning, and Preservation of Stein Pianofortes."

*Steinway and Sons, of New York, Hamburg, and London. This world-renowned house was founded by Heinrich Engelhard Steinweg (the name Steinway was taken when establishing the business in New York), b. Feb. 15, 1797, Wolfshagen, in the Hartz Mountains, Brunswick, Germany; d. Feb. 7, 1871, New York. He had learned cabinet making and organ building in Goslar; tried, later, his luck in making guitars and cithers. Opened a piano business (1835) at Seesen, but, having settled in Brunswick, resolved to build square, upright, and grand pianos. The business soon increased; but, owing to the political events of 1848, he was obliged to emigrate (1850) to America, with his four sons: I., Charles (b. Jan. 4, 1829, Seesen, Brunswick; d. there, March 31, 1865, while on a trip to Germany). II., Henry, jun. (b. Oct., 1829, Seesen; d. March 11, 1865, New York). III., William, present head of the house (b. March 5, 1836, Seesen). IV., Albert (b. June 10, 1840, Seesen; d. May 14, 1877, New York). The eldest son, Theodore (b. Nov. 6, 1825, Seesen; d. March 26, 1889, Brunswick), remained in Europe, in order to continue the Brunswick business; but transferred it (1865) to Grotrian, Helfferich, and Schulz, the firm becoming Theodor Steinweg Nachfolger (see Steinweg). The New York house, founded 1853, after Steinway and several of his sons had worked in other American factories, soon took the lead in New York—indeed, in America. A factory of grand dimensions, to which was added the Steinway Hall for concerts, was built, but soon found insufficient, and at present the different factories are: Steinway, Astoria (opposite New York), covering twelve acres, and employing 650 workmen; the factory of New York, covering the square between the Park and Lexington Avenue, where about 60 instruments per week are finished and 650 workmen employed; the Steinway Hall, which had room for 2,400 seats, but since 1890 has been used for purposes of manufacture; and the warerooms, offices, &c., where about 250 persons work. 1880, a factory was opened in Hamburg (Neue Rosenstrasse, 20-24), in which 300 workmen are employed; the pianos sent from New York are finished there. Of the five sons of the founder, Theodor and William took the most important part in furthering the progress of the firm. Theodor was Member of the Academies of Paris, Berlin, and Stockholm; whilst William is the founder of different institutions for the benefit of his workmen. He built a school, in which 800 children are taught; opened a library; erected a fine church, with a good organ; opened bath-rooms; and laid out a fine garden. Among the rewards given to the firm are—Gold medals: 1854 and 1855, for squares. Prize medal, with particular mention of excellence, London, 1862; Paris, 1867; Stockholm, 1868; Philadelphia, 1876; London, 1885, with an especial gold medal of the Society of Arts. The firm received the patent as manufacturer to the English and German Courts, and the German Emperor received William Steinway in a private audience, and conferred on him the Order of the Red Eagle. The present active members of Steinway and Sons are: William, head of the firm; Charles H. (b. June 3, 1857, New York), and Fr. T. (b. Feb. 9, 1860, New York), both sons of the late Charles Steinway; Henry Ziegler (b. Oct. 30, 1857, New York), nephew of William; George A. (b. June 4, 1865, New York), son of William; Charles F. Tretbar (b. Feb. 13, 1832, Brunswick); and Nahum Stetson (b. Dec. 5, 1856, Bridgewater, Mass.). The London warehouse, with an adjoining concert-room for 700 persons, is in Lower Seymour Street.

*Steinweg, C. F. Th. Nachfolger (successor), of Brunswick. Founded (1859) by Theodor Steinweg as a branch of the firm Steinway and Sons, of New York. The American firm altered the German name Steinweg into Steinway. 1865, the Brunswick business was taken over by Grotrian, Helfferich, and Schulz, as G. H. and S. Theodor Steinweg Nachfolger (registered 1869). The firm produces grand and upright pianos, and has received many (everywhere the highest) medals. Among these are the medal and diploma of honour at the Chicago Exhibition, 1893. The excellence and solidity of construction, beauty and evenness of tone, and perfection of repetition mechanism of the Brunswick firm are everywhere recognised.

Stodart and Sons, a firm of eminent pianoforte makers in London, from 1776 to 1861. Robert Stodart, the founder of the business, was a pupil of John Broadwood, and, with him, assisted Americus Backers in the invention of the so-called English action. In 1777 Stodart took out a patent, in which "grand," as applied to a pianoforte, first appears. In 1795 William Stodart took out a patent for an upright grand in the form of a bookcase. The most important patent acquired by this firm was that of James Thom and William Allen, taken out in 1820, in which metal was for the first time successfully introduced in the framing. This patent gave a great impulse to the Stodart business, and, yet more, it entirely revolutionised pianoforte making.

Stodart, Worcester, and Dunham, of New York. Founded, about 1836, by Adam Stodart, Horatio Worcester, and John B. Dunham, successors of John Osborn. Adam Stodart was a nephew of Robert Stodart; John B. Dunham (b. 1799, d. 1873) settled (1834) in New York, and was first employed by Nunns, Clark, and Co. as case maker. Horatio Worcester left the association, the firm being then styled Stodart and Dunham. 1849, Stodart withdrew, when the firm became (1867) Dunham and Sons. Their "boudoir grands" are widely known.

Streicher, J. B., und Sohn, of Vienna. This celebrated manufactory was originally founded in Augsburg by Johann Andreas Stein (*see* this name), organ builder, a pupil of Silbermann. Stein's daughter, Nanette, an excellent piano player, to whom Mozart refers in his letters, was also taught piano making by her father (*see* Stein, Nanette), married (1794) Andreas Streicher, and settled with him in Vienna. For many years she was alone in the supervision of her small business; but when this increased, she was joined by her husband, who gave up his work as a teacher. The firm was, from 1794, Nanette Streicher geb. Stein. When she had instructed her only son, Johann Baptist (b. 1796), for ten years (1812-22) he, having also extensively travelled and gathered rich experiences, was taken, in 1822, as partner, the firm becoming Nanette Streicher und Sohn. After the death of his parents (1833) he remained sole proprietor until his death, March 28, 1871, although the firm was, from 1857, J. B. Streicher und Sohn (Emil). The firm was intimately connected with famous musicians, such as Beethoven, Hummel, Cramer, Moscheles, Henselt, Kullak, &c., whilst both Mozart and Beethoven early speak of the excellent qualities of Stein's pianos. The eminent qualities and great solidity of the Streicher pianos were almost universally acknowledged. Gold medals and different diplomas were received. The patent as Kaiserl. Königl.-Hof und Kammer Piano Fabrikant and the Order of Francis Joseph was bestowed by the Emperor of Austria on both father and son, and it may be asserted that the name "Vienna" pianos was formerly synonymous with that of Streicher.

V.

Vose and Sons, of Boston, Mass. Founded (1851) by J. W. Vose (b. 1818, Milton, Mass.), now consists of the founder, Irving B. Vose (b. 1850), Willard A. Vose (b. 1852), and Julian W Vose (b. 1859). The firm's instruments enjoy great popularity. The partners are all practical piano makers.

W.

*Waters, H., and Co., of New York. Founded (1845) by Horatio Waters; is now a company, and his son, J. Lands Waters, is president. "The specialty of the firm is high-grade upright and small grand pianos."

Weber, A., of New York. The firm was founded by Albert Weber (b. 1829, in Bavaria; d. June 25, 1879, New York). He went (1845) to America, worked in the shops of Holder and Van Winckle, then started his business, and achieved such eminent success that (1860) he was able to open the great Weber warerooms. His instruments enjoy a great and well-deserved reputation. He was succeeded by his son, Albert (b. 1858, New York), who started a branch establishment in Chicago. He built the Weber Hall in 1883, and this enterprise proved in every respect a successful one. 1887, he exhibited in London, and his popular bijou instrument, called the "Baby Grand," excited general curiosity and obtained general approbation. The Weber Hall proving inadequate, he opened a much larger hall in Wabash Avenue. The firm received a great number of exhibition honours.

*Westermayer, Edouard, of Berlin. He founded the business, 1863 (b. Aug. 20, 1824, Meiningen, Bavaria; d. Jan. 6, 1891), Berlin. He studied at Vienna, Paris, Berlin, and Philadelphia, and resided for some time as a tuner in Buenos Ayres. The specialty of his grands and uprights is a patent repetition mechanism, entirely different to that of Erard and other makers. His adopted son, Paul Westermayer, is at present principal of the firm.

*Wheelock, William E., and Co., of New York. The business was started (1877) under the supervision of Charles Borst, and soon grew to considerable importance. 1880, W. Lawson, of Brooklyn, became a partner, and (1890) D. Lazelle was taken as a partner for the retail trade. Branch establishment in Chicago. "Their instruments hold a high position."

*Wornum, Robert, and Sons, of London. This eminent and well-known firm, founded (1777) by Robert Wornum, attained its celebrity under the guidance of Robert Wornum, jun. (b. 1780, London; d. there 1852), who took out the first patent for a small upright piano with oblique stringing in 1811. He was associated with

George Wilkinson, but the partnership was dissolved (1812). 1813, he introduced a small upright with vertical strings (called the "Harmonic"), now generally termed "Cottage" piano. 1829, he made the "Piccolo" pianoforte; for this the patent had already been taken out in 1826, and vastly improved by the introduction of the double-check action, used at present by the pianoforte makers of France and Germany. After the death of Robert Wornum, jun., he was succeeded by his son, A. N. Wornum, who made great improvements in the grand pianoforte. He died 1888, his successors being his son-in-law, Augustus Mongredien, in conjunction with the former manager of the works, A. J. Brown. Patents were taken out in 1811, 1820, 18__, 1828, 1842, 1862, 1867, 1871, and 1__. Prize medals were awarded in 18__, 1862, 1867, and 1878. The London manufacture of upright pianos be__ with Wornum's invention in 1811.

Z.

Zeitter und Winkelmann, of Brunswick, manufacturers to the Court. The firm was founded in 1837 and has adopted the "Steinway" system for their grands and uprights. Medals were received in London, 1851, 1884, and 1885; Brunswick, 1877; Melbourne, 1881 and 1889; Porto Allegre, 1882; Amsterdam, 1883; Calcutta, 1884.

Zumpe, Johann, the inventor of the square pianoforte, as known in this country for many years. According to Burney he had long worked for the harpsichord maker, Shudi, and was the first to construct small pianos of the size and shape of the virginal. There are several of these instruments still existing, the oldest in Messrs. Broadwood's possession, dated 1766. In 1769, the firm had become Zumpe and Buntebart; in 1776, it was Zumpe and Mayer. No personal record remains of Zumpe, his birth, death, or country; but that he was a German, as many of the early pianoforte makers in England were, there can be no doubt.

www.ingramcontent.com/pod-product-compliance
Lightning Source LLC
Chambersburg PA
CBHW030250170426
43202CB00009B/690